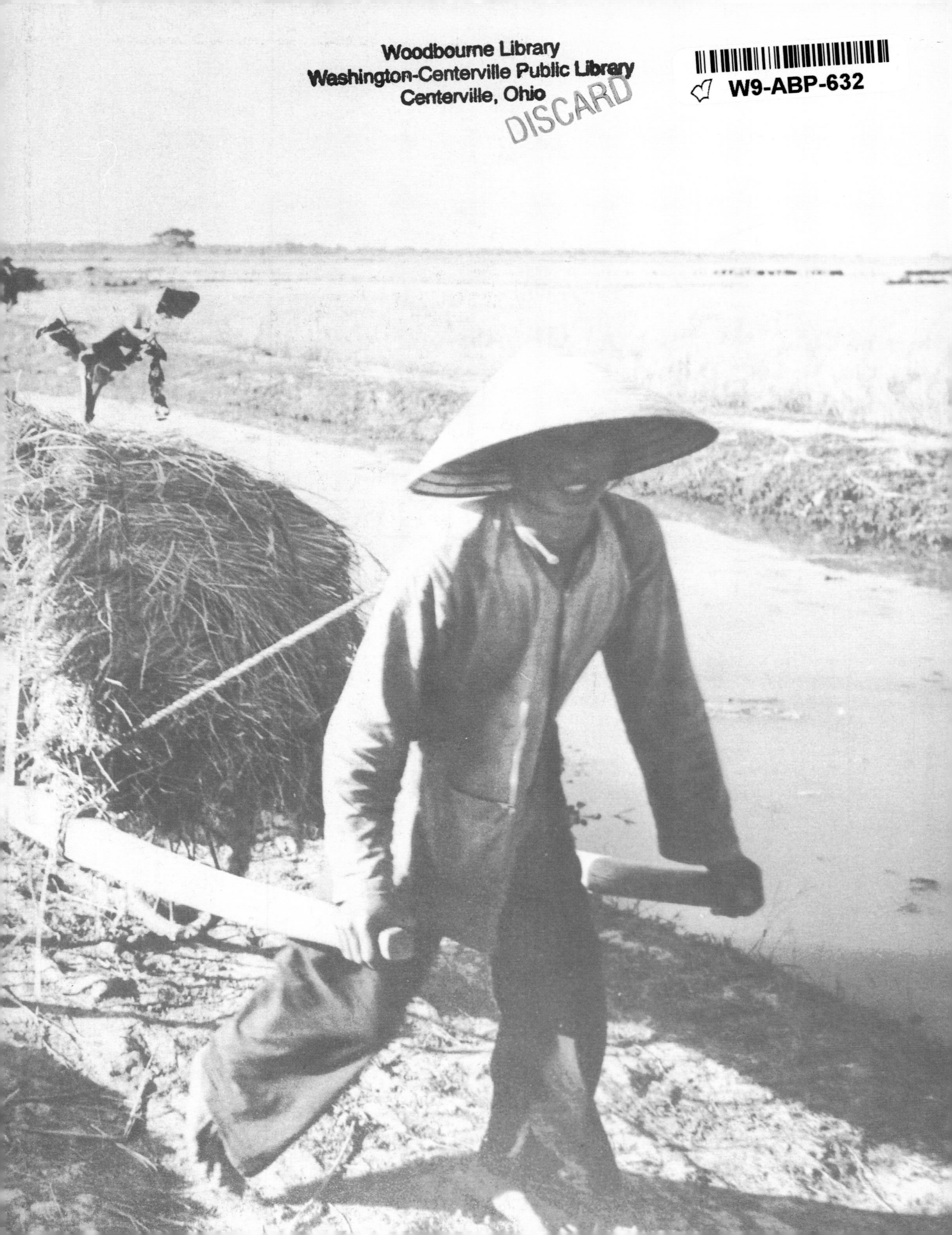

HISTORICAL
ATLAS
OF THE
VIETNAM
WAR

HARRY G. SUMMERS, JR.

INTRODUCTION AND EPILOGUE BY
STANLEY KARNOW

HOUGHTON MIFFLIN COMPANY
BOSTON   NEW YORK
1995

Library of Congress Cataloging-in-Publication Data

Summers, Jr., Harry G.
Historical atlas of the Vietnam war / Harry G. Summers, Jr.:
introduction and epilogue by Stanley Karnow.
p.   cm.
Includes index.
ISBN 0-395-72223-3
1. Vietnamese Conflict, 1961–1975—Campaigns.   2. Vietnamese Conflict,
1961–1975—United States.   3. Vietnam—Politics and government—
1945–1975.   I. Title
DS557.7.S93   1995   95–22200
959.704'34'0223—dc20   CIP

R
959.704
34
Summ

For information about this and other Houghton Mifflin
trade and reference books and multimedia products, visit
The Bookstore at Houghton Mifflin on the World Wide Web at
http://www.hmco.com./trade/.

There, where a French legionnaire
once walked patrol
Around the flightline perimeter of the airfield
at Nha Trang,
ten years later I walked,
an American expeditionary forces
soldier on night guard duty
at Nha Trang,
occupied even earlier,
twenty years before
(a year more than my nineteen),
by the Japanese.

Unhaunted by the ghosts, living and dead
among us
in the red tile-roofed French barracks
or listening in on the old Japanese telephone line
to Saigon,
we went about our military duties,
setting up special forces headquarters
where once a French Foreign Legion post had been,
oblivious to the irony
of Americans walking in the footsteps
of Genghis Khan.

Unencumbered by history,
our own or that of 13th-century Mongol armies
long since fled or buried

by the Vietnamese,
in Nha Trang, in 1962, we just did our jobs:
replacing kepis with berets, "Ah so!" with "Gawd!
Damn!"

In the Footsteps of Genghis Khan
Jan Berry

Contents

Foreword by Colonel H. G. Summers, Jr.

"How long do you think this fascination with Vietnam is going to last?" asked war correspondent Peter Arnett during a 1993 symposium on the war at Hampden-Sydney College in Virginia. "Well," I replied, "in April 1865, just down the road at Appomattox Court House, 110 years before the fall of Saigon, the Civil War came to an end. Yet over a century later we're still publishing books and magazines and making motion pictures and television documentaries about that conflict. Like the Civil War, Vietnam will probably still be with us for a while yet."

Evidencing that prediction was the furor raised by the 1995 publication of former secretary of fefense Robert McNamara's contemptible book, *In Retrospect: The Tragedy and Lessons of Vietnam.* The savage reaction from the whole of the political spectrum to what former senator Eugene McCarthy called McNamara's "Presbyterian confession"—his way of discreetly praising himself while blaming everyone else for his failures—was proof of the intensity of the emotions still just under the skin over two decades after the war came to an end.

Those emotions extend well beyond the Vietnam generation. At a conference on the war at the U.S. Air Force Academy in October 1990, Oklahoma teacher Bill McCloud told of the great interest in the war among his junior high school students. "They know there's a skeleton in the family closet," he said, "and now they want in on the secret."

But it is difficult to convey the realities of the Vietnam War. One of the main complaints of the more than 100,000 subscribers to *Vietnam* magazine, of which I am the founding editor, is the lack of adequate maps on the war. For those who served there, where you were and when you were there made an enormous difference, for the swamps of the Mekong delta were as different from the mountains of the Central Highlands and the trenches of the DMZ as the terrain of the European–African–Middle Eastern battlefields of World War II were different from those of the South Pacific.

The *Historical Atlas of the Vietnam War* is designed to fill that void. For that we have Malcolm A. Swanston, managing director of Swanston Publishing Limited in Great Britain, to thank, for he was the original inspiration for this work. Thanks also to the distinguished author and war correspondent Stanley Karnow for providing the book's introduction and epilogue.

Special thanks to Elizabeth Wyse, Rhonda Carrier, and the production team of Swanston Publishing, who combined the text with maps and pictures to provide a clear picture of what the war was all about, and to Jennifer S. Keen, former photo and art research editor for *Vietnam* magazine, who helped to track down those illustrations.

In expressing my thanks to those who helped, I must add that such errors as the book may contain are solely my responsibility.

Harry G. Summers, Jr.
Bowie, Maryland
September 1, 1995

In Honor of
"Dracula Six"
Major Richard DeWyatt Clark
and his 290 fellow soldiers
of the
1st Battalion, 2nd Infantry
First Infantry Division

MORT POUR LA PATRIE

Introduction by Stanley Karnow

As chief Asia correspondent for *Time* and *Life* magazines, I was visiting Saigon on July 8, 1959, when I heard that two American military advisers had been killed at Bien Hoa, the headquarters of a South Vietnamese army division about 20 miles north of the city. The next morning I drove there through the oppressive tropical heat and humidity. Along the road old French bunkers stood as reminders of France's futile war to retrieve its colonial hold over Vietnam, which had ended six years before. Peasants in black pajamas and conical straw hats bent over flooded paddy fields, carefully transplanting tender rice stalks, and bustling market towns reflected the country's fertility. Six years later, Bien Hoa would become a mammoth base as the United States pumped men, money, and materiel into Vietnam, but now it was a sleepy little provincial seat, its mildewed church, stucco villas, and tree-lined streets the quaint relics of nearly a century of French rule.

In May 1954, after protracted fighting, Communist-led Viet Minh troops had overrun the beleaguered French garrison at the battle of Dien Bien Phu. An international diplomatic conference assembled at Geneva partitioned Vietnam into two zones, ceding the north to the Communists and the south to a rival regime until elections scheduled for 1956 determined who would control the entire country. Having vanquished the French, the Communists were widely admired as the only true nationalists, and they would almost certainly have won had the election not been shelved. Disappointed, they organized an insurgency in the south. The term Viet Cong—a pejorative word conceived by Saigon government propagandists to brand the rebels as Communists—had not yet been coined, and they were still known as the Viet Minh.

The evening before my arrival, six of the eight U.S. advisers based at Bien Hoa had settled down in their mess after supper to watch a film. When one of them switched on the lights to change a reel, guerrillas poked their weapons through the screened windows and riddled the room with automatic fire, instantly slaying Major Dale R. Buis and Master Sergeant Chester M. Ovnand. My report on the incident earned only a few paragraphs in *Time*; it deserved no more. Nobody could have imagined then that 3 million Americans would eventually serve in Vietnam, and that the names Buis and Ovnand would one day head the list of almost 60,000 others etched into the stark black marble Vietnam Memorial in Washington. Nor could I, examining the bullet-pocked scene at Bien Hoa, even remotely envisage the holocaust that would devastate Vietnam over the subsequent 16 years.

The longest war in America's history, and its first defeat, the conflict continues to haunt the United States. Nor has it been forgotten by the Vietnamese. Some 4 million Vietnamese soldiers and civilians on both sides—nearly 10 percent of the population—either were wounded or died.

So in human terms, at least, the war was a war that nobody won—a struggle between victims. Its origins were complex, its lessons disputed, its legacy still to be fully assessed. But whether it was a justifiable venture or a misguided endeavor, it was a tragedy of epic dimensions.

It is commonly believed that President John F. Kennedy first involved the United States in Southeast Asia, but President Harry S. Truman actually took the initial step in June 1950. He had been alarmed the year before by Mao Zedong's conquest of China; the Korean War had just erupted; and he was under intense pressure in Washington from political conservatives who taunted him as being "soft on Communism." Also faced by the Soviet threat to Western Europe, he sought to induce the French to agree to the rearmament of West Germany by promising them $15 million in exchange for financing their Vietnam war. Though State Department specialists cautioned his successor that the French cause was hopeless, President Dwight D. Eisenhower amplified the aid. He articulated the domino theory: the idea that the rest of Asia would topple if Vietnam fell to Communism. By 1954, America had squandered $3 billion on the French war.

Underpinning this misguided policy was an almost total lack of understanding of the Vietnamese. Despite portrayals of them as primitive, they were a remarkably refined people who had borrowed their cultural institutions from China, which over the centuries had occupied their land. They were also atavistic warriors, having repeatedly struggled against the Chinese for freedom. During a talk in Hanoi in 1990, General Vo Nguyen Giap, the brilliant Communist commander, told me, "Our profoundest ideology is patriotism."

Consistent with their *grande mission civilisatrice*, the French had exported the lofty ideals of *liberté*, *égalité*, and *fraternité* to the Vietnamese, then denied them the right to practice those tenets. Frustrated, many young Vietnamese embraced Communism, which promised them emancipation from imperialism. The most influential of these was Ho Chi Minh, who lived in Paris from 1917 to 1923. While there he joined the French Communist Party and later became a Soviet agent. But he would always maintain that "it was nationalism that made me a Communist."

By 1946, with French diehards foiling Ho's attempts to avert a clash with France, he warned a French official, "If we go to war, we will lose ten men for every one you lose, but in the end we will win." His grisly equation proved accurate, dramatizing a tragic reality that both the French and, later, the Americans would disregard to their peril: here was an enemy prepared to make enormous sacrifices to achieve victory. General Giap emphasized that thesis when I asked him how long he would have continued fighting against the United States: "Another ten, twenty years, maybe a hundred years," he thundered, "regardless of cost."

Eisenhower spurned pleas from the French to rescue them at Dien Bien Phu—a decision partly influenced by his Joint Chiefs of Staff, who estimated that Vietnam was "devoid of decisive military objectives" and that intervention "would be a serious diversion of limited U.S. capabilities." After the creation of the South Vietnamese regime, however, Eisenhower strongly supported its president, Ngo Dinh Diem. Kennedy, inheriting the commitment, sent helicopters and other equipment, and steadily increased the corps of U.S. military advisers. But the Viet Cong quickly adapted to the new circumstances and in January 1963 struck what proved to be a major embarrassment to Diem's army in a minor engagement at Ap bac.

Diem had solid nationalist credentials, but he had been a peculiar choice for the position. He viewed himself as a mandarin who demanded absolute obedience, a trait that put him out of touch with the people. A devout Catholic, he was distrusted by the Buddhists, and, suspecting everyone except his family, he relied for advice solely on his brother Nhu, an odd pseudointellectual—and, it was said, an opium addict. Soon he alienated the Saigon elite, who resented his autocratic style, as well as his own senior army officers, who despite their own shortcomings blamed him for the growing Viet Cong challenge.

In 1963, after narrowly surviving two attempted coups, Diem was confronted by Buddhist dissidents. His generals started to conspire against him, with the connivance of Henry Cabot Lodge, the American ambassador in Saigon, who argued that Diem could not cope with either the inter-nal crisis or the Viet Cong menace. On November 1, the generals overthrew Diem and murdered him and his brother. Enthusiastic, Lodge cabled Kennedy: "The prospects now are for a shorter war."

The episode was a turning point. From then on South Vietnamese leaders would increasingly rely on the United States to defend their country—and in the process their initiative waned.

Three weeks after Diem died, Kennedy was assassinated in Dallas. During his brief term in office he had doubled the number of American military advisers, to 16,300, and raised U.S. assistance to Vietnam to $0.5 billion a year. Lyndon B. Johnson, his vice–president, entered the White House and inherited the Vietnam War.

Johnson's priority was the Great Society, the liberal social programs that he dreamed would surpass the New Deal of his idol, Franklin D. Roosevelt. But he could not duck Vietnam, where the situation swiftly degenerated as the generals who had displaced Diem squabbled among themselves. Johnson feared that he might be the first president to lose a war; he was also worried that the right wing in Congress would subvert his Great Society proposals unless he adopted a firm stance toward Communism. Senator Barry Goldwater, the Republican presidential candidate, denounced him as well for waffling on Vietnam.

Early in August 1964, a murky event in the Gulf of Tonkin, off North Vietnam, provided Johnson with a riposte. After receiving reports that a U.S. destroyer deployed there had been attacked by a Communist patrol boat, he asked Congress to pass a resolution authorizing him to introduce American forces into Southeast Asia. Most of the evidence suggests that the attack never occurred, yet except for two senators, both chambers unanimously approved the request. The bipartisan vote silenced Goldwater, and Johnson won the election by a landslide. One of Johnson's legal aides later called the resolution "the moral equivalent of a declaration of war." But in a memoir published in April 1995, his former defense secretary, Robert S. McNamara, stressed that Johnson should have sought a real declaration of war before sending combat troops to Vietnam.

Johnson hesitated to use his new powers until February 1965, when, reacting to the deaths of eight American advisers during a Viet Cong raid against an outpost at Pleiku, in the Central Highlands, he started the bombing of North Vietnam. A month later he sustained the air campaign under the code name Rolling Thunder. At the same time he ordered two U.S. marine battalions to Da Nang to secure the airfields located there. The moves were largely designed to bolster the bickering Saigon leaders, but their feuds continued as they shifted responsibility for the war to the Americans.

In July 1965, Johnson fulfilled a request from General William C. Westmoreland, the U.S. commander in Vietnam, for 125,000 men. Westmoreland brought them over three months later without a proper logistical system, an extraordinary feat. Lifted by helicopter, they plunged into action in the Ia Drang Valley, where, with the support of B-52 bombers, they prevented a Communist sweep from the Central Highlands down to the populated coast. By the end of the year there were nearly 200,000 American troops in Vietnam, and their superior firepower imposed horrendous losses on the enemy. Johnson, convinced that Westmoreland's search-and-destroy missions were effective, continued to reinforce him, so that by late 1967, Westmoreland had nearly half a million men.

Westmoreland was persuaded that the immense weight of U.S. technology would grind down the Communists and inevitably break their morale. With the exception of nuclear weapons, he had at his disposal everything in America's gigantic arsenal, from supersonic aircraft and modern artillery to sophisticated electronic devices. He inflicted horrendous casualties on the Communists, whose corpses, piled up after every battle, convinced him that his strategy of attrition could not fail. But the "body count," his grim barometer of success, was meaningless, as fresh enemy waves kept coming back to supplant those he had slaughtered.

By 1967, President Johnson was worried that support at home for the apparently interminable war was dwindling. Even though he sounded optimistic in public, Robert McNamara was expressing doubts privately—as he did in August in closed hearings before a congressional committee. Johnson, enraged by what he regarded as McNamara's betrayal, pondered dropping him. He also summoned General Westmoreland to Washington to reassure the nation that all was well. Dutifully declaring that "we have reached an important point when the end begins to come into view," Westmoreland defied the Communists to stage a massive attack, asserting: "I hope they try something because we are looking for a fight." General Giap was indeed preparing a big assault, but not the one Westmoreland anticipated.

For months Communist troops had been hitting a series of isolated American outposts scattered across the Central Highlands, among them Khe Sanh. Westmoreland saw Khe Sanh as a showdown battleground, a potential Dien Bien Phu. He called in B-52s, which ravaged the enemy. But, as Giap later told me, his threat to Khe Sanh was a diversion. His plan was to draw the Americans into the interior so he could attack the heavily populated coast—which he did.

On the night of January 31, 1968, approximately 70,000 North Vietnamese and Viet Cong soldiers launched a colossal offensive. Violating a truce that they had vowed to observe during Tet, the lunar New Year, they surged into more than a hundred towns and cities, including Saigon. The war had shifted for the first time from its rural setting into a new arena—the supposedly impregnable urban areas. A Viet Cong suicide squad even stormed the American embassy in Saigon, a hideous ultramodern building shielded by thick walls. The Communist leaders had counted on triggering uprisings throughout the south, but they failed, suffering huge losses. Still, their audacious move shattered Westmoreland's rosy forecasts and the impact in the United States, where Americans watched the events on television, was cataclysmic.

Contrary to popular belief, the Tet Offensive did not suddenly turn the U.S. public against the war. Support for the conflict had been steadily declining for two years as Americans increasingly felt that the growing expenditure in blood and treasure were not achieving results. Nor did "anti-war" necessarily mean "pro-peace." The prevailing opinion was that the war should be prosecuted more dynamically. Or, as bumper stickers summed it up, "We should not have gotten involved in the first place but now that we are there let's win—or get out."

By 1968, an election year, some 16,000 Americans had died in Vietnam, and the war had become a domestic political liability. In the New Hampshire Democratic Party primary election conducted in March, the peace candidate, Senator Eugene McCarthy, nearly defeated Johnson—a stunning blow to an incumbent president. The Democratic convention opened in Chicago in August amid chaos as police fought antiwar demonstrators. The Democrats nominated Vice President Hubert Humphrey as their candidate. The Republican contender, Richard Nixon, campaigned on a pledge of "peace with honor," and in January 1969 entered the White House accompanied by a former Harvard professor, Henry Kissinger, as his national security adviser.

Nixon was, very much like Johnson, a consummate politician who had clawed his way to the top, often by devious means. And like Johnson, he dreaded the possibility that he might be the first president to lose a war. But, recognizing that America was squandering its resources in Vietnam, he shaped a dual policy designed to extract the United States without tarnishing its image. He would withdraw the U.S. ground forces while preparing the Vietnamese army to fight more effectively—a program known as "Vietnamization." At the same time he instructed Kissinger to initiate negotiations in the hope of inducing the Communists to concede to a compromise. But his approach was flawed.

However much the United States trained and equipped the South Vietnamese troops, they could not deal with the enemy as long as they were led by incompetent, corrupt officers. Kissinger's negotiations meanwhile dragged as the Communists realized that they had only to stall until the Americans departed, leaving a vacuum that would enable them to crush the weak Saigon regime. Growing more and more impatient as time passed, Nixon secretly ordered his aides to ferret out his antiwar opponents—a gambit that was to lead to the Watergate scandal. Late in April 1970 he invaded adjacent Cambodia, igniting a storm of protest that left him feeling besieged even though most Americans—the "silent majority"—continued to trust him.

In 1972 Nixon embarked on a diplomatic venture that was to have an indirect, though momentous, impact on the Vietnam situation. In February he visited China, becoming the first American president to meet Mao Zedong, and shortly afterward traveled to Moscow to see Leonid Brezhnev, the Soviet Communist Party boss. That their powerful allies were willing to entertain their chief adversary distressed the Vietnamese Communists. Isolated, they decided to come to terms with Kissinger. But in May, in an effort to improve

their negotiating posture, they launched an ambitious offensive. Pounded by B-52s, their forces failed, and in October they offered Kissinger a compromise. They would drop their demand that the Saigon government be dismantled on condition that the United States permit some 300,000 North Vietnamese soldiers already in the South to remain in place.

Kissinger agreed despite the objections of Nguyen Van Thieu, the South Vietnamese president, who viewed the accord as treachery. To reassure Thieu, and also as a warning to the Communists not to break the arrangement, Nixon unleashed the B-52s against North Vietnam during the Christmas season. In January 1973 a ceasefire was signed in Paris, but soon both the Communists and the Saigon government started to violate it. Nixon could do nothing. Congress had passed a resolution that barred him from bombing North Vietnam, and he was also entangled in the Watergate scandal, which would shortly spell his downfall as president.

By April 1975, with the American forces gone, the South Vietnamese were naked. The Communist legions rolled down from the North and, at the end of the month, captured Saigon. Nixon's successor, President Gerald Ford, had relegated Vietnam to the history books a week earlier in an address at Tulane University in New Orleans: "Today, Americans can regain a sense of pride that existed before Vietnam. But it cannot be achieved by fighting a war that is finished … These events, tragic as they are, portend neither the end of the war nor of America's leadership in the world."

Members of the 1st Brigade, 25th Infantry Division make ready to come ashore from LCMs at Vung Tau in April 1966.

Key to Maps

Size of military units

■ **ARMY** NAME   or   ☐ XXXX 1   Army

■ **I CORPS**   or   ☐ XXX   Corps

☐ XX   Division

☐ X   Brigade

☐ III   Regiment

☐ II   Battalion

☐ I   Company

Type of military units

⊠ Infantry   ∞ Air Cavalry

⊘ Cavalry (mechanized)   ⊠ Airmobile Infantry

◻ Armored   ▽ ⌢ Parachute/ air landing

⊠ Armored Cavalry

⊠ Motorized   → Airforce unit

▣ Artillery   ⊥ Naval troops

⊠ Rangers   ⊓ Engineers

Military movements

➚ Attack or advance

⇢ Retreat or withdrawal

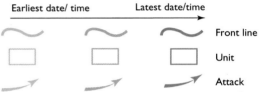

Earliest date/ time   Latest date/time

~ ~ ~   Front line

☐ ☐ ☐   Unit

➚ ➚ ➚   Attack

National colors

■ United States and allies   □ Japanese

■ North Vietnamese   ■ Koreans

■ Chinese   ■ French

General military symbols

⚑ Headquarters

Machine-gun post

Barbed wire

✕✕✕ Roadblock

⊓⊔⊓ --- Defensive line

—— Trenches

▽ Parachute landing

◯ Parachute landing area/drop zone

Tank/armored concentration

✳ Raid/bombing/attack/naval bombardment

Ⓗ Helicopter landing pad

△ Airfield/air base

⊙ Radar station

✈ Air attack

Mines

▣ Fire Support Base

▲ Hill (strategic)

— XXX — Corps boundary

Aircraft

Bomber

Fighter

Jet fighter or fighter bomber

B–52

Helicopter

Warships

Aircraft carrier

Cruiser

Destroyer

Transport/support ship

Fire support ships

Landing Craft

Ship attacked and sunk

Other symbols used on maps

Town/settlement/urban area

Prominent building

International border

Provincial border

Major road

Road (alternative)

Railway

Bridge

Trees/vegetation (town/village plans)

Land tints

Paddy field

Jungle/forest

Swamps

Beaches

Plantation

Abbreviations on maps

AA	Antiaircraft (artillery)
ACR	Armored Cavalry Regiment
ATF	Australian Task Force
ARVN	Army of the Republic of Vietnam
ATC	Armored Troop Carrier
BM	*Bataillon de Marche*
Brig	Brigade
CAG	Combined Action Group
CAP	Combined Action Platoon
CAV	Cavalry
CIA	Central Intelligence Agency
CIDG	Civilian Irregular Defense Group
COSVN	Central Office of South Vietnam
CP	Command Post
Div	Division
DMZ	Demilitarized Zone
Elts	Elements
FFV	Field Force Vietnam
FSB	Fire Support Base
Fwd	Forward
GM	*Groupement Mobile*
HQ	Headquarters
LZ	Landing zone
MAF	Marine Amphibious Force
MAR	Marine
MACV/MCV	Military Assistance Command Vietnam
MP	Military Police
MR	Military Region
MRF	Mobile Riverine Force
NVA	North Vietnamese Army
POW	Prisoner-of-war
PT	Patrol torpedo boat
Regt	Regiment
RC	*Route Coloniale*
RF	Regional Force
ROK	Republic of Korea
SAM	Surface-to-air missile
SOG	Studies and Observation Group
TF	Task Force
USAF	United States Air Force
USN	United States Navy
VC	Viet Cong
VNN	South Vietnamese Navy

Chronology

1945

February — Yalta Conference: World War II Allies plan defeat of Germany and Roosevelt discusses Indochina with Chiang Kai-shek.

March 9 — Japanese coup against French. Bao Dai proclaims Vietnam's independence under Japanese "protection".

July — Potsdam Conference divides Vietnam into two zones.

August 15 — World War II ends.

August 22 — Emperor Bao Dai abdicates.

September 2 — Japanese sign surrender agreement. Ho Chi Minh proclaims Vietnamese independence and declares himself president of new republic

September 23 — First U.S. death in Vietnam during fall of Saigon to French forces.

1946

February — Chinese agree to withdraw from North Vietnam and allow a French return to Tonkin in exchange for certain treaty concessions.

March 6 — The Democratic Republic of Vietnam becomes a "free state" within the French Union.

September — Ho Chi Minh signs agreement with French in Paris.

October — Fighting breaks out in Haiphong.

December 19 — First Viet Minh attack on French in Hanoi begins First Indochina War.

1947

May 11 — Laos is proclaimed an independent state within the French Union.

October 7–December 22 — Operation Lea: French launch attacks on Viet Minh positions near Chinese border.

1949

March — French install Bao Dai as puppet head of state.

July — French found Vietnamese National Army.

October — Mao Zedong's Communist forces defeat Chiang Kai-shek's Nationalist Army in Chinese civil war.

1950

January — People's Republic of China and Soviet Union recognize Democratic Republic of Vietnam. China begins to provide arms to Viet Minh.

February — Giap begins offensive against French border posts.

May — Truman authorizes $10 million in U.S. military aid to French—U.S. involvement in Vietnam begins.

June 27 — Truman sends U.S. troops into Korea—Korean War begins.

September 16 — Viet Minh launch second attack on Dong Khé.

September 27 — MAAG–Indochina established.

1951

January 13 — Viet Minh attack Vinh Yen outpost.

March 23–24 — Viet Minh attack Mao Khé outpost.

May 29 — Giap renews attempt to seize De Lattre line.

June 9 — Giap orders Viet Minh withdrawal from Red River delta.

June 18 — Red River campaign ends.

November 16 — French assault forces link up at Hoa Binh.

December 9 — Giap's attack on Tu Vu outpost begins Black River fights.

1952

January 12 — Viet Minh cut French supply lines to Hoa Binh.

February 22–26 — French withdraw from Hoa Binh.

October 29 — French launch Operation Lorraine against Viet Minh supply bases.

November 14 — Operation Lorraine canceled. French withdraw.

1953

March — Stalin dies; his death leads to Geneva Conference in 1954.

November 20 — French begin Operation Castor: the construction of a fortified airhead at Dien Bien Phu.

December 8 — French begin Operation Pollux: the evacuation of the Tai Highlands and Lai Chi outpost to Dien Bien Phu.

1954

March 13–17 — Viet Minh launch assaults on French outpost at Dien Bien Phu.

March 30–May 1 — Dien Bien Phu is besieged.

May 7 — French are defeated at Dien Bien Phu. Geneva Conference begins.

June 24–July 17 — G.M. 100 is ambushed three times during retreat to Pleiku.

August 1 — Armistice declared. Geneva accords divide Vietnam at 17th parallel and Diem is made head of state in South Vietnam. Laos and Cambodia are granted full independence from French.

October — French leave Hanoi. Ho Chi Minh's forces gain control of North.
President Eisenhower backs Diem's regime and offers military aid to Diem.

1955

January — First U.S. military supplies reach Saigon.

May — Clashes between Diem's forces and anti-government sects begin. Diem exiles head of Binh Xuyen group.

October 26 — Diem defeats Bao Dai in referendum and proclaims the Republic of Vietnam with himself as president. RVNAF founded.

1956

February — Leader of Cao Dai sect flees to Cambodia.

April 28 — Last French soldier leaves South Vietnam; French High Command for Indochina is dissolved.

July — Deadline passes for elections set by Geneva Conference.

July 13 — Leader of Hoa Hao sect is beheaded.

November	Peasant discontent in North is put down by force. Land Reform campaign fails.

1959

March	North Vietnamese Politburo orders shift from political to military struggle—the "armed revolution" begins.
May	North Vietnamese Communist Party's 15th Plenum establishes COSVN. Construction of Ho Chi Minh Trail begins.
June	4,000 Viet Minh troops are sent to South.
July	Group 579 formed to move North Vietnamese arms and equipment down coast to the South.

1960

December	National Liberation Front is founded in Hanoi to coordinate war in South.

1961

November	Kennedy writes to Diem offering military assistance and sends first U.S. advisers to South Vietnam, opening the way for a U.S. combat role.
December	White Paper sets out U.S. intentions in Vietnam.

1962

February	MACV replaces MAAG–Vietnam. First CIDG camps established.
March	Operation Sunrise begins Strategic Hamlets resettlement program.
May	Australia sends team of jungle warfare specialists to Vietnam.
July 23	Geneva Conference on Laos forbids U.S. invasion of eastern Laos (site of Ho Chi Minh Trail).
August	U.S. Special Forces CIDG camp set up at Khe Sanh to monitor NVA infiltration down Ho Chi Minh Trail.

1963

January	Battle of Ap Bac draws U.S. public attention to Vietnam.
May	Duc Lap designated a strategic hamlet. Diem's forces break up Buddhist celebration in Hue, triggering a wave of suicides in protest. Pressure mounts on U.S. government to disassociate itself.
November 2	Assassination of Diem creates power vacuum in which a series of military and civilian governments take control.
November 22	President Kennedy assassinated.
December	SOG transferred from CIA to MACV control.

1964

January	President Johnson approves covert operations against North Vietnam. Operation Plan 34A (DeSoto) raids and cross-border operations against North Vietnamese infiltration routes in Laos begin.
July	First New Zealand forces arrive in Vietnam.
August 2–4	Attacks reported on U.S. vessels in Gulf of Tonkin.
August 7	Congress overwhelmingly passes Gulf of Tonkin Resolution allowing president to use

	unlimited military force to prevent attacks on U.S. forces.
November	Johnson reelected.
December	One regiment of NVA 325th Division arrives in Central Highlands, with two more regiments enroute, changing the nature of the war.

1965

January	Operation Game Warden begins riverine operations in South Vietnam.
February	First contingent of Korean troops arrives in Vietnam. Operation Flaming Dart, the bombing of targets in North Vietnam, begins.
March	First U.S. air strikes against Ho Chi Minh Trail.
March 2	Rolling Thunder air campaign begins.
March 8	U.S. Marines land at Da Nang and become first U.S. combat troops in Vietnam.
March 11	Market Time naval interdiction begins.
April 6	President Johnson authorizes use of ground troops in combat operations.
May	First pause in U.S. bombing announced. U.S. combat troops in action for first time 1st RAR Battalion arrives in Vietnam.
July 28	Johnson sends additional 50,000 ground troops.
July 31	Coastal Surveillance Force (Task Force 115) formed.
August	Combined Action platoons begin on ad hoc basis.
August 18–24	Operation Starlite begins major U.S. ground combat operations.
October	NVA attacks U.S. Special Forces camp at Plei Me.
November	Antiwar demonstrations in United States.
November 14–16	Battle of the Ia Drang marks NVA shift toward use of conventional military forces.
November 17	NVA ambush of 2nd Battalion, 7th Cavalry at LZ Albany.
December 24	Second pause in bombing of North Vietnam.
December 25	U.S. troop levels in Vietnam reach 184,300.

1966

January	Bombing of North Vietnam resumes. President Johnson announces his "Fourteen Points." Concept of Combined Action platoons is formalized.
January 28–March 6	Operation Masher/White Wing is first U.S. search-and-destroy operation.
April	1st Australian Task Force is formed.
August 18	Battle of Long Tan, the most important Australian engagement, begins.
September 14– November 24	Operation Attleboro shows that the Viet Cong will fight to protect its base areas.
December 19	U.S. troop levels reach 389,000.

1967

January 2	Operation Bolo against North Vietnamese MiG-21 interceptors begins.
January 8–26	Operation Cedar Falls to clear "Iron Triangle" begins.
February 22–May 14	Operation Junction City becomes largest U.S. military offensive of war.
April	Antiwar demonstrations in New York and San Francisco.
April 24–May 11	Hill fights rage at Khe Sanh.

May 9	Komer becomes deputy commander of MACV and forms CORDS.
June	Mobile Riverine Force supplements River Patrol Force; Coronado operations begin.
July 7	General Offensive/General Uprising conceived.
September	First Thai troops arrive in Vietnam.
September–October	Con Thien outpost besieged.
October 21–23	"March on the Pentagon" draws 50,000 protestors.
December 25	U.S. troop levels reach 463,000.

1968

January 5	Operation Niagara I to locate NVA around Khe Sanh begins.
January 21	Siege of Khe Sanh begins. Aerial bombardment and resupply (Niagara II) set in motion.
January 30	NVA begins premature attacks in II Corps.
January 31	Tet Offensive launched: Viet Cong enter U.S. Embassy grounds in Saigon and battle for Hue begins.
February 1	U.S. troops drive NVA from Tan Son Nhut.
February 24	Imperial Palace at Hue recaptured.
March 1	McNamara replaced by Clark Clifford.
March 2	Battle for Hue ends.
March 7	Battle for Saigon ends.
March 12	Eugene McCarthy wins 42 percent of vote in New Hampshire Democratic primary elections.
March 16	300–400 civilians slaughtered at My Lai.
March 28	Report on My Lai makes no mention of civilian casualties.
March 31	Johnson announces cessation of bombing of targets north of 20th parallel and decision not to stand in election.
April 1	Operation Pegasus to reopen Route 9 and end siege of Khe Sanh begins.
April 8	Siege of Khe Sanh ends.
April 16	Pentagon announces "Vietnamization" of the war.
May 12	Kham Duc CIDG border post evacuated.
May 13	Peace talks begin in Paris but soon stall. NVA "Mini Tet" offensive begins.
July 1	President Thieu establishes Phung Hoang plan (Phoenix program).
July 3	Abrams replaces Westmoreland as U.S. commander.
October 8	Operation Sealord launched against NVA supply lines and base areas.
October 31	U.S. bombing of North Vietnam halted.
November	Colby replaces Komer as head of CORDS.
November 4	Nixon beats Humphrey in U.S. presidential election.
December 1	U.S. troop levels reach 495,000.

1969

January	Sealords barrier system is completed.
March	Letters from Ronald Ridenhour trigger investigation into My Lai massacre.
March 18	Nixon authorizes Operation Menu—the "secret" bombing of Cambodia.
April 9	U.S. troop levels peak at 543,400.
May	"Hamburger Hill" ends large-scale U.S. engagements.
June 5	Lieutenant Calley returns to United States as suspect in mass murder inquiry.
June 8	First U.S. troop cuts of 25,000 announced—Vietnamization begins.
August	Sihanoukville closed to Communist shipping.

September 3	Ho Chi Minh dies.
September 6	Calley charged with 109 murders.
December 5	Calley refuses to testify.

1970

March	Prince Sihanouk of Cambodia deposed by General Lon Nol.
March 31	Captain Medina charged with murder of 175 people in My Lai.
April 30	Nixon orders invasion of Cambodia to disrupt NVA base areas.
May 4	U.S. National Guard kills four students during antiwar protest at Kent State University.
June 24	U.S. Senate repeals 1964 Gulf of Tonkin Resolution.
June 30	U.S. troops withdraw from Cambodia.
November 20	Troop levels drop to 334,600.
December	Cooper–Church Amendment to defense appropriations bill forbids U.S. ground troops in Laos.

1971

January 30–April 6	Lam Son 719 results in appalling South Vietnamese losses.
February	Nixon visits China to forge new links.
March 29	Calley found guilty of murder of 22 civilians and assault with intent to murder a child.
April 1	Nixon orders Calley's release pending appeal.
June	George Jackson replaces Colby as head of CORDS.
August 20	Cambodian military launches series of operations against Khmer Rouge.
September 22	Medina acquitted of all charges.
October 3	Operation Chenla II against the Khmer Rouge ends in disaster for FANK.
December 17	U.S. troop levels drop to 156,800.

1972

March 30	First nationwide NVA offensive since 1968 begins.
April 2	U.S. 7th Fleet ordered to strike DMZ area.
April 4	Massive U.S. air campaign authorized.
April 12	Attack on Kontum begins.
April 19	Attack on An Loc begins.
April 30	U.S. troop levels drop to 69,000.
May	Nixon orders mining of northern ports (Operation Linebacker I) and intensified bombing of the North.
May 1	Quang Tri abandoned to NVA.
May 30	NVA attack on Kontum thwarted.
June	weyand replaces Abrams as U.S. commander
June 9	John Paul Vann killed in helicopter crash.
July 11	95-day siege of An Loc ends.
September 16	Quang Tri recaptured from NVA.
October 17	Peace talks between Pathet Lao and Royal Lao government begin.
October 22	Operation Linebacker I ends.
December 13	Peace talks collapse again.
December 18	Christmas bombing (Operation Linebacker II) begins.
December 26	Peace negotiations resume.
December 29	Operation Linebacker II ends.

1973

January 27	Paris peace accords signed; U.S. agrees to withdraw all remaining troops within 60 days.

February 21	Peace agreement between Pathet Lao and Royal Lao government signed. U.S. air strikes in Laos end next day.
March	Operation Homecoming ends: Nixon claims that all U.S. POWs have returned to U.S.A.
March 29	Last U.S. troops withdraw.
June 19	Case–Church Amendment prevents further U.S. military involvement in Southeast Asia.
August 14	U.S. "secret" bombing of Cambodia ends.

1974

January 14	Schlesinger accuses Congress of reneging on Paris peace accords.
April	Coalition government formed in Laos: Pathet Lao hold key positions.
August	U.S. military contribution to South Vietnam set at $1 billion.
August 4	Nixon resigns as result of Watergate scandal.
September	House and Senate appropriate only $700 million for South Vietnam.
October	North Vietnamese Politburo meeting begins— Le Duan makes his "resolution".
November 9	Calley freed.
December 13	NVA contravene Paris accords with attack on Phuoc Long.

1975

January 8	20-day Politburo meeting ends. General Staff draft plan approved.
January 21	President Ford gives press conference stressing unwillingness to reenter war.
March	Khmer Rouge mines Mekong River in Cambodia, ending FANK resupplies.
March 10	NVA attacks Ban Me Thuot—final offensive begins.
March 11	Ban Me Thuot falls.
March 13	President Thieu decides to abandon Central Highlands and northern provinces.
March 16	Evacuation from Pleiku begins.
March 17	Refugees from Hue begin to flee to Da Nang.
March 19	Quang Tri City falls to NVA.
March 24	Tam Ky overrun by NVA.
March 25	Hue abandoned.
March 26	Chu Lai evacuated.
March 28	NVA begin to shell Da Nang.
March 30	Da Nang falls.
March 31	NVA open fire on Tuy Hoa.
April 12	NVA close in on Xuan Loc. U.S. staff evacuated from Phnom Penh.
April 17	Phnom Penh falls to Khmer Rouge.
April 21	President Thieu resigns, condemning the United States.
April 22	Xuan Loc falls to NVA.
April 23	President Ford gives speech at Tulane University.
April 27	Saigon encircled. NVA fires rockets into downtown Saigon.
April 28	"Big Minh" becomes president. NVA attacks Tan Son Nhut air base.
April 29	U.S. Embassy evacuated.
April 30	420 evacuees accidentally left behind at U.S. Embassy. NVA enters Independence Palace; President Minh surrenders and war ends.
May 15	U.S. merchant ship *Mayaguez* recaptured from Khmer Rouge.
August 23	Laotian capital, Vientiane, falls to Pathet Lao.

	War ends in Laos but ruthless massacres result in mass exodus.
December 3	Lao monarchy abolished. People's Democratic Republic of Laos proclaimed.

1976

July	Vietnam united as Socialist Republic of Vietnam, with Le Duan holding power as general secretary of Communist Party. Saigon renamed Ho Chi Minh City.

1978

December 5	Vietnam launches full-scale invasion of Cambodia.

1979

January 5	Vietnam occupies Phnom Penh. Pol Pot is ousted and a friendly regime is installed.
February 17–March 16	China wages a "pedagogical" war against Vietnam; an international crisis is created by the exodus of the "boat people".

1986

	Nguyen Van Linh becomes general secretary of the Communist Party in Vietnam. A liberal economic renovation (*doi moi*) policy is introduced.

1988

	The "screening" of Vietnamese boat people begins; they must explain their reasons for emigration.

1989

	Vietnam withdraws from Cambodia.

1990

	U.K. government begins the forced repatriation of boat people.

1991

	Anti-Communist dissent becomes a criminal offense.
December	Vietnam renews links with United States when the dissolution of the Soviet Union means it no longer counterbalances Chinese domination.

1992

	The revised constitution allows foreign investment in Vietnam.

1993

May	U.N.-sponsored elections are held in Cambodia and a coalition government is formed in Phnom Penh.
September 24	Sihanouk reinstalled as king of Cambodia.

1995

July 11	Full diplomatic relations are established between the United States and Vietnam.

Part I: The Setting

During the Vietnam War, it was said, only half in jest, that the reason for the dissent on campus was that many students were afraid that if they were sent off across the seas to fight there, they would fall off the edge of the earth. Be that as it may, Americans knew, and know, almost nothing about Vietnam. Even after the long U.S. military involvement there, the vast majority of students cannot locate Vietnam on a world map.

The notion persists that Vietnam is a small country. Yet it is a small country only in the same sense as Germany, with whom we fought two world wars. With a total land area of 127,248 square miles, it is only slightly smaller than Germany, which measures 137,736 square miles. Its population of 73 million is not far from the 81 million inhabitants of a newly unified Germany. Like Germany, it is homogeneous. Just as Germany is 95 percent ethnic German, so Vietnam is 85–90 percent ethnic Vietnamese. Both peoples have a strong sense of national identity and pride in nationhood.

Some have carried the analogy even further. Douglas Pike, director of the Indochina Studies Program at the University of California at Berkeley, has called the Vietnamese the "Prussians of Asia." Quoting Hanoi historian Le Dinh Sy, Pike notes that "Vietnam's national tradition is that every Vietnamese is a soldier, the model citizen being the farmer in the field who is ever ready to drop his hoe and march off to battle. Over the centuries the Vietnamese have endured warfare no more incessantly than have most of their Asian neighbors [but] that is not what the Vietnamese tell themselves today, not what is taught in their schools, and not what they believe. The theme of their history—like Prussia's in Europe—is that Vietnam is the most fought over ground. Vietnamese battled China with amazing determination for centuries."

That fact was lost on many Americans, including some in the highest reaches of the government, who saw Vietnam as a "new" country. But Vietnam's recorded history goes back to 111 BC—over 1,500 years before America was discovered and a half century before the Roman legions landed on the island of Britain. For the first thousand years, Vietnam was administered as a

Native workers in Son La Province in the former North Vietnam. Despite such idyllic scenes, the forced resettlement of lowlanders in mountain regions to reduce overcrowding in the north is putting pressure on limited farming resources.

province of China, and even after it won independence, it remained under Chinese influence as a suzerain state until almost the beginning of this century.

While historians dwell on China's military aggression, it was its cultural aggression that had the most profound effect on the evolution of Vietnamese social and political institutions. To the Chinese it was axiomatic that there were two ways to conquer another nation. One way was through *wu* [武], or military means. This was always seen as transitory. The other way was through *wen* [文], or culture, which was seen as enduring. That was certainly true in Vietnam, where Chinese culture shaped Vietnamese language, writing, religion, and views on the role and structure of government.

This heritage shaped the fundamental philosophies and attitudes of the Vietnamese in much the same way as Greek and Roman philosophies form our attitudes toward government and society, as our Judeo-Christian heritage undergirds our system of laws, and as the English evolution of democratic ideals, including the 13th-century Magna Carta, became the basis for our constitutional liberties. It was the Magna Carta that overturned the idea that kings and princes rule by divine right, an idea that, according to some sociologists, survives until this day in Vietnam in the Chinese concept of the "mandate of heaven."

South Vietnamese president Ngo Dinh Diem was described in his day as "the last Confucian," and his Communist successors resemble the mandarins who ruled Imperial China, and Imperial Vietnam, for thousands of years. There is some truth in the cynical remark that the only way America could succeed in democratizing Vietnam was to declare a Magna Carta and wait 700 years, since Vietnamese culture, both Communist and otherwise, was resistant to such changes.

It can be argued that by ignoring these cultural realities and promoting its own Western democratic model as the only acceptable one for the Republic of Vietnam, the United States weakened and undermined the very government it was attempting to strengthen and support. But it also can be argued that the North Vietnamese, by adopting the Western developmental model of Marxism-Leninism, also doomed itself to eventual destruction. That model failed in the Soviet Union and in Eastern Europe, and brought Vietnam itself to the brink of economic collapse.

For many years, the Chinese, sensitive to the impact of the ancient concept of *wu* by which they extended their sway over East Asia, have accused the United States of "cultural imperialism." That charge mystified most Americans, who were not aware that we even had a culture, and who were sure that we were not imperialists. But American culture has proved to be the most insidious in the world. Moving on what one French critic called "wheels lubricated by Coca-Cola," it subverts and undermines traditional cultures without even being aware of doing so. Vietnam is no exception. America unconsciously planted its cultural seeds in Vietnam during its stay there, and those seeds continue to sprout. T-shirts, rock records, and free market economics may yet succeed in doing what bullets and bombs failed to do a quarter century ago.

Despite a slow growth rate in comparison with Ho Chi Minh City, Hanoi is also embracing free enterprise. As foreign money pours in, cars and vans will no doubt soon replace the three-wheeled pedicabs and motorcycles which throng the busy streets.

Geography

Lying entirely below the Tropic of Cancer, Vietnam has a tropical climate in the south and a monsoonal climate in the north. A hot, rainy season extends from May to mid-September and a warm, dry season from mid-October to mid-March. Occupying a land area of 127,246 square miles, Vietnam is roughly the size of California. But that comparison is misleading—South Vietnam alone, if superimposed on a map of the United States, would extend from Pittsburgh, Pennsylvania, to Savannah, Georgia.

Occupying the eastern portion of the Southeast Asian Indochina peninsula, Vietnam has a 2,386-mile land boundary, with an 800-mile border with China to the northwest, a 972-mile border with Laos to the southwest, and a 614-mile border with Cambodia to the southwest. To the east it has a 2,152-mile coastline extending along the Gulf of Tonkin and the South China Sea.

Described as resembling a carrying-pole with containers of rice at each end, the fertile rice-growing Red River delta occupies the northern portion of Vietnam. The central area consists of a mountainous coastal strip and an inland highland. The even more fertile Mekong delta, one of the world's great rice-growing areas, comprises the southern portion. Only about 22 percent of Vietnam is arable, however. Except for the two deltas and several enclaves along the coast suitable for wet-land rice farming, most of the country is dominated by the Chaîne Annamitique, a north-south mountain range originating in Tibet and China and extending the length of Vietnam from the Chinese border to about 50 miles north of Saigon.

With peaks ranging from 5,000 to 8,521 feet, the Chaîne Annamitique forms the western border with Laos and Cambodia. Irregular in height and form, it breaks off into numerous spurs that divide the coastal strip and make communication between the north and the south difficult. In the middle of what was South Vietnam, the Chaîne Annamitique forms a plateau area known as the Central Highlands. About 100 miles wide and 200 miles long, this sparsely settled region covers approximately 20,000 square miles.

Geography played a key role in the conduct of military operations in Vietnam. During the war with the French, the Viet Minh were able to use the mountain fasts of the Chaîne Annamitique and the border areas with China to stage their forces for attacks against French positions in the Red River delta. During the Second Indochina War they used not only the border areas in Laos and Cambodia as staging areas, but also the Ho Chi Minh Trail along the Chaîne Annamitique, which gave them the advantage of interior lines.

To understand this advantage, one must visualize South Vietnam as a long bow, with South Vietnam's north-south road networks, which followed the curvature of the coastline, forming the bow, and the Ho Chi Minh Trial, which followed the relatively straight line of the mountains, forming the bow-string. North Vietnamese forces could thus move more quickly than the South Vietnamese defenders to almost any point in South Vietnam. The advantage of interior lines was offset by the tactical mobility provided by U.S. helicopter and fixed-wing airlifts but proved critical in the final 1975 offensive, when that airlift was no longer available to South Vietnamese forces.

The Nha Trang shore forms part of the narrow coastal strip known as the Central Lowlands, where torrential rivers produce fertile delta regions well suited to rice cultivation. Fishing, especially along the coast, remains crucial to Vietnam's economy.

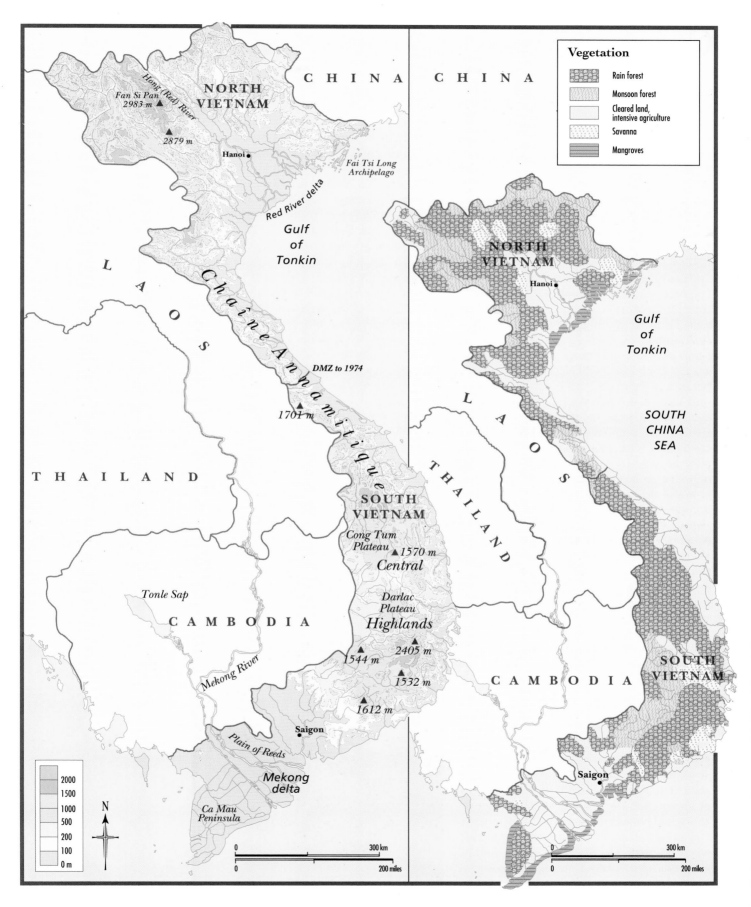

Vegetation

- Rain forest
- Monsoon forest
- Cleared land, intensive agriculture
- Savanna
- Mangroves

Left map:

CHINA

NORTH VIETNAM

Hong (Red) River

Fan Si Pan
2983 m ▲

▲ 2879 m

Hanoi ●

Fai Tsi Long Archipelago

Red River delta

Gulf of Tonkin

L A O S

Chaîne Annamitique

T H A I L A N D

DMZ to 1974

▲ 1701 m

SOUTH VIETNAM

Cong Tum Plateau ▲ 1570 m

Central

Tonle Sap

C A M B O D I A

Darlac Plateau

Highlands

▲ 1544 m

2405 m ▲

Mekong River

▲ 1532 m

▲ 1612 m

Saigon ●

Plain of Reeds

Mekong delta

Ca Mau Peninsula

2000
1500
1000
500
200
100
0 m

N

0 ___ 300 km

0 ___ 200 miles

Right map:

CHINA

NORTH VIETNAM

Hanoi ●

Gulf of Tonkin

L A O S

T H A I L A N D

SOUTH CHINA SEA

C A M B O D I A

SOUTH VIETNAM

Saigon ●

0 ___ 300 km

0 ___ 200 miles

Culture, People, and Language

The geographic realities of Vietnam had a determining influence on the evolution of Vietnamese culture. The north-south mountains of the Chaîne Annamitique turned Vietnam into a cultural peninsula by blocking the eastward flow of Indian culture and encouraging the southward flow of Chinese culture, just as they protected and channeled the prehistoric migration from the southern part of China. Thus Vietnam, alone of the nations of Southeast Asia, was primarily influenced by Chinese rather than Indian culture.

This Chinese culture shaped Vietnamese language, writing, and political institutions. Like Chinese, the Vietnamese language is tonal, with the meaning of words changed by their inflection. Vietnamese was written in Chinese ideographs until the 17th century, when it was transcribed into the Roman alphabet by a French priest, Alexandre de Rhodes, who added a series of diacritical marks to this alphabet to indicate the five tones that characterize the Vietnamese language. The Burmese, Cambodian, Thai, and Lao languages, by comparison, are written in a form of Pali script derived from religious Indian texts.

While the remainder of Southeast Asia is dominated by Hinayana Buddhism, which remains closer to the Indian Hindu roots of the religion, most Vietnamese people follow Mahayana Buddhism, which is practised in China, Japan and Korea. Preceding Buddhism, however, was Chinese Confucianism, the philosophies behind which profoundly influenced Vietnamese political institutions. As early as the 1st century AD, Vietnam had a sophisticated governmental structure and a civil service system based on the Chinese system, where mandarins (government officials) were selected through countrywide exams.

Between 85 and 90 percent of Vietnamese people are ethnic Vietnamese who, along with the 3 percent ethnic Chinese minority, live primarily in the Red River and Mekong River delta areas, and in rice-growing enclaves along the coast. The sparsely settled mountainous areas of the interior are populated by a number of aboriginal tribes known as the Montagnards ("mountain people"). The tribes in the former North Vietnam are primarily of mongoloid extraction, and like the Vietnamese themselves, emigrated from China. The tribes in what was South Vietnam, however, are of Austroasiatic, Malayo-Polynesian and Mon-Khmer ethnic extraction, indicating that they originally emigrated to Indochina from the south and west.

Whatever their origin, the Montagnards had one trait in common—their hatred for the Vietnamese. The White Tai tribesmen in North Vietnam, for example, teamed with the French against the Viet Minh in the First Indochina War. In the Second Indochina War, the U.S. Special Forces recruited many Montagnard tribes in the south to guard against North Vietnamese infiltration.

It has been argued that Vietnam's Sinitic culture, especially its "mandate of heaven" concept, under which a ruler governed by divine right, predisposed it to the Communist model of the "dictatorship of the proletariat" and the hierarchical governmental structure of "democratic centralism." But these arguments do not survive the passage of time. In retrospect, it is obvious that it was not the force of Communist ideas but the force of Communist arms that overwhelmed South Vietnam. It seems highly unlikely that Vietnam (or China either) will long tolerate being misgoverned by Marxism-Leninism, a failed 19th-century Western philosophy that has been thoroughly repudiated by most of the world.

The pace of life is slow and most areas of Vietnam remain largely unspoilt, despite industrial growth.

The principles underpinning Vietnamese political and social institutions are often derived from the thought of the Chinese philosopher Confucius (551–479 BC), who strove to perfect government by perfecting a benign class of scholars

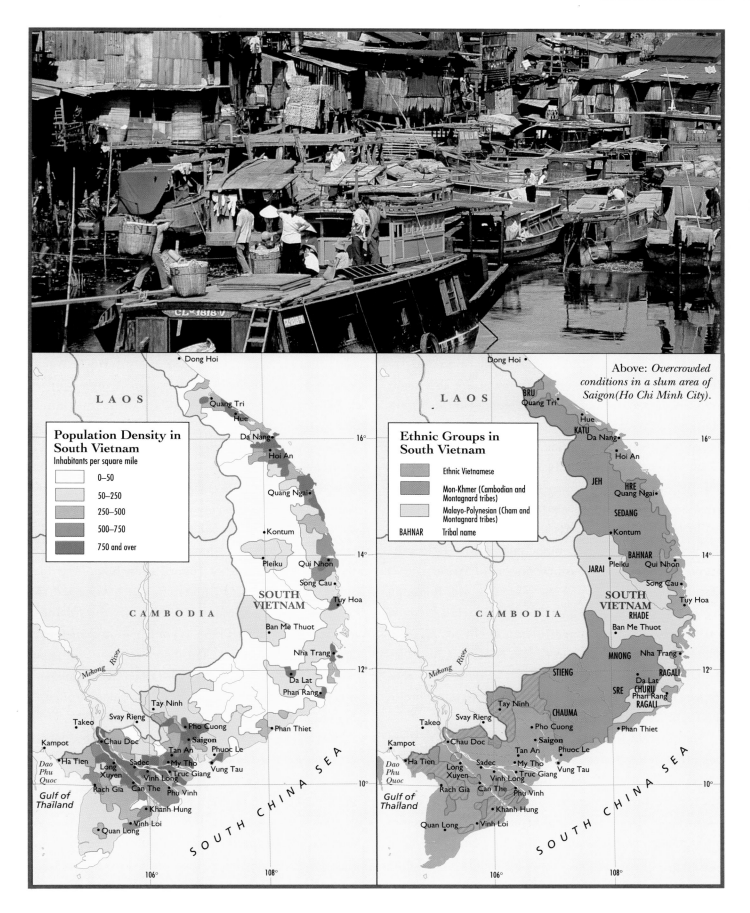

Above: *Overcrowded conditions in a slum area of Saigon (Ho Chi Minh City).*

Population Density in South Vietnam
Inhabitants per square mile
- 0–50
- 50–250
- 250–500
- 500–750
- 750 and over

Ethnic Groups in South Vietnam
- Ethnic Vietnamese
- Mon-Khmer (Cambodian and Montagnard tribes)
- Malayo-Polynesian (Cham and Montagnard tribes)

BAHNAR   Tribal name

Part II: The Legacy of History

"When it came to Vietnam, we found ourselves setting policy for a region that was terra incognita," wrote former defense secretary Robert S. McNamara, in *In Retrospect: The Tragedy and Lessons of Vietnam*, his 1995 apologia for his feckless conduct. "Worse, our government lacked experts for us to consult to compensate for our ignorance about Southeast Asia. The irony of this gap was that it existed largely because the top East Asian and China experts in the State Department—John Paton Davies Jr., John Stewart Service, and John Carter Vincent—had been purged during the McCarthy hysteria of the 1950s. Without men like these to provide sophisticated, nuanced insights, we—certainly I—badly misread China's objectives and mistook its bellicose rhetoric to imply a drive toward regional hegemony. We also totally underestimated the nationalistic aspect of Ho Chi Minh's movement. We saw him first as a Communist and only second as a Vietnamese nationalist."

McNamara's attempt to blame his failures on others, like his strategies for the war, does not bear close scrutiny. How did the "sophisticated, nuanced insights" provided by his East Asian experts affect President Franklin D. Roosevelt's policy toward Indochina? At the 1945 Yalta Conference, where the Allied powers of World War II decided on the makeup of the postwar world, Roosevelt asked China's generalissimo Chiang Kai-shek if he wanted Indochina. The Generalissimo declined. As John Paton Davies himself says in *Dragon by the Tail*, his excellent 1972 account of 20th-century U.S.–East Asian relations, "Roosevelt's China policy does not contribute to his reputation as a great president."

Having knowledgeable experts and listening to them are two different things. With his overweening arrogance, McNamara would not even listen to his military experts, preferring instead the mathematical formulas of his "whiz kids." There is no reason to believe, his present protestations notwithstanding, that he would have been any more willing to listen to the "old China hands" than Roosevelt had been.

Davies called Roosevelt's policies "illusioned and credulous." They were, like subsequent Vietnam policies, a continuation of the policies the United States had practiced in East Asia since the turn of the century. During the Boxer Rebellion in 1900, for example, the United States had "spacious commitments—to 'preserve,' to 'protect,' and to 'safeguard'" China. "These undertakings," noted Davies, "were unsupported by the determination and the necessary means to make good so extravagant a policy. At best this was diplomacy by incantation."

Secretary of State Dean Rusk, McNamara's Vietnam War contemporary, was certainly not unaware of East Asian history. A Rhodes Scholar and pre-World War II college professor, Rusk served as an Army major on General "Vinegar Joe" Stilwell's staff in the China–Burma–India theater (CBI) during World War II.

One anecdote from that period is revealing. In his autobiography, *As I Saw It*, Rusk tells of how, when French intelligence officers began to ask the CBI to parachute them into Indochina, he repeatedly questioned Washington about U.S. policy toward that area. "Finally, in early 1945, the Joint Chiefs of Staff sent us a paper on that subject, 'U.S. Policy Toward Indochina.' The first sheet said, 'The Joint Chiefs of Staff have asked the President for a statement of U.S. Policy toward Indochina. The President's reply is contained in Annex A.' I flipped over to Annex A, and there was a sheet of paper that said, 'When asked by the Joint Chiefs for a statement of U.S. policy toward Indochina, the President replied, "I don't want to hear any more about Indochina."'"

After the war, Rusk served as deputy undersecretary of state, assistant secretary of state for Far Eastern affairs during the Korean War, and secretary of state during much of the Vietnam War. Significantly, he did not buy McNamara's argument that the government lacked Southeast Asia experts. "I worked with John Service and John Paton Davies when they were General Stilwell's political advisers in CBI and I knew … many of the old

China hands," Rusk noted in 1990. "They were fine Foreign Service officers, entirely loyal to the United States, and their reports about China have stood history's tests well." I testified in Service's loyalty hearings, and Davies as well, but to no avail.

What McNamara called the McCarthy hysteria of the 1950s did not "mean that Foreign Service officers became afraid to report candidly their views about policy," said Rusk. "Those who rose to the top of the Foreign Service throughout this period expressed themselves freely and forcibly, whether or not their views meshed with existing policy. While the careers of some very able men were tarnished or ruined, the claim that McCarthyism stifled the Foreign Service has been exaggerated." That said, how could the United States, and Rusk in particular, have disregarded the lessons of history, especially the centuries of Sino-Vietnamese hostility, to such a degree? How could they have taken seriously Secretary of State John Foster Dulles' statement that North Vietnam was a proxy for Communist China, and that any extension of North Vietnam's control in Vietnam would mean a dangerous enlargement of China's effective control?

The reason, surprisingly enough, is that the Communists told us this was the case. The most trenchant analysis of Cold War misperceptions was Professor John H. Kautsky's March 1965 article, "Myth, Self-Fulfilling Prophecy, and Symbolic Reassurance in the East-West Conflict" in the *Journal of Conflict Resolution.* An example of myth, defined as "a complex of remote goals, tense moral moods and expectations of apocalyptic success," was the Marxist tenet that the common interests of the working class transcend nationalism. The party line was that the class struggle had replaced historical antagonisms between nation-states and that Socialist brotherhood had erased all national boundaries within the Communist sphere.

The Korean War, as President Truman and his advisers believed, was thus the work of "monolithic world Communism" directed by Moscow, not (as later evidence proved) primarily the brainchild of North Korea's Kim Il-sung. North Vietnam's later aggression was seen in exact-

ly the same light. With this reasoning, John Foster Dulles' belief that North Vietnam was a Chinese proxy became a self-fulfilling prophecy ("a false definition of the situation evoking a new behavior that makes the originally false conception come true"), as did the resulting fear of Chinese intervention, which was reinforced by the symbolic reassurance ("emotional commitment to a symbol") of the Korean War.

"Our China specialists stated almost unanimously that if we sent American ground troops into North Vietnam, the chances of Chinese intervention were high," Rusk wrote. The United States thus tried "to avoid threatening the Chinese or leaving our intentions unclear, as had been done by General MacArthur's advance to the Yalu. The possibility of Chinese intervention definitely influenced how we fought the war."

Professor Kautsky explained that "myths, no matter how untrue, do have very real consequences; that

The Museum of History in Hanoi, where the rich diversity of Vietnam's cultural, mythological, and military past lives on.

prophecies based on initially false perceptions can produce conditions which really exist (and thus fulfill the prophecy); that men react to symbols by real behavior, be it activity or quiescence ... If men define situations as real, they are real in their consequences."

Thirty years after these words were written, their truths are glaringly apparent. The Sino-Soviet split, the reemergence of fiercely nationalistic independent states in Eastern Europe, the 1978 invasion of Communist Cambodia by its Vietnamese Communist "brothers," and the 1979 Sino-Vietnamese border war all give the lie to the fanciful notion that the common interests of the proletariat transcend nationalism and that Communism renders historical antagonisms meaningless.

While this section also explores the legacy of French colonialism, the legacy of China remains much more important. As Stanley Karnow reports, when Ho Chi Minh had to choose between allowing the French to return to Indochina after World War II and expelling the Chinese, who had occupied the northern part of Vietnam in order to disarm the Japanese, he had no difficulty in making a decision. "You fools!" he said. "Don't you realize what it means if the Chinese remain? Don't you remember your history? The last time the Chinese came, they stayed a thousand years. The French are foreigners. They are weak. Colonialism is dying. The white man is finished in Asia. But if the Chinese stay now, they will never go. As for me, I prefer to sniff French shit for five years than eat Chinese shit for the rest of my life."

During my visits to Hanoi between 1975 and 1985 as a negotiator on the POW/MIA issue, a regular feature of the official itinerary was a tour of the historical museum, where elaborate models of Vietnamese battles with the Chinese were on display, as well as a visit to the "Restored Sword" park and a recounting of the Vietnamese version of the Arthurian legend. According to mythology, Le Loi was a simple fisherman who cast his net into the lake and brought up a magic sword that made him invincible. In fact, Le Loi led a revolt against the Chinese Ming invaders, routing them at the battle of Tot Dong and ending centuries of direct Chinese rule.

One of the main streets in Saigon, Hai Ba Trung, was named after the Trung sisters, who also won fame for their battles against the Chinese. Trung Trac and her sister Trung Nhi raised a revolt against the Chinese in AD 40 and set up an independent state. When the Chinese crushed the rebellion two years later, the sisters committed suicide rather than surrender.

"Vietnamese seem particularly proud of figures from antiquity who were the cleverest in combat or who threw themselves away in some grand battlefield *beau geste*," wrote Douglas Pike. "Hanoi historians today treat this spirit mostly as the manifestation of exemplary behavior ... It is the spirit of *chinh nghia*, literally 'just cause,' connoting a highly moral act, rooted in rationality, compassion, and responsibility. It was this spirit that motivated the Vietnamese in the struggle against Mongol barbarism and against *Han-hwa* (Sino-ization) efforts by the sons of Han, as even today it motivates Vietnamese against perceived Chinese hegemonism."

The legacy of history lives on. Ironically, with the 1991 dissolution of the Soviet Union, Vietnam's former counterweight to Chinese hegemony, the country has now turned to its erstwhile American adversary to provide the power balance essential to national survival.

Both France and China have held Vietnam under their sway during the country's tumultuous history. The two invading cultures clashed at the battle of Son Tay in 1883 (right), when Admiral Amedee Courbet's troops drove the forces of Lui Yung-fu from the Red River delta.

" THE ' BLACK FLAG ' SOLDIER . . . DIED WITH HIS FACE TO THE FOE " (p. 392).

Chinese Invaders 500 BC—1427

Chinese accounts mention a Viet kingdom that existed in about 500 BC south of the Yangtse River. This kingdom fell in 333 BC and its inhabitants, one of the many tribal peoples in southern China at the time, moved farther south. United in 207 BC as the Kingdom of Nam ("Southern") Viet, it was overthrown in 111 BC by the armies of the Chinese Han Dynasty. Nam Viet became Giao Chi, the southernmost of the Chinese provinces. A revolt in AD 39 led by two sisters, Trung Trac and Trung Nhi, gained brief independence, but after four years of independent rule, the Chinese gained control again and the sisters committed suicide rather than submit to foreign domination.

Chinese rule survived the fall of the Han Dynasty in AD 220 and the ensuing period of confusion. In 679 the T'ang Dynasty made the province of Giao Chi a protectorate and renamed it Annam ("pacified south"). In 938 the dynasty began to disintegrate, and Vietnamese general Ngo Quyen led a revolt. At the battle of Bach Dang, near present-day Haiphong, he drove the Chinese imperial forces from the Red River delta. Driving iron-tipped stakes into the bed of the tidal Bach Dang River, he provoked a Chinese attack at high tide. When the tide ebbed, the Chinese fleet became impaled and were destroyed by the Viet forces. Ngo Quyen founded the Ngo Dynasty in 946 and the first independent Vietnamese state was formed.

In 968, Dinh Bo Linh seized power and renamed the country Dai Co Viet ("Kingdom of the Watchful Hawk"). He then sent an emissary to the Chinese court requesting confirmation of his authority to rule, making Dai Co Viet one of the first suzerain states of the Chinese empire. The Dinh Dynasty was succeeded by the Ly Dynasty in 1009, which in 1069 changed the country's name to Dai Viet ("Greater Viet"), a name which survived until 1802. Yet another Chinese invasion was repelled in 1076.

In 1225, the throne was seized by the Tran Dynasty which held power for the next 175 years. Using guerrilla tactics, Vietnamese general Tran Hung Dao repulsed three Mongol invasions by the armies of Kublai Khan in 1257, 1284, and 1287 respectively. In the last of these battles in the Red River valley in 1287, Tran Dung Dao's forces routed 300,000 Mongol troops. Later, however, Dai Viet resumed its

status as a suzerian state of the Mongol Yuan Dynasty that then ruled China.

In 1400 an ambitious regent, Ho Qui Ly, usurped the Dai Viet throne, giving the Chinese Ming Dynasty an excuse to intervene on the pretext of restoring the Tran Dynasty to power. Within a year of the Chinese invasion in 1406, Dai Viet was once again a province of China. The Ming were harsh overseers, and their oppression sparked a Vietnamese national resistance movement, led by an aristocratic landowner called Le Loi.

In a tale that recalls the British Arthurian legend, Le Loi, one of the great heroes of Vietnamese history, received a magic sword from what is now called the "Restored Sword Lake" in Hanoi. His guerrilla army seized control of the countryside, forcing the Chinese to retreat into the cities. After wearing the enemy down with his guerrilla tactics, Le Loi attacked directly, using elephants against their horse cavalry. In 1426, at Tot Dong west of Hanoi, he routed the Chinese armies and forced their withdrawal. In a signed accord in 1427, the Chinese recognized Vietnamese independence.

Le Loi established his capital at Hanoi, naming it Dong Kinh, which, as Tonkin, became the name for northern Vietnam. Although he immediately resumed the tributary ties to China, ties that would continue into the late 19th century, the battle of Tot Dong marked the end of 15 centuries of Chinese attempts to conquer Vietnam by force of arms.

The Hoān Kiem or "Restored Sword Lake" in Hanoi, from which Le Loi, the self-proclaimed "Prince of Pacification" and a guerrilla warrior of immense courage and compassion, is said to have received a magic sword that endowed him with supernatural powers.

"The rule of the Ming was probably worse than anything Vietnam had ever experienced. The country was bled white. Battalions of forced laborers were sent into mines, forests, and to the bottom of the sea to extract Vietnam's natural wealth for China ... The women were made to dress in the Chinese mode and men forced to let their hair grow long ... In these years of Ming rule, the Vietnamese people learned to live with burning hatred in their hearts and to conceal their anguish until the time was ripe for revenge."

—Joseph Buttinger

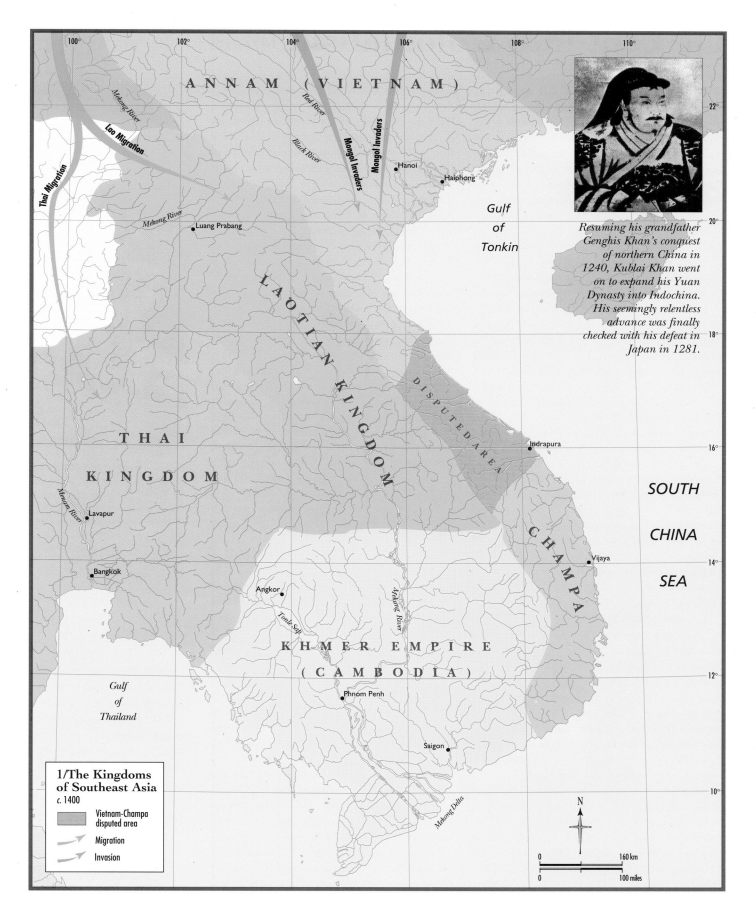

A N N A M   (V I E T N A M)

Mekong River

Lao Migration

Thai Migration

Red River

Black River

Mongol Invaders

Mongol Invaders

● Hanoi

● Haiphong

Mekong River

● Luang Prabang

L A O T I A N   K I N G D O M

T H A I

K I N G D O M

Menam River

● Lavapur

● Bangkok

D I S P U T E D   A R E A

● Indrapura

C H A M P A

● Vijaya

Gulf
of
Tonkin

SOUTH

CHINA

SEA

*Resuming his grandfather
Genghis Khan's conquest
of northern China in
1240, Kublai Khan went
on to expand his Yuan
Dynasty into Indochina.
His seemingly relentless
advance was finally
checked with his defeat in
Japan in 1281.*

● Angkor

Tonle Sap

Mekong River

K H M E R   E M P I R E

(C A M B O D I A)

● Phnom Penh

Gulf
of
Thailand

● Saigon

Mekong Delta

**1/The Kingdoms
of Southeast Asia**
c. 1400

Vietnam-Champa
disputed area

Migration

Invasion

N

0   160 km
0   100 miles

Descent into Colonialism 1427–1893

With the Chinese defeat at Tot Dong, Le Loi ascended the throne as Le Thai To and founded the Le Dynasty. He began the "March to the South" in earnest, as the Dai Viet expanded south from the Red River delta, defeating the Kingdom of Champa in 1471 and driving the Cambodians from the Mekong delta. The southern tip of the Indochinese peninsula was finally brought under Dai Viet control in 1780.

After Le Thai To's death in 1497, the Le Dynasty was wracked by internal dissent. The throne was usurped in 1527 by General Mac Dang Dung, who was in turn deposed in 1592 by the Trinh family, who "restored" the Ly Dynasty by placing a Trinh puppet on the throne. This claim was challenged by the Nguyen family, who created a government in exile south of the 17th parallel (the dividing line between North and South Vietnam from 1954–1975). After half a century of fighting, a truce was concluded which divided Vietnam at the 17th parallel for the next century. Both families ruled nominally under the Le Dynasty, which was actually under their control.

This period ended with the Tay Son uprising, a revolt by the Nguyen brothers against the unrelated ruling Nguyen family. In 1778, the eldest brother, Ngac, proclaimed himself emperor over the southern Dai Viet. His younger brother, Hue, defeated the Trinh family in the north in 1786, and in 1788 expanded his power to the south at the expense of his brother. Vietnam was once again united. But Hue's reign was destined to be brief.

The last descendant of the Nguyen lords, Nguyen Anh, survived the Tay Son rebellion with the help of a missionary, Pigneau de Béhaine. This French bishop raised a small group of Frenchmen to aid Anh, and the last king of the Tay Son was defeated in 1802. Anh became Emperor Gia Long and founded the Nguyen Dynasty, which renamed the country Vietnam ("Viet of the South"). In 1803 it was formally recognized by the Ch'ing Dynasty as a suzerain state under Chinese protection.

Gia Long had reunified Vietnam, but had made a fatal mistake in allowing the French to help him gain the throne. France wanted to establish its own Asian empire to rival those of the Dutch and the British. The conquest of Indochina began with the capture of Tourane (now Da Nang) in 1858, ostensibly to protect

missionaries there. Saigon was captured in February 1859, and after a brief diversion to fight the Second Opium War with China, the French completed their conquest in 1861. In June 1862 the Vietnamese court at Hue ceded Saigon and surrounds. The western part of the Mekong delta was annexed in 1867, completing the territorial formation of what became the French colony of Cochin China. In August 1883 the French fleet attacked Hue and forced a treaty recognizing a French protectorate over Tonkin (northern Vietnam) and Annam (central Vietnam). The Imperial capital at Hue was ostensibly left in charge of internal affairs, but it was the French who exercised real control.

France now turned to Chinese claims of suzerainty over Vietnam. In 1865, Liu Yung-fu, the self-proclaimed "General of the Black Flags," had established a fortified camp at Son Tay. The Chinese government ordered its armies in Kwangsi and Yunnan to cooperate with Liu's Black Flags, reinforcing the 3,000-man garrison with 1,500 troops. In November 1883, French troops were ordered to occupy this base. The 5,500-strong force moved up the Red River in December and a violent assault by French Foreign Legionnaires and Marines, supported by a massive artillery barrage, drove the Chinese from the city.

The "Black Flag Wars" were over, but the "Tonkin Wars," the most famous of which was the battle of Tuyen Quang, now began. After distinguishing themselves at Son Tay, the 600 men of the Foreign Legion's 1st and 2nd companies were garrisoning the border fort at Tuyen Quang when it came under attack by 20,000 Chinese regular troops. On January 23, 1885, a ferocious battle began. Experienced sappers, the Chinese invested the fort with a band of trenches from which they mounted their assault. Just when it appeared that the garrison would be overwhelmed, a relief column arrived, and on March 3 the Chinese withdrew.

While France was celebrating this victory, a series of humiliating defeats took place elsewhere in Tonkin, including the fall of Lang Son on March 28. But before the Chinese could exploit their successes, an armistice was declared in April. On June 9 the Treaty of Tientsin was signed, whereby China renounced its suzerainty and recognized the French protectorate over what became French Indochina.

A French print of 1888 shows an idealized vision of tirailleurs tonkinois, *the name given to native troops serving under the colonial administration. Tonkin was officially a French protectorate at this time, but actually came under direct French rule.*

"The occupation became a prolonged warfare, in which 25,000 French, compelled to guard innumerable posts, had to oppose an intangible enemy, appearing by night, vanishing by day, and practising brigandage rather than war."

—De Lanessan,
La colonialisation française en Indo-chine, 1895

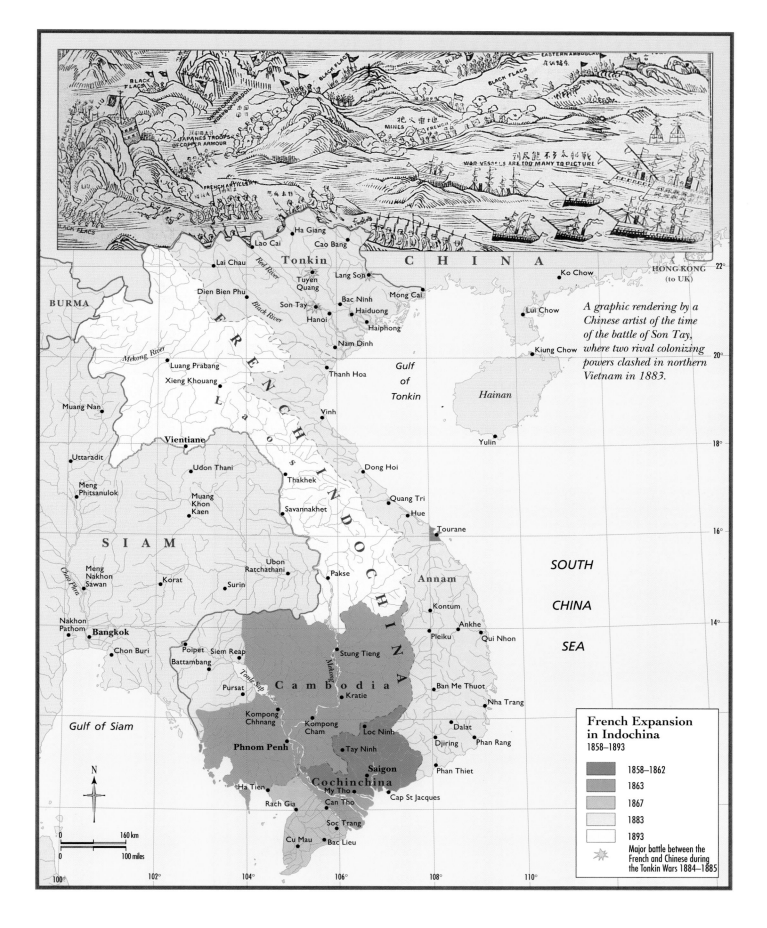

A graphic rendering by a Chinese artist of the time of the battle of Son Tay, where two rival colonizing powers clashed in northern Vietnam in 1883.

BLACK FLAGS
LIU
JAPANES TROOPS OF COPPER ARMOUR
MINES
FRENCH
EASTERN AMBUSCADE
BLACK FLAGS
WAR VESSELS ARE TOO MANY TO PICTURE
FRENCH ARTILLERY
BLACK FLAGS

CHINA

HONG KONG
(to UK)

Ha Giang
Lao Cai
Cao Bang
Tonkin
Lai Chau
Red River
Tuyen Quang
Lang Son
Mong Cai
Ko Chow
Dien Bien Phu
Black River
Son Tay
Bac Ninh
Haiduong
Lui Chow
Hanoi
Haiphong
Nam Dinh
Kiung Chow
BURMA

Mekong River
Luang Prabang
Thanh Hoa
Gulf
of
Tonkin
Xieng Khouang
Hainan
Muang Nan
Vinh
Yulin
Vientiane
Uttaradit
Dong Hoi
Meng Phitsanulok
Udon Thani
Thakhek
Quang Tri
Muang Khon Kaen
Savannakhet
Hue
Tourane
SIAM
Ubon Ratchathani
Meng Nakhon Sawan
Korat
Pakse
Annam
SOUTH
Surin
Kontum
Chao Phra
Nakhon Pathom
Bangkok
Ankhe
Pleiku
Qui Nhon
CHINA
Chon Buri
Poipet
Siem Reap
Stung Tieng
SEA
Battambang
Mekong
Cambodia
Ban Me Thuot
Pursat
Tonle Sap
Kratie
Nha Trang
Kompong Chhnang
Kompong Cham
Loc Ninh
Dalat
Gulf of Siam
Phnom Penh
Tay Ninh
Djiring
Phan Rang
Ha Tien
Saigon
Phan Thiet
Cochinchina
My Tho
Rach Gia
Can Tho
Cap St Jacques
N
Soc Trang
Cu Mau
Bac Lieu

French Expansion in Indochina
1858–1893

	1858–1862
	1863
	1867
	1883
	1893

⁕ Major battle between the French and Chinese during the Tonkin Wars 1884–1885

0   160 km
0   100 miles

100°   102°   104°   106°   108°   110°

French Indochina 1858–1941

In Asia the 18th and 19th centuries were a time of empire for the Western powers. Beginning with the establishment of the East India Company in 1609, the British gradually gained control of India (including present-day Bangladesh, Myanmar [Burma] and Pakistan) by the mid-19th century and of Malaysia in 1867. The Netherlands gained territorial power over Java in 1750 and gradually brought the rest of Indonesia (then called the Dutch East Indies) under its sway. As the Manchu Dynasty disintegrated, China, once the master of East Asia, was itself divided up into Russian, British, French, and Portuguese spheres of influence. Even the supposedly anti-colonialist United States was not immune, gaining the Philippines from Spain in 1898.

Not to be outdone, France too acquired an Asian empire in what became known as French Indochina. Cambodia became a French protectorate in 1863, and Laos in 1893. But the heart of the empire was Vietnam. Using the pretext of protecting French missionaries, the French conquest of Vietnam began in 1858. The southern portion of Vietnam, including the Mekong delta, was ceded to the French by the Vietnamese Imperial Court in 1862, becoming the French colony of Cochin China (named after "Giao Chi," the Chinese characters for the area). The central portion, Annam, became a French protectorate in 1883, and with the battle of Tuyen Quang, Tonkin was also confirmed as a French protectorate.

Vietnamese independence was at an end, and the name "Vietnam" was officially eliminated. In Annam, the emperor and his officials at the Imperial Court at Hue were left in charge of internal affairs, but functioned under close French scrutiny. Active armed resistance to French control, however, continued into the early 20th century. The final phase of the French consolidation was the formation of the Indochinese Union in 1887, consisting of Tonkin, Annam, Cochin China, and Cambodia, joined by Laos in 1893. The Indochinese Union was administered under a French governor-general who was directly responsible to the minister of culture in Paris.

When U.S. president Woodrow Wilson's call for self-determination after World War I was rejected by the architects of the 1919 Treaty of Versailles, many Asian nationalists, including Ho Chi Minh, then living in France, turned to the successful 1917 Russian Revolution as a model for the future. Within Vietnam many anti-French secret societies sprang up, and in 1930 an uprising was staged at Yen Bay, north of Saigon. In the repression that followed, the nationalist movement was forced underground and came under the control of the Indo-Chinese Communist Party. The French had unwittingly set the stage for what was to follow.

"The soldiers had pinioned her on her back, gagged her and then bayoneted her over and over again … until she was effectively dead. After which, they cut off her finger to retrieve a ring and her head to acquire a necklace. On the open stretch of salt-marsh the three bodies were left: the naked corpse of the little girl, the young woman disemboweled and with her right stiffened forearm clenched up into heaven, and the body of the old man: this one particularly horrible, naked like the others, distorted by the roasting, glistening with melted fat that had run out and congealed on the stomach, now scorched and gilded like the skin of a roast pig."

—"Annamite Women under French Rule," article by Ho Chi Minh in *Le Paria*, August 1, 1922

Left: *Hanoi was the starting point for the extension of French colonial power throughout Tonkin and the capital of French Indochina from 1887 to 1946.*

Top right: *Founded in the 3rd century AD, the imperial capital of Hue was to see turbulent times. Occupied by the French in 1883, it was also the scene of bloody battles during the Tet Offensive, when much of the city, with its magnificent palace and tombs, was destroyed.*

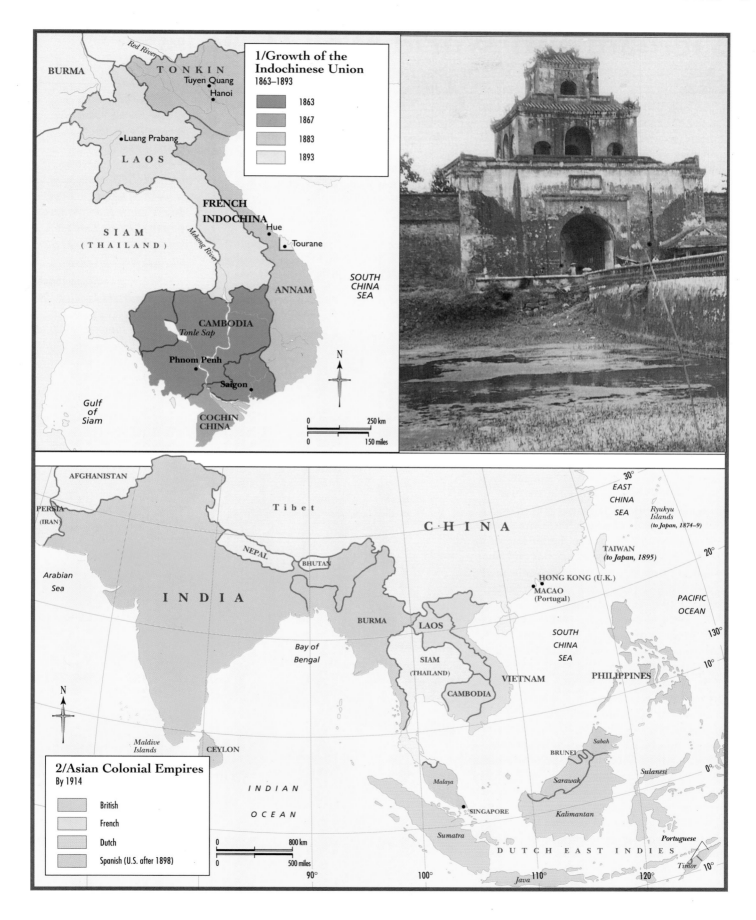

1/Growth of the Indochinese Union
1863–1893

- 1863
- 1867
- 1883
- 1893

BURMA

TONKIN

Red River

Tuyen Quang
Hanoi

Luang Prabang

LAOS

FRENCH INDOCHINA

SIAM (THAILAND)

Mekong River

Hue

Tourane

ANNAM

SOUTH CHINA SEA

CAMBODIA

Tonle Sap

Phnom Penh

Saigon

Gulf of Siam

COCHIN CHINA

N

0   250 km
0   150 miles

2/Asian Colonial Empires
By 1914

- British
- French
- Dutch
- Spanish (U.S. after 1898)

AFGHANISTAN

PERSIA (IRAN)

Arabian Sea

Tibet

CHINA

NEPAL

BHUTAN

INDIA

BURMA

Bay of Bengal

LAOS

SIAM (THAILAND)

CAMBODIA

VIETNAM

SOUTH CHINA SEA

30°

EAST CHINA SEA

Ryukyu Islands
(to Japan, 1874–9)

TAIWAN
(to Japan, 1895)

HONG KONG (U.K.)
MACAO
(Portugal)

PACIFIC OCEAN

130°

20°

10°

PHILIPPINES

N

Maldive Islands

CEYLON

INDIAN OCEAN

0   800 km
0   500 miles

Malaya

SINGAPORE

Sumatra

DUTCH EAST INDIES

Java

BRUNEI

Sabah

Sarawak

Kalimantan

Sulanesi

Portuguese

Timor

0°

10°

90°   100°   110°   120°

Vietnam and World War II 1941–1945

With the Russo-Japanese War of 1904–1905, Japan began the destruction of the myth of European superiority. It finished the job with its early victories in World War II. After the fall of France in June 1940, the craven nature of the French Vichy government was revealed when it acceded to Japanese demands that ultimately led to Japanese control of all of Indochina. In August 1940, the Vichy authorities agreed to accept Japan's "pre-eminent" position in the Far East and agreed to grant Japan transit facilities in Tonkin in return for its recognition of French sovereignty in Indochina. But it was a Faustian bargain.

Japan's position was further consolidated in July 1941 when the French and Japanese governments signed military agreements providing for the "common defense of French Indochina." Japan was permitted to station troops in Indochina and to control all important railroads and port facilities as well as virtually all airfields in the south. These airfields—including, by some accounts, Tan Son Nhut air base in the suburbs of Saigon—were used by the Japanese to launch strikes that sank the British battleship HMS *Prince of Wales* and the battle cruiser HMS *Repulse* on December 10, 1941.

A month later, in January 1942, aircraft of General Claire Chennault's China-based American Volunteer Group, better known as the Flying Tigers, launched air raids on Hanoi. When the United States lost its bases in southern China these raids ceased, only to resume in January 1945 with U.S. Navy and Army Air Force strikes from carriers offshore and from the newly liberated Clark Field in the Philippines. These closed Japanese rail and sea lines through Indochina.

In December 1944, the Tokyo government, alarmed over growing anti-Vietnamese activities in Indochina, including those of the U.S. Office of Strategic Services (OSS), decided to displace the French and grant independence to the Vietnamese. On March 9, 1945, the emperor Bao Dai, at the instigation of the Japanese, proclaimed Vietnam's independence under Japanese "protection."

In Hanoi, meanwhile, the Viet Minh, under the leadership of Ho Chi Minh, announced the formation of the Committee for the Liberation of the Vietnamese People. Assuming this movement had allied support, on August 25, 1945,

Bao Dai abdicated and handed over his imperial seal and other symbols of office to Ho Chi Minh. The latter proclaimed the independence of Vietnam and the establishment of the Democratic Republic of Vietnam on September 2, 1945—the same day as the surrender of Japan was formally signed in Tokyo Bay.

Japanese troops move into Indochina under the pretext of a "common defense." Troops were stationed throughout the country by August 4, 1941, and Indochina became part of the "Greater East Asia Co-Prosperity Sphere," a Japanese slogan which was fast becoming reality.

"After the Japs came in, 60,000 French colonials went on living much as before. Little of the old grand manner had to be foregone. Even business went on much as usual … In all Asia, French Indochina was the one efficient Japanese political success. The French did their work for them."

—William Lederer,
The Anguished American, 1969

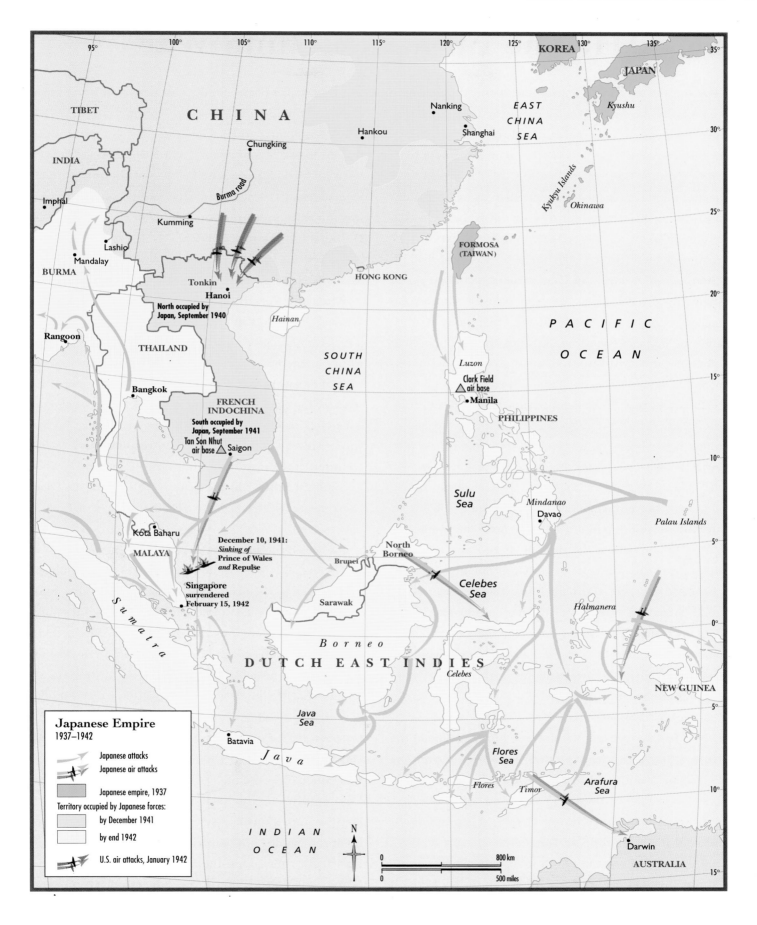

TIBET

CHINA

Nanking

KOREA

JAPAN

EAST CHINA SEA

Kyushu

Hankou

Shanghai

INDIA

Chungking

Imphal

Burma road

Kumming

Kyukyu Islands

Okinawa

Lashio

Mandalay

BURMA

Tonkin

Hanoi

North occupied by Japan, September 1940

Hainan

HONG KONG

FORMOSA (TAIWAN)

PACIFIC OCEAN

Rangoon

THAILAND

SOUTH CHINA SEA

Luzon

Clark Field △ air base

Manila

Bangkok

FRENCH INDOCHINA

South occupied by Japan, September 1941

Tan Son Nhut air base △ Saigon

PHILIPPINES

Sulu Sea

Mindanao

Davao

Palau Islands

Kota Baharu

MALAYA

December 10, 1941:
Sinking of **Prince of Wales** *and* Repulse

Brunei

North Borneo

Celebes Sea

Halmanera

Singapore surrendered February 15, 1942

Sarawak

Borneo

NEW GUINEA

S u m a t r a

DUTCH EAST INDIES

Celebes

Java Sea

Batavia

J a v a

Flores Sea

Flores

Timor

Arafura Sea

INDIAN OCEAN

N

Darwin

AUSTRALIA

Japanese Empire
1937–1942

↦ Japanese attacks

✈ Japanese air attacks

▨ Japanese empire, 1937

Territory occupied by Japanese forces:

☐ by December 1941

☐ by end 1942

✈ U.S. air attacks, January 1942

0   800 km

0   500 miles

Part III: The First Indochina War

"For the United States," cynics have said, "the main lesson of the Vietnam War is to never again become involved in an armed conflict in a former French colony in Indochina." That is a good lesson, although certainly one of rather limited application. And it would have been a good lesson for France in 1945 as well, for their post-World War II attempt to reestablish their colonial empire in Indochina proved to be a tragic mistake.

America had tried to tell them so. Not surprisingly, given its own origins, the United States had always been staunchly anti-colonialist. Even its own foray into colonialism with the annexation of the Philippines in 1898, after the Spanish–American War, was bitterly opposed at home by the Anti-Imperialism League, whose ranks included, among others, the author Mark Twain.

"We hold that the policy known as imperialism is hostile to liberty and tends toward militarism, an evil of which it has been our glory to be free,' read their platform in 1899. "We regret that it has become necessary in the land of Washington and Lincoln to reaffirm that all men, of whatever race or color, are entitled to life, liberty and the pursuit of happiness ... We insist that the subjugation of any people is 'criminal aggression' and open disloyalty to the principles of our Government.

"We hold, with Abraham Lincoln, that 'no man is good enough to govern another man without that man's consent,'" they said, urging "that Congress be promptly convened to announce to the Filipinos our purpose to concede to them the independence for which they have so long fought and which of right is theirs." Seventeen years later, in August 1916, the Jones Act declared that "it is, as it has always been, the purpose of the people of the United States to withdraw their sovereignty over the Philippine Islands and to recognize their independence as soon as a stable government can be established."

It would be another 18 years before this promise was fulfilled in the Philippine Independence Act of 1934, and another 13 years until full independence was granted, on July 4, 1947. But the American anti-colonialist

sentiment was clear. It was eloquently expressed by President Woodrow Wilson in January 1918, in his "Fourteen Points," which formed the basis of peace negotiations to end World War I. Point Five called for "a free, open minded, and absolutely impartial adjustment of all colonial claims," a statement that was interpreted as calling for self-determination for all peoples. As David Halberstam relates, Ho Chi Minh, then in Paris, "prepared his own eight-point program for freedom in Vietnam, based on Wilson's Fourteen Points."

When the Versailles Peace Conference swept aside Wilson's (and Ho Chi Minh's) anti-colonialist proposals, a massive backlash followed. The May 4th Movement in China, named after the 1919 student uprisings against what they saw as their betrayal at Versailles, sowed the seeds of the Communist Party in China and elsewhere in Asia. Ho Chi Minh "turned from the ideologue and the young student rebel into the real revolutionary ... He founded the Inter-colonial Union in 1921 as a Communist Front." In the pages of his paper, *Le Paria*, "he repeatedly attacked the entire structure of French colonialism."

Ironically, the foundation of the First Indochina War had been laid in part by the United States, whose inflated anti-colonialist rhetoric—another example of what John Paton Davies labeled "diplomacy by incantation"—had raised false expectations throughout Asia. When these expectations were not realized, there was a rejection of "Mr. Science and Mr. Democracy," as the American model was then known, and a move toward the model provided by Vladimir Lenin, who had led the successful October 1917 Communist revolution in Russia. As Ho Chi Minh wrote in a 1960 article, "The Path Which Led Me to Leninism," "At first patriotism, not yet Communism, led me to have confidence in Lenin ... Step by step, along the struggle, by studying Marxism-Leninism parallel with participating in practical activities, I gradually came upon the fact that only Socialism and Communism can liberate the oppressed nations and

Amidst the mud and trenches of Dien Bien Phu, France's misguided attempt to reclaim its former colony culminated in a bloodbath, as 10,000 troops under General DeCastries were besieged by the Viet Minh.

working people of the world from slavery."

But Lenin was not Ho's only inspiration. As Stanley Karnow writes, Ho "had been inspired by the Atlantic Charter, issued during the summer of 1941, in which President Franklin D. Roosevelt and British Prime Minister Winston Churchill pledged 'to see sovereign rights and self-government restored to those who have been forcibly deprived of them.'" But, continues Karnow, Roosevelt's position was not entirely clear, despite his anti-colonial reputation. In 1942, he told General Charles de Gaulle, then head of the Free French, that all of France's overseas possessions would be restored after the war. The next year he told his son that he would work "with all [his] might and main" against any plan to "further France's imperialistic ambitions." A year later he

proposed an international trusteeship for Indochina, saying that France had "milked it for one hundred years" and left its people "worse off than they were at the beginning." He later changed his mind yet again, saying that the French could reoccupy Indochina if they pledged to eventually give it its independence.

With much greater issues occupying his attention, in January 1945, three months before his death, Roosevelt told Edward R. Stettinius, his secretary of state, that he "still [did] not want to get mixed up in any Indochina decision,"—the same answer that Major Dean Rusk received when he questioned Washington about the president's Indochina policy.

America's anti-colonial attitudes were sometimes reflected in strange ways. Rush describes the controversy over the shoulder patch for the China–Burma–India theater, which showed the star of India and the sun of China alongside red and white stripes for the United

States. Only Americans could wear it, for it was intended to symbolize that the United States was there to fight the Japanese, not to restore British colonial rule. When the British commander, General William Slim, asked that his troops be allowed to wear it, he was turned down. "That patch and the attitude it represented," said Rusk, "led to some friction with the British." But it was not the only reason for the friction. "Roosevelt strongly believed that the major colonial areas of Asia—India, Burma, Malaya and Indonesia—should emerge from World War II as independent nations. He pressed Churchill hard to promise that Britain would grant India its independence at the end of the war, but Churchill was very resistant.

"I believe that President Roosevelt gave up this idea of an independent Asia around the beginning of 1945," Rusk went on to say. "Perhaps he was growing old and sick; perhaps he was tired of butting his head against Churchill." A year-long gap developed in U.S. policy toward Asia, and in the interim, the British returned to India, Burma, and Malaya, the Dutch returned to Indonesia, and the French returned to Indochina. This, said Rusk, "had major consequences for the future of Southeast Asia."

The beginning of the Cold War between the Soviet Union and the Western democracies further limited the U.S. ability to shape events in Indochina. As Rusk, by then undersecretary of state, explained, "French participation in both the Marshall Plan and the North Atlantic Treaty Organization was indispensable. This meant that Indochina stayed on the back burner. Good Franco-American relations were vital ... and we could not allow these relations to be disrupted over Indochina."

When arguments broke out within the State Department between the European and Far Eastern bureaus over Indochina policy, the European bureau usually won, because it had Secretary of State Dean Acheson's support. "Basically a 'North Atlantic' man," said Rusk, "Acheson was a superb secretary of state, and yet he really didn't give a damn about the brown, yellow,

By 1952 the 90,000-strong French Expeditionary Force was backed up by 100,000 Vietnamese National Army troops (left). But although well-equipped by the French, the men proved highly unreliable.

black and red peoples of the world. He wanted full co-operation with the French." This would come at what would prove to be a terrible price. Interestingly, the major opposition to U.S. support for the French return to Indochina came from the military. As he reports in *The 25-Year War*, in the fall of 1951 Colonel Bruce Palmer, Jr., a student at the Army War College, was part of a work group assigned to do a study on U.S. policy in Southeast Asia. Palmer, who later rose to four-star rank and served as the commander of U.S. Army Vietnam from 1967 to 1968, and as Army vice chief of staff from 1968 to 1973, found that a large majority of the students opposed any U.S. involvement there.

Among the conclusions of their study were that "(1) The United States had probably made a serious mistake in agreeing with its allies to allow French power to be restored in Indochina ... (2) Indochina was of only secondary strategic importance to the United States. The economic and military value of Vietnam, the most important state in the region, was not impressive [and] in any event did not warrant the commitment of U.S. force to its defense ... (3) General war planning by the U.S. Joint Chiefs of Staff envisioned a strategic defense in the Pacific, drawing the U.S. forward defense line to include Japan, South Korea, and the offshore island chain (Okinawa–Taiwan–the Philippines). But in Southeast Asia the line was drawn through the Isthmus of Kra on the mainland, excluding all of Indochina and most of Thailand ... (4) Militarily, the region in general and Vietnam in particular would be an extremely difficult operational area, especially for U.S. forces. Unlike the relatively narrow Korean peninsula, Vietnam presented very long land and coastal borders that would be almost impossible to seal against infiltration and difficult to defend against overt military action ... (5) Politically and psychologically the United States, if it were to become involved, would have to operate under severe disadvantages, for it would inherit the taint of European colonialism. The United States should not become involved in the area beyond providing material aid."

The study accurately reflected the temper of the times as far as the Army was concerned, for then Army chief of staff General Matthew B. Ridgway was adamantly opposed to any U.S. military involvement in Southeast Asia. In March 1954, General Paul Ely, the French chief of staff, asked for American military help to lift the siege of Dien Bien Phu. As Stanley Karnow reveals, Admiral Arthur Radford, the chairman of the Joint Chiefs of Staff, proposed that 60 Air Force B-29 bombers based in the Philippines, escorted by Navy carrier-based fighters, conduct night raids against the Viet Minh perimeter around Dien Bien Phu. While Air Force chief of staff General Nathan Twining agreed, Ridgway was totally opposed.

In his 1956 autobiography, *Soldier: The Memoirs of Matthew B. Ridgway*, Ridgway discussed his analysis of the situation. The Hanoi Delta planning force consisted of eight U.S. Army divisions and 35 engineer battalions and other auxiliary units, almost the same size as the force committed to the Korean War. "As soon as the full report was in," Ridgway said, "I lost no time in having it passed up on the chain of command. It reached President Eisenhower. To a man of his military experience its implications were immediately clear. The idea of intervening was abandoned, and it is my belief that the analysis which the Army made and presented to high authority played a considerable, perhaps a decisive part in persuading our government not to embark on that tragic adventure."

Given the ultimate rationale for the later U.S. intervention discussed in Part IV, an interesting aspect of the Army's analysis was the attention given to China. "The more we studied the situation," wrote Lieutenant General James Gavin, then the Army's deputy chief of staff for plans and operation, "the more we realized that we were, in fact, considering going to war with China … If we would be, in fact, fighting China, then we were fighting her in the wrong place on terms entirely to her advantage … It seemed to U.S. military planners that if an effort were made by the United States to secure Vietnam from Chinese military exploitation, and that if force on the scale that we were talking about were to be employed, then the Chinese would very likely reopen the fighting in Korea."

But the Sino-Vietnamese alliance was not nearly the "lips to teeth" relationship both sides then publicly portrayed, and China was not the "fraternal socialist brother" it appeared to be at the time. Reverting to the centuries-old foreign policy tactic of "using barbarians to control barbarians," China was exploiting Vietnam for its own ends. As Stanley Karnow writes, Chinese premier Zhou En-lai "had concluded by 1953 that France would, sooner or later, scuttle its commitments in Indochina. He estimated, however, that the United States might step in, thus menacing China on its own doorstep. So he favored a negotiated settlement … He would work for just such an accord even at the expense of the Viet Minh. A divided Vietnam suited the Chinese better than a unified neighbor—particularly one that had quarreled with China for two thousand years."

Thus it was that China sold North Vietnam down the river at the 1964 Geneva Conference. As Douglas Pike notes, "Sino-Vietnamese relations during the Vietnam War were complex … China wanted the Vietnamese communists to win but also to follow cautious policies that would not endanger China or threaten to provoke a Chinese–U.S. confrontation." Looking back, Pike wrote, Vietnamese leaders would argue that the fundamental Chinese orientation throughout was a mixture of ideological commitment and selfish national interests, "with the latter always dominating the former;" that their material support was always conditional and never certain; that at critical moments, such as when U.S. air strikes against North Vietnam began, they stood by and did nothing; and that "the Chinese never did care deeply about the Vietnamese and their cause."

A key center of gravity in war, said the great military theorist Karl von Clausewitz, is the community of interests among alliances. The United States was so mesmerized by the delusion of "monolithic world communism" that it did not spot the fissures in the Sino-Vietnamese alliance until the Nixon–Kissinger initiatives in the 1970s. By that time, it was too late to make a difference.

Despite resounding successes, such as this surprise parachute raid on a Viet Minh supply base at Lang Son in 1953, the French engagement in Indochina was destined to end in tragedy.

The Independence Struggle Begins   1945

Long before the defeat of Japan, the groundwork was laid for the struggle which would ultimately result in the end of French rule in Indochina. On May 10, 1941, the Vietnamese Communist Party held a conference chaired by Ho Chi Minh, then known by his cover name of Nguyen Ai Quoc.

Breaking with the existing restriction of party membership to workers' organizations, Ho broadened the movement to include all anti-colonial forces. He called this new organization the Vietnam Doc Lap Dong Minh (Vietnam Independence League), but it is better known as the Viet Minh. As in Stalin's national front anti-fascist coalitions of the 1930s, Communist ideology was played down in favor of nationalism and independence. Adherence to party doctrine was not necessary for membership or participation.

Another important aspect of the new strategy was the development in Vietnam of guerrilla bases patterned on Mao Zedong's guerrilla base in Yenan. Ho wanted to establish bases in a remote area from which to spread Communist influence and to serve as a model for a liberated Vietnam. Cao Bang Province on the Sino-Vietnamese border was selected, and by the end of 1941 training bases had been estab-

After training in Moscow, Ho Chi Minh (1890–1969) returned to Vietnam via China in 1941 to establish the Viet Minh.

lished there to provide cadres for the forthcoming independence struggle.

Playing down his Communist background—he had been a founding member of the French Communist Party in 1920 and had founded the Vietnamese Communist Party in 1930—Ho stressed his anti-Japanese and anti-French credentials, and portrayed the Viet Minh as a nationalist rather than a Communist movement. The best organized of the resistance groups, the Viet Minh dominated the new government that came to power after the Japanese surrender. On August 22, 1945, Emperor Bao Dai asked the Viet Minh to form a government, and abdicated to become its adviser. As Stanley Karnow noted, "Nothing reinforced the Viet Minh cause more than the mercurial Bao Dai's decision to abdicate. For his gesture conferred the 'mandate of heaven' on Ho, giving him a legitimacy that, in Vietnamese eyes, had traditionally resided in the emperor."

An interim government was formed, with Ho Chi Minh as president. Striking a deal with the Chinese Nationalist general, Lu Han, who favored a rival Vietnamese party, the Viet Nam Quon Dan Dang, Ho dissolved his party in November 1945, in return for Lu Han's agreement to elections that would yield a Viet Minh/VNQDD coalition government. This deal was overtaken in February 1946 by a Chinese agreement to withdraw their troops and to allow a French return to Tonkin in exchange for the French abandonment of its old treaty port concessions in China.

Earlier, in his speech of September 2, 1945, in which he announced the liberation of Vietnam, Ho Chi Minh had said, "'We hold truths that all men are created equal, that they are endowed by their Creator with certain unalienable Rights.' This immortal statement is extracted from the Declaration of Independence of the United States of America in 1776. These are undeniable truths."

This cynical attempt to gain the support of the United States in the battle for independence from France would not succeed, but with the establishment of guerrilla base areas and the training of Communist cadres, as well as his successful garnering of the 'mandate of heaven' concept to win public support, Ho Chi Minh had laid the basis for victory in his forthcoming struggle.

"How many times in my life I've been asked: you who know Ho Chi Minh so well, can you say whether he is a nationalist or a communist? The answer is simple: Ho Chi Minh is both. For him, nationalism and communism, the end and the means, complement one another; or rather, they merge inextricably."

—Tran Ngoc Danh,
Histoire du Président Ho

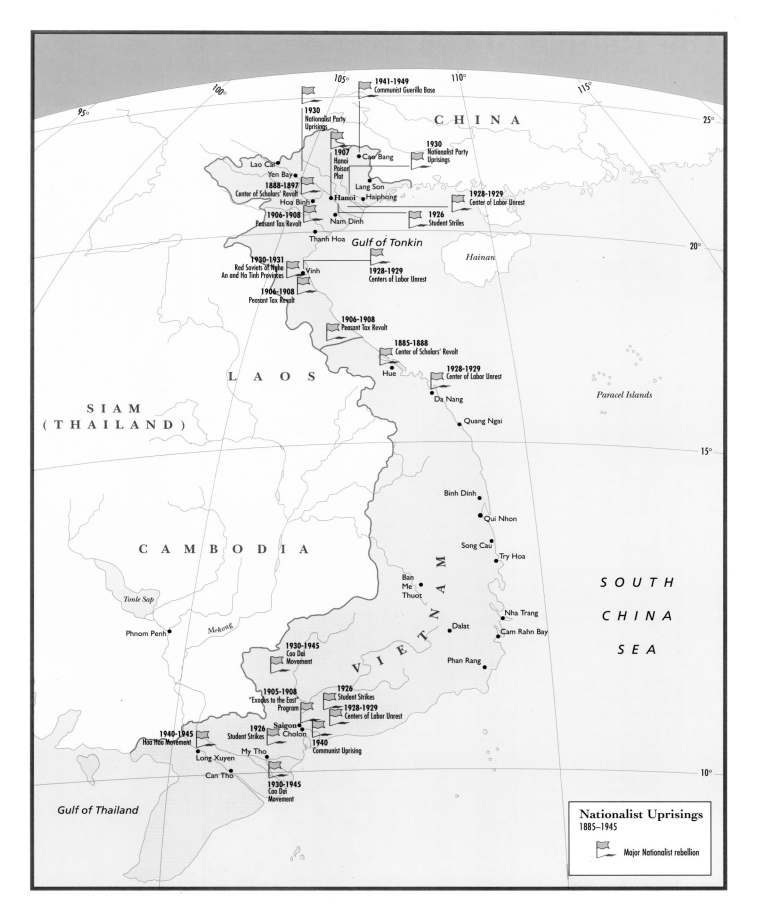

1941-1949
Communist Guerilla Base

C H I N A

1930
Nationalist Party
Uprisings

1907
Hanoi
Poison
Plot

Cao Bang

1930
Nationalist Party
Uprisings

Lao Cai

Yen Bay

Lang Son

1888-1897
Center of Scholars' Revolt

Haiphong

Hoa Binh

Hanoi

1928-1929
Center of Labor Unrest

1906-1908
Peasant Tax Revolt

Nam Dinh

1926
Student Strikes

Thanh Hoa

Gulf of Tonkin

Hainan

1930-1931
Red Soviets of Nghe
An and Ha Tinh Provinces

Vinh

1928-1929
Centers of Labor Unrest

1906-1908
Peasant Tax Revolt

1906-1908
Peasant Tax Revolt

1885-1888
Center of Scholars' Revolt

L A O S

Hue

1928-1929
Center of Labor Unrest

Da Nang

Paracel Islands

Quang Ngai

S I A M
(T H A I L A N D)

Binh Dinh

Qui Nhon

Song Cau

Try Hoa

C A M B O D I A

Ban
Me
Thuot

S O U T H

Tonle Sap

Dalat

Nha Trang

Cam Rahn Bay

C H I N A

Phnom Penh

Mekong

V
I
E
T
N
A
M

Phan Rang

S E A

1930-1945
Cao Dai
Movement

1905-1908
"Exodus to the East"
Program

1926
Student Strikes

1928-1929
Centers of Labor Unrest

Saigon
Cholon

1940-1945
Hoa Hao Movement

1926
Student Strikes

My Tho

1940
Communist Uprising

Long Xuyen

Can Tho

1930-1945
Cao Dai
Movement

Gulf of Thailand

Nationalist Uprisings
1885–1945

Major Nationalist rebellion

The Return of the French 1945–1946

"Do you want Indochina?" President Roosevelt asked Chinese leader Chiang Kai-shek at the Yalta Conference in February 1945. "We don't want it," Chiang Kai-shek replied, with full knowledge of Sino-Vietnamese history. "They are not Chinese. They would not assimilate into the Chinese people."

In principle the United States favored the formation of a provisional international trusteeship for Vietnam, and as a result the question of whether France would be allowed to repossess its colonies was kept deliberately ambiguous at the Potsdam Conference in July 1945. The Allies agreed that the British were to accept the surrender of the Japanese south of the 16th parallel, and that the Chinese would do the same to the north.

Ironically, U.S. involvement in Vietnam began with the same concern for U.S. POWs that still marked its concerns half a century later. Preceding the British was a U.S. OSS team headed by Army Major A. Peter Dewey, sent to liberate U.S. prisoners-of-war held in Japanese camps in the Saigon area. These POWs included 120 survivors of the Texas National Guard's antiaircraft battalion that had been captured in Java in 1942, as well as 86 survivors of the cruiser U.S.S *Houston* which had been sunk off Java that same year. Arriving at Tan Son Nhut on September 4, the OSS team quickly accomplished its mission, and the POWs were flown out of Vietnam the next day.

On September 12, 1945, a British Gurkha division from Rangoon arrived to disarm the Japanese. They were accompanied by a company of French paratroopers from Calcutta. On September 23, French forces took control of all the main buildings in Saigon. In the Viet Minh uprising that followed, Dewey, mistaken for a French officer, was killed in an ambush, becoming the first American soldier to die in the Indochinese wars.

Like the British in the south, who were concerned with their own Asian empire, the Chinese in the north were driven by their own interests. In February 1946, a Franco-Chinese agreement allowed the return of the French to Indochina in exchange for various concessions, including the renunciation of French extraterritorial claims in China. The United States, now led by Harry S. Truman, was more concerned with securing French cooperation in Europe to meet the growing Soviet threat than with Asian anti-colonialism.

Faced with this loss of outside support, the Viet Minh had to reconsider their policy toward France. In March 1946, Ho Chi Minh signed an agreement by which the Democratic Republic was recognized as a "free state" within the French Union. As a result of this agreement, French forces were allowed to land in the north. Differences between the French government and the Democratic Republic of Vietnam immediately developed over the definition of "free state." A Vietnamese delegation headed by Ho Chi Minh was sent to Paris, and in September 1946 he signed an agreement designed to facilitate French economic and cultural activities in return for promises to liberalize the Indonesian regime.

Conditions continued to deteriorate. In October 1946, French attempts to enforce customs controls aroused further hostility. In November, shooting broke out in Haiphong, and subsequent house-to-house fighting and bombardment by the cruiser *Suffren* drove the Viet Minh from the city. The French demands that followed the fighting were so unacceptable that the Democratic Republic of Vietnam decided to go to war rather than accede to them. On December 19, 1946, the Viet Minh launched their first attack on the French, beginning what was to become the eight-year First Indochina War.

> "*This agreement that had been fought over for six months in an atmosphere of hate, distrust and imminent carnage was finally signed (6 March 1946) amidst the jingle of champagne glasses. Ho knew how to accept the inevitability of ceremony as well as of compromise. The spectre at the feast was [Viet Minh General] Giap, whose sister had died in a French prison and his wife on a French scaffold.*"
>
> —Charles Fenn

The Potsdam Conference between the United States, the United Kingdom, and the Soviet Union called for the unconditional surrender of Japan and divided Indochina into two zones, which came under Chinese and British control. The question of a French return was left unresolved.

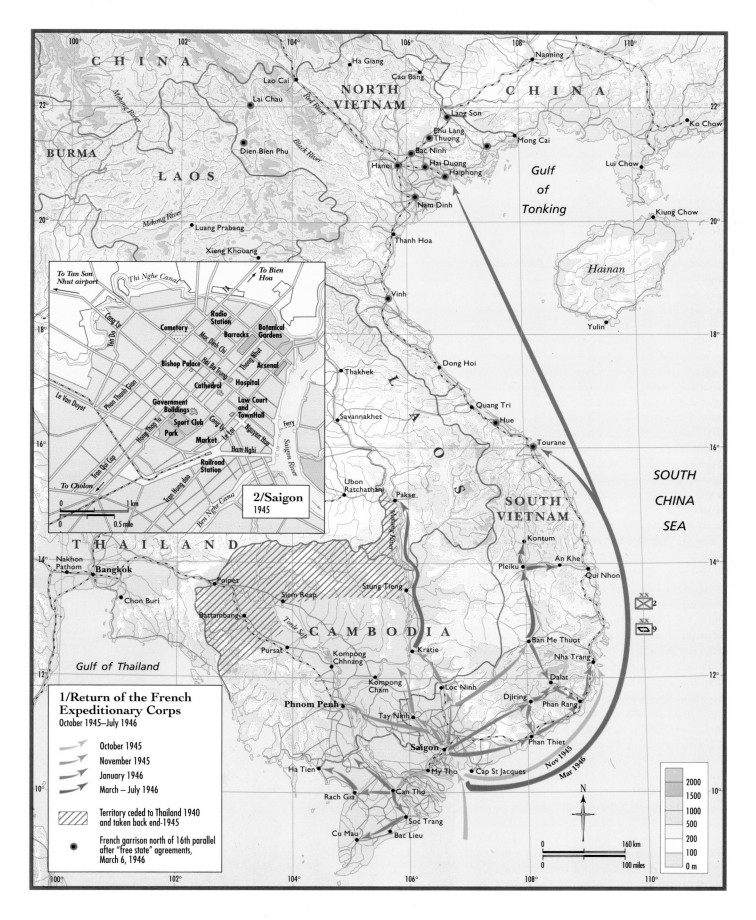

CHINA

Ha Giang
Nanning
NORTH
VIETNAM
Lao Cai
Cao Bang
CHINA
Lai Chau
Lang Son
Ko Chow
Phu Lang
Thuong
Mong Cai
Dien Bien Phu
Bac Ninh
Lui Chow
Hanoi
Hai Duong
Haiphong
Gulf
of
Tonking
Nam Dinh
Kiung Chow
Luang Prabang
LAOS
BURMA
Hainan
Mekong River
Xieng Khouang
Black River
Red River
Yulin
Vinh

Inset: 2/Saigon 1945

To Tan Son
Nhut airport
Thi Nghe Canal
To Bien
Hoa
Cong Ly
Van Do
Cemetery
Radio
Station
Mac Dinh Chi
Barracks
Botanical
Gardens
Bishop Palace
Hai Ba Trung
Thong Nhut
Arsenal
Cathedral
Hospital
Phan Thanh Gian
Le Van Duyet
Government
Buildings
Law Court
and
TownHall
Hong Thap Tu
Sport Club
Cong Ly
Nguyen Hue
Park
Market
Le Loi
Tran Qui Cap
Ham Nghi
Saigon River
To Cholon
Tran Hung dao
Railroad
Station
Ben Nghe Cana
Ferry

**2/Saigon
1945**

0   1 km
0   0.5 mile

Thakhek
Dong Hoi

L
A
O
S

Savannakhet
Quang Tri
Hue

Ubon
Ratchathani
Pakse
Tourane

THAILAND

SOUTH
CHINA
SEA

Nakhon
Pathom
Bangkok
Mekong River
SOUTH
VIETNAM
Kontum

Chon Buri
Poiper
An Khe
Pleiku
Siem Reap
Qui Nhon

Gulf of Thailand
Stung Treng
XX 2

Battambang
Tonle Sap
CAMBODIA
Kratie
Ban Me Thuot
9

Pursat
Nha Trang
Kompong
Chhnang
Dalat

Kompong
Cham
Loc Ninh
Djiring
Phan Rang

**1/Return of the French
Expeditionary Corps**
October 1945–July 1946

Phnom Penh
Tay Ninh
Phan Thiet

October 1945
November 1945
January 1946
March – July 1946

Ha Tien
Saigon
My Tho
Cap St Jacques
Nov 1945
Mar 1946
Rach Gia
Can Tho

Territory ceded to Thailand 1940
and taken back end-1945

French garrison north of 16th parallel
after "free state" agreements,
March 6, 1946

Cu Mau
Soc Trang
Bac Lieu

N

0   160 km
0   100 miles

2000
1500
1000
500
200
100
0 m

The Rise of the Viet Minh 1946–1947

On the evening of December 19, 1946, the Viet Minh military commander, General Vo Nguyen Giap, issued what amounted to a declaration of war. "I order all soldiers and militia … to stand together, go into battle, destroy the invaders, and save the nation," he said. "The resistance will be long and arduous, but our cause is just and we will surely triumph."

The battle for Hanoi began with a Viet Minh attack on the municipal power plant and on French homes in the city and raged throughout December 1946, with the Viet Minh militia fighting from street to street against French regulars. But in the end they were forced to retreat into the Viet Bac, a mountainous region 80 miles north of Hanoi.

Giap began in December 1944 as the commander of a 34-man "armed propaganda brigade for the liberation of Vietnam," the first formal standing military force of the Viet Minh, and went on to organize this force into fighting units. At the lowest level were the *dan quan*, 30-man local part-time militia platoons. Next were the *dia phuong*, 85-man regional strike force companies at the district level and 300-man battalions at the province level. Finally there were the *chuc luc*, 400-man main force units organized as mobile light infantry battalions armed with recoilless rifles and 60mm mortars.

In the fall of 1947, French General Etienne Valluy attempted to mount a *coup de main* that would destroy these forces in one stroke. Called Operation Lea, it would involve 20 battalions and support units, with 15,000 men organized into three columns or *groupements*. Groupement S, named after its commander, Lieutenant Colonel Sauvagac, consisted of the Airborne Half-Brigade. Groupement B, under Colonel Beuffre, was made up of three armored, three infantry and three artillery battalions reinforced by an engineer and a transport battalion. Groupement C, under Lieutenant Colonel Communal, comprised a three-battalion shipborne force. In support was the 4th Fighter Group, with Spitfire fighters and a variety of transport aircraft.

Groupement S began the operation on October 7, 1947, with a 1,137-man parachute assault directly on Viet Minh positions at Bac Kan, Cho Moi, and Cho Don, almost capturing Ho Chi Minh and General Giap. Meanwhile, Groupement B attacked northwest from Lang Son along Route Coloniale RC4 toward Cao Bang, which had been seized in an airborne assault, to seal off the China–Vietnam border. After linking up on October 12, Beuffre pushed part of the motorized Moroccan Colonial Infantry Regiment southwest in order to relieve Groupement S, then under heavy attack.

After three days of hard fighting the Moroccans broke through to Sauvagac's forces, which had held out on their own against heavy odds for nine days. Meanwhile Groupement C was moving up the Red and Clear rivers aboard French Navy LCTs (Landing Craft Tank). Leaving one battalion at Tuyen Quang, site of a famous battle in 1885, the task force pushed northward toward Chiem Hoa, 120 miles inside the Viet Minh lines, where they were met by an armored column from Groupement B.

The Viet Minh suffered heavily, losing a reported 9,500 casualties, as well as their main headquarters and many of their supply depots. Their main redoubt had been encircled, but in this kind of war that proved meaningless. Between the French forces along the perimeter were large gaps where most of the 40,000-man Viet Minh force could and did slip away. One month after it had begun, Operation Lea was called off, and on December 22, 1947, the French pulled most of their forces back to the lowlands, leaving behind a string of border forts along the China–Vietnam border.

"To resist the planes and artillery of the enemy we had only bamboo slivers. But our party is a Marxist–Leninist party, we don't see only the present, we also see the future and we put our confidence in the morale and strength of the masses."

—Ho Chi Minh

A revolutionary from the age of 14, Giap, seen here with members of his armed forces, studied guerrilla tactics in China. Chosen to manage Ho Chi Minh's network of guerrilla troops, he transformed the force into a powerful organization with substantial public backing.

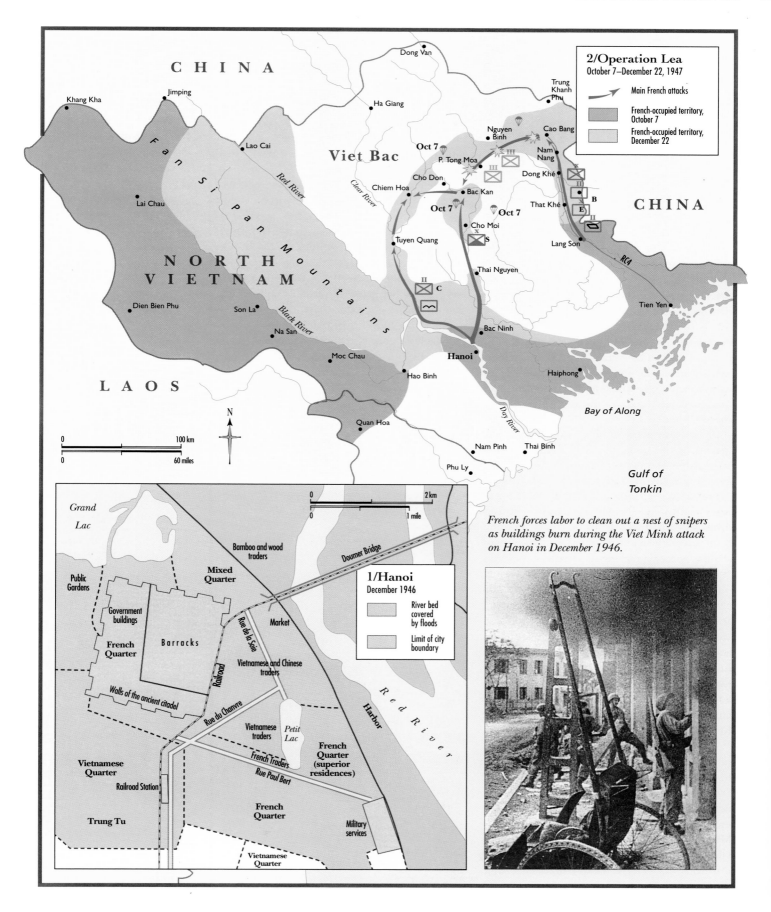

2/Operation Lea
October 7–December 22, 1947

→ Main French attacks

French-occupied territory, October 7

French-occupied territory, December 22

CHINA

Dong Van

Khang Kha

Jimping

Ha Giang

Trung Khanh Phu

Lao Cai

Viet Bac

Nguyen Binh

Cao Bang

Oct 7

P. Tong Moa

Nam Nang

III

Chiem Hoa

Cho Don

Dong Khé

CHINA

Lai Chau

Red River

Clear River

Bac Kan

That Khé

B

Oct 7

E

Cho Moi

Oct 7

II

NORTH

Tuyen Quang

S

Lang Son

RC4

VIETNAM

Thai Nguyen

Dien Bien Phu

Son La

Black River

II C

Tien Yen

Na San

Moc Chau

Bac Ninh

Hanoi

LAOS

Hao Binh

Haiphong

Day River

N

0   100 km
0   60 miles

Quan Hoa

Bay of Along

Nam Pinh

Thai Binh

Phu Ly

Gulf of Tonkin

Grand Lac

0   2 km
0   1 mile

Bamboo and wood traders

Doumer Bridge

Mixed Quarter

Public Gardens

Government buildings

Market

1/Hanoi
December 1946

River bed covered by floods

Limit of city boundary

French Quarter

Barracks

Rue de la Soie

Vietnamese and Chinese traders

Railroad

Walls of the ancient citadel

Rue du Chanvre

Vietnamese traders

Petit Lac

French Quarter (superior residences)

Red River

Harbor

Vietnamese Quarter

French Traders

Rue Paul Bert

Railroad Station

French Quarter

Trung Tu

Military services

Vietnamese Quarter

French forces labor to clean out a nest of snipers as buildings burn during the Viet Minh attack on Hanoi in December 1946.

The Sino-Vietnamese Border Fights   1950

"When the smoke had cleared," wrote Bernard Fall of the 1950 debacle along the Chinese border on Route Coloniale 4, "the French had suffered their greatest colonial defeat since Montcalm had died in Quebec." Those defeats, rather than the later battle at Dien Bien Phu, were the real death knell for France in Indochina, for with the loss of the frontier the end was foreordained.

This loss was significant because, during the preceding year, Mao Zedong's Chinese Communist armies had routed the Chinese Nationalist armies of Chiang Kai-shek to win the civil war, and had moved their forces into Kwangsi (now Guangxi) and Yunnan provinces, across the border from Vietnam. "This great historical event," said General Giap in a masterpiece of understatement, "exerted a considerable influence on the war … Vietnam was no longer in the grip of enemy encirclement, and was henceforth geographically linked to the socialist bloc."

China could provide the Viet Minh with automatic weapons, mortars, howitzers, and trucks. With this military aid, Giap transformed his guerrilla army into a conventional military organization, expanding his battalions and regiments into five 10,000-man light infantry divisions (the 304th, 308th, 312th, 316th, and 320th), as well as a heavy division consisting of artillery and engineering regiments.

His immediate target was the series of French outposts along the border. These posts from east to west included the main base at Lang Son with its 4,000-man garrison, the 4,000-man base at Cao Bang, with two or three battalions and outposts at Dong Khé and That Khé, each held by a battalion of the French Foreign Legion, and the base at Lao Cai with its 2,000–3,000-man garrison, including its four company-sized outposts at Muong Khuong, Pa Kha, Nghia Do, and Pho Lu.

After initial probes in 1949, Giap began his offensive in February 1950, massing nine to ten battalions—5,000–6,000 men—of his 308th Division against the 150-man French company defending the outpost at Pho Lu. Next to fall was Dong Khé, overrun by a five-battalion Viet Minh assault. Although recaptured three days later by a surprise French parachute assault, it did not long survive. Giap's main offensive came on September 16, 1950, with a renewed attack on Dong Khé. Odds were eight to one in his favor, and the outpost fell to a massive artillery barrage and human-wave infantry attack. Instead of counterattacking, the French commander, General Carpentier, decided to abandon the border defenses.

The retreat was a debacle. The Cao Bang and That Khé garrisons were cut to pieces as they attempted to withdraw. Lang Son, the bastion of the border defenses, was abandoned without a fight. Only the garrison at Lao Cai fought their way to safety in good military order.

Six thousand of the 10,000 defenders of the border outposts had been lost, as well as large amounts of military stores. At Lang Son alone some 13 howitzers, 940 machine guns, 4,000 submachine guns, 8,000 rifles, and more than 1,000 tons of ammunition fell into enemy hands. More important, any chance of victory in Indochina had been lost.

"Giap could feel satisfied with his achievements in 1950. He demonstrated the effectiveness of his Main Force units; he seized the initiative; and he demoralized the French command. Beyond that, he had unnerved the French government, which now realized that there was no way to win Indochina without a massive effort, and this was politically impossible."

—Lieutenant General Phillip B. Davidson, former MACV intelligence chief

Weary Legionnaires in North Vietnam, where the French border posts, linked by poor roads and separated by miles of deserted countryside, were highly vulnerable to Viet Minh attack.

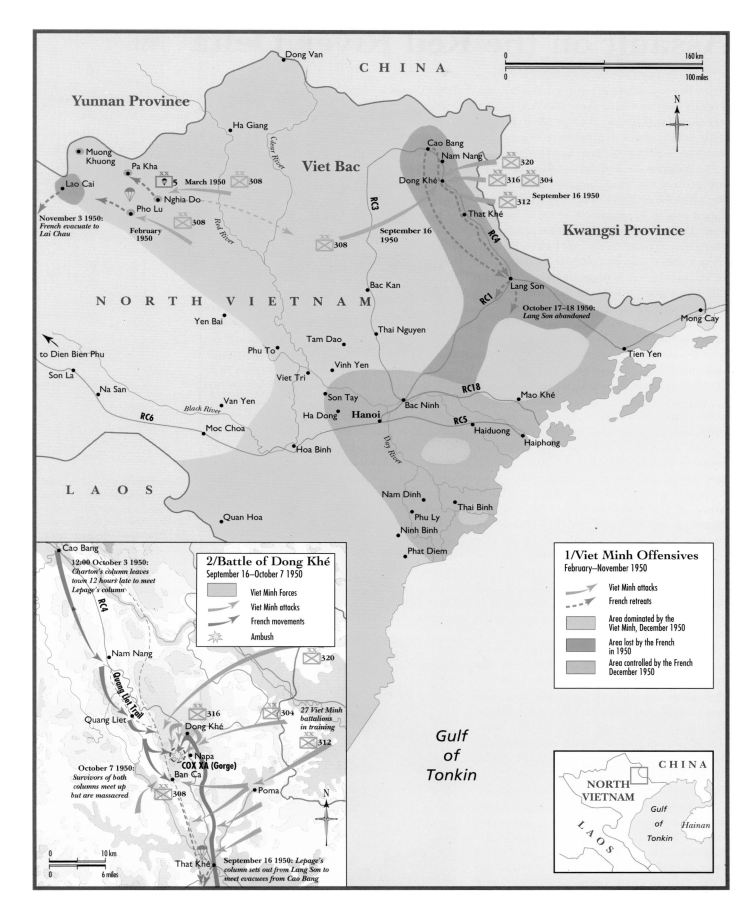

CHINA

Dong Van

Yunnan Province

Ha Giang

Clear River

Viet Bac

Cao Bang

Nam Nang

XX 320

Muong Khuong

Pa Kha

XX 5 March 1950

XX 308

Dong Khé

XX 316   XX 304

Lao Cai

Nghia Do

That Khé

XX 312   September 16 1950

Kwangsi Province

November 3 1950: *French evacuate to Lai Chau*

Pho Lu

February 1950

XX 308

Red River

September 16 1950

RC3

XX 308

RC4

NORTH VIETNAM

Bac Kan

Lang Son

RC1

October 17–18 1950: *Lang Son abandoned*

Mong Cay

Yen Bai

Thai Nguyen

to Dien Bien Phu

Tam Dao

Phu To

Vinh Yen

Tien Yen

Son La

Na San

Van Yen

Viet Tri

Son Tay

RC18

Mao Khé

Black River

RC6

Moc Choa

Ha Dong

Hanoi

Bac Ninh

RC5

Haiduong

Haiphong

Hoa Binh

Day River

LAOS

Nam Dinh

Thai Binh

Quan Hoa

Phu Ly

Ninh Binh

Phat Diem

Gulf of Tonkin

Cao Bang

12:00 October 3 1950: *Charton's column leaves town 12 hours late to meet Lepage's column*

RC4

2/Battle of Dong Khé
September 16–October 7 1950

	Viet Minh Forces
	Viet Minh attacks
	French movements
	Ambush

Nam Nang

Quang Liet Trail

XX 320

Quang Liet

XX 316   XX 304

Dong Khé

27 Viet Minh battalions in training

XX 312

Napa

October 7 1950: *Survivors of both columns meet up but are massacred*

COX XA (Gorge)

Ban Ca

XX 308

Poma

N

0   10 km

0   6 miles

That Khé

September 16 1950: *Lepage's column sets out from Lang Son to meet evacuees from Cao Bang*

1/Viet Minh Offensives
February–November 1950

	Viet Minh attacks
	French retreats
	Area dominated by the Viet Minh, December 1950
	Area lost by the French in 1950
	Area controlled by the French December 1950

CHINA

NORTH VIETNAM

LAOS

Gulf of Tonkin

Hainan

0   160 km

0   100 miles

N

Assault on the Red River Delta 1951

After the loss of their border outposts, the French withdrew into their Red River delta defenses. For their part the Viet Minh, flushed with victory, made a premature decision to attack these French defenses head on.

But the open areas of the Red River delta did not provide the cover and concealment that the jungles had done; in the delta the French superiority in firepower could be brought to bear. The incompetent General Carpentier was also gone, replaced by one of France's best soldiers, General Jean de Lattre de Tassigny. One of his first acts was to begin construction of the "De Lattre line," a series of fortified positions to protect the delta from Viet Minh attack.

On January 13, 1951, Giap launched his first attack at Vinh Yen, a key road junction about 25 miles northwest of Hanoi. The town was defended by two French groupement mobiles (G.M.), each with three infantry battalions and an artillery battalion. Against this 6,000-man force Giap committed the 20,000 men of his 308th and 312th divisions.

After some initial successes, the Viet Minh were beaten back with terrible losses. Taking personal command of the battle, de Lattre launched the most intensive aerial bombardment of the war, reinforced by the two Moroccan battalions and one parachute battalion of G.M. 2. The Viet Minh suffered terrible casualties—6,000 dead and another 500 captured—but Giap was undeterred.

On the night of March 23–24, he launched another attack on Mao Khé, 20 miles north of Haiphong. With his 316th Division leading the attack, and the partially rebuilt 308th and 312th divisions in reserve, Giap had some initial successes against the lightly defended town, but naval gunfire support was available to the defenders from three French destroyers and two landing craft which had steamed from the Gulf of Tonkin into the nearby Da Bac River. Their intense bombardment, combined with French air strikes, broke the back of the Viet Minh attack. By March 28 the fighting was over. Again Giap withdrew, leaving some 3,000 dead.

Giap's last attempt to breach the De Lattre line was an ambitious assault on its northwestern side in the Day River area. He had already infiltrated two regiments behind the French lines, the independent 42nd Regiment and the 320th Division's 64th Regiment. The 304th and 308th divisions would launch secondary attacks at Phu Ly and Ninh Binh, while the main attack would be by the 320th Division at Phat Diem. The goal was to seize and hold the rice-rich southern corner of the Red River delta.

The attack began on May 29, and again Giap enjoyed initial success. But de Lattre (whose only son had been killed in the initial Viet Minh attack) reacted quickly, rushing three mobile groups, four artillery groups, an armored group, and a paratroop battalion to the area. A key element was the resistance of the Catholic militia in the area, which slowed the Viet Minh attack. Another factor was the *dinassauts* (Division navale d'assaut), the armed French river craft that operated along the Day River. These craft, along with the French air force, cut Giap's lines of supply and communication, sinking the boats and sampans that Giap was using to reinforce and resupply his units across the river.

By June 6, 1951, the French controlled the battle and Giap began to withdraw. The Day River campaign ended on June 18, with Viet Minh losses estimated at some 10,000 killed and captured. Giap's disastrous 1951 offensive had cost him around 20,000 men and, temporarily, the initiative.

Although North Vietnamese leaders later blamed the failure of their 1951 offensive on their Chinese military adviser, General Lo Guipo, for pressuring them to escalate too soon from guerrilla to conventional war, General Giap cannot avoid responsibility for this colossal miscalculation.

"Our resistance war will be long and painful, but whatever the sacrifices, however long the struggle, we shall fight to the end, until Vietnam is fully independent and reunified."

—Ho Chi Minh

The temperamental but talented French general Jean de Lattre de Tassigny, who gave his name to the De Lattre line encircling the Red River delta. Constructed in 1951 and consisting of concrete watchtowers and fortifications at intervals of one or two miles, the line was largely ineffective in preventing infiltration by Viet Minh troops.

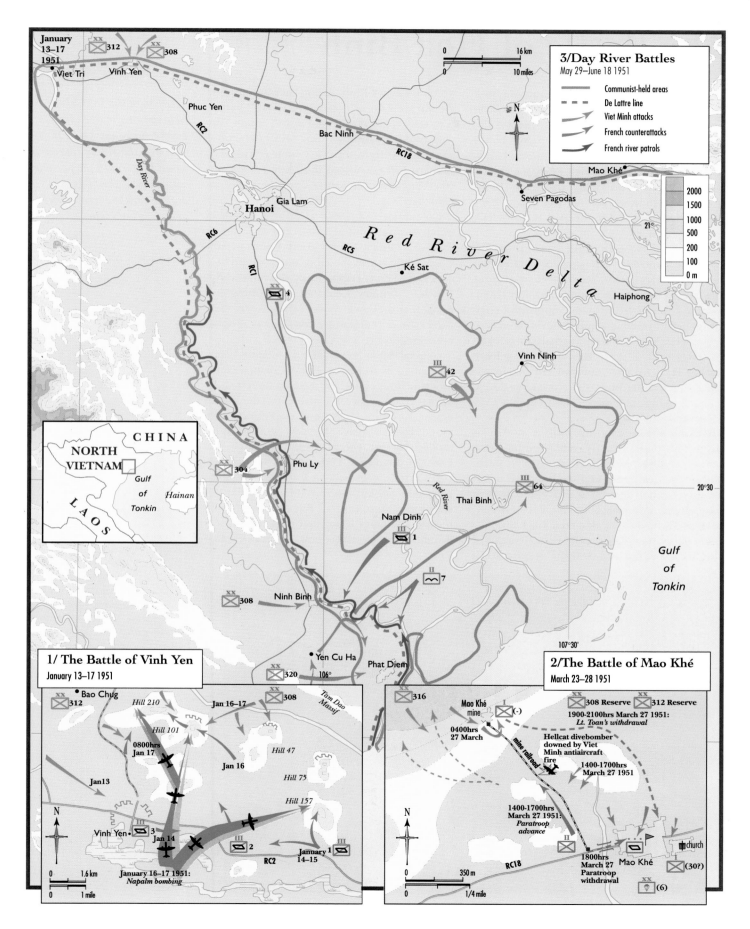

January
13–17
1951

Viet Tri

Vinh Yen

312

308

Phuc Yen

RC2

Bac Ninh

RC18

Mao Khé

Seven Pagodas

3/Day River Battles
May 29–June 18 1951

Communist-held areas

De Lattre line

Viet Minh attacks

French counterattacks

French river patrols

0   16 km

0   10 miles

N

21°

2000
1500
1000
500
200
100
0 m

Day River

Gia Lam

Hanoi

Red River Delta

RC6

RC5

Ké Sat

Haiphong

RC1

4

42

Vinh Ninh

CHINA

NORTH
VIETNAM

*Gulf
of
Tonkin*

Hainan

LAOS

304

Phu Ly

Red River

Thai Binh

64

20°30

Nam Dinh

1

7

308   Ninh Binh

*Gulf
of
Tonkin*

107°30'

Yen Cu Ha

Phat Diem

106°

320

1/ The Battle of Vinh Yen
January 13–17 1951

312   Bao Chug

Hill 210

Jan 16–17

308

*Tam Dao
Massif*

Hill 101

0800hrs
Jan 17

Jan 16

Hill 47

Jan13

Hill 75

Hill 157

N

Vinh Yen   3

Jan 14

2

RC2

January
14–15

1

January 16–17 1951:
Napalm bombing

0   1.6 km

0   1 mile

2/The Battle of Mao Khé
March 23–28 1951

316

Mao Khé
mine

308 Reserve   312 Reserve

1900-2100hrs March 27 1951:
Lt. Toan's withdrawal

0400hrs
27 March

mine railroad

Hellcat divebomber
downed by Viet
Minh antiaircraft
fire

**1400-1700hrs
March 27 1951**

N

**1400-1700hrs
March 27 1951:**
*Paratroop
advance*

**1800hrs
March 27
Paratroop
withdrawal**

Mao Khé

RC18

church

(30?)

(6)

0   350 m

0   1/4 mile

The Battle of Hoa Binh   1951–1952

Seeking to exploit his success in turning back the Viet Minh's 1951 offensive, General de Lattre set out to lure Giap into a set-piece battle where the superior French firepower could again be brought to bear. The chosen battle-ground was the town of Hoa Binh, the capital of the intensely loyal Moung tribesmen. It was situated on the west bank of the Black River, about 25 miles outside the Red River delta's defensive line.

On November 14, 1951, the 1st, 2nd, and 7th Colonial Parachute battalions dropped on the airstrip at Hoa Binh. Meanwhile, a ground force of 15 infantry battalions, 7 artillery battalions, 2 armored groups and supporting engineers began pushing down Route Coloniale 6 from Xuan Mai, and a naval assault force of 20 *dinassauts* sailed down the Black River from Trung Ha. On November 16, all the forces linked up at Hoa Binh. On November 20, de Lattre, dying of cancer, was replaced by General Raoul Salan.

Taking his time, Giap took a month to perfect his plans. First he committed his 316th and 320th divisions to pin down French forces within the delta. He then deployed his 308th Division around Hoa Binh, his 304th Division along Route Coloniale 6, its land line of supply, and his 312th Division along the Black River, its water supply line. On December 9, elements of the 312th Division attacked the outpost at Tu Vu on the Black River, fading back into the jungle when the French counterattacked. This pattern was repeated time and again. Supply convoys could get through only with heavy *dinassaut* escorts fighting every inch of the way. Bernard Fall was to call the Black River fights "the bloodiest river battles since the American Civil War."

On January 12, 1952, after an ambush in which six river craft were lost, the river line of supply was finally cut for good. Coincidentally Route Coloniale 6, the land line of supply, was also cut when a regiment of the 304th NVA Division occupied Kem Pass, ambushing and destroying a French road-clearing force. Only the airfield remained open, but it too was under enemy fire.

General Salan launched a 12-infantry battalion task force to reopen Route Coloniale 6 for long enough to withdraw the Hoa Binh defenders back within the De Lattre line. The pullout began on February 22, and on February 26, aided by a massive French 30,000-round artillery barrage, the last of the defenders, the Foreign Legion's 13th Half-Brigade (*13e DBLE*), fought its way back to friendly lines. Each side had lost over 5,000 men in what Fall called the "Meatgrinder." But the French were the big losers, for it was now obvious they had lost the ability to project power outside the Red River delta.

"Although the Viet Minh held nothing materially except the countryside, they also had the greatest weapon of all time (with the possible exception of the H–bomb): a leader with the fixed belief that he would win."

—Charles Fenn

Viet Minh troops patrol the Black River, one of three French supply routes to Hoa Binh. Bordered by dense jungle, the river banks were riddled with North Vietnamese soldiers brandishing bazookas and recoilless cannon, and the supply artery was soon cut.

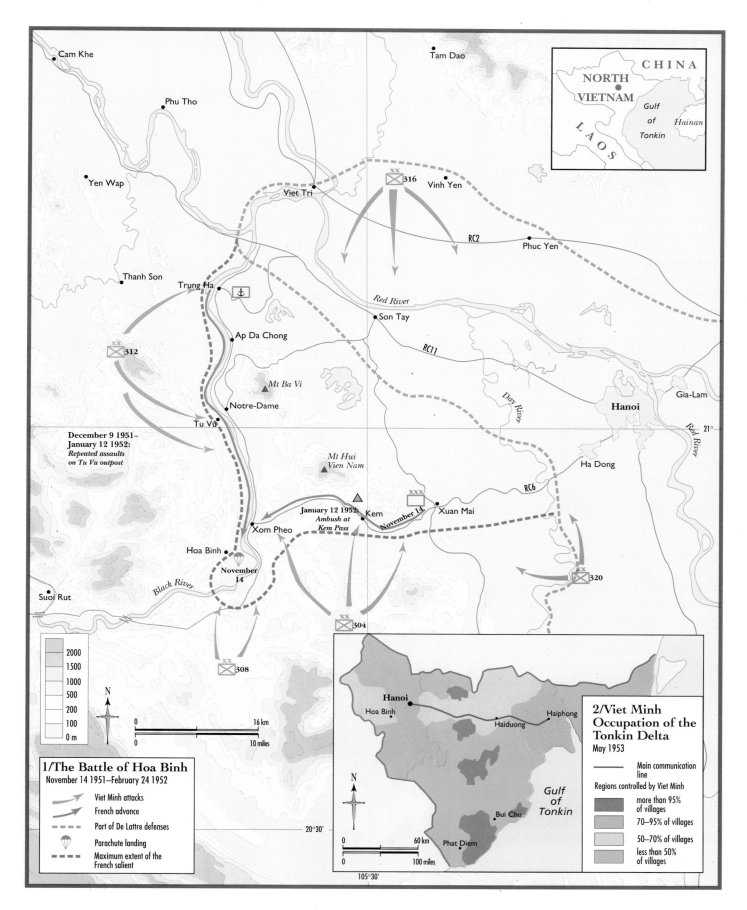

CHINA

NORTH VIETNAM

LAOS

Gulf of Tonkin

Hainan

Cam Khe

Tam Dao

Phu Tho

Yen Wap

Viet Tri

316

Vinh Yen

Phuc Yen

RC2

Thanh Son

Trung Ha

Red River

Son Tay

312

Ap Da Chong

RC11

Day River

Hanoi

Gia-Lam

Mt Ba Vi

Red River

21°

Notre-Dame

Tu Vu

Ha Dong

**December 9 1951–
January 12 1952:**
*Repeated assaults
on Tu Vu outpost*

Mt Hui
Vien Nam

RC6

January 12 1952:
*Ambush at
Kem Pass*

Kem

November 14

Xuan Mai

Xom Pheo

Hoa Binh

November
14

320

Black River

Suoi Rut

304

2000
1500
1000
500
200
100
0 m

N

0   16 km

0   10 miles

308

Hanoi

Hoa Binh

Haiduong

Haiphong

Bui Chu

*Gulf
of
Tonkin*

Phat Diem

**2/Viet Minh
Occupation of the
Tonkin Delta**
May 1953

Main communication
line

Regions controlled by Viet Minh

more than 95%
of villages

70–95% of villages

50–70% of villages

less than 50%
of villages

N

0   60 km

0   100 miles

105°30'

20°30'

1/The Battle of Hoa Binh
November 14 1951–February 24 1952

Viet Minh attacks

French advance

Part of De Lattre defenses

Parachute landing

Maximum extent of the
French salient

Operation Lorraine OCTOBER–NOVEMBER 1952

By the fall of 1952 the combat power ratio had shifted radically in favor of the Viet Minh. With about 125,000 men in his Main Force units, another 60,000–75,000 regional guerrillas, and yet another 120,000–200,000 local militias, Giap had a significant advantage over the French. By mid-1952 the French Expeditionary Force numbered about 90,000 men; some 50,000 were French, the rest were Foreign Legionnaires, North Africans, and French-led Vietnamese. They were backed up by a 100,000-man Vietnamese National Army of doubtful reliability.

In late 1951, Giap had formed a sixth light infantry division, the 325th, and in 1952 he formally organized his heavy forces as the 351st Division. It included an engineer regiment and two artillery regiments equipped with 120mm mortars and 105mm howitzers. The division also contained some antiaircraft artillery (AAA) units equipped with 20mm and 40mm guns.

On October 11, 1952, Giap, seeking to draw the French into operations at a maximum distance from their fortified De Lattre line, launched a three-division assault along the Fan Si Pan mountain range between the Red and Black rivers, which would threaten the Tai tribesmen, who were longtime French allies, as well as French outposts in Laos. In response, the French launched Operation Lorraine, a drive against Giap's supply bases in the Viet Bac, which they thought would force him to break off his attack. One mobile force would cross the Red River at Trung Ha and move northwest to Phu To. A second column, advancing from Viet Tri, would link up with them there. Both would then move toward Phu Doan, the site of a known Viet Minh supply point. A three-battalion parachute group would then drop on the town and be joined by a riverine *dinassaut* force.

Beginning on October 29, 1952, this complex operation remarkably came off without a hitch. There was only one problem: Giap refused to take the bait. Instead, he ordered two of his regiments then in the area to stop the French advance before it reached either Yen Bai or Thai Nguyen, his two main supply depots in the area, and continued his Black River operations.

A fateful French decision was made on November 13, 1952, when the lead elements of their task force reached the junction of Highways 157 and 13A. The latter led to the major Viet Minh supply base at Yen Bai, some 15 miles away. But the French failed to move in that direction, evidently fearing stiff opposition from the 316th Division's 176th Regiment, which blocked the way.

On November 14, General Salan canceled the operation. The only major fight came during the French withdrawal, when, on November 17, the French column was ambushed at the Chan Muong gorge on Route Coloniale 2 by the 308th Division's 36th Regiment. After a bayonet attack by the Batallion de Marche Indochinoise, the ambush was cleared and the French retreated back into the De Lattre line. Operation Lorraine had been a mere diversion. It failed to force Giap to pull back from his Black River positions and it did no serious damage to the Viet Minh's logistical system.

The French Expeditionary Force of the early 1950s was well-trained and well-armed, and could boast many competent leaders, but it was undermined by the Vietnamese National Army, in which a shortage of manpower at all levels was exacerbated by continual desertions.

"[Giap's] foremost achievement in countering Lorraine was his correct assessment of the true French intentions and capabilities. From his intelligence (or from deduction), Giap estimated that the French would not try to break into his critical supply areas, but intended primarily to make a demonstration to draw him back from the Black River … Buttressed by his recognition of the limited nature of French intentions and the thinness of their real capabilities, Giap contemptuously allowed them to run up the road to Phu Yen Binh and back again before he struck at Chan Muong."

—Lieutenant General Phillip B. Davidson

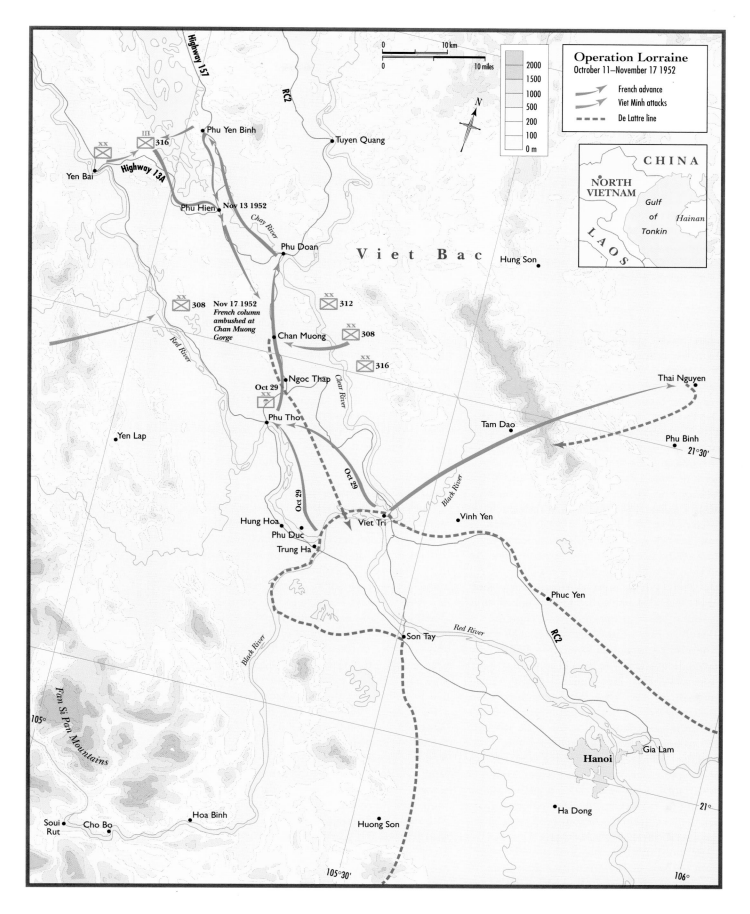

Highway 157

RC2

Phu Yen Binh

Tuyen Quang

xx

III 316

Yen Bai

Highway 13A

Phu Hien

Nov 13 1952

Chay River

Phu Doan

Viet Bac

Hung Son

CHINA

NORTH VIETNAM

Gulf of Tonkin

Hainan

LAOS

Operation Lorraine
Octrober 11–November 17 1952

French advance
Viet Minh attacks
De Lattre line

2000
1500
1000
500
200
100
0 m

10 km

10 miles

N

xx 308

Nov 17 1952
French column
ambushed at
Chan Muong
Gorge

Red River

xx 312

xx 308

Chan Muong

xx 316

Ngoc Thap

Clear River

Thai Nguyen

Oct 29

xx

Phu Tho

Yen Lap

Tam Dao

Phu Binh

21°30'

Oct 29

Oct 29

Black River

Vinh Yen

Hung Hoa

Phu Duc

Trung Ha

Viet Tri

Son Tay

Red River

Phuc Yen

RC2

Fan Si Pan Mountains

105°

Black River

Hanoi

Gia Lam

Ha Dong

21°

Soui Rut

Cho Bo

Hoa Binh

Huong Son

105°30'

106°

Dien Bien Phu   MARCH–MAY 1954

The French defeat at Dien Bien Phu in May 1954 was the denouement of the eight-year First Indochina War and dealt the *coup de grâce* to faltering French public support for hostilities. Ironically, the battle had been deliberately staged by the French military commander, General Henri Navarre, who had replaced General Salan the year before. The intent was to use Dien Bien Phu to provide the basis for "une solution politique honorable" to the war.

Codenamed Operation Castor, the plan called for placing a *herisson*, a fortified "hedge-hog" airhead, at Dien Bien Phu, located 183 miles from the French bases at Hanoi, astride Giap's lines of supply into Laos. It began on November 20, 1953, with a three-battalion parachute assault, reinforced over the next two days by three additional parachute battalions. The Viet Minh defenders, a battalion of the independent 148th Infantry Regiment, put up stiff resistance before fleeing. At his headquarters in the Viet Bac, 375 miles northwest of Dien Bien Phu, Giap immediately saw a critical opportunity. His 148th Regiment, which was already in the area, and the 316th Division, then en route, were ordered to attack French positions at Lai Chau, some 40 miles north of Dien Bien Phu, so as to isolate the battlefield. At the same time Giap ordered the 308th and 312th divisions, as well as artillery and engineer regiments of the heavy 351st Division, to move from the Viet Bac to Dien Bien Phu as quickly as possible.

Aware of these moves through radio intercepts, Navarre made the fateful decision to accept a battle in the northeast "centered on Dien Bien Phu, which must be held at all costs." The French launched Operation Pollux, the evacuation of the Tai highlands to the "more defensible" Dien Bien Phu. Lai Chi, the main outpost in the area, was abandoned on December 8, 1953, when elements of the 316th Division were detected in the area. Regular troops were evacuated to Dien Bien Phu by air, and the 2,100 Tai partisans in the area began to move toward Dien Bien Phu on foot. Only 185 finally made it two weeks later. French attempts to link up with them by relief columns from Dien Bien Phu were beaten back with heavy losses. The noose was tightening.

Joining the 316th Division, the 308th Division arrived in the Dien Bien Phu area on December 20, 1953, followed by the 312th Division. The 57th Regiment of the 304th Division arrived from the southern Red River delta on January 23, 1954, and by the end of January 1954, the 351st Division had its field artillery and antiaircraft guns in position.

Against this corps-sized 33-battalion force, the French commander, Colonel Christian DeCastries, had only 12 infantry battalions, two 105mm artillery battalions, and a battery of 155mm howitzers. With the enemy occupying the high ground around the base, outgunned by the Viet Minh artillery, and outnumbered five-to-one in infantry, the French could not hope to win.

The Viet Minh assault began on March 13, 1954, with an attack on the French battalion-sized outposts of Gabrielle and Béatrice, north of the main defensive positions. Under cover of an intense artillery barrage, Giap massed two infantry battalions against each French company. Béatrice fell on March 13 and Gabrielle on March 15. Even worse, Viet Minh artillery closed the French airstrip for good. Resupply and reinforcement could be only by parachute, but Viet Minh antiaircraft guns made even this a tricky business, shooting down several French transports over the drop zones.

The last of the northern outposts, Anne Marie, fell on March 17 when it was abandoned by its Tai partisan defenders. A lull fell over the battlefield, as Giap, who had taken heavy losses in the assaults, consolidated his forces. On March 30, he resumed the attack. This time his objective was the eastern outposts, Eliane and Dominique, and Hugette and Claudine to the west. After overrunning most of these outposts and isolating outpost Isabelle to the south, Giap settled into a classic siege, digging mines, saps, and approach trenches to turn the French defenses. On May 1, the final attacks began.

By May 7, 1954—the very day that the Geneva Conference to decide the fate of French Indochina began—it was all over. Militarily, it had been a bloodbath. While Viet Minh casualty figures have never been released, it was estimated in 1994 that at least 8,000 of their men were killed during their attacks. Although the French forces suffered only a quarter as many killed, 6,452 wounded, and 10,000 captured, their actual loss was much higher. They had not only lost Dien Bien Phu—they had lost an empire as well.

"Historically this battle might take its place alongside Creasey's Fifteen Decisive Battles of the World. *It was the first time in three centuries of colonialism that Asian troops defeated a Western conqueror in open battle."*

—Charles Fenn

The impenetrable jungle terrain surrounding the outposts at Dien Bien Phu allowed the enemy, who had concentrated their artillery by hauling weaponry and supplies along jungle trails by night, to easily encircle the French forces stationed there.

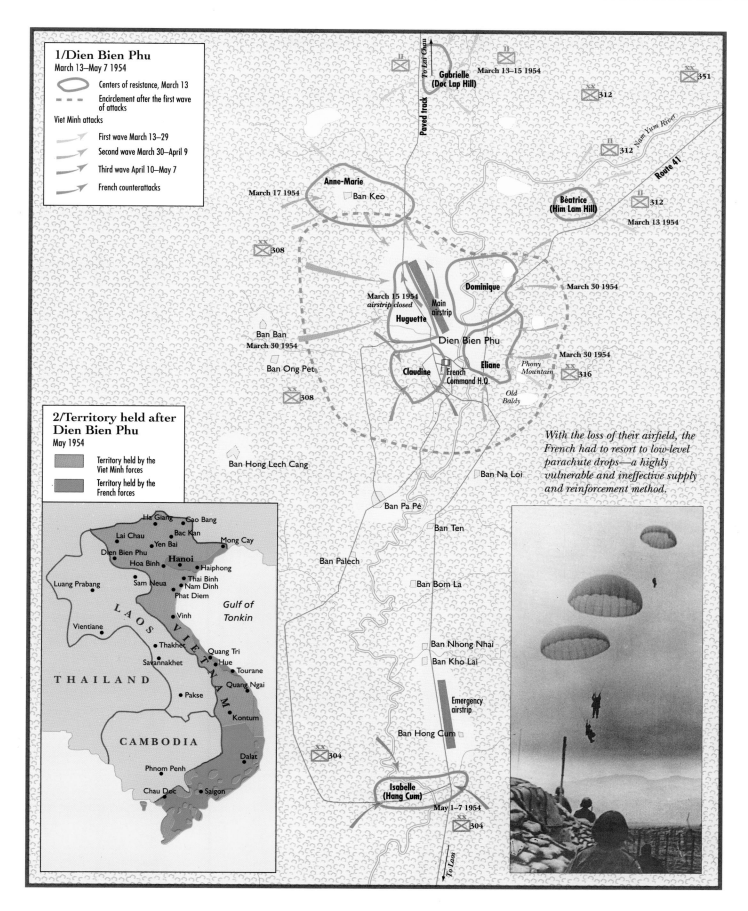

1/Dien Bien Phu
March 13–May 7 1954

◯ Centers of resistance, March 13

- - - Encirclement after the first wave of attacks

Viet Minh attacks

⟶ First wave March 13–29

⟶ Second wave March 30–April 9

⟶ Third wave April 10–May 7

⟶ French counterattacks

2/Territory held after Dien Bien Phu
May 1954

▨ Territory held by the Viet Minh forces

▨ Territory held by the French forces

To Lai Chau

Gabrielle (Doc Lap Hill)

March 13–15 1954

351

312

Nam Yum River

312

Route 41

Paved track

Anne-Marie

Ban Keo

March 17 1954

Béatrice (Him Lam Hill)

312

March 13 1954

308

Dominique

March 30 1954

March 15 1954 airstrip closed

Main airstrip

Huguette

Ban Ban
March 30 1954

Dien Bien Phu

Ban Ong Pet

Claudine

French Command H.Q.

Eliane

Phony Mountain

March 30 1954

316

Old Baldy

308

Ban Hong Lech Cang

Ban Na Loi

With the loss of their airfield, the French had to resort to low-level parachute drops—a highly vulnerable and ineffective supply and reinforcement method.

Ban Pa Pé

Ban Ten

Ban Palech

Ban Bom La

Ban Nhong Nhai

Ban Kho Lai

Emergency airstrip

Ban Hong Cum

Isabelle (Hang Cum)

May 1–7 1954

304

304

To Laos

(inset map — Territory held)

Ha Giang

Cao Bang

Lai Chau

Bac Kan

Yen Bai

Mong Cay

Dien Bien Phu

Hanoi

Hoa Binh

Haiphong

Luang Prabang

Sam Neua

Thai Binh

Nam Dinh

Phat Diem

LAOS

VIETNAM

Vinh

Gulf of Tonkin

Vientiane

Thakhet

Quang Tri

Hue

Savannakhet

Tourane

THAILAND

Quang Ngai

Pakse

Kontum

CAMBODIA

Dalat

Phnom Penh

Chau Doc

Saigon

The Death of G.M. 100   JUNE–JULY 1954

A month after the fall of Dien Bien Phu the tragic finale of the French experience in Vietnam played itself out, three days before the ceasefire that was to bring the First Indochina War to an end. On July 17, 1954, at Chu Dreh Pass on Route Coloniale 14 in the Central Highlands, the 1st Bataillon de Corée (1st Korea Battalion) ceased to exist.

The 1st Korea Battalion and its sister unit, the 2nd Korea Battalion, had been formed from the French battalion that had fought with the U.S. 2nd Infantry Division in the Korean War, winning three U.S. Presidential Unit citations for bravery in the process. On November 15, 1953, they became part of Groupement Mobile 100, along with Commando Bergerol, the Bataillon de Marche (B.M.) of the 43rd Colonial Infantry, and the 2nd Group of the 10th Colonial Artillery Regiment.

On June 24, 1954, G.M. 100 received orders to abandon its defensive positions at Ankhe and fall back to Pleiku, some 50 miles away over Route Coloniale 19. At road marker "Kilometer 15" the column was ambushed by the Viet Minh's 803rd Regiment. Suffering heavy losses, the remnants of G.M. 100, including the 1st Korea Battalion, broke through, only to be ambushed again on June 28 at Dak Ya-Ayun by the Viet Minh 108th Regiment.

The survivors of Groupement Mobile 100 finally reached Pleiku on June 29. The 1st Korea, the 2nd Korea, and the 43rd's Bataillon de Marche, which numbered 834 men each at the outset, now mustered 452, 497, and 345 men respectively, and the 2nd Group of the 10th Colonial Artillery, reduced to fighting as infantry after the loss of its guns, had shrunk from 475 to 215 men.

But the ordeal was not over. The 1st Korea Battalion was ordered to take part in Operation Forget-Me-Not to open RC14 between Pleiku and Ban Me Thuot. "My God, they want to kill us to the last man," said Corporal Cadiergue. "Haven't we done enough?" But his protestations were in vain. On July 17, the column was ambushed at Chu Dreh Pass. When the survivors, including Corporal Cadiergue, finally straggled in, there were only 107 men left, and of those 53 were in hospital at Ban Me Thuot.

On July 20, 1954, a battlefield ceasefire was announced, and on August 1, 1954, the armistice that was to end the First Indochina War went into effect. On September 1, 1954, G.M. 100 was officially dissolved. But it was not forgotten. As late as 1964, there was a simple memorial to G.M. 100 at the road marker on the Ankhe–Pleiku road. It read simply, *Mort pour la Patrie* ("Fallen for the Fatherland").

"Soldiers of Mobile Group 100! Your friends at Dien Bien Phu have not been able to resist the victorious onslaught of the Vietnam People's Army. You are much weaker than Dien Bien Phu! You will die, Frenchmen, and so will your Vietnamese running dogs!"

—Loudspeaker message
to G.M. 100, May 8, 1954

In the wake of the terrible losses suffered at Dien Bien Phu and in the Central Highlands, French forces withdraw from the Red River delta. By 1954, French public and government support for what has become known as the "sale guerre" (dirty war) had almost entirely evaporated.

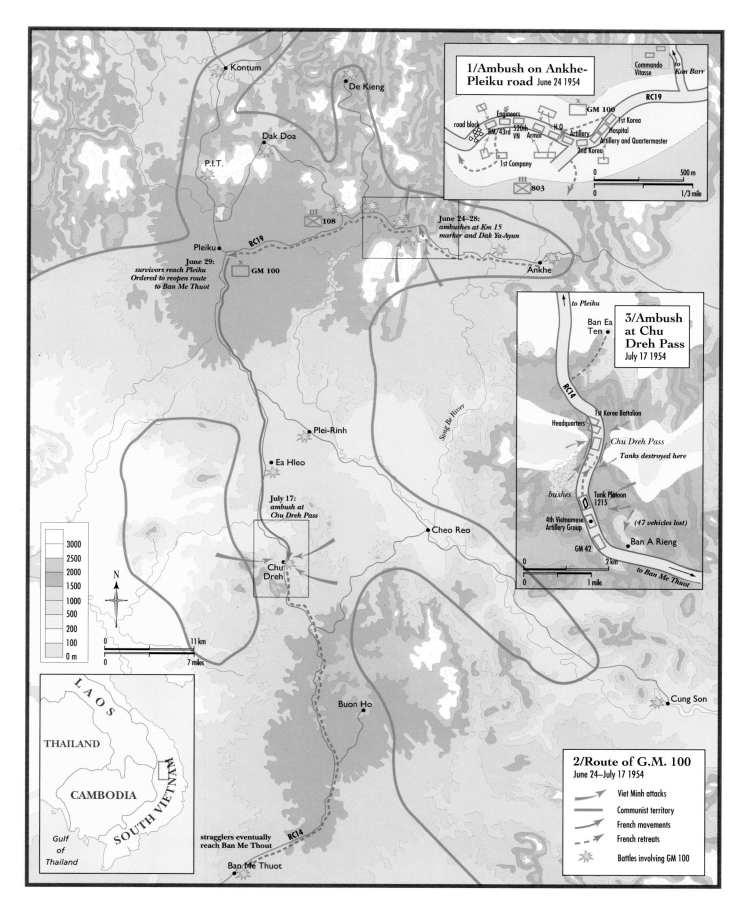

1/Ambush on Ankhe-Pleiku road June 24 1954

Commando Vitasse
to Kon Barr
RC19
GM 100
Engineers
road block
BM/43rd
520th VN
Armor
H.Q.
Artillery
1st Korea
Hospital
Artillery and Quartermaster
2nd Korea
1st Company
803
0   500 m
0   1/3 mile

Kontum
De Kieng
Dak Doa
P.I.T.
108
June 24–28:
ambushes at Km 15
marker and Dak Ya-Ayun
Pleiku
RC19
GM 100
June 29:
survivors reach Pleiku
Ordered to reopen route
to Ban Me Thuot
Ankhe

3/Ambush at Chu Dreh Pass July 17 1954

to Pleiku
Ban Ea Ten
RC14
1st Korea Battalion
Headquarters
Chu Dreh Pass
Tanks destroyed here
bushes
Tank Platoon 1215
4th Vietnamese Artillery Group
(47 vehicles lost)
GM 42
Ban A Rieng
to Ban Me Thuot
0   2 km
0   1 mile

Song Be River

Plei-Rinh
Ea Hleo
July 17:
ambush at
Chu Dreh Pass
Chu Dreh
Cheo Reo

3000
2500
2000
1500
1000
500
200
100
0 m

N

0   11 km
0   7 miles

Buon Ho
Cung Son

LAOS
THAILAND
CAMBODIA
SOUTH VIETNAM
Gulf
of
Thailand

2/Route of G.M. 100
June 24–July 17 1954

Viet Minh attacks
Communist territory
French movements
French retreats
Battles involving GM 100

stragglers eventually
reach Ban Me Thuot
RC14
Ban Me Thuot

Part IV: The Second Indochina War

"Vietnam would find more ways of breaking one's heart than anyone could ever have conceived," said former secretary of state Henry Kissinger. His words could well serve as the motto for the 25-year American travail there. One reason for the heartbreak is that the involvement throughout was based, like unrequited love, on self-delusions and false premises.

It was just such a false premise in June 1950 that led to the initial U.S. involvement. "The attack upon Korea makes it plain beyond all doubt that Communism has passed beyond the use of subversion to conquer independent nations and will now use armed invasion and war," said President Harry S. Truman on June 27, 1950, as he committed U.S. forces to battle in Korea. As well as beginning the massive U.S. military buildup in NATO, Truman ordered the Seventh Fleet to prevent any attack on Taiwan, and increased U.S. aid to the Philippines, which was then battling against the Communist-led Hukbalahap uprising. Most significantly, he increased the flow of military aid to France and its associated forces in Indochina, and sent a military mission to form "close working relations" with them.

With the opening of the archives of the former Soviet Union, it has become clear that Moscow, and Beijing as well, far from being the instigators of the attack, were at best reluctant partners to Pyongyang's decision to unify Korea by force. China's role, as discussed in the introduction to Part III, was far more ambiguous and convoluted than simply the "taking over [of] its neighbor to the south." Nevertheless, the U.S. government was blinded by Cold War rhetoric, and the fear of Chinese expansion played a large part in its calculations.

If keeping China out of Southeast Asia was truly the primary U.S. objective, success came not through U.S. efforts but through the efforts of the Vietnamese themselves. Contrary to what was thought at the time, Communism did not transcend the 2,000-year legacy of Sino-Vietnamese hostility. And Communist rhetoric misled the United States as to the very nature of the war.

As Clausewitz warned over a century earlier, "the first, the supreme, the most far-reaching act of judgment that the statesman and commander have to make is to establish ... the kind of war on which they were embarking; neither mistaking it for, nor trying to turn it into ... something that is alien to its nature. This is the first of all strategic questions and the most comprehensive."

In the wake of the Korean War, which was ended in part by President Dwight D. Eisenhower's veiled threat to escalate the conflict to the nuclear level if a ceasefire was not forthcoming, the Soviet Union and China were faced with a major strategic problem. While both were rapidly developing their nuclear arsenals, which would eliminate their vulnerability to U.S. intimidation, the immediate challenge was to develop a counter to the nuclear-based U.S. strategy of massive retaliation.

Their answer was what the Soviet Union called "wars of national liberation," and the Chinese labeled "the people's war." Instead of challenging the United States at the upper end of the conflict spectrum, they would do so at the lower end. Announced by Soviet premier Nikita Khrushchev in January 1961, the eve of Kennedy's inauguration, this strategy was essentially a low-cost effort which used surrogate forces to wear the United States down while avoiding direct armed confrontation.

This Communist strategy, which was seemingly validated by the Chinese Communist successes in winning the Chinese mainland through people's war strategies, and by Fidel Castro's humiliating successes in Cuba, fell on fertile ground in Washington. Returning from his browbeating by Khrushchev at the 1961 Vienna summit meeting, Kennedy gave his direct endorsement to a "new kind of warfare." Under the influence of advisers like former Army chief of staff General Maxwell D. Taylor, who had retired in protest against Eisenhower's emphasis on nuclear weaponry, Kennedy emphasized the need for a U.S. counterinsurgency capability. "In the 1940s and early fifties, the great danger was from Communist armies marching across free borders, which we saw in

Korea," he said. "Now we face a new and different threat. We no longer have a nuclear monopoly. Their missiles, they believe, will hold off our missiles, and their troops can match our troops should we intervene in so-called wars of national liberation. Thus, the local conflict they support can turn in their favor through guerrillas or insurgency or subversion."

"It is clear," he continued, "that this struggle in this area of the new and poorer nations will be a continuing crisis of this decade." He later said that he "would bet nine-to-one that they would be the most likely wars of the future." These words became a self-fulfilling prophecy, as Kennedy made Vietnam the test case for this "new kind of warfare." As Douglas Blaufarb noted in *The Counterinsurgency Era* in 1977, Kennedy himself "took the lead in formulating the [counterinsurgency] programs, pushing both his own staff and the government establishment to give the matter priority attention." He sent a letter to the Army pointing out the need for a new doctrine and new tactics, and brought General Taylor out of retirement to serve as his special military representative and to monitor the counterinsurgency effort.

It is difficult now, a generation later, to comprehend the massive impact that counterinsurgency doctrine had on the military, and on the Army in particular. "A national military policy and strategy relying upon massive nuclear retaliation for nearly all the uses of force left the Army uncertain of its place in the policy and strategy, uncertain that civilians recognized a need even for the Army's existence and uncertain therefore of the service's whole future," wrote historian Russell F. Weigley in *The American Way of War*. "The Army ... needed a newly defined raison d'être."

Counterinsurgency doctrine filled that void. Its impact was revealed in the March 1962 edition of *Army*, the influential magazine of the Association of the U.S. Army. Devoted to "spreading the gospel" of counterinsurgency, it told how Army chief of staff George Decker, a World War II combat infantryman, resisted that gospel and

A descendant of the ancient Hue dynasty, the playboy emperor Bao Dai was used as a puppet head of state by both the Japanese and the French. In 1955 he was replaced by Ngo Dinh Diem.

Having campaigned against the French since 1946, Ho Chi Minh became president and prime minister of North Vietnam in 1954. He resigned as prime minister in 1955 but remained president until his death in 1969.

"stood stoutly up to the President with the assurance [later validated on the battlefield] that 'any good soldier can handle guerrillas.'" The president's response was "a brisk homily to the effect that guerrilla fighting was a special art." Six months later, on October 1, 1962, Decker was out, replaced by General Earle Wheeler, a consummate and compliant staff officer. That same day, counterinsurgency guru General Maxwell Taylor was appointed chairman of the Joint Chiefs of Staff.

The Army leadership got the message, especially when, as reported in *Army* magazine in March 1962, "Kennedy dropped a broad hint that future promotions of high-ranking officers would depend upon their demonstration of experience in the counter-guerrilla or sublimited war field."

"There was a time," Blaufarb wrote, "when military intellectuals were advancing the notion that the U.S. Army was the arm of the government best equipped to carry out in the field the entire range of activities associated with 'nation-building.'" Counterinsurgency appeared to give the Army a whole new lease of life, one in which their traditional role as fighters was abandoned. The Army's *Field Service Regulations* now stated that "the fundamental purpose of U.S. military forces is to preserve, restore or create an environment of order or stability within which the instrumentalities of government can function effectively under a code of laws."

Gone were the initial U.S. military efforts to build a South Vietnamese military along conventional military lines. From 1954 to 1960, U.S. military assistance programs had concentrated on preparing the RVNAF for a conventional delaying action against what was regarded as the most serious threat—an NVA cross-border blitzkrieg by regular, rather than guerrilla, forces supported by tanks and heavy artillery. Had the U.S. military followed the pre-Chinese intervention strategy implemented in the Korean War, its response to such an attack would have included the early seizure of air and port facilities and the phased deployment of American ground combat units, first to block the North Vietnamese invasion and then to launch a joint airborne, amphibious, and ground counterattack into North Vietnam to reunify Vietnam under South Vietnamese control.

All this came to an end when counterinsurgency replaced counterattack as the watchword. In August 1962, the National Security Council directed that plans of action be drawn up which were "consistent with the doctrines of counterinsurgency." In accordance with these plans, U.S. military assistance to Vietnam shifted from the external enemy to counterinsurgency.

A major flaw in this new doctrine was its failure to distinguish the truly revolutionary First Indochina War, between France and the Viet Minh, from the Second Indochina War, between North Vietnam and South

Vietnam. This led to a further failure to distinguish between the military actions appropriate for a colonial power like France in Indochina (or Great Britain in Malaya, also held up as a model) and the actions appropriate for the United States, a coalition partner whose ally, the Republic of Vietnam, was faced with both an internal and an external threat.

The result was massive overinvolvement in the internal affairs of South Vietnam. In pursuit of its own objective of limiting worldwide Communist expansion through a defensive military policy of containment, the United States forced the South Vietnamese government onto the defensive too. Offensive actions by the South Vietnamese to unify their country were deliberately forbidden, lest

Right: *The youngest U.S. president (1961–1963), John F. Kennedy offered increased military aid to Diem and promoted a new doctrine of counterinsurgency, for which Vietnam was the testing ground.*

Below: *President Diem (second from right, shown with his family,) had begun to show a dangerous degree of independence. His assassination in 1963 was greeted with relief by the U.S. government.*

they involve the United States in a war with China, as had been the case in the Korean War. The result was that South Vietnamese president Ngo Dinh Diem, who was certainly as ardent a nationalist as Ho Chi Minh, was stripped of those credentials and made to seem a puppet of the United States.

But the fiercely independent Diem was never that. When his handling of the Buddhist uprisings in 1963 appeared to be at odds with the emphasis on "winning the hearts and minds" of the Vietnamese people as the key to victory, the counterinsurgency crowd in Washington and Saigon conspired to have him removed from office. As General Westmoreland noted, "that action morally locked us in Vietnam."

For their part, the North Vietnamese had launched one of the most effective deception operations in history. As they now freely admit, they had been determined from the start to unify the country under their control. When it became apparent that South Vietnam was not going to fall of its own weight after the 1954 Geneva accords, North Vietnam gradually began to raise the ante. In March 1959 it activated the guerrilla cadres left behind in the South, and in May it established the Central Office of South Vietnam (COSVN) to run the war in the South. In December 1960, it formed the National Liberation Front to keep up the pretense that the war in South Vietnam was a true revolutionary war, rather than a guerrilla or partisan war.

The difference between the two is critical. Sir Robert Thompson explains, in *Revolutionary War in World Strategy*, that "guerrilla warfare is designed merely to harass and distract the enemy so that the regular forces can reach a decision in conventional battles ... Revolutionary war on the other hand is designed to reach a decisive result on its own." If his book, *In Retrospect*, is any guide, Robert McNamara, the U.S. secretary of defense during that period, is still gulled by this North Vietnamese propaganda line, and still sees the war there as a primarily internal affair. But Hanoi has long since acknowledged its successful deception, bragging that the Communist forces in the South were always a single military entity kept tightly on Hanoi's leash.

As the State Department's Norman Hannah put it, "In South Vietnam we responded mainly to Hanoi's simulated insurgency rather than to its real, but controlled, aggression, as a bull charges the toreador's cape, not the toreador."

Right: *Defense Secretary Robert McNamara and JCS chief of staff Maxwell Taylor at a press conference following a fact-finding tour of Vietnam for President Kennedy in October 1963. When President Diem was assassinated a month later, McNamara described developments within Vietnam as "very disturbing," adding "We should watch the situation very carefully, running scared, hoping for the best, and preparing for more forceful moves."*

Below: *A U.S. Special Forces adviser sports an ARVN Rangers red beret and a MACV shoulder insignia. The Special Forces evolved in response to Kennedy's new doctrine of counterinsurgency warfare.*

Two Nations: the Geneva Conference 1954

"You don't win at the conference table what you've lost on the battlefield," said General Walter Bedell Smith, the head of the U.S. delegation to the Geneva Conference on Indochina. But having won on the battlefield with the capture of Dien Bien Phu on May 7, 1954, the very day that the conference began, the Viet Minh no doubt expected to win at the conference table as well.

Co-chaired by Great Britain's Anthony Eden and the Soviet Union's Vyacheslav Molotov, the conference included the U.S.'s John Foster Dulles (soon succeeded by General Smith), France's Georges Bidault, China's Chou En-lai (Zhou Enlai), the Viet Minh's Pham Van Dong, and the South Vietnamese prime minister Ngo Dinh Diem.

The Viet Minh expected support from their Communist brethren for their claims to all of Vietnam. But that was not to be. Concerned less with Vietnam than with the threat to their own security posed by the expanding U.S. anti-Communist defense network, the Soviet Union and China sought to undercut that expansion by presenting themselves as champions of world peace. Believing that in any case a government in South Vietnam built around former emperor Bao Dai and pro-French Vietnamese would not long survive, they pressured the Viet Minh to accept half a victory. Instead of the whole of Vietnam, Ho Chi Minh had to settle for the portion north of the 17th parallel.

The only documents signed at Geneva were ceasefire agreements between France and the Democratic Republic of Vietnam (DRV), as the Viet Minh now called itself. These provided for the temporary division of Vietnam at the 17th parallel pending elections to be held in the summer of 1956. Much has been made of the refusal of South Vietnam (the Republic of Vietnam or RVN) to hold those elections—elections to which they had not agreed and which, along with the rest of the accords, they had rejected at the time. The reason for this was simple. Given the fact that the population of North Vietnam exceeded that of South Vietnam by 2 million people, the result would have been a foregone conclusion.

Neither the Soviet Union nor China protested too loudly, since in the two other countries divided by the Cold War—Germany and Korea—the population imbalance was not in

their favor and the Communists would have lost free elections in both countries. Far from pressing for unification, in 1957 the Soviet Union proposed that North and South Vietnam be admitted to the United Nations as "two separate states [which] differ from each other in political and economic structure."

During the regroupment process following the Geneva Conference, some 900,000 people, primarily Catholics, fled North Vietnam and were resettled in the South. Conversely, 80,000-90,000 Viet Minh troops moved from the South to the North. Significantly, however, 10,000 Viet Minh troops were told to quietly remain in place in remote areas in the South.

Both sides were now consolidating their power. Ho Chi Minh showed his true colors by moving to eliminate all non-Communist elements in society. This included a "land reform" program to eliminate "landlord" bourgeoisie. Thousands were executed (including loyal Viet Minh veterans) and thousands more were imprisoned in the frenzied quest for ideological purity. Blaming these excesses on his Chinese advisers, Ho Chi Minh publicly confessed that "errors had been committed," but when a rebellion broke out in his home province of Nhge An in November 1956, Ho put it down ruthlessly, killing or deporting more than 6,000 people in the process.

In the South, Ngo Dinh Diem defeated former emperor Bao Dai in a referendum in October 1955 and proclaimed the Republic of Vietnam (RVN) on October 27, 1955, with himself as president. The initial anti-government opposition in the South came not from the Communists, who had been ordered by Hanoi to lay low, but from the Cao Dai and Hoa Hao religious sects and the criminal Binh Xuyen force that controlled much of Saigon.

In May 1955, even before becoming president, then prime minister Diem had ignored Bao Dai's orders and routed the 40,000-man Binh Xuyen thugs, forcing their leader into exile in Paris. Attention was then turned against the Cao Dai and Hoa Hao, which Diem, with the help of the CIA's Colonel Edward G. Lansdale, subdued in early 1956. To the surprise and consternation of many, including Ho Chi Minh, who had counted on his quick collapse, Ngo Dinh Diem was firmly in control of South Vietnam.

"Unfortunately, French pressure will be exerted at the conference for negotiation and the end of the fighting. The British will take a similar position, because of mounting Labour Party pressure and defections in the Conservative ranks ... This country is the only nation strong enough at home to take a position that will save Asia."

—Vice-President Richard Nixon, April 1954

A woman and her son flee for their lives as bloody battles rage in Saigon between anti-government sects and the forces of Diem's newly proclaimed Republic in May 1955.

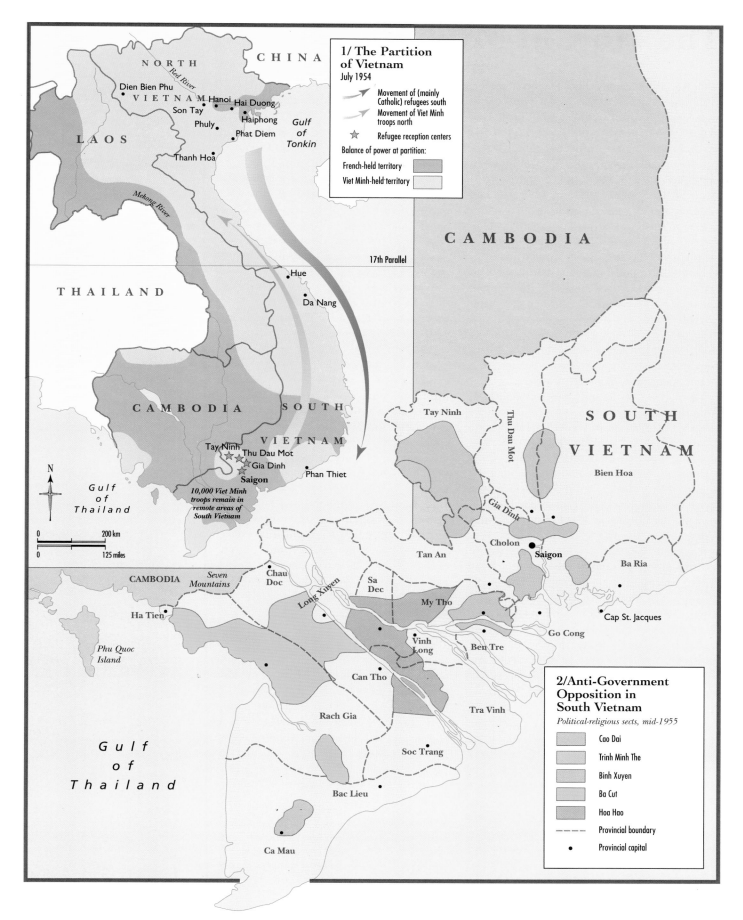

1/ The Partition of Vietnam
July 1954

→ Movement of (mainly Catholic) refugees south
→ Movement of Viet Minh troops north
★ Refugee reception centers

Balance of power at partition:
French-held territory
Viet Minh-held territory

CHINA

NORTH VIETNAM

Dien Bien Phu
Hanoi
Son Tay
Hai Duong
Phuly
Haiphong
Phat Diem
Thanh Hoa

Red River

LAOS

Gulf of Tonkin

Mekong River

17th Parallel

THAILAND

Hue

Da Nang

CAMBODIA

SOUTH VIETNAM

Tay Ninh
Thu Dau Mot
Gia Dinh
Saigon
Phan Thiet

10,000 Viet Minh troops remain in remote areas of South Vietnam

N

Gulf of Thailand

0   200 km
0   125 miles

CAMBODIA

Seven Mountains

Chau Doc

Sa Dec

Long Xuyen

My Tho

Vinh Long

Ben Tre

Go Cong

Ha Tien

Phu Quoc Island

Can Tho

Rach Gia

Tra Vinh

Soc Trang

Bac Lieu

Ca Mau

Gulf of Thailand

Tay Ninh

Thu Dau Mot

SOUTH VIETNAM

Bien Hoa

Gia Dinh

Cholon

Saigon

Ba Ria

Tan An

Cap St. Jacques

2/Anti-Government Opposition in South Vietnam
Political-religious sects, mid-1955

Cao Dai
Trinh Minh The
Binh Xuyen
Ba Cut
Hoa Hao
- - - Provincial boundary
• Provincial capital

The Ho Chi Minh Trail   1959–1975

With Ngo Dinh Diem's consolidation of power, it became obvious to the North Vietnamese that South Vietnam would not fall of its own accord. How then should the struggle (*dau tranh*, in Vietnamese) proceed? Political *dau tranh*—organizing people in Communist-controlled areas of the South, proselytizing to Army of the Republic of Vietnam troops, and winning over the people who were not under Communist control through propaganda, disinformation, and terror—had not been enough.

In early 1956, having destroyed his non-Communist opposition, Diem had turned on the Communists and by the end of the year had smashed 90 percent of the former Viet Minh guerrilla bands in the Mekong delta. In March 1959, with the Communist organization in the South on the verge of extinction, the North Vietnamese Politburo ordered a change from political *dau tranh* to military *dau tranh*.

The "armed revolution" had begun, and in May 1959 the North Vietnamese Communist Party's 15th Plenum in Hanoi established the Central Office in South Vietnam (COSVN) to run the war in the South. In July, 4,000 Communist cadres, recruited from among the southern Viet Minh veterans who had moved north in 1954, were dispatched to the South to become the nucleus of Viet Cong Main Force battalions and regiments.

The 15th Plenum also formed a series of logistics groups to support these forces: Group 579 to control sea routes of supply; Group 959 to support Communist forces in Laos; and Group 559, under the command of General Vo Bam, to construct and operate the Truong Son Route, better known as the Ho Chi Minh Trail, which ran down the spine of the Chaîne Annamitique mountains in eastern Laos to supply depots in the jungles of South Vietnam. Construction of the trail began in May 1959, and by the height of the war Group 559 had some 50,000 transport workers, another 50,000 North Vietnamese Army (NVA) engineer troops to maintain the route, and yet another 12,000 NVA infantry and antiaircraft artillery forces to provide security.

The word "trail," however, soon became a misnomer. It was more like a superhighway, literally a lifeline to victory. NVA General Van Tien Dung described the 12,500-mile-long, 22-foot-wide route as "our pride. With 5,000 kilo-

meters [3,125 miles] of pipeline laid through deep rivers and streams and on the mountains more than 1,000 meters [3,300 feet] high, we were capable of providing enough fuel for the various battlefields." According to Vietnamese sources, 2 million people moved up or down the trail during the war, and peak traffic ranged above 20,000 tons a month. "Freight went by six-wheel-drive truck, reinforced bicycle, and elephants," said a December 1994 Associated Press report, "But the mainstay was a steady stream of human beasts of burden, men and women humping 100-pound packs."

In March 1965, six years after construction of the trail had begun, the United States began attempting to interdict it through air strikes by Air Force B-52 bombers and Air Force, Navy, and Marine fighter bombers, and by attacks on NVA truck convoys by Air Force fixed-wing gunships. The movement of NVA supplies and reinforcements was slowed, but despite the thousands of tons of bombs and millions of rounds of ammunition expended, the trail could never be closed by air operations alone.

Ground operations that could have severed it were precluded by the terms of the 1962 Geneva Conference on Laos, where U.S. ambassador Averill Harriman had foolishly agreed to Communist guarantees of the neutrality of western Laos, which had no great strategic value to the United States, in exchange for U.S. guarantees not to invade eastern Laos, the site of the strategic Ho Chi Minh Trail. The NVA's supply lifelines were thus assured.

Even more damagingly, the Ho Chi Minh Trail gave the NVA the advantage of interior lines. Using the relatively straight supply lines down the mountains, they could concentrate their forces anywhere in the South more quickly than the ARVN, who had to move along the curvature of the coast. Negated by U.S. helicopter and fixed-wing air mobility while the Americans were in the war, this advantage proved decisive in the NVA's final 1975 campaign, after the United States had withdrawn.

In 1964, the arduous march from the northern to the southern tip of the Ho Chi Minh Trail took four months. By 1975, the trail consisted of six main north–south routes and 21 east–west arteries, and an army corps could cover its length in 12 days.

"When marching leave no tracks, when cooking make no smoke, when resting build no house."

—North Vietnamese slogan on the Ho Chi Minh Trail

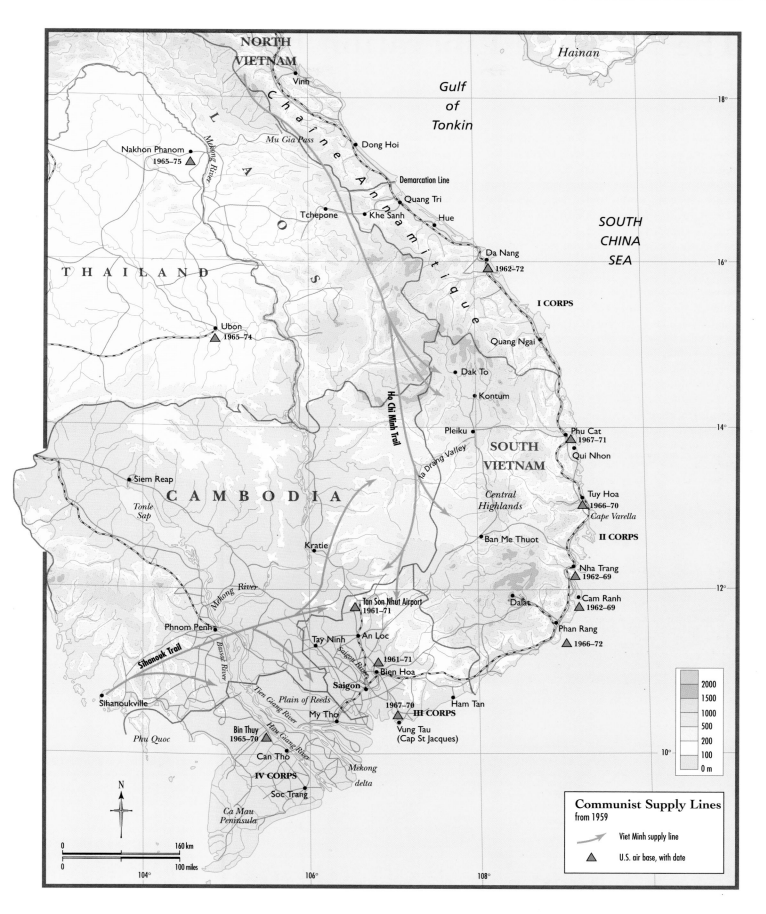

NORTH VIETNAM

Vinh

Gulf of Tonkin

Hainan

Nakhon Phanom
1965–75 ▲

Mekong River

Mu Gia Pass

● Dong Hoi

L A O S

Chaîne Annamitique

Demarcation Line

Quang Tri

Tchepone ● ● Khe Sanh ● Hue

T H A I L A N D

Ubon
▲ 1965–74

Da Nang
▲ 1962–72

SOUTH CHINA SEA

I CORPS

Quang Ngai

● Dak To

● Kontum

● Pleiku

SOUTH VIETNAM

Ho Chi Minh Trail

Ia Drang Valley

Phu Cat
▲ 1967–71
● Qui Nhon

● Siem Reap

C A M B O D I A

Tonle Sap

Central Highlands

Tuy Hoa
▲ 1966–70
Cape Varella

II CORPS

● Ban Me Thuot

● Kratie

Mekong River

Nha Trang
▲ 1962–69

● Dalat

Cam Ranh
▲ 1962–69

Phnom Penh ●

Bassac River

Tan Son Nhut Airport
▲ 1961–71

Tay Ninh ● ● An Loc

Phan Rang
▲ 1966–72

Sihanouk Trail

Saigon River

▲ 1961–71
Bien Hoa ●

Sihanoukville ●

Tien Giang River

Plain of Reeds

Saigon

Ham Tan ●

Phu Quoc

Bin Thuy
1965–70 ▲

Hau Giang River

My Tho ●

1967–70
▲ III CORPS

Vung Tau
(Cap St Jacques)

● Can Tho

Mekong delta

IV CORPS

Soc Trang ●

Ca Mau Peninsula

N

| | 2000 |
| 1500 |
| 1000 |
| 500 |
| 200 |
| 100 |
| 0 m |

0 ————— 160 km
0 ————— 100 miles

Communist Supply Lines
from 1959

⟶ Viet Minh supply line

▲ U.S. air base, with date

104°   106°   108°

18°

16°

14°

12°

10°

The National Liberation Front 1960

One of the most successful deception operations of the Second Indochina War was the North Vietnamese Politburo's decision in December 1960 to create a classic Communist front organization to mask its control of the war in the South. Titled the National Liberation Front (NLF), this organization convinced many, especially in the United States, that the war in South Vietnam was entirely a home-grown nationalist insurgency.

Taking its orders from the Politburo in Hanoi, the NLF brought together a variety of anti-Diem groups in the South, including former Viet Minh peasant, youth, religious and cultural associations as well as the remnants of the Cao Dai, Hoa Hao and Binh Xuyen groups that Diem had decimated five years before. It was ostensibly headed by Nguyen Huu Tho, a French-educated South Vietnamese lawyer, but he was only a figurehead.

Since the end of the war, North Vietnam has completely changed its story. While during the 1960s and early 1970s Hanoi vehemently denied any direct involvement in the war, now, as historian Douglas Pike has noted, "Hanoi's historians not only acknowledge, they boast that the Communist force in the South was always regarded by Hanoi's High Command as a single military entity … kept under tight leash, using northern cadre structure and logistic support as the means."

These historians virtually deny that the NLF and Viet Cong made any contribution, and give all credit for victory to the NVA. The NLF thus emerge as the great losers of the war. Almost destroyed when they emerged from cover at Hanoi's bidding during the 1968 Tet Offensive, their bid for political power in postwar Vietnam was thwarted too. Talking with former war correspondent Morley Safer in 1989, Dr. Duong Quynh Hoa, one of the 16 founders of the NLF, was thoroughly disillusioned. "I thought I was making a revolution for the people," she said. "I discovered I made a revolution for a cause, for a discipline, for an ideology. The people had nothing to do with it."

"The Viet Cong never mention the subject of Communism. The whole thing is infinitely more simple than that. Their political staff don't hold meetings of the peasants to conduct seminars in political theory. What they do is propose concrete solutions to concrete problems. These problems are not difficult to state. They are, in the order of their importance: the return of peace; the reestablishment of law and order; the better management of public affairs."

—Max Clos,
The Situation in Vietnam

Right: *Young Viet Cong guerrillas display a submachine gun and an automatic pistol constructed from scraps of weapons and parts made by villagers in local jungle arsenals.*

Left: *Male and female volunteers are taught the rudiments of jungle guerrilla warfare by North Vietnamese veterans of the war against the French. Seen here near the U.S. air base at Da Nang and recruited locally, the troops can easily pass for farmers and merchants if approached by government forces.*

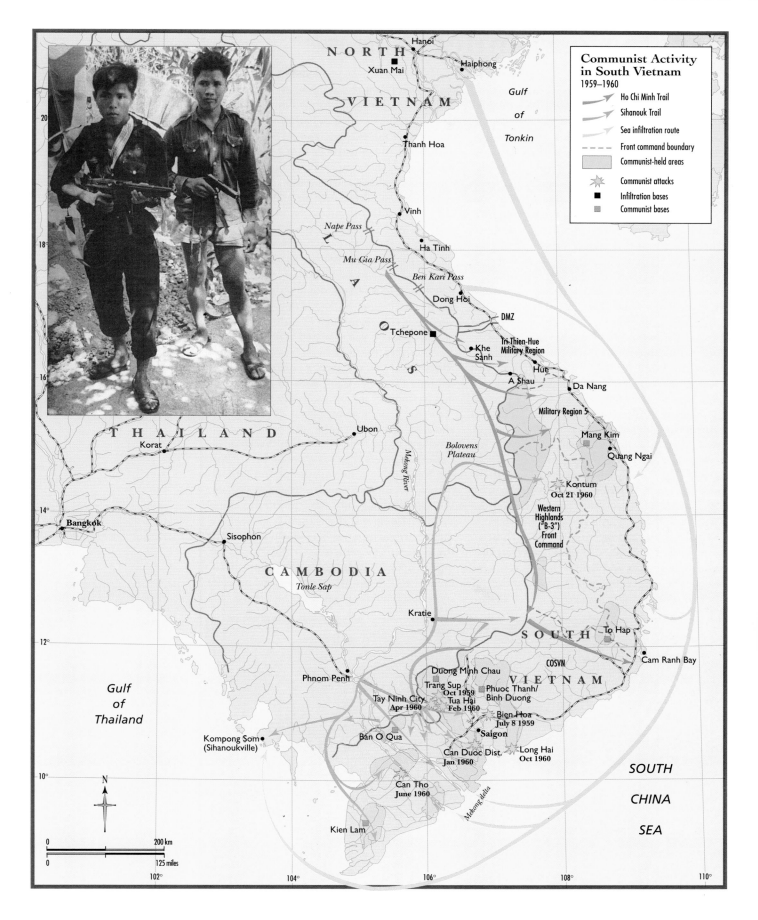

**Communist Activity
in South Vietnam**
1959–1960

→ Ho Chi Minh Trail
→ Sihanouk Trail
→ Sea infiltration route
- - - Front command boundary
▨ Communist-held areas
✦ Communist attacks
■ Infiltration bases
▨ Communist bases

NORTH

VIETNAM

Hanoi

Xuan Mai

Haiphong

*Gulf
of
Tonkin*

Thanh Hoa

Vinh

Nape Pass

Ha Tinh

Mu Gia Pass

Ben Kari Pass

Dong Hoi

DMZ

L

Tchepone

Khe
Sanh

Tri-Thien-Hue
Military Region

A

Hue

A Shau

Da Nang

Military Region 5

O

Ubon

Korat

*Bolovens
Plateau*

Mang Kim

Quang Ngai

S

Mekong River

Kontum
Oct 21 1960

Western
Highlands
("B-3")
Front
Command

THAILAND

Bangkok

Sisophon

CAMBODIA

Tonle Sap

Kratie

SOUTH

To Hap

VIETNAM

Cam Ranh Bay

COSVN

Phnom Penh

Duong Minh Chau

Trang Sup
Oct 1959
Tua Hai
Feb 1960

Phuoc Thanh/
Binh Duong

Tay Ninh City
Apr 1960

Bien Hoa
July 8 1959

*Gulf
of
Thailand*

Ban O Qua

Saigon

Kompong Som
(Sihanoukville)

Can Duoc Dist.
Jan 1960

Long Hai
Oct 1960

SOUTH

N

Can Tho
June 1960

CHINA

Mekong delta

SEA

0   200 km

Kien Lam

0   125 miles

Strategic Hamlets   1962–1966

In 1959, as North Vietnam stepped up its attacks on South Vietnam with its Viet Cong guerrilla force, President Ngo Dinh Diem announced the *Khu Tru Mat* program, the construction of a series of *agrovilles* or farm communities to isolate the people from the Communist guerrillas. This scheme died aborning, but was resurrected three years later as the "strategic hamlet" program. Encouraged by British counterinsurgency expert Sir Robert Thompson, who had overseen a similar project during the successful British counterinsurgency operation in Malaya, this involved the construction of armed hamlets where local farmers and their families would be housed free of Viet Cong intimidation.

The program began in March 1962 with Operation Sunrise in Binh Duong Province north of Saigon, and by September it was claimed that one-third of the South Vietnamese population—4,322,034 people—were in strategic hamlets. Although popular with American statisticians such as Defense Secretary Robert McNamara, who praised its progress in "countering insurgency," the program was immensely unpopular with farmers removed from their ancestral lands. Described by Stanley Karnow as "Potemkin villages mainly designed to impress visiting dignitaries," the program soon crumbled through lack of adequate government resources, which had been siphoned off by corrupt local officials and by the lack of adequate arms and equipment for self-defense.

The village of Duc Lap south of Cu Chi in Hau Nghia Province was a case in point. In May 1963, Duc Lap was transformed into a "strategic hamlet" by the erection of barbed wire fortification around the existing hamlets of Duc Lap A and B and the construction of housing for a thousand of its farmers. But from the beginning, the government failed to provide adequate security. Even after an ARVN battalion was stationed in the village, security remained tenuous. Whenever the battalion left the village to conduct combat operations in the area, the Viet Cong would move in to terrorize the inhabitants. After one hamlet chief was assassinated by the Viet Cong, the other resigned and government supervision virtually ceased. Duc Lap was finally abandoned in early 1966.

This pattern was repeated across the country. After the assassination of President Diem in November 1963, the strategic hamlet program fell into disrepute. U.S. efforts to revive it with massive military aid proved counterproductive. "The Viet Cong claim we use U.S. barbed wire and iron stakes to confine the people in U.S. military bases," wrote South Vietnamese General Nguyen Huu Co early in 1964. "With the loathing and hatred the people already have, when they hear the seemingly reasonable Viet Cong propaganda, they turn to the side of the Viet Cong and place their confidence in them." An attempt was later made to resurrect the program by renaming it the "New Life" hamlet plan. But despite an infusion of $40 million in U.S. aid, that program was no more successful than its predecessor.

"Many times the recruiters for the NVA would come into a village, take the oldest person and string him up, slit his stomach open and let the wild pigs eat him alive while he was dying. Then they say, 'Who wants to come with us?' God help you if you don't."

—U.S. soldier

South Vietnamese soldiers look on as Operation Sunrise, a mass resettlement project designed to hamper Viet Cong guerrilla activities and intimidation of the rural population, gets under way. Local people's belongings are loaded onto an ox-cart during the evacuation of their village.

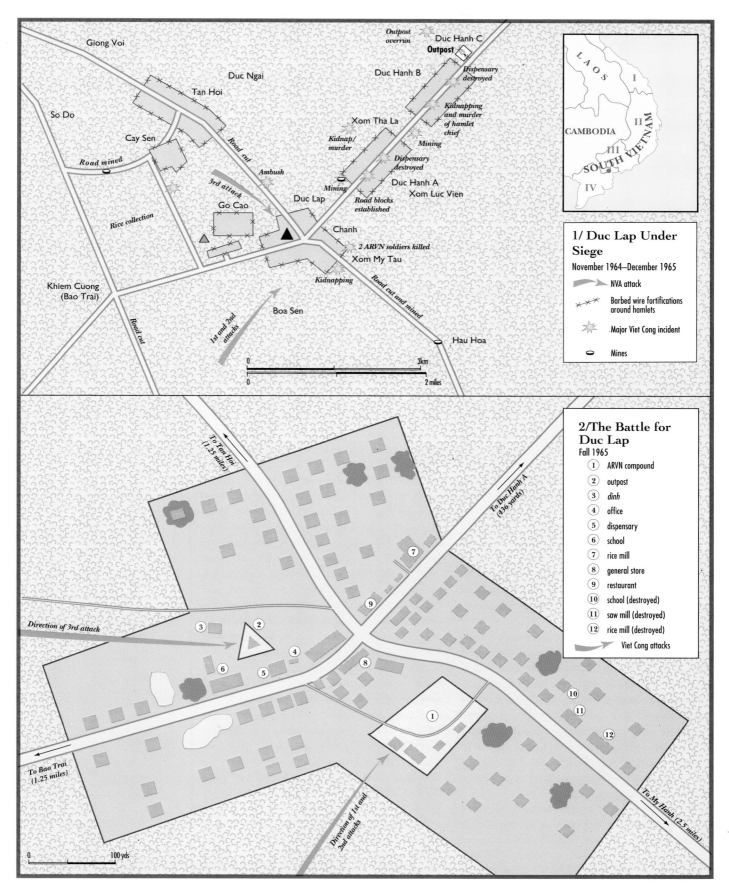

Giong Voi

Duc Ngai

Tan Hoi

So Do

Cay Sen

Road mined

Road cut

Ambush

3rd attack

Go Cao

Rice collection

Khiem Cuong
(Bao Trai)

Road cut

1st and 2nd attacks

Boa Sen

Road cut and mined

Duc Lap

Chanh

Xom My Tau

2 ARVN soldiers killed

Kidnapping

Hau Hoa

Outpost overrun

Duc Hanh C

Outpost

Dispensary destroyed

Duc Hanh B

Xom Tha La

Kidnap/murder

Mining

Kidnapping and murder of hamlet chief

Mining

Dispensary destroyed

Duc Hanh A
Xom Luc Vien

Road blocks established

Mining

LAOS

I

II

CAMBODIA

III

SOUTH VIETNAM

IV

0   3km
0   2 miles

1/ Duc Lap Under Siege

November 1964–December 1965

NVA attack

Barbed wire fortifications around hamlets

Major Viet Cong incident

Mines

2/The Battle for Duc Lap

Fall 1965

1. ARVN compound
2. outpost
3. *dinh*
4. office
5. dispensary
6. school
7. rice mill
8. general store
9. restaurant
10. school (destroyed)
11. saw mill (destroyed)
12. rice mill (destroyed)

Viet Cong attacks

To Tan Hoi
(1.25 miles)

To Duc Hanh A
(436 yards)

Direction of 3rd attack

To Bao Trai
(1.25 miles)

Direction of 1st and 2nd attacks

To My Hanh (2.5 miles)

0   100 yds

MACV 1962

On June 27, 1950, President Harry S. Truman delivered his war message on Korea. Seeing the war there as an attempt by "monolithic world communism" directed by Moscow to expand its empire by force of arms, Truman not only sent American troops into Korea but also began the buildup of U.S. forces in Western Europe to guard against a Soviet attack there, sent the U.S. Seventh Fleet into the Taiwan Straits to prevent the Chinese Communists from attacking Taiwan, and increased aid to the Philippine government who were then fighting a Communist insurgency. He also "directed acceleration in the furnishing of military assistance to the forces of France and the Associated States of Indochina and the dispatch of a military mission to provide close working relations with those forces." Although it would later turn out that "monolithic world communism" was more illusory than real, the misperception would determine U.S. actions in Indochina for the next quarter century.

Military Assistance Advisory Group (MAAG) Indochina was established in Saigon on September 27, 1950. After the French withdrawal, the name was changed to MAAG-Vietnam and the mission was expanded to the provision of training and assistance as well as military aid and support for the fledgling Republic of Vietnam Armed Forces (RVNAF.) From around 900 U.S. military personnel assigned when President Eisenhower left office in 1961, MAAG-Vietnam grew to 3,205 personnel by February 1962, when it was superseded by a new headquarters, U.S. Military Assistance Command Vietnam (MACV).

Faced with the growing Communist insurgency in Vietnam, President Kennedy increased MACV's strength to 16,300 by the time of his death in November 1963. As part of the U.S. ambassador's country team, MACV served as a high-level adviser to the Government of the Republic of Vietnam, and its Field Advisory Group provided military advisers down to battalion level within the RVNAF. But its main function was to be the command of the enormous U.S. buildup in Vietnam.

In the Korean War, the Korean Military Advisory Group was subordinate to the Eighth U.S. Army headquarters, which was in charge of all air and ground combat operations. No such theater army headquarters was established in Vietnam, and MACV's attention was thus split between its advisory functions and its theater army duties. Furthermore, unlike the Eighth Army in the Korean War, which had command authority over all allied forces, MACV commanded only the U.S. forces and had no authority over RVNAF or other allied forces. Combined operations were therefore on a cooperative rather than a directed basis.

Unlike his North Vietnamese counterpart, General Giap, who was a North Vietnamese Politburo member, the minister of defense, and commander-in-chief of the North Vietnamese armed forces, the MACV commander was the ground commander only. He had no command over air operations outside South Vietnam, including strikes against enemy supply lines in Laos, or over naval operations outside South Vietnamese waters, which were under the control of the commander-in-chief of Pacific Command in Honolulu. This convoluted command chain had a highly adverse impact on the U.S. conduct of the war.

A little known aspect of MACV was its clandestine force, innocuously titled "Studies and Observation Group" (SOG), which had its origins in President Kennedy's 1961 decision to launch secret operations against North Vietnam and Laos. Initially run by the CIA, in December 1963 it was transfered to MACV control. Its official mandate was President Johnson's Operations Plan 34A of January 1964. Under that authority, the DeSoto raids on the North Vietnamese coast that triggered the Gulf of Tonkin incident were conducted, and cross-border operations such as Prairie Fire and Nickel Steel were mounted against North Vietnamese infiltration routes in Laos.

While its advisory strength remained relatively constant, the commitment of U.S. ground combat forces in May 1965 increased MACV's size dramatically. It reached a peak in April 1969, at 543,400 men and women in the Army, Navy, Air Force, Marine Corps and Coast Guard, before troop withdrawals began later that year. MACV was commanded by General Paul D. Harkins from February 1962 to June 1964, by General William C. Westmoreland until July 1968, by General Creighton W. Abrams until June 1972, and by General Fred C. Weyand until March 1973, when it was disestablished by the Paris Peace Accords.

"He [President Kennedy] compromised between withdrawal and full Americanization of the war by steadily increasing the teams of American military 'advisers,' who, it soon became known, were more and more actively engaged in combat direction, and he lavishly supplied the South Vietnamese army with modern equipment."

—Joseph Buttinger

A U.S. adviser instructs a South Vietnamese Guardsman in the use of an automatic rifle. By 1962, the increased effectiveness of the South Vietnamese forces had become glaringly apparent to the Viet Cong.

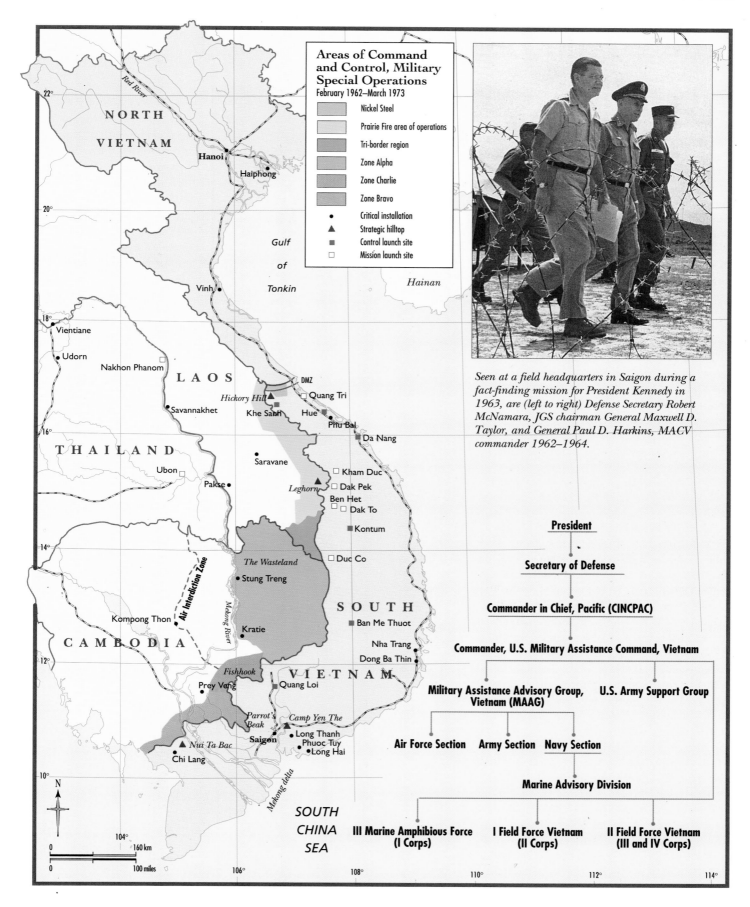

Areas of Command and Control, Military Special Operations
February 1962–March 1973

- Nickel Steel
- Prairie Fire area of operations
- Tri-border region
- Zone Alpha
- Zone Charlie
- Zone Bravo

- • Critical installation
- ▲ Strategic hilltop
- ■ Control launch site
- □ Mission launch site

NORTH VIETNAM

Red River

Hanoi

Haiphong

Gulf

of

Tonkin

Hainan

Vinh

Vientiane

Udorn

Nakhon Phanom

LAOS

Savannakhet

DMZ

Hickory Hill

Quang Tri

Khe Sanh

Hue

Phu Bai

THAILAND

Saravane

Ubon

Pakse

Leghorn

Da Nang

Kham Duc

Dak Pek

Ben Het

Dak To

Kontum

The Wasteland

Duc Co

Stung Treng

SOUTH

Air Interdiction Zone

Kompong Thon

Mekong River

Kratie

CAMBODIA

Ban Me Thuot

Nha Trang

Dong Ba Thin

Fishhook

VIETNAM

Prey Veng

Quang Loi

Parrot's Beak

Camp Yen The

Saigon

Long Thanh

Phuoc Tuy

Long Hai

Nui Ta Bac

Chi Lang

Mekong delta

N

SOUTH CHINA SEA

0   160 km
0   100 miles

104°

106°

108°

110°

112°

114°

22°

20°

18°

16°

14°

12°

10°

Seen at a field headquarters in Saigon during a fact-finding mission for President Kennedy in 1963, are (left to right) Defense Secretary Robert McNamara, JGS chairman General Maxwell D. Taylor, and General Paul D. Harkins, MACV commander 1962–1964.

President

Secretary of Defense

Commander in Chief, Pacific (CINCPAC)

Commander, U.S. Military Assistance Command, Vietnam

Military Assistance Advisory Group, Vietnam (MAAG)   **U.S. Army Support Group**

Air Force Section   **Army Section**   **Navy Section**

Marine Advisory Division

III Marine Amphibious Force (I Corps)   **I Field Force Vietnam (II Corps)**   **II Field Force Vietnam (III and IV Corps)**

The Green Berets   FEBRUARY 1962–FEBRUARY 1971

One of the unique aspects of the Vietnam War was the role played by U.S. Army Special Forces, better known as the Green Berets. Organized in 1952 at Fort Bragg, North Carolina, these were the Army's answer to President John F. Kennedy's fascination with counterinsurgency warfare. As early as 1957, elements of the 1st Special Forces Group on the island of Okinawa trained 58 South Vietnamese soldiers at the Commando Training Center at Nha Trang. These were to become the nucleus of the South Vietnamese Special Forces or *Luc Luong Dac Biet*.

Although often portrayed as Rambo-type commandos, the Green Berets were actually designed to organize and train guerrilla bands behind enemy lines. It was that task that first drew them to Vietnam. The main Green Beret effort during the war was the organization of Civilian Irregular Defense Groups (CIDG) among South Vietnam's Montagnard population and the establishment of CIDG camps along the mountainous border areas to guard against NVA infiltration. Beginning in February 1962 at the Rhade village of Buon Enao in the Central Highlands, by the end of the year the program had expanded to 24 such camps in 1962, each with a basic 12-man Special Forces A-Team as cadre.

Until the 5th Special Forces Group (Airborne) set up headquarters at Nha Trang on October 1, 1964, Green Berets had been assigned to Vietnam only on temporary duty. At peak strength the 5th Special Forces Group controlled 84 CIDG camps with more than 42,000 CIDG strike forces and Regional Force and Popular Force local militias. They also raised several mobile guerrilla forces that conducted raids into Communist-controlled areas and provided personnel for the strategic reconnaissance units of the super-secret MACV-SOG (Military Assistance Command Vietnam, Studies and Observation Group) which conducted cross-border operations into North Vietnam, Laos, and Cambodia.

The CIDG program ended in December 1970 with the transfer of 14,534 CIDG troops, organized into 37 light infantry battalions, to the South Vietnamese Ranger Command. In February 1971, the 5th Special Forces Group left Vietnam as part of the U.S. withdrawal from the war.

Above: *This locally devised shoulder patch, although not officially authorized, shows the famous green beret from which Special Forces deriverd its nickname.*
Below: *U.S. Special Forces members on jungle patrol, armed with M-16 automatic rifles.*

"When they talk of the montagnards—uncorrupted by the cities, physically superior to most South Vietnamese, less sophisticated in their outlook—the Americans are fiercely possessive. They remind a visitor of the manner in which the British military once talked of the Gurkhas of Nepal.
Because the Green Berets enjoy their own toughness, they appreciate some of the more primitive aspects of the montagnards' habits. They even exaggerate them, and they hope the montagnards will never change."

—**New York Times,**
August 10, 1970

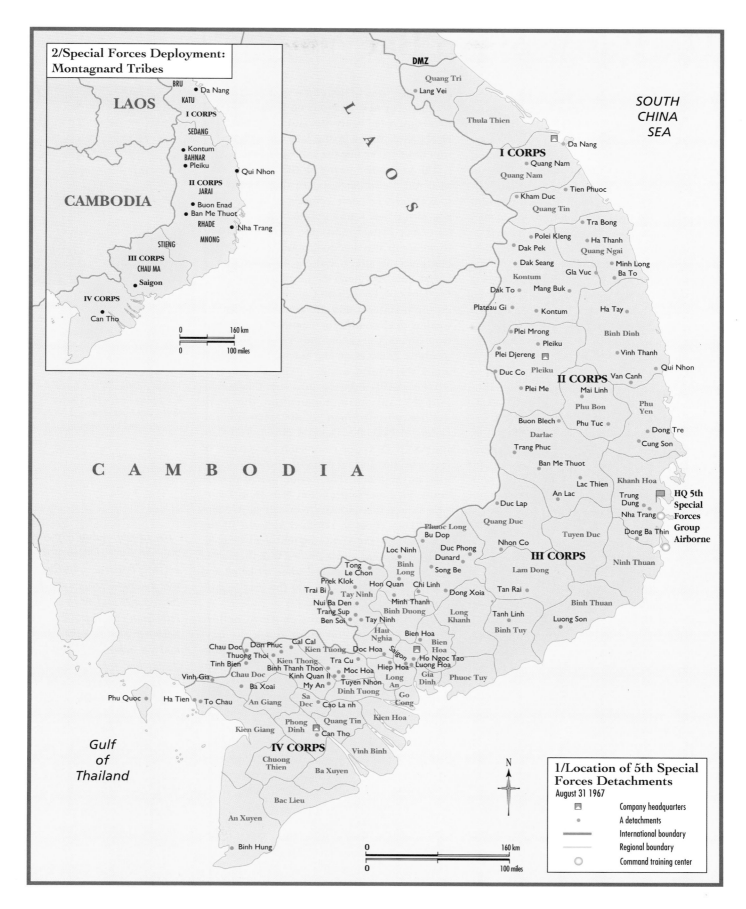

2/Special Forces Deployment: Montagnard Tribes

LAOS
BRU
• Da Nang
KATU
I CORPS
SEDANG
• Kontum
BAHNAR
• Pleiku
CAMBODIA
II CORPS
JARAI
• Buon Enad
• Ban Me Thuot
RHADE
• Nha Trang
MNONG
STIENG
III CORPS
CHAU MA
• Saigon
IV CORPS
• Can Tho
• Qui Nhon

0   160 km
0   100 miles

LAOS

DMZ
• Quang Tri
• Lang Vei

Thula Thien

SOUTH
CHINA
SEA

I CORPS
• Da Nang
• Quang Nam
Quang Nam
• Tien Phuoc
• Kham Duc
Quang Tin
• Tra Bong
• Polei Kleng
• Ha Thanh
• Dak Pek
Quang Ngai
• Dak Seang
• Gla Vuc
• Minh Long
Kontum
• Ba To
• Dak To
• Mang Buk
• Plateau Gi
• Kontum
• Ha Tay
• Plei Mrong
Binh Dinh
• Pleiku
• Plei Djereng
• Vinh Thanh
• Duc Co   Pleiku
II CORPS
• Van Canh
• Qui Nhon
• Plei Me
• Mai Linh
Phu
• Buon Blech
Phu Bon   Yen
• Phu Tuc
• Dong Tre
Darlac
• Cung Son
• Trang Phuc
• Ban Me Thuot
• Lac Thien   Khanh Hoa
• An Lac   Trung   **HQ 5th**
• Duc Lap   Dung   **Special**
Quang Duc   Nha Trang   **Forces**
Phuoc Long   **Group**
Bu Dop   Tuyen Duc   Dong Ba Thin   **Airborne**
• Duc Phong   Nhon Co
• Loc Ninh   Dunard
Binh   • Song Be   **III CORPS**   Ninh Thuan
Tong   Long
Le Chon   • Hon Quan   Lam Dong
Prek Klok   • Chi Linh
Trai Bi   • Dong Xoia   • Tan Rai
Nui Ba Den   Tay Ninh   Minh Thanh   Binh Thuan
Trang Sup   Binh Duong   Long   • Tanh Linh   • Luong Son
Ben Soi   Tay Ninh   Khanh   Bien Hoa
Hau   • Binh Tuy
Nghia   • Bien Hoa
Cal Cal   Doc Hoa   Hoa
Chau Doc   Don Phuc   Kien Tuong   Saigon   Ho Ngoc Tao
Thuong Thoi   Tra Cu   Luong Hoa   Phuoc Tuy
Tinh Bien   Kien Thong   Hiep Hoa   Gia
Binh Thanh Thon   Moc Hoa   Long   Dinh
Vinh Gia   Chau Doc   Kinh Quan II   Tuyen Nhon   An   Go
Ba Xoai   My An   Dinh Tuong   Dinh
Phu Quoc   Ha Tien   To Chau   An Giang   Sa   Cao La nh   Go
Dec   Kien Hoa   Cong
Phong   Quang Tin
Kien Giang   Dinh   Can Tho   Vinh Binh
IV CORPS
Chuong
Thien   Ba Xuyen

Gulf
of
Thailand

Bac Lieu

An Xuyen

• Binh Hung

N

0   160 km
0   100 miles

1/Location of 5th Special
Forces Detachments
August 31 1967

▭ Company headquarters
• A detachments
━━ International boundary
── Regional boundary
◯ Command training center

The Battle of Ap Bac 1963

As a battle it did not amount to much, but Ap Bac would have profound consequences for the later prosecution of the war. On December 28, 1962, the ARVN 7th Infantry Division, headquartered at My Tho in the Mekong delta, received orders from the Republic of Vietnam Armed Forces (RVNAF) Joint General Staff (JGS) in Saigon to seize a Viet Cong radio transmitter that was operating from the hamlet of Tan Thoi, about 14 miles to the northwest.

At that time there were only 11,000 U.S. troops in Vietnam, most of whom were serving as advisers, administrators, and aviators. Among them was an Army Security Agency team from the 3rd Radio Research Unit, whose aircraft interceptors had located the transmitter. This information was relayed to MACV who in turn passed it on to the RVNAF JGS.

MACV had been formed in February 1962 to control the buildup of U.S. troops ordered by President John F. Kennedy. From the 900 U.S. personnel in Vietnam in 1960, when JFK was elected, the force had grown to 11,300 by December 1962. Commanded by Army General Paul D. Harkins, MACV included some 300 field advisers who were working directly with ARVN troops, including Lieutenant Colonel John Paul Vann, senior adviser to the 7th ARVN Division.

Believing the transmitter to be protected by about 100 men of the Viet Cong 514th Regional Battalion, then resting in nearby Ap Bac ("ap" means village), Vann saw an opportunity to use the ARVN's advantages in mobility, firepower, and armor to destroy a Viet Cong unit. The plan was to use H-21 cargo helicopters (known as "flying bananas" because of their shape) to land one infantry battalion of the 7th ARVN Division north of Tan Thoi and Bac, while two Civil Guard battalions moved up from the south to block any Viet Cong attempt to withdraw in that direction. The western flank would be covered by an infantry company in M-113 armored personnel carriers, leaving the open rice paddies to the east as a killing zone for fleeing Viet Cong troops.

The plan began to unravel from the start. There were 350 rather than 100 enemy troops in the area, including elements of the Viet Cong's 261st Main Force Battalion. They were dug in and ready to fight, having learned from radio intercepts that an attack was imminent.

When the first helicopters approached the landing zone at 0730 hours on January 3, 1963, they confronted heavy fire, and three of the ten H-21s and one escorting UH-1 gunship were shot down in the first five minutes of the battle.

The remainder of the H-21s had also taken hits, and the infantry aboard dismounted and took immediate cover, refusing to move for the rest of the day. Running into opposition from Viet Cong security units, the Civil Guard units to the south also went to ground and refused to continue the attack. Calling for artillery and aerial bombardment of the entrenched Viet Cong troops, Lieutenant Colonel Vann exhorted the infantry inside the armored personnel carriers to close with the enemy. But as enemy fire systematically killed the exposed 50-caliber machine gunners on the tracks, the armored attack also came to a halt.

When ARVN airborne units were finally committed to regain the momentum, they were deliberately dropped to the west—on the orders of Brigadier General Huyen Van Cao, the ARVN IV Corps commander in charge of forces in the Mekong delta—rather than to the east, as requested. The reason was to placate South Vietnamese president Ngo Dinh Diem, who wanted to avoid ARVN casualties. As Vann said, "They chose to reinforce defeat." By the next morning the Viet Cong units had escaped, taking their dead and wounded with them. The South Vietnamese suffered some 80 killed and more than 100 wounded, but the most significant casualty was the truth.

While General Harkins chose to believe General Cao, who faked an attack the next morning against the abandoned Viet Cong positions and reported that a victory had been won, Vann briefed the press on what had really happened. The credibility gap that would plague the future prosecution of the Vietnam War had begun.

Harkins did not want to hear the truth, and neither did his superiors in Washington. Vann's testimony to the Joint Chiefs of Staff was blocked by General Maxwell D. Taylor, chairman of the JCS. "It is impossible to resist the conclusion," wrote General Bruce Palmer, Jr., who served on the JCS, "that Taylor and [Defense Secretary] McNamara were playing U.S. presidential politics—the 1964 elections were only a year away."

Rifle at the ready, a U.S. soldier stands guard as his compatriots work to attach a hoisting sling from an H-37 to an H-21 cargo helicopter, which has been downed in the swamps of the Mekong delta. Of the 4,869 helicopters lost by the United States during the war, 2,382 were downed by enemy fire.

"Because of Vann, Ap Bac was, for better or worse, a decisive battle ... Ap Bac was putting Vietnam on the front pages and on the television evening talk shows with a drama no other event had yet achieved. The dispatches, replete with details of cowardice and bumbling, were describing the battle as the worst and most humiliating defeat ever inflicted on the Saigon side ... Ap Bac was a sharp picture that discredited the big picture that Harkins and [U.S. Ambassador to South Vietnam] Nolting were projecting."

—Neil Sheehan, *New York Times*

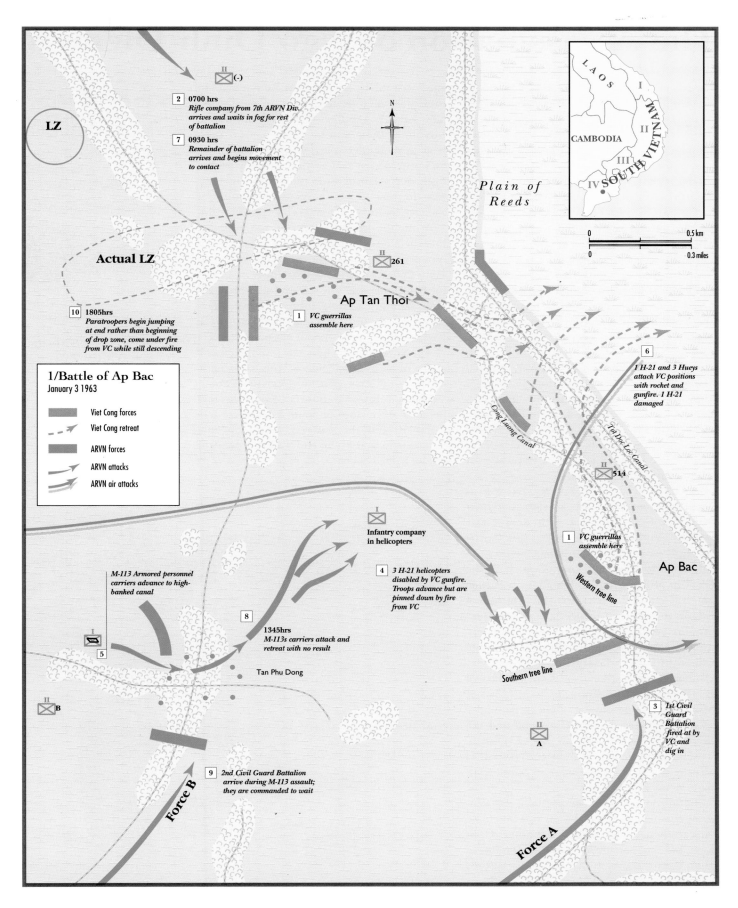

LZ

2 0700 hrs
*Rifle company from 7th ARVN Div.
arrives and waits in fog for rest
of battalion*

7 0930 hrs
*Remainder of battalion
arrives and begins movement
to contact*

N

Plain of
Reeds

LAOS

CAMBODIA

SOUTH VIETNAM

I

II

III

IV

0   0.5 km

0   0.3 miles

Actual LZ

II 261

Ap Tan Thoi

1 *VC guerrillas
assemble here*

10 1805hrs
*Paratroopers begin jumping
at end rather than beginning
of drop zone, come under fire
from VC while still descending*

6
*1 H-21 and 3 Hueys
attack VC positions
with rocket and
gunfire. 1 H-21
damaged*

1/Battle of Ap Bac
January 3 1963

	Viet Cong forces
	Viet Cong retreat
	ARVN forces
	ARVN attacks
	ARVN air attacks

Cong Luong Canal

Tot Doc Loi Canal

II 514

1 *VC guerrillas
assemble here*

Ap Bac

I
Infantry company
in helicopters

4 *3 H-21 helicopters
disabled by VC gunfire.
Troops advance but are
pinned down by fire
from VC*

Western tree line

*M-113 Armored personnel
carriers advance to high-
banked canal*

8

I
5

1345hrs
*M-113s carriers attack and
retreat with no result*

Tan Phu Dong

Southern tree line

II A

3 *1st Civil
Guard
Battalion
fired at by
VC and
dig in*

II B

9 *2nd Civil Guard Battalion
arrive during M-113 assault;
they are commanded to wait*

Force B

Force A

The Assassination of Ngo Dinh Diem 1963

"In his zeal the young president [John F. Kennedy] made a grievous mistake in assenting to the overthrow of South Vietnamese president Ngo Dinh Diem in 1963," said General William C. Westmoreland, the U.S. military commander in Vietnam from 1964 to 1968. "In my view that action morally locked us in Vietnam. If it had not been for our involvement in the overthrow of President Diem, we could perhaps have gracefully withdrawn our support when South Vietnam's lack of unity and leadership became apparent."

Ironically, Kennedy had been an early supporter of his fellow Catholic president. The ties between them reached back to 1951, when Diem had lived in a Maryknoll seminary in the United States. When Diem returned to Vietnam in 1954, he became prime minister in the Bao Dai government in the newly formed South Vietnam. In a referendum in October 1955, he defeated Bao Dai and became president. An ardent nationalist, Diem had earlier refused an offer to become Ho Chi Minh's minister of the interior when the Viet Minh proclaimed the Democratic Republic of Vietnam in 1945.

Diem, described by Stanley Karnow as "America's mandarin," was an autocratic ruler who had little patience with democratic niceties. Although he was locked in a mortal struggle with the Communists, it was the Buddhists who brought him down. With the breakup of a Buddhist celebration in Hue in May 1963, and the self-immolation of several Buddhist monks in protest at the incident, pressure began to mount on Washington to disassociate itself from such repression. While General Paul D. Harkins, the U.S. military commander in Vietnam, and General Maxwell D. Taylor, the chairman of the Joint Chiefs of Staff, opposed the ousting of Diem, the under secretary of state Averill Harriman and the head of the Far East Bureau, Roger Hilsman, were adamant that Diem must be replaced, as was the new U.S. ambassador to South Vietnam, Henry Cabot Lodge.

In Saigon, with the complicity of the CIA, Army commander General Tran Van Don, military academy commandant General Le Van Kim, and "special adviser" General Duong An Minh (better known as Big Minh) were already plotting a coup d'état. After receiving assurances that the United States would not stand in their way, they set their plan in motion on November 1. The next day, on the orders of Big Minh, Diem and his brother, Ngo Dinh Nhu, were murdered in cold blood. Having set events in motion that would eventually lead to his nation's defeat, it was fitting that Big Minh was the one to surrender the Republic of Vietnam to the NVA invaders on April 30, 1975.

While the United States had not intended that Diem be executed, there is no doubt about American involvement in the coup. As Ambassador Lodge told President Kennedy in a cable on November 6, "The ground in which the coup seed grew into a robust plant was prepared by us, and the coup would not have happened [as] it did without our preparation."

On November 22, Kennedy too became the victim of an assassin's bullet. With his acquiescence in the American involvement in South Vietnam's internal affairs, Kennedy had doomed any chance of South Vietnamese self-reliance, and the country would become increasingly, and in the end fatally, dependent on the United States.

> "If the Buddhists want to have another barbecue, I will be happy to supply the gasoline."
>
> —Ngo Dinh Nhu,
> brother of President Diem

Moments after this extreme display of anti-government feeling—the sixth suicide by a Buddhist monk in less than a month in protest at Diem's policies—three U.S. newsmen who had witnessed the tragic sight on the busy streets of Saigon were set upon by members of the Vietnamese secret police.

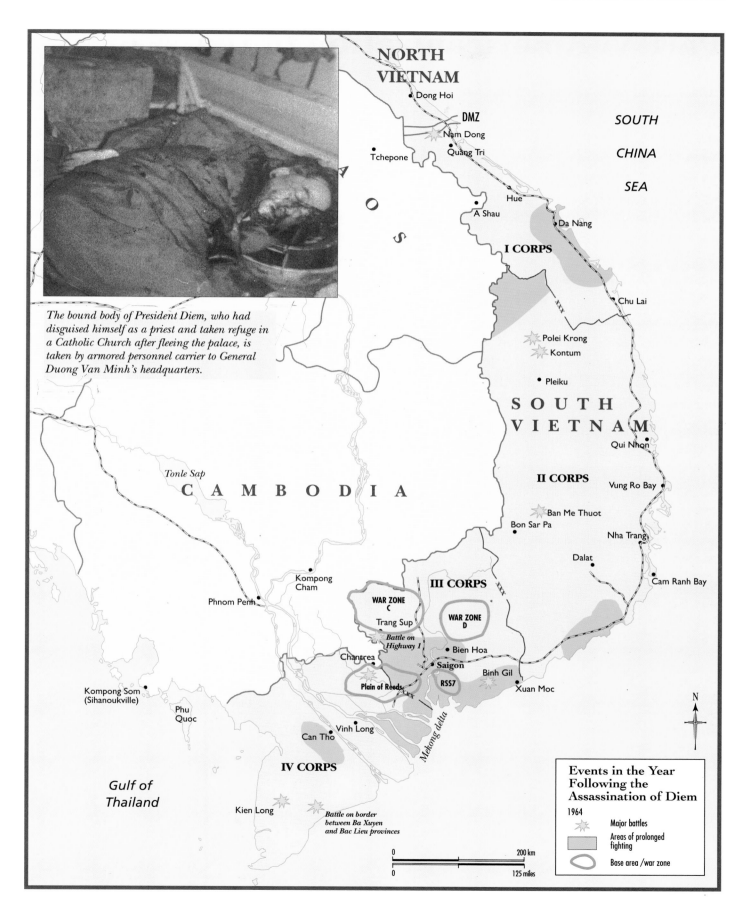

The bound body of President Diem, who had disguised himself as a priest and taken refuge in a Catholic Church after fleeing the palace, is taken by armored personnel carrier to General Duong Van Minh's headquarters.

NORTH VIETNAM

Dong Hoi

DMZ

Nam Dong

Tchepone

Quang Tri

L A O S

A Shau

Hue

Da Nang

I CORPS

Chu Lai

Polei Krong

Kontum

Pleiku

S O U T H V I E T N A M

Qui Nhon

II CORPS

Vung Ro Bay

Ban Me Thuot

Bon Sar Pa

Nha Trang

Dalat

Cam Ranh Bay

SOUTH CHINA SEA

Tonle Sap

C A M B O D I A

Kompong Cham

Phnom Penh

III CORPS

WAR ZONE C

Trang Sup

WAR ZONE D

Battle on Highway 1

Bien Hoa

Chantrea

Saigon

Binh Gil

Kompong Som (Sihanoukville)

Phu Quoc

Plain of Reeds

RSS7

Xuan Moc

Mekong delta

Vinh Long

Can Tho

IV CORPS

Gulf of Thailand

Kien Long

Battle on border between Ba Xuyen and Bac Lieu provinces

N

Events in the Year Following the Assassination of Diem

1964

✶ Major battles

Areas of prolonged fighting

Base area / war zone

0   200 km

0   125 miles

Part V: Americanization of the War

"When the day comes to face my Maker and account for my actions, the thing I would be most humbly proud of," said Matthew B. Ridgway, chief of staff of the United States Army from 1953 to 1955, "was the fact that I fought against … the carrying out of some harebrained tactical schemes which would have cost the lives of thousands of men. To that list of tragic accidents that fortunately never happened, I would add the Indo-China intervention." A decade later, the Gulf of Tonkin incident provoked an entirely different response and the United States not only intervened militarily in Vietnam, but ended up Americanizing the war as well.

McNamara later complained that "our government lacked experts for us to consult." But all he had to do was to dig back in the files of his own Defense Department and resurrect the study Ridgway had commissioned in 1954 or, better yet, the Army War College study by Bruce Palmer and others in 1951. The conclusions of that study

(see preface to Part III) all came to pass. But what was then seen as a war was by 1964 seen as a counterinsurgency, a new kind of limited war where the old rules no longer applied.

Instead of World War II combat veterans, McNamara relied on civilian dilettantes for advice. These systems analysts had, like McNamara, an almost pathological disdain for all things military. As Alain C. Enthoven and K. Wayne Smith pontificated in *How Much is Enough?*, the bible of the McNamara years, "What is commonly called 'military science' is not scientific in the same sense as law or medicine or engineering. It encompasses no agreed-upon body of knowledge, no prescribed curriculum, no universally recognized principles that one must master to

U.S. war photographers in the midst of an operation against the Viet Cong in 1968. Press and television coverage of the war had an enormous bearing on the attitude of the American public toward the conflict in Vietnam.

qualify as a military professional. The so-called 'principles of war,'" they sniffed, as they violated every one of them, "are really a set of platitudes that can be twisted to suit any situation … Modern day strategy … has become largely an analytical process … and civilians are often better trained in modern analytical techniques."

These analysts had fallen into a trap described by Karl von Clausewitz over a century earlier. "The conduct of war branches out in almost all directions and has no definite limits," he wrote, "while any system, any model, has the finite limit of a synthesis … An irreconcilable conflict exists between this type of theory and actual practice." His words were later validated by the Vietnam War.

During the debate on the Rolling Thunder campaign, the argument had revolved around both whether to bomb and how to go about it. As Dave Palmer pointed out in *Summons of the Trumpet*, "Civilian planners wanted to start out softly and gradually increase the pressure by precise increments which could be unmistakenly recognized by Hanoi. Ho Chi Minh would see the tightening pattern, the theory went, and would sensibly stop the war against South Vietnam in time to avoid devastation of his homeland." John T. McNaughton, a Harvard Law School professor whom McNamara had brought in to serve as an assistant secretary of defense, "dubbed the strategy 'slow squeeze' and explained it in musical terms—an orchestration of activities which would proceed in crescendo fashion toward a finale. 'The scenario,' he wrote, 'would be designed to give the United States the option at any point to proceed or not, to escalate or not, and to quicken the pace or not.'"

This "strategy" flew in the face of all conventional military wisdom. Both the generals and the intelligence community argued that if force were to be used at all, it ought to be applied hard and fast to obtain maximum impact. If the purpose was to affect Hanoi's will, "the U.S. would have to hit hard at vital points and demonstrate a willingness to apply unlimited force." But these arguments fell on deaf ears. As Palmer relates, "President Johnson overrode the objections of his intelligence and military advisers. Indeed, it is not at all clear whether Secretary McNamara ever bothered to convey their argu-

ments to him. Ambassador Taylor, still addressed as 'General,' had given his blessings to their theory, approval which apparently cancelled out the objections of the Joint Chiefs of Staff."

Commenting on the impact that these civilians had on military strategy, Henry Kissinger noted that "there was a truth which senior military officers had learned in a lifetime of service that did not lend itself to formal articulation: that power had a psychological and not only a technical component … In the final analysis the military profession is the art of prevailing, and while in our time this required more careful calculations than in the past, it also depends on elemental psychological factors that are difficult to quantify. The military found themselves … carrying out strategies in which they did not really believe, and ultimately conducting a war that they did not understand. To be sure, the military brought on

Committed to a struggle in which final victory was precluded from the outset, thousands of American men and women fell victim to the undermining of U.S. military and psychological strength by a defeatist general-in-chief, Defense Secretary Robert McNamara.

some of their own troubles. They permitted themselves to be co-opted too readily."

One cannot imagine World War II military leaders tolerating the strategies for the war being set up by McNaughton, Enthoven, and Smith. But to their discredit, the Vietnam-era military leaders did just that. As General Bruce Palmer, a member of the Joint Chiefs of Staff, admitted, the JCS "lost control of the overall strategic direction of American armed forces [and] seemed unable to articulate an effective military strategy that they could persuade the commander-in-chief and secretary of defense to adopt." In the face of the obviously flawed civilian strategies, "not once during the war did the JCS advise the commander-in-chief or the secretary of defense that the strategy being pursued most probably would fail and that the United States would be unable to achieve its objectives."

But they did come close. Almost 10 years after the retirement of General Harold K. Johnson, Army chief of staff from 1964 to 1969, a colleague asked him "If you had your life to live over, what would you do differently?" Johnson replied, "I remember the day I was ready to go over to the Oval Office and give my four stars to the president and tell him, 'You have refused to tell the country they cannot fight a war without mobilization; you have required me to send men into battle with little hope of their ultimate victory; and you have forced us in the military to violate almost every one of the principles of war. Therefore I resign and will hold a press conference after I walk out your door.'" With anguish on his face, he concluded, "I made the typical mistake of believing I could do more for the country and for the Army if I stayed in than if I got out. And now I am going to my grave with that burden of lapse of moral courage on my back."

General George C. Marshall would have had no problems communicating his misgivings to President Roosevelt in World War II. Omar Bradley would have spoken openly to Truman during the Korean War, as would Colin Powell to Bush during the Persian Gulf War, for that matter. All these presidents welcomed military advice. But Lyndon Johnson was another story. In *Strategy for Tomorrow*, Hanson Baldwin, the military analyst for the

New York Times, notes that President Johnson mistrusted the military, and that the close contact between Roosevelt and Marshall, and Truman and Bradley, was missing between President Johnson and General Johnson.

"The Chairman of the Joint Chiefs of Staff was the only member of the Joint Chiefs who saw the president with any regularity in the crucial years 1965–1968 [but even he] was always accompanied by the Secretary of Defense or his deputy who never hesitated to 'second guess' the Chairman and to dilute and contradict his statements," wrote Baldwin. "In the crucial twelve months from June 1965 to June 1966, when large numbers of U.S. ground troops were committed to Vietnam … the Chief of Staff of the Army saw the president privately twice." One reason for this was that there was not the sense of urgency, requiring close consultation with the military, that there had been in World War II and Korea. As Samuel Johnson observed 200 years ago, "Depend upon it, Sir, when a man knows he is to be hanged in a fortnight it concentrates his mind wonderfully."

The U.S. defeats at the hands of the Japanese at Bataan and Corregidor, in the Philippines, and by the Germans at the Faid and Kasserine passes in North Africa, left no doubt that failure to "concentrate our minds wonderfully" could lead to an Allied defeat. There was no such warning in Vietnam. The first battle in the Ia Drang Valley was a resounding victory, the tragedy at LZ Albany notwithstanding, and the civilian theorists of limited war had removed fighting from the very definition of war. In his perceptive article "Vietnam and the American Theory of Limited War" in the fall 1982 issue of *International Security*, Harvard's Stephen Peter Rosen noted that these theorists shared "the happy belief that the study of limited war in no way depended on any actual knowledge about war." According to Robert Osgood, a limited-war theorist, "military problems are no proper part of a theory of limited war … limited war is an essentially diplomatic instrument, a tool for bargaining with the enemy."

Outstanding feats of military skill and bravery, such as the taking of Hill 875 at Dak To (right), were rendered meaningless by the theorists of limited war.

General Westmoreland told of one memorable application of such theories of limited war. "In 1965, we observed the construction of the first surface-to-air missile [SAM] sites in North Vietnam and the military sought permission to attack them before they were completed to save American casualties. McNaughton ridiculed the idea. 'You don't think the North Vietnamese are going to use them!' he scoffed to [Seventh Air Force commander] Joseph Moore. 'Putting them in is just a political ploy by the Russians to appease Hanoi.' It was all a matter of signals for the clever civilian theorists in Washington. We won't bomb the SAM sites, which signals the North Vietnamese not to use them."

But the enemy was not playing Washington's silly games. A month later the United States lost its first aircraft to a SAM. The United States was sending signals, just as the limited-war theorists had recommended. But the signal was that the United States was a paper tiger. Unlike North Vietnam, the United States was never serious about fighting. General Taylor told the Senate in 1966 that the United States was not trying to "defeat" North Vietnam, only "to cause them to mend their ways." Taylor likened the concept of defeating the enemy to "Appomattox or something of that sort." But "Appomattox" was exactly the way in which the war ended, for the North Vietnamese were playing by the old rules, where the very object of war is victory.

U.S. Marines in action in Hue in 1968. Distressing television pictures of the Tet Offensive ended hopes of a U.S. victory and fatally sapped both public and government morale.

This was not so for the Americans. "The greater the costs and risks of a military measure," Rosen noted, "the greater the tendency for the men at the higher levels of government to talk and act as if they were guided by the academic theory of limited war [which] appeared to minimize the risk and offer victory without combat. This [was] true for the civilians, but, to a surprising extent, also true of military men, particularly Maxwell Taylor." But as Clausewitz once warned generals who won battles without bloodshed, "Sooner or later someone will come along with a sharp sword and lop off your arms." And General Vo Nguyen Giap, a member of the North Vietnamese Politburo, minister of defense and commander of the NVA, was precisely that man.

The comparison between Giap and his American counterparts is almost painful to relate. While Giap remained as minister of defense and NVA commander during the entire Second Indochina War, there was a succession of American defense secretaries, who were also, like Giap, the generals-in-chief of the armed forces. Of these, only James Schlesinger, who served in that office from July 1973 to November 1975, was worthy of the name. Melvin Laird, who served from 1969 to 1973, was a political hack. His successor, Elliot Richardson, served only four months and was not in office long

The 173rd Airborne Brigade, (seen here in June 1966) was one of several units to gain a reputation for excellent service in the Vietnam War. Others included the Army's 1st Infantry Division and 1st Cavalry Division (Airmobile) and the 1st and 3rd Marine Divisions.

enough to make a difference. Clark Clifford, a Demo-cratic Party insider and influence peddler, was brought in after the 1968 Tet Offensive to bulwark the president's Vietnam policies. But he deliberately set out to sabotage them instead, "poisoning the well" with the "wise men" of the president's senior advisory group. Their pessimistic assessment in March 1968 led Johnson to call a bombing halt and to fail to seek re-election.

As Phillip Davidson explains in *Vietnam at War,* "Johnson had fired a doubting Thomas (McNamara) only to replace him with a Judas." But McNamara was far more than a doubting Thomas. He cynically betrayed his president and the American people, and he treacherous-ly betrayed to their deaths the men and women of the American armed forces under this command, who looked to him for leadership and protection.

Adopting the role of the imperial eunuchs of ancient

China, who isolated the emperor from outside influence, McNamara froze out the Joint Chiefs of Staff. He then deliberately undermined President Johnson's order to "win the war." During his testimony in the CBS–Westmoreland libel trial in 1984, he admitted for the first time that he had come to the belief as early as 1965 or 1966—before the American military buildup in Vietnam even began—that the war could "not be won militarily." He repeated this self-fulfilling prophecy in his memoirs. As the general-in-chief of the American military, in direct command of all armed forces in the field, his will was crucial. As Clausewitz pointed out, "If you want to over-come your enemy you must match your effort against his power of resistance, which can be expressed as the prod-uct of two inseparable factors, viz. the total means at his disposal and the strength of his will."

When it came to the "total means at his disposal," there was no contest. A bitter story circulating in the Pentagon in the closing days of the Vietnam War told that when President Nixon took office in 1969, all the data on North Vietnam and the United States—population size, GNP, manufacturing capacity, number of combat air-craft, warships, tanks, etc.—was fed into a Pentagon com-puter. The computer was then asked, "When will we win?" The answer was instantaneous. "You won in 1964!"

When it came to strength of will, however, there was also no contest. When Stanley Karnow asked General Giap how long he would have continued fighting against the United States, Giap replied, "Another ten, twenty years, maybe 100 years, regardless of cost." McNamara's will, by his own admission, was broken before the Americanization of the war even began. As Napoleon observed, the moral is to the physical as three to one, and no amount of physical strength or battlefield sacrifice could compensate for the lack of will of the U.S. general-in-chief. To add insult to injury, McNamara kept his misgivings to himself, courting the antiwar move-

A smoke flare marks the landing spot for helicopters arriving to evacuate 1st Cavalrymen wounded in the strategic A Shau Valley. The 1st Air Cavalry Division was the most controversial unit deployed in Vietnam, since the airmobile concept was untested in battle. But the division soon set the standards for the rest of the Army.

ment while continuing to send American soldiers to their deaths in what he was convinced was an unwinnable war. By his actions he made it so.

"His regret cannot be huge enough to balance the books for our dead soldiers," emphasized an April 12th 1995, *New York Times* editorial in the wake of the publication of McNamara's memoirs. "The ghosts of those unlived lives circle close around Mr. McNamara. Surely he must in every quiet and prosperous moment hear the ceaseless whisper of those poor boys in the infantry, dying in the tall grass, platoon by platoon, for no purpose … Mr. McNamara says he weeps easily and has strong feelings when he visits the Vietnam Memorial. But he says he will not speak of those feelings. Yet someone must, for that black wall is wide with the names of people who died in a war that he did not, at first, carefully research nor, in the end, believe to be necessary."

A harrowing scene from "Hamburger Hill," the bloody 10-day battle that provoked a public outcry resulting in the end of U.S. ground combat operations in Vietnam. Wounded troops from the ARVN's 3rd Infantry Regiment and the U.S. 101st Airborne Division descend Hill 937, which finally fell to their combined assault on May 20, 1969.

Free World Military Forces   1964

During the Korean War the United States had a United Nations mandate and the direct support of almost all of its NATO allies, but neither was true in Vietnam. The Soviet Union was one of North Vietnam's major allies and would have vetoed any attempt to gain UN approval for the war. Despite President Johnson's efforts, none of the NATO allies would agree to commit troops to Vietnam—even though 374,000 U.S. military personnel were deployed in Western Europe in 1964 to protect NATO from Communist attack.

The American public has always insisted on the appearance of multilateral support, even if it is only a veneer. To provide such a multilateral cover, in April and December 1964 President Johnson publicly called for members of the free world to unite in the effort to stop the spread of Communism. Members of this so-called Free World assistance program included several NATO allies, including Belgium, Canada, and the United Kingdom. In all, 39 nations, including Japan, Pakistan, Iran, Israel, Turkey, Liberia, Tunisia, Ireland, Venezuela, and Brazil, sent relief or commodity aid. But when it came to troops, only five nations responded—Australia, New Zealand, the Republic of Korea, Thailand, and the Philippines.

Australia was first on the scene, sending a team of jungle warfare specialists in 1962 to advise the South Vietnamese Army. They were followed by an aviation detachment and an engineer civic action team in 1964, and then by the 1st Battalion, Royal Australian Regiment (RAR) in May 1965. Establishing their own base camp at Ba Ria in Phuoc Tuy Province in III Corps, the 1st Australian Task Force grew to a two-infantry battalion force, augmented by Special Air Service (SAS) commandoes, a medium tank squadron and a helicopter squadron.

Reinforcing the Australians were forces from New Zealand, which deployed an engineer platoon and a surgical team in July 1964 to assist in civic action projects. These were replaced in July 1965 by the Royal New Zealand Artillery's 161st Battery, V and W companies of the Royal New Zealand Infantry Regiment, and a platoon from New Zealand's Special Air Service. Australia also dispatched its Royal Australian Air Force (RAAF) No. 9 Squadron of *Iroquois* helicopters, No. 35 Squadron of *Caribou* transport aircraft, and No. 2 Squadron of *Canberra*

bombers, which flew 11,963 sorties. Australian naval deployments included the destroyer HMAS *Hobart* and several other warships.

The largest allied contingent was from the Republic of Korea (ROK). A "dove" unit of engineers and medical personnel was dispatched in February 1965, followed by the ROK Marine Corps' 2nd (Blue Dragon) Brigade in October 1965. The ROK Army's Capital Division arrived in April 1966, and the 9th (White Horse) Division in September 1966. While the ROK Marine Brigade established its base camp at Hui An in I Corps, the two ROK army divisions established base camps in II Corps at Binh Khe near Qui Nhon and at Ninh Hoa near Cam Ranh Bay to protect these key ports.

In addition to permitting the use of their air bases during the air war over North Vietnam, Thailand contributed 11,568 combat soldiers. First to arrive were the Queen's Cobras Regiment in September 1967, which was stationed at Bear Cat near Bien Hoa in III Corps. They were replaced by the Royal Thai Volunteer Force in July 1968, consisting of the Black Panther Division with two infantry brigades, three artillery battalions, and an armored cavalry squadron. In July 1964, the Philippines sent a medical contingent to Vietnam to aid in civic actions. This was followed in 1966 by the 1,500-man Philippine Civic Action Group, stationed at Tay Ninh in III Corps and conducted pacification operations in the surrounding area.

A total of 4,407 ROK soldiers and marines, 469 Australians and New Zealanders, and 351 Thai soldiers were killed in action in Vietnam.

"The Australian approach to the tactics of the Vietnam War was honed in jungle warfare against the Japanese in World War II and the Communists in Malaya. Their credo: avoid trails, avoid villages, avoid resupply; slide into the jungle like a snake and hide, then terrorize the enemy at will ... No enemy dead is ever claimed unless an Aussie can walk up and put his foot on the body; no wounded counts unless he can be trailed 300 yards, with blood seen all the way."

—New York Times, May 7, 1966

The Royal Australian Air Force flew alongside the U.S. Army in many operations in South Vietnam and their heliborne and airborne tactics were based to a large degree on American experience.

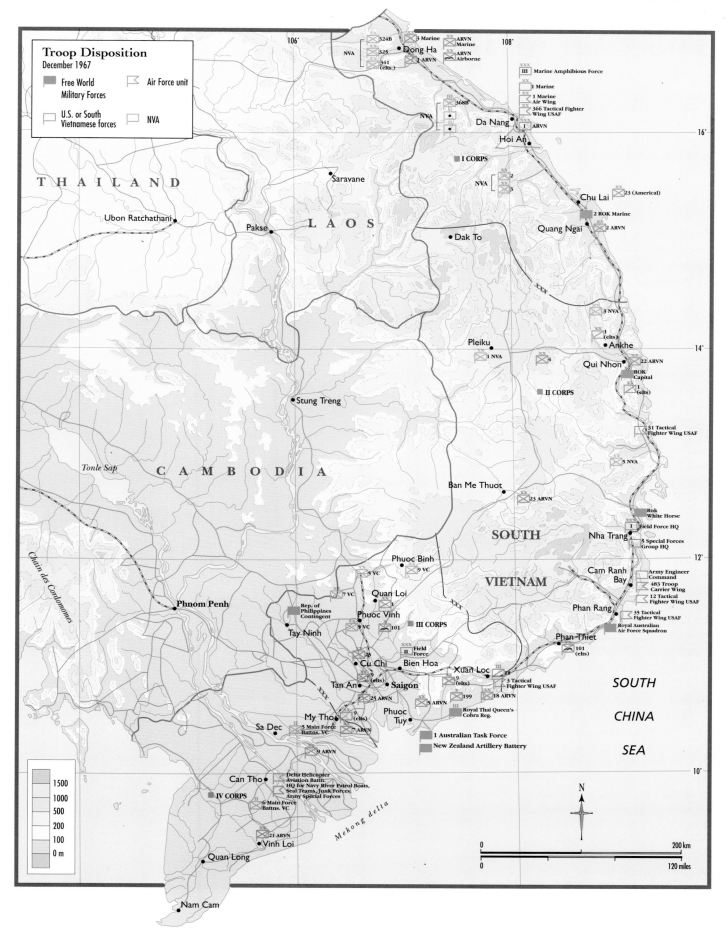

Troop Disposition
December 1967

Free World Military Forces

U.S. or South Vietnamese forces

Air Force unit

NVA

The Gulf of Tonkin Incident   AUGUST 1964

The precipitate cause of direct U.S military involvement in the Vietnam War did not happen on land, where most of the subsequent action took place, but at sea. And like the war itself, it was shrouded in controversy.

On July 28, 1964, the Navy destroyer USS *Maddox* (DD 731), commanded by Captain John Herrick, was ordered to sail from Taiwan to the Gulf of Tonkin to support the highly secret Operation Plan 34A, or "DeSoto" operations. These involved CIA-sponsored commando raids by fast gunboats along the North Vietnamese coast to gather intelligence on radar sites and other defenses.

On August 1, the *Maddox* was on station at Point Charlie, about four miles off the coast of Hon Me, the site of a radar station and home port for North Vietnamese patrol torpedo (PT) boats, which had been bombarded in a DeSoto operation the day before. On August 2, three of these PT boats launched an attack on the *Maddox*, but all the torpedoes missed their target. The *Maddox* returned fire, and after receiving several hits the PT boats broke contact. Under fire from Navy F-8 Crusader fighters from the aircraft carrier USS *Ticonderoga* (CVA 14), which was also in the area, they returned to their base at Hon Me.

On August 3, the *Maddox* was joined by another destroyer, the USS *Turner Joy* (DD 951). A further PT boat attack on these ships was reported on August 4, but subsequent investigation has suggested that this second incident may have been a false alarm triggered by skittish and overexcited sonar operators. Be that as it may, President Lyndon B. Johnson used the second attack as a *casus belli*, and asked Congress to give him the power to "take all necessary measures to repel an armed attack against the forces of the United States and to prevent further aggression."

On August 7, this Southeast Asia Resolution, better known as the Gulf of Tonkin Resolution, passed the Senate by a vote of 88 to 2 and the House by a unanimous 416 to 0 vote. Some senators later complained that they had been misled by President Johnson and had not intended to authorize the bombing of North Vietnam and the commitment of U.S. ground troops to the war. But they were being disingenuous, for on March 1, 1966, long after the bombing had begun and long after U.S. troops

had been committed to combat, an attempt in the Senate to repeal the resolution was defeated by a vote of 92 to 5.

With minimal threat from the North Vietnamese Navy, the long-range missiles of U. S. cruisers and destroyers proved more than a match for enemy aircraft attacks and could be deployed only a few miles from the coast. The USS Ticonderoga *is seen here on patrol in the South China Sea.*

> *"Entire action leaves many doubts except for apparent attempt to ambush at the beginning."*
>
> **—Captain Herrick, reporting to his superiors a few hours after the incident**

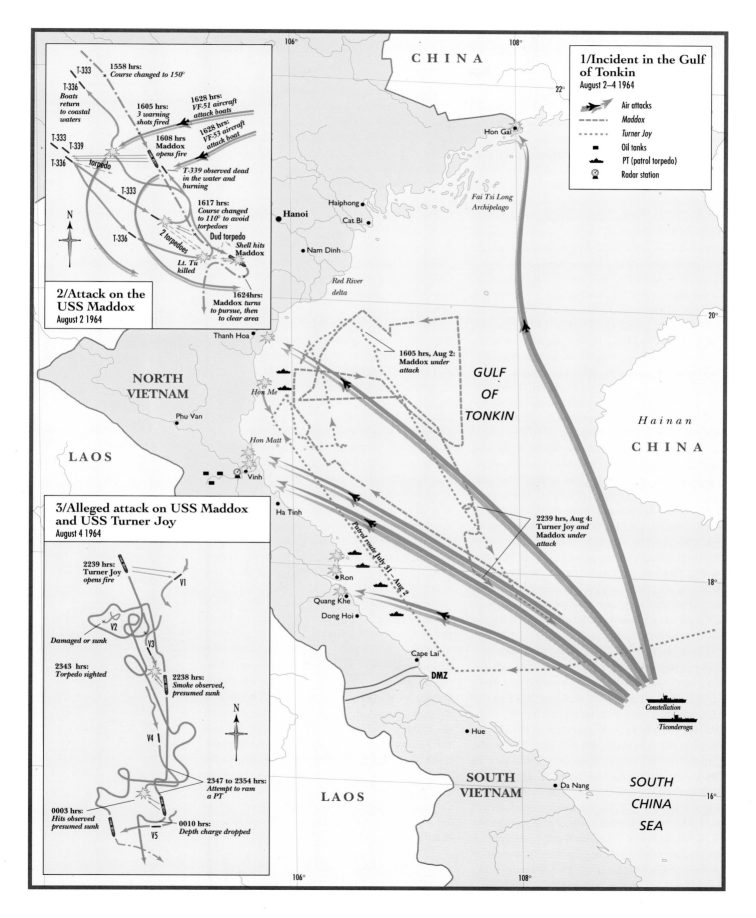

1/Incident in the Gulf of Tonkin
August 2–4 1964

- Air attacks
- Maddox
- Turner Joy
- ■ Oil tanks
- PT (patrol torpedo)
- Radar station

CHINA

Hon Gai

Fai Tsi Long Archipelago

Haiphong

Cat Bi

Hanoi

Nam Dinh

Red River delta

Thanh Hoa

NORTH VIETNAM

Hon Me

Phu Van

Hon Matt

LAOS

Vinh

Ha Tinh

Ron

Quang Khe

Dong Hoi

Cape Lai

DMZ

Hue

SOUTH VIETNAM

LAOS

Da Nang

GULF OF TONKIN

Hainan

CHINA

SOUTH CHINA SEA

1605 hrs, Aug 2: Maddox *under attack*

2239 hrs, Aug 4: Turner Joy *and* Maddox *under attack*

Patrol route July 31 – Aug 2

Constellation

Ticonderoga

2/Attack on the USS Maddox
August 2 1964

T-333
T-336

1558 hrs: *Course changed to 150°*

Boats return to coastal waters

T-333
T-339
T-336

torpedo

T-333

T-336

1605 hrs: *3 warning shots fired*

1628 hrs: *VF-51 aircraft attack boats*

1628 hrs: *VF-53 aircraft attack boat*

1608 hrs Maddox *opens fire*

T-339 *observed dead in the water and burning*

1617 hrs: *Course changed to 110° to avoid torpedoes*

Dud torpedo

2 torpedoes

Shell hits Maddox

Lt. Tú killed

1624hrs: Maddox *turns to pursue, then to clear area*

N

3/Alleged attack on USS Maddox and USS Turner Joy
August 4 1964

2239 hrs: Turner Joy *opens fire*

V1

V2

V3

Damaged or sunk

2343 hrs: *Torpedo sighted*

2238 hrs: *Smoke observed, presumed sunk*

V4

N

2347 to 2354 hrs: *Attempt to ram a PT*

0003 hrs: *Hits observed presumed sunk*

V5

0010 hrs: *Depth charge dropped*

Rolling Thunder   MARCH 1965–OCTOBER 1968

The military response to the Gulf of Tonkin incident was not long in coming. On August 4, 1964, hours after the alleged second attack by North Vietnamese PT boats on U.S. destroyers in the gulf, fighter bombers from the aircraft carriers USS *Ticonderoga* and *Constellation* struck at North Vietnamese patrol boat bases along the coast and at the oil storage depot at Vinh. The U.S. bombing campaign against North Vietnam had begun and would not end, despite intermittent halts, until the "Christmas bombing" more than eight years later.

In February 1965, in retaliation for Viet Cong attacks on U.S. installations in the South, Operation Flaming Dart was launched, with air strikes by U.S. Air Force (USAF) and South Vietnamese Air Force (VNAF) fighter bombers on targets in the North. These strikes were followed on March 2 by the beginning of the Rolling Thunder air campaign, which continued until October 31, 1968, when President Lyndon B. Johnson announced a halt to the bombing of North Vietnam.

The Navy strikes were flown by Navy and Marine Corps fighter bombers from aircraft carriers at Yankee Station, an operational staging area in the Gulf of Tonkin. They were joined by shore-based Marine fighter bombers from Chu Lai and Da Nang air bases in South Vietnam. Air Force fighter bomber strikes were flown primarily from bases at Don Muang, Korat, Nakhon Phanom, Takhli, Udorn, and Ubon in Thailand, and B-52 strategic bombers flew from Andersen air base on Guam, Kadena air base on Okinawa, and later from U-Tapao air base in Thailand.

Targets were divided into Air Force and Navy geographical route packages. Route Package I, just north of the Demilitarized Zone (DMZ), was seen as part of the ground war in the South and was controlled by the U.S. Military Assistance Command (MACV) in Saigon. All remaining routes were under the control of Pacific Command (PACOM) in Honolulu, with route packages II, III, IV, and VIB the responsibility of the U.S. Navy Seventh Fleet's Task Force 77, and route packages V and VIA the responsibility of the combined U.S. 7th Air Force/13th Air Force headquarters in Thailand. B-52 bomber operations remained under the command of the Strategic Air Command in Omaha, Nebraska.

These convoluted command relationships were a reflection of the vacuity of Rolling Thunder itself. Instead of a coordinated air campaign, as in World War II, which would destroy the enemy's ability to wage war and break their will to resist, air operations over the North were designed as a diplomatic "slow squeeze" signaling device. As Defense Secretary Robert S. McNamara said on February 3, 1966, "U.S. objectives are not to destroy or to overthrow the Communist government of North Vietnam. They are limited to the destruction of the insurrection and aggression directed by North Vietnam against the political institutions of South Vietnam."

Throughout Rolling Thunder, seven bombing halts were imposed, all intended to signal the U.S. willingness to negotiate. But in each case North Vietnam used the halts to rebuild air defenses and increase the flow of arms and equipment to the war in the South. The "signal" that the U.S. was unwittingly sending out was that it was not serious about waging war. The bombing campaign was intended to weaken North Vietnamese public support for the war, but instead it undercut U.S. resolve. On April 1, 1968, President Johnson, under increasing domestic political pressure, announced the cessation of operations north of the 20th parallel, thereby excluding Hanoi and the Red River delta from attack. On October 31, a week before the presidential elections of 1968, he ordered a halt to Rolling Thunder.

From 1965 to 1968, at a cost of 922 aircraft lost to enemy action, the Navy and Air Force flew 304,000 fighter bomber and 2,380 B-52 bomber sorties over North Vietnam and dropped 643,000 tons of bombs—more than the 537,000 tons dropped in the entire Pacific theater in World War II and the 454,000 tons dropped during the Korean War. But it was all for naught. "Rolling Thunder must go down in the history of aerial warfare as the most ambitious, wasteful, and ineffective campaign ever mounted," said former CIA analyst Raphael Iungerich. "While damage was done to many targets in the North, no lasting objective was achieved. Hanoi emerged as the winner of Rolling Thunder."

A U.S. Navy F-8 Corsair takes off from the deck of the USS Coral Sea *to take part in the bombing of targets in selected areas of North Vietnam.*

"Senior airmen pressed for the extension of Rolling Thunder into an air strategy focused upon the heart of North Vietnam. But neither the President, the Secretary of State, nor the Secretary of Defense yet conceived of Rolling Thunder as a strategic air offensive. The Secretary of Defense continued to maintain that the primary role for airpower should be to support ground forces in South Vietnam [and believed that] the size and frequency of these strikes, as well as the targets, should be selected in Washington."

—General William W. Momyer,
Airpower in Three Wars,
USAF

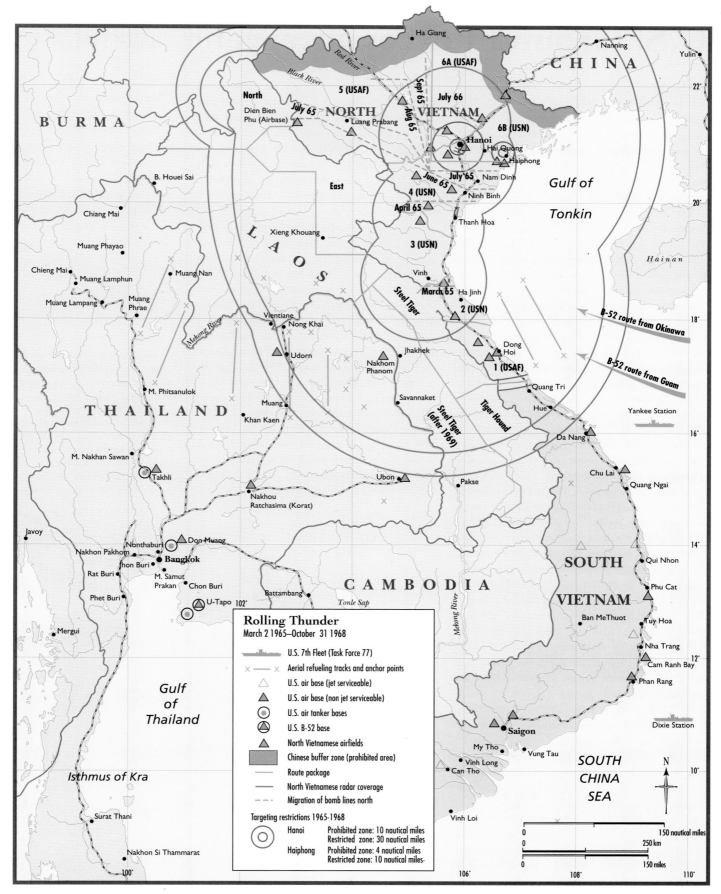

Ha Giang

Nanning

Yulin

Red River

6A (USAF)

CHINA

Black River

5 (USAF)

Sept 65

July 66

BURMA

North

July 65

Dien Bien
Phu (Airbase)

Luang Prabang

NORTH

Aug 65

VIETNAM

6B (USN)

Hanoi

B. Houei Sai

Hai Quong

Haiphong

Chiang Mai

East

June 65

July 65

Nam Dinh

Gulf of

Muang Phayao

4 (USN)

Ninh Binh

Tonkin

Chieng Mai

Xieng Khouang

April 65

Muang Lamphun

Muang Nan

Thanh Hoa

Hainan

Muang Lampang

LAOS

Muang
Phrae

3 (USN)

Vinh

Mekong River

Vientiane

Nong Khai

Steel Tiger

March 65

Ha Jinh

2 (USN)

M. Phitsanulok

Udorn

Jhakhek

Dong
Hoi

B-52 route from Okinawa

THAILAND

Nakhom
Phanom

1 (USAF)

B-52 route from Guam

Khan Kaen

Muang

Savannaket

Quang Tri

M. Nakhan Sawan

Ubon

Pakse

Steel Tiger
(after 1969)

Tiger Hound

Hue

Yankee Station

Da Nang

Takhli

Nakhou
Ratchasima (Korat)

Chu Lai

Quang Ngai

Javoy

Nonthaburi

Don Muang

SOUTH

Qui Nhon

Nakhon Pakhom

CAMBODIA

Jhon Buri

Bangkok

Phu Cat

Rat Buri

M. Samut
Prakan

Chon Buri

Battambang

Tonle Sap

VIETNAM

Ban MeThuot

Tuy Hoa

Phet Buri

U-Tapo

Mekong River

Nha Trang

Mergui

Cam Ranh Bay

Phan Rang

Gulf
of
Thailand

Dixie Station

Rolling Thunder
March 2 1965–October 31 1968

Saigon

My Tho

Vung Tau

SOUTH

U.S. 7th Fleet (Task Force 77)

Vinh Long

CHINA

Isthmus of Kra

Can Tho

SEA

N

Aerial refueling tracks and anchor points

U.S. air base (jet serviceable)

U.S. air base (non jet serviceable)

U.S. air tanker bases

U.S. B-52 base

North Vietnamese airfields

Chinese buffer zone (prohibited area)

Route package

North Vietnamese radar coverage

Migration of bomb lines north

Surat Thani

Vinh Loi

Targeting restrictions 1965-1968

Hanoi   Prohibited zone: 10 nautical miles
           Restricted zone: 30 nautical miles

Haiphong   Prohibited zone: 4 nautical miles
           Restricted zone: 10 nautical miles

0   150 nautical miles

0   250 km

Nakhon Si Thammarat

0   150 miles

106°   108°   110°

U.S. Ground Forces Intervene   MARCH 1965

On March 8, 1965, the war in Vietnam entered a new phase when elements of the U.S. 9th Marine Expeditionary Force came ashore at Da Nang, ostensibly to provide protection for the air base there. Their mission was expanded on April 6, 1965, when President Johnson authorized the use of U.S. ground troops for offensive combat operations in Vietnam.

The U.S. military buildup in Vietnam had begun. From 23,300 U.S. military personnel in Vietnam on January 1, 1965, troop strength increased to 184,300 by the end of the year. It would peak at 543,400 on April 30, 1969. U.S. ground forces were deployed in each of the four corps tactical zones, later called military regions, into which South Vietnam was organized. Each military region was commanded by an ARVN general officer, while a counterpart U.S. corps-level headquarters was established in three of the four corps areas. I Corps, with headquarters at Da Nang, included the Demilitarized Zone between North and South Vietnam and the five northern provinces of South Vietnam. ARVN forces included the 1st, 2nd, and 3rd ARVN divisions and, at times, the Airborne and Marine divisions.

At their peak in 1968, U.S. forces included the corps-level III Marine Amphibious Force headquarters at Da Nang, the 1st and 3rd Marine divisions, and the 1st Marine Aircraft Wing. In August 1968 they were joined by the Army's XXIV Corps with its American Division, 101st Airborne Division (Airmobile), and 1st Brigade, 5th Infantry Division (Mechanized). The 1st Cavalry Division (Airmobile) was also there for a time during the 1968 Tet Offensive.

II Corps, with headquarters at Pleiku, encompassed all of central Vietnam, including the Central Highlands. South Vietnamese forces included the 22nd and 23rd ARVN divisions. The U.S. corps-level I Field Force Vietnam was established at Nha Trang, with its 4th Infantry Division and, until its transfer to I Corps in 1968, the 1st Cavalry Division (Airmobile) and the 1st Brigade, 101st Airborne Division, which was replaced by the 173rd Airborne Brigade from III Corps.

With headquarters at Bien Hoa, III Corps was responsible for the approaches to and the defense of Saigon, the capital of the Republic of Vietnam. South Vietnamese forces included the 5th, 18th, and 25th ARVN divisions and the

home bases of the mobile ARVN Airborne and Marine divisions. The U.S. corps-level II Field Force headquarters was located at Long Binh, with its 1st Infantry Division, 25th Infantry Division, 11th Armored Cavalry Regiment, and 199th Light Infantry Brigade. In 1967, its 173rd Airborne Brigade was redeployed to II Corps, and was only replaced in May 1969 by the 1st Cavalry Division (Airmobile).

II Field Force also augmented IV Corps, which included the Mekong delta and the country's southernmost portions. South Vietnamese forces included the 7th, 9th, and 21st ARVN divisions. In addition to an Army aviation group, the U.S. 9th Infantry Division conducted riverine operations in the delta.

Ground forces comprised the bulk of the American military buildup in Vietnam. During the war the U.S. Army deployed 81 infantry battalions, 3 tank battalions, 12 cavalry squadrons, 70 artillery battalions, and 142 aviation companies and air cavalry troops to Vietnam. The U.S. Marine Corps deployed 24 infantry battalions, 2 tank battalions, 2 antitank battalions, 3 amphibious tractor battalions, 2 reconnaissance battalions, 10 artillery battalions and 26 helicopter and fixed-wing flying squadrons.

"Making do with a bad situation is what it was all about. Making do with nothing, on your own. You get young kids, throw them into general chaos, they make do with it. You get stable right away, or you don't make it at all."

—U.S. soldier

In the first exercise involving all elements of the 173rd Airborne Brigade, coordinated war zone training is undertaken in Bien Hoa in May 1965. The elite brigade had been dispatched to Bien Hoa and Vung Tau from Okinawa earlier that month to reinforce the 3rd Marine Regiment, which was the first ground combat unit in Vietnam.

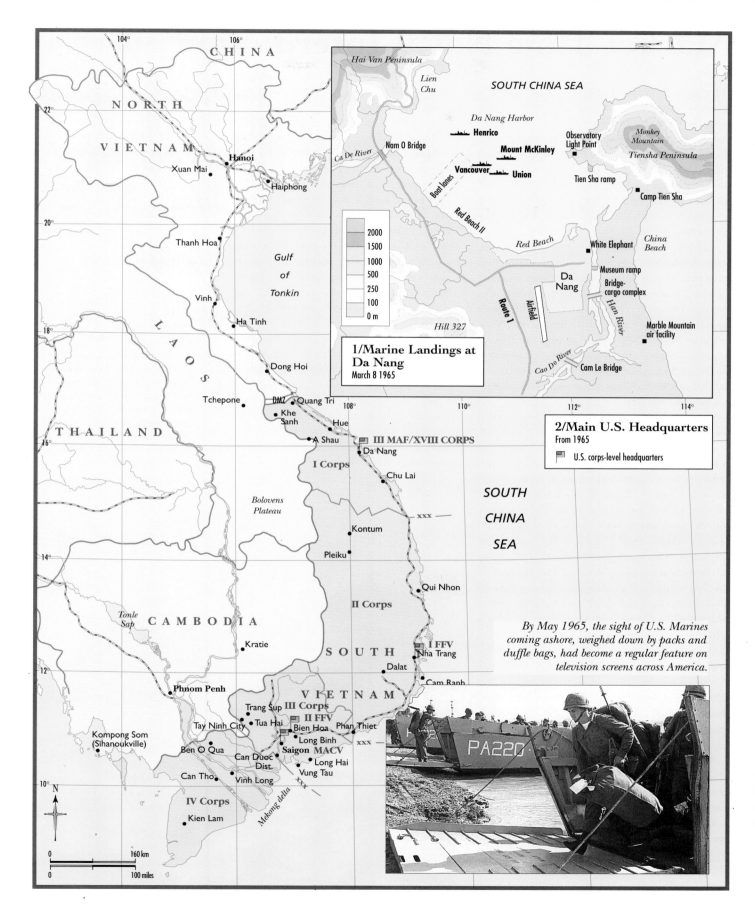

CHINA

NORTH

VIETNAM

Xuan Mai

Hanoi

Haiphong

Thanh Hoa

Gulf
of
Tonkin

Vinh

Ha Tinh

L A O S

Dong Hoi

Tchepone

DMZ Quang Tri
Khe
Sanh Hue

T H A I L A N D

A Shau

Da Nang

I Corps

Chu Lai

Bolovens
Plateau

Kontum

Pleiku

SOUTH
CHINA
SEA

Qui Nhon

II Corps

Tonle
Sap

C A M B O D I A

Kratie

S O U T H

I FFV
Nha Trang

Dalat

Cam Ranh

Phnom Penh

V I E T N A M

Trang Sup III Corps

Tay Ninh City Tua Hai II FFV
Bien Hoa

Kompong Som
(Sihanoukville)

Ben O Qua

Long Binh

Saigon MACV

Can Duoc
Dist.

Can Tho

Vinh Long

Long Hai

Vung Tau

Phan Thiet

IV Corps

Kien Lam

Mekong delta

N

0   160 km
0   100 miles

1/Marine Landings at Da Nang
March 8 1965

Hai Van Peninsula

Lien
Chu

SOUTH CHINA SEA

Da Nang Harbor

Henrico

Mount McKinley

Ca De River Nam O Bridge

Vancouver Union

Observatory
Light Point

Monkey
Mountain

Tiensha Peninsula

Tien Sha ramp

Camp Tien Sha

Boat lanes

Red Beach II

Red Beach

White Elephant

China
Beach

2000
1500
1000
500
250
100
0 m

Da
Nang

Museum ramp
Bridge-
cargo complex

Han River

Marble Mountain
air facility

Route 1

Airfield

Hill 327

Cao Do River

Cam Le Bridge

2/Main U.S. Headquarters
From 1965

U.S. corps-level headquarters

III MAF/XVIII CORPS

*By May 1965, the sight of U.S. Marines
coming ashore, weighed down by packs and
duffle bags, had become a regular feature on
television screens across America.*

PA220

Market Time Naval Interdiction   1965–1971

The 15th Plenum of the North Vietnamese Communist Party in May 1959 authorized not only the construction of the Ho Chi Minh Trail for the land movement of arms and equipment to the South, but also the creation of sea lines of supply. In July 1959, Group 579 was formed under the command of Rear Admiral Tran Van Giang to move arms and equipment along the coast of the South China Sea to support the war in the South.

General William C. Westmoreland, the U.S. commander in Vietnam at the time, estimated that prior to 1965, the Viet Cong had received about 70 percent of its supplies by sea. On March 11, 1965, Operation Market Time, a combined U.S. Navy (USN) and South Vietnamese Navy (VNN) effort to stop the flow of supplies, began. Organized around nine patrol sectors, Operation Market Time covered the 1,200-mile South Vietnamese coast and extended 40 miles out to sea.

On July 31, 1965, the Coastal Surveillance Force (Task Force 115) was formed, with headquarters at Cam Ranh Bay. Three zones of interdiction were established. At the farthest edge, 100–150 miles out to sea, was an air surveillance zone. Closer to land was an outer surface barrier patrolled initially by 15 destroyers or minesweepers and later by radar picket escorts (DER). In May 1965, U.S. Coast Guard Squadron Three, equipped with 82-foot cutters, arrived on station to patrol this barrier, and by February 1966, 26 Coast Guard cutters were in operation. Between 1967 and 1971 the force was augmented by three Royal Australian Navy guided-missile destroyers.

Nearest to shore was an inner or shallow-water barrier. Here, in addition to the South Vietnamese Junk Force (later renamed the Coastal Force), the Navy deployed 84 Swift boats—50-foot vessels armed with .50 caliber machine guns and mortars that could navigate in shallow coastal waters.

From January 1966 to July 1967, Market Time forces sank several North Vietnamese steel-hulled trawlers and inspected or boarded more than 700,000 vessels in South Vietnamese waters. Except for five enemy ships that were either sunk or turned back while attempting to resupply their forces in the aftermath of the 1968 Tet Offensive, no other enemy trawlers were spotted from July 1967 to August 1969.

Operation Market Time had succeeded in closing down North Vietnam's lines of supply by sea. Unfortunately this success was overshadowed by the failure of efforts to close down the land lines of supply down the Ho Chi Minh Trail through "neutral" Laos and by the overt transshipment of arms and equipment to the Viet Cong through the "neutral" Cambodian port of Sihanoukville. When this port was closed to Communist shipping in August 1969, the North Vietnamese made an attempt to resume their trawler traffic. But of the 15 trawlers detected moving south between August 1969 and late 1970, one was sunk, 13 were turned back, and only one got through.

As part of the "Vietnamization" of the war, the VNN took charge of the inner screen in September 1970, and all Swift boats were transferred to their control. While combined operations continued into 1971, when 10 out of 11 enemy trawlers were either sunk or turned back, the Vietnamization of the outer barrier continued. Between 1971 and 1972 all 26 Coast Guard cutters from that screen were turned over to the VNN.

"We search a junk or a sampan an average of every minute and a half. And that is 24 hours a day and 365 days a year."

—U.S. naval officer, 1966

Helicopters prepare to take off for Chu Lai from the the flight deck of the amphibious assault ship USS Princeton. *Market Time was a highly effective if relatively unsung operation, which began with a modest commitment of six radar picket destroyers to patrol the coast of South Vietnam and succeeded in cutting Viet Cong sea lines of supply.*

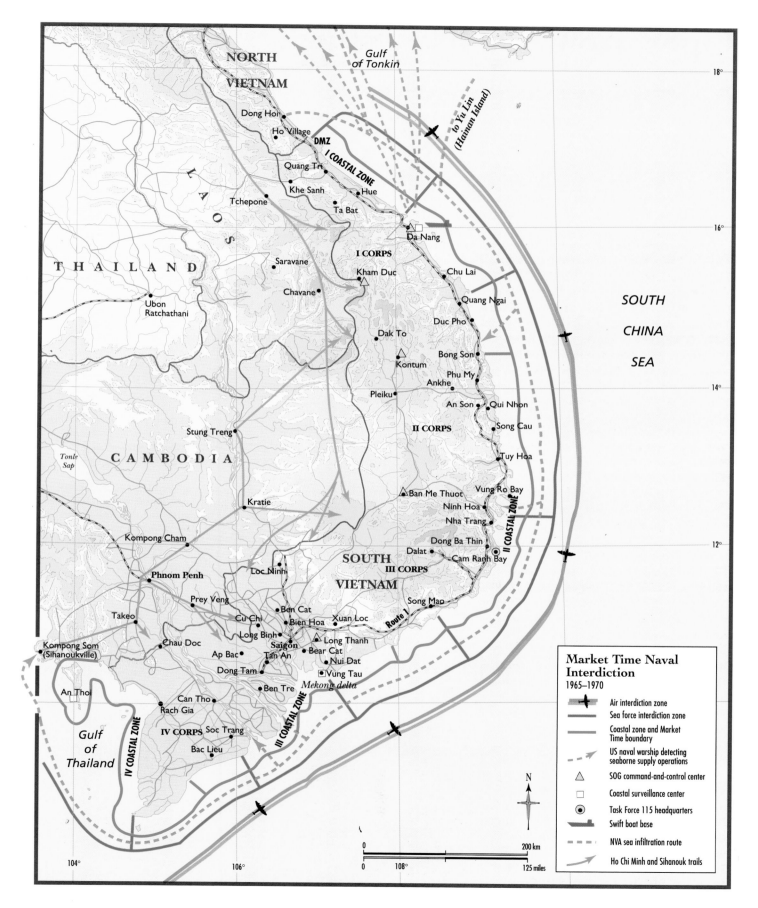

NORTH VIETNAM

Gulf
of Tonkin

to Yu Lin
(Hainan Island)

Dong Hoi
Ho Village
DMZ
I COASTAL ZONE
Quang Tri
Khe Sanh
Hue
Tchepone
Ta Bat

LAOS

Da Nang

I CORPS
Saravane
Kham Duc
Chu Lai
Chavane
Quang Ngai
Duc Pho

THAILAND

Ubon
Ratchathani

Dak To
Bong Son
Kontum
Phu My
Ankhe
Pleiku
An Son   Qui Nhon
Song Cau

II CORPS

SOUTH

CHINA

SEA

Stung Treng

Tuy Hoa

CAMBODIA

Tonle
Sap

Vung Ro Bay
Ban Me Thuot
Ninh Hoa
Nha Trang
II COASTAL ZONE
Kratie
Dong Ba Thin
Dalat
Cam Ranh Bay

Kompong Cham

Phnom Penh

Loc Ninh
**SOUTH
VIETNAM**
III CORPS
Song Mao
Prey Veng
Ben Cat
Xuan Loc
Takeo
Cu Chi
Bien Hoa
Route 1
Long Binh
Chau Doc
Ap Bac
Long Thanh
Dong Tam
Saigon
Bear Cat
Nui Dat
Tan An
Vung Tau
Ben Tre
Mekong delta

Kompong Som
(Sihanoukville)

An Thoi
Can Tho
Rach Gia
III COASTAL ZONE

Gulf
of
Thailand

IV COASTAL ZONE
IV CORPS   Soc Trang
Bac Lieu

N

0   200 km
0   125 miles

104°   106°   108°

18°
16°
14°
12°

Market Time Naval
Interdiction
1965–1970

✈ Air interdiction zone

— Sea force interdiction zone

— Coastal zone and Market
  Time boundary

- - → US naval warship detecting
  seaborne supply operations

△ SOG command-and-control center

□ Coastal surveillance center

⊙ Task Force 115 headquarters

⛴ Swift boat base

- - - NVA sea infiltration route

→ Ho Chi Minh and Sihanouk trails

Operation Starlite AUGUST 1965

The first major U.S. ground combat operation of the Vietnam War began when a Viet Cong deserter revealed that the 1,500-strong main force VC 1st Regiment, with its 60th and 80th battalions and 52nd Company, was planning an attack on the airfield at Chu Lai. When Major General Lewis W. Walt, commander of the III Marine Amphibious Force based at Chu Lai, was informed, he decided to preempt the Viet Cong with a spoiling attack of his own.

The Marines, under the command of Colonel Oscar E. Peatross, would make a two-battalion assault on the VC force, which was bivouaced at the village of Van Tuong, 12 miles south of Chu Lai. One battalion, the 3rd Battalion, 3rd Marine Regiment (3/3), would make an amphibious landing on the beach and the other, the 2nd Battalion, 4th Marine Regiment (2/4), would land by helicopter further inland. Afloat would be the Special Landing Force's 3rd Battalion, 7th Marine Regiment (3/7).

August 18, 1965, was selected as D-Day, with 3/3 (less M Company) plus three flame-thrower tanks and a platoon of five M-48 medium tanks landing at Green Beach to block VC avenues of escape to the south. M Company would move overland from Chu Lai to a blocking position on a ridgeline four miles northwest of the landing area, and close off the VC retreat in that direction. Meanwhile 2/4 would land at Landing Zones (LZ) Red, White, and Blue, about 2,000 yards apart and approximately one mile inland from the coast. Link-up between the two forces would be outside the hamlet of An Cuong, about one mile inland.

After an artillery preparation by 155mm howitzers firing from Chu Lai and air strikes by Marine fighter bombers on the LZs, the assault began. Green Beach was secured without opposition, and there was only light resistance at LZ Red and LZ White. But at LZ Blue the assault force landed almost on top of the VC 60th Battalion, entrenched on nearly Hill 43.

A bitter fight ensued, but the hill was soon overrun. Meanwhile elements of the 3/3 landing party attacked the fortified hamlet of An Cuong. As the LZ Blue force moved to link up with the force from Green Beach they came under heavy fire from the hamlet of Nam Yen and were forced to withdraw to LZ Blue. A Marine supply convoy was ambushed near An

Cuong. A company from 3/7 was then landed, and after hard fighting the 60th Viet Cong Battalion broke contact. After the commitment of the rest of 3/7, the attack continued on August 19, and by nightfall the sweep of the area was completed.

Operation Starlite officially ended on August 24, 1965. The 1st VC Regiment had been rendered, temporarily at least, ineffective, with the 60th Battalion destroyed and its 80th Battalion badly mauled. The Marines had suffered 45 dead and 120 wounded, while 614 VC bodies were found and 9 VC were taken prisoner. One reason for the disparity in casualties (which would continue throughout the war) was the intensity of U.S. fire support. Marine artillery at Chu Lai had fired more than 3,000 rounds, and the mortar battery with the assault force fired over 2,400 rounds. Marine fighter bombers flew some 290 sorties, and the destroyers U.S.S. *Orleck* (DD 886) and *Prichett* (DD 561) and the cruiser *Galveston* (CLG-3), lying offshore, fired 1,562 rounds of naval gunfire support.

"Perhaps the most important outcome of Operation Starlite was its psychological lift," wrote historians Edward Doyle and Samuel Lipsman. "In the first major engagement between American forces and Main Force Vietcong soldiers, the Americans had been victorious. Had the Americans lost—a real possibility given their inexperience—the effects may have been severe indeed."

"It became a way of life. I didn't even know where those shells were going. I didn't even know what they was. But every death sound there is, you start to detect it—you know it. You start to know if death is going over you or if it's coming right at you."

—U.S. soldier

Even when fire fights raged within 50 yards of the pickup point, Marine Aircraft Group 16 pilots managed to land their helicopters in the fields and evacuate their wounded compatriots during Operation Starlite. The Viet Cong, concealed in hillside bunkers and tunnels, assailed their enemy with a constant rain of mortars, grenades, and small-arms fire, but the Marines could always count on the pilots to answer their requests for assistance.

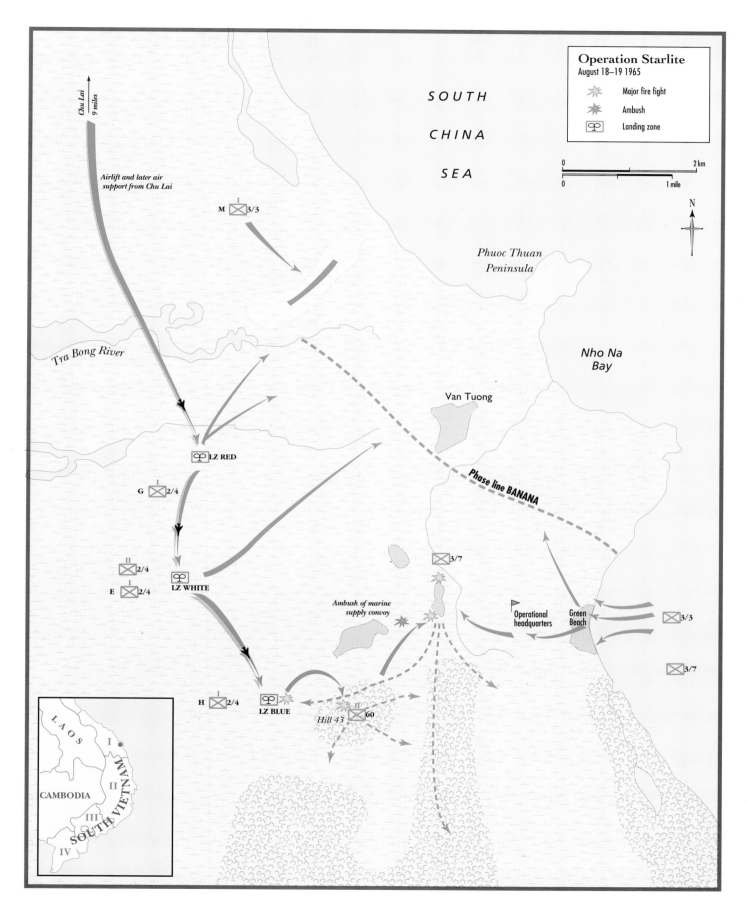

Operation Starlite
August 18–19 1965

Major fire fight

Ambush

Landing zone

SOUTH

CHINA

SEA

Phuoc Thuan
Peninsula

Nho Na
Bay

N

Chu Lai
9 miles

Airlift and later air
support from Chu Lai

M 3/3

Tra Bong River

Van Tuong

LZ RED

Phase line BANANA

G 2/4

3/7

II 2/4

E 2/4

LZ WHITE

Ambush of marine
supply convoy

Operational
headquarters

Green
Beach

3/3

3/7

H 2/4

LZ BLUE

Hill 43

60

LAOS

I

II

CAMBODIA

SOUTH VIETNAM

III

IV

Battle of the Ia Drang   OCTOBER–NOVEMBER 1965

"This could be the most significant battle of the Vietnam War," said *New York Times* war correspondent Neil Sheehan, reporting from the Ia Drang Valley in South Vietnam's Central Highlands. This was the scene, on November 14–16, 1965, of a battle between the U.S. Army's 1st Cavalry Division (Airmobile) and the 33rd and 66th regiments of the NVA.

For the NVA, the battle marked a shift from reliance solely on Viet Cong guerrilla forces to the use of the conventional military forces of the regular army. For the United States, it was the beginning of direct massive involvement in ground combat operations, as well as a test of the heliborne airmobility tactics that were to become a hallmark of the war.

Deciding that the Viet Cong guerrillas alone could not topple the South Vietnamese government, the North Vietnamese Politburo had begun committing its regular armed forces to the struggle in the South a year before the landing of U.S. ground troops in March 1965. During 1964, some 10,000 soldiers, including the NVA 320th Regiment, had moved down the Ho Chi Minh Trail. By June 1965, the 320th Regiment was besieging the Special Forces camp at Duc Co on Route 19 in the Central Highlands, in the same area where France's Groupement Mobile 100 had come to grief a decade before.

More NVA forces were on the way. In July 1965, the NVA's 33rd Regiment left Quang Ninh in North Vietnam on its two-month-long march down the Ho Chi Minh Trail, followed by the NVA 66th Regiment, which began its trek in August. NVA plans were for a coordinated attack against Pleiku in the Central Highlands, then along Route 19 to Qui Nhon and the South China Sea. South Vietnam would be cut in half and victory assured.

The battle began in October 1965 with an attack on the U.S. Army Special Forces camp at Plei Me, south of Pleiku. The NVA commanders believed that a South Vietnamese relief column which was sure to follow would be destroyed by a regimental-sized NVA ambush. The way would then be open for their drive to the coast. But a new dimension had been added to the war. The U.S. Army's 1st Cavalry Division (Airmobile) arrived in Vietnam in September 1965 and by late October had established a base camp at Pleiku. Pioneering a new concept of warfare,

the 1st Cavalry Division used helicopters to fly over enemy ambush positions and land troops directly in the battle area.

On November 14, 1965, the division's 1st Battalion, 7th Cavalry made a heliborne combat assault into LZ X-Ray 14 miles east of Plei Me, near the Cambodian border. Unknowingly, they landed in the middle of the assembly area for the NVA 66th Regiment, and a major two-day battle ensued. The Americans, reinforced by the 2nd Battalion, 7th Cavalry and the 2nd Battalion, 5th Cavalry, held on. They were supported by massive artillery and air strikes. This included the first use of B-52 strategic bombers flying from their base on Guam, each with a load of 200 tons of 500-pound bombs.

By November 16, the fight for LZ X-Ray had ended. The NVA quit the battlefield, some heading across the border into sanctuaries in Cambodia and others into the jungles of the Ia Drang. It was estimated that they had lost 2,000 men (killed and wounded), while American casualties stood at 79 killed and 121 wounded in action. The battle of the Ia Drang revealed that the war's true center of gravity was not the Viet Cong guerrillas but the regular forces of North Vietnam. Ten years later, beginning with an attack on nearby Ban Me Thuot, the NVA succeeded in cutting South Vietnam in two and bringing the war to a close.

"Never before had the Vietnamese enemy carried the fight to an American Army unit with such tenacity. None of the common wisdom born of the American experience in Vietnam to date applied to this enemy. We were locked in a savage battle, of fire and manuever, a battle for survival, which only one side would be permitted to win."

—We Were Soldiers Once...and Young, Lt. Col. Harold G. Moore Commanding, 1st Battalion, 7th Cavalry

The Americans brought vast firepower to bear in the isolated Ia Drang Valley, using B-52s or 'big birds' for the first time and sending the enemy scuttling back into their jungle hide-outs.

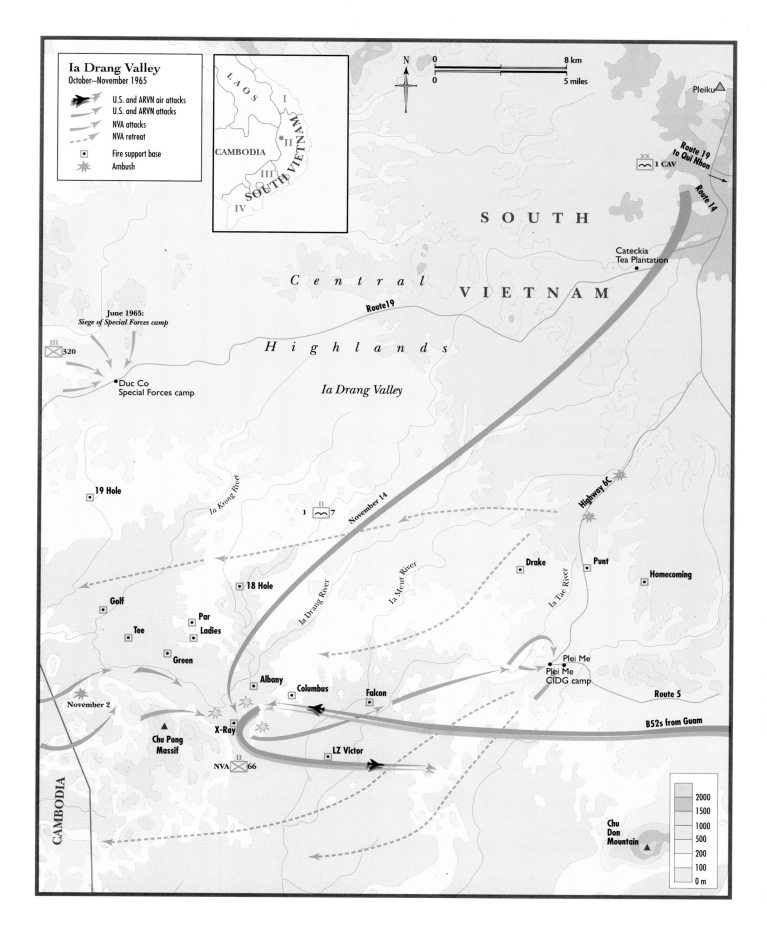

Ia Drang Valley
October–November 1965

→ U.S. and ARVN air attacks
→ U.S. and ARVN attacks
→ NVA attacks
⤏ NVA retreat
⊡ Fire support base
✳ Ambush

LAOS

CAMBODIA

SOUTH VIETNAM

N

0   8 km
0   5 miles

Pleiku

SOUTH

Route 19 to Qui Nhon

Route 14

XX 1 CAV

Cateckia Tea Plantation

Central   VIETNAM

Route 19

Highlands

June 1965:
Siege of Special Forces camp

III 320

Ia Drang Valley

•Duc Co
Special Forces camp

Highway 6C

19 Hole

Ia Krong River

1 II 7

November 14

Drake

Punt

Homecoming

Ia Meur River

Ia Tae River

18 Hole

Golf

Par
Ladies

Tee

Green

Plei Me

Albany

Columbus

Falcon

Plei Me
CIDG camp

Route 5

November 2

X-Ray

B52s from Guam

Chu Pong
Massif

NVA II 66

LZ Victor

CAMBODIA

Chu
Don
Mountain

	m
	2000
	1500
	1000
	500
	200
	100
	0 m

The Tragedy at LZ Albany   NOVEMBER 1965

"No matter what you did you got hit," wrote Jack Smith, son of the famous news commentator Howard K. Smith, then a soldier with the 2nd Battalion, 7th Cavalry, about the NVA ambush of his unit near Landing Zone Albany on November 17, 1965. "The snipers in the trees just waited for someone to move, then shot him. I could hear the North Vietnamese entering the woods from our right. They were creeping along, arguing and babbling among themselves, calling to each other when they found a live G.I. Then they shot him."

This was the tragic postlude to the victory at LZ X-Ray the day before. As the NVA withdrew, the 1st Cavalry Division (Airmobile)'s 2nd Battalion, 7th Cavalry was ordered to move overland some two miles northwest to a jungle clearing called "LZ Albany". It was seen as a "walk in the sun". Unbeknown to the 7th Cavalry, however, the NVA had staked out all the clearings in the area, and its 8th Battalion, 66th Regiment, which had been held in reserve during the fight at LZ X-Ray, was alerted to their approach. Strung out for 550 yards along the line of march, the NVA sprang the ambush as the column reached the edge of LZ Albany. Thus began what one observer called "the most savage one-day fight of the Vietnam War."

The 400 men of the 2nd Battalion, 7th Cavalry were both surprised and outnumbered. Enemy forces included both the 550-man NVA 8th Battalion, 66th Regiment and remnants of the 1st and 3rd NVA battalions, 33rd Regiment, which had retreated from Landing Zone X-Ray the day before. When the battle ended the next morning, 155 U.S. soldiers had been killed and another 124 wounded.

The Americans were not the only ones whose tactics were put to the test in the Ia Drang. "We had to study how to fight the Americans," NVA historian Major General Hoang Phuong told U.S Lieutenant General Harold G. Moore in an interview in 1990.

"I think this fight was the most important of the entire campaign," said the NVA battlefield commander Lieutenant General (then Senior Lieutenant Colonel) Nguyen Huu An. "I gave my orders to the battalion: 'Move inside the column, grab them by the belt, and thus avoid casualties from the artillery and air.' We consider [LZ Albany] our victory," he continued, echoing the sentiments of the Americans after their win at LZ X-Ray. "This was the first time [we] fought the Americans and we defeated Americans, caused big American losses. As military men we realize it is important to win the first battle. It raised our soldiers' morale and gave us many good lessons."

Well-trained, well equipped, and highly motivated, the 1st U.S. Cavalry Division was the U.S. Army's elite division. Its 7th Cavalry, which experienced such tragic losses in the wake of victory in the Ia Drang, is most famous for its part in the Battle of Little Big Horn, where it met both death and glory under General Custer in 1876.

"It ran through my mind for a moment, 'Did his mother feel something, did his father feel something, did anybody? Was she reaching for a can of peas in the supermarket and feel a tug or a jolt and not know what it was? Does anybody close to him know that he just died?'"

—U.S. soldier

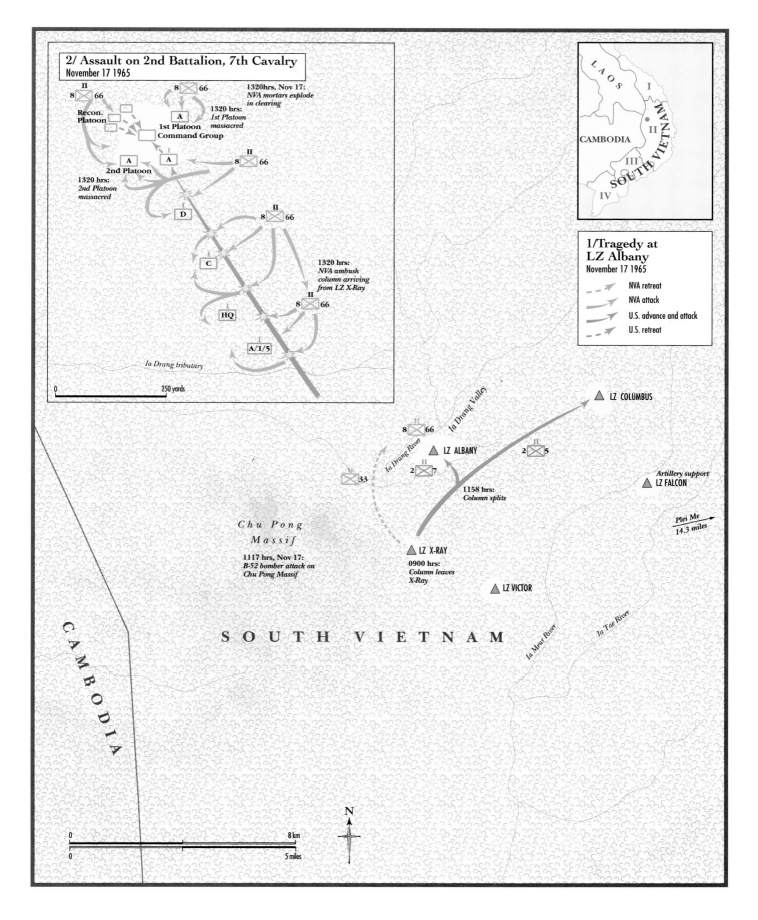

2/ Assault on 2nd Battalion, 7th Cavalry
November 17 1965

II 8 ⊠ 66

8 ⊠ 66

1320hrs, Nov 17:
*NVA mortars explode
in clearing*

Recon.
Platoon

A

1320 hrs:
*1st Platoon
massacred*

1st Platoon
Command Group

A A

2nd Platoon

II 8 ⊠ 66

1320 hrs:
*2nd Platoon
massacred*

D

II 8 ⊠ 66

C

1320 hrs:
*NVA ambush
column arriving
from LZ X-Ray*

HQ

II 8 ⊠ 66

A/1/5

Ia Drang tributary

0 —————— 250 yards

**1/Tragedy at
LZ Albany**
November 17 1965

→ → → NVA retreat
——→ NVA attack
══→ U.S. advance and attack
– – → U.S. retreat

LZ COLUMBUS

8 II ⊠ 66   *Ia Drang Valley*

II
2 ⊠ 5

Ia Drang River   ▲ LZ ALBANY

II
⊠ 33

II
2 ⊠ 7

Artillery support
▲ LZ FALCON

1158 hrs:
Column splits

Plei Me
14.3 miles

*Chu Pong
Massif*

1117 hrs, Nov 17:
*B-52 bomber attack on
Chu Pong Massif*

▲ LZ X-RAY

0900 hrs:
*Column leaves
X-Ray*

▲ LZ VICTOR

S O U T H   V I E T N A M

Ia Meur River   *Ia Tae River*

C A M B O D I A

0 —————— 8 km
0 —————— 5 miles

N

Combined Action Platoons   JANUARY 1966

One of the major controversies of the war was the question of how to deal with the Viet Cong guerrillas. The Army, faced primarily by VC Main Force battalions and regiments in II Corps and III Corps, favored the use of conventional military "search-and-destroy" tactical combat operations to defeat these units by force of arms. The Marine Corps, faced with VC insurgents in the heavily populated coastal areas of I Corps, favored an "ink blot" pacification strategy, whereby government control would be gradually extended from a pacified hamlet to the surrounding countryside by means of "clear-and-hold" operations.

"The first Marines who came to Vietnam learned quickly that the Vietnamese peasant was tired of war, hungry for a little tranquility, and terrified of the Vietcong guerrillas who ... murdered their village mayors, extracted rice and tribute, labor and information ... and impressed their children into the Vietcong ranks," said Marine Lieutanant General Victor H. Krulak. "All the common people could fall back on for direct protection were local volunteers, the Popular Forces. These were boys from the village, miserably equipped, ill-paid, poorly led, poorly trained, and frightened. They were no match for the hardened Vietcong guerrilla ... They had just one thing going for them: they were fighting for their homes, their mothers, their sweethearts."

Combined Action platoons (CAPs) were begun on an ad hoc basis in the Phu Bai area by the 3rd Battalion, 4th Marine Regiment, in August 1965. One Marine rifle squad, with a Navy medical corpsman attached, was assigned to each of these Popular Force local home guard militia units. Their mission was both to provide local security for the villagers and to conduct civic action projects to improve the quality of life in the villages.

The concept was formalized in January 1966, when Combined Action companies, each containing several CAPs, were created. By the end of 1968, there were 102 CAPs, organized into four Combined Action groups (CAG), which had their headquarters at Chu Lai, Da Nang, Phu Bai, and Quang Tri. Until 1969, the CAPs maintained fixed positions in their villages. In mid-1969, however, mobile CAPs began to set up temporary command posts within their areas of operations, and used these

as bases from which to launch aggressive patrols. By the end of 1969, 145,000 patrols had been conducted, resulting in the deaths of 1,938 VC guerrillas and the capture of a further 425, and the confiscation of 939 weapons.

At its height, 42 Marine officers and 2,000 enlisted men were involved in the program, as were 2 Navy officers and 126 Navy medical corpsmen. They operated in conjunction with more than 3,000 South Vietnamese Regional Force local militia as well as the Popular Force home guard. It was, says historian Ronald Spector, "among the most effective, imaginative, and humane approaches to the Vietnam struggle the Americans ever devised. In a war where the United States and the South Vietnamese frequently waged war *on* the villages, Combined Action opted for war *in* the villages."

But the CAP program had a fatal flaw. Its tactical success only served to highlight the deficiencies of the South Vietnamese political system and to further alienate the villagers from the Saigon government, when the strategic purpose of U.S. involvement was in fact to strengthen that very government.

"The survivors wandered dazedly through the smoldering ruins of their homes. One old dwarf carried two severed hands wrapped in paper—all that he could find of his twelve-year-old son, who was in one of the bunkers. Even as the people of Thanh My mourned their dead, the women of a village controlled by the Viet Cong only a few miles away showed up to carry off the 16 Communists killed during the attack. Neither group of mourners disturbed the other."

—Time, June 22, 1970

Members of a Combined Action Company head for a VC village.

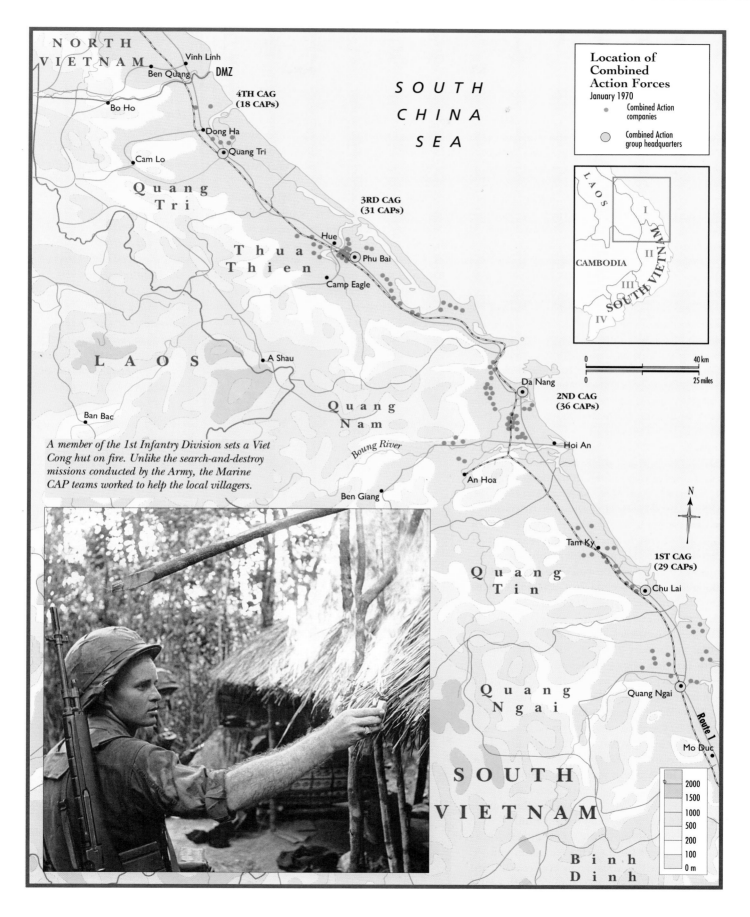

NORTH VIETNAM

Vinh Linh

Ben Quang

DMZ

Bo Ho

Dong Ha

Cam Lo

Quang Tri

4TH CAG
(18 CAPs)

SOUTH
CHINA
SEA

Location of
Combined
Action Forces
January 1970

• Combined Action
companies

⊙ Combined Action
group headquarters

LAOS

CAMBODIA

SOUTH VIETNAM

I

II

III

IV

0   40 km

0   25 miles

Thua
Thien

Hue

Phu Bai

Camp Eagle

3RD CAG
(31 CAPs)

LAOS

A Shau

Quang
Nam

Da Nang

2ND CAG
(36 CAPs)

Hoi An

Boung River

A member of the 1st Infantry Division sets a Viet
Cong hut on fire. Unlike the search-and-destroy
missions conducted by the Army, the Marine
CAP teams worked to help the local villagers.

Ban Bac

An Hoa

Ben Giang

N

Tam Ky

Quang
Tin

1ST CAG
(29 CAPs)

Chu Lai

Quang
Ngai

Quang Ngai

Route 1

Mo Duc

SOUTH
VIETNAM

Binh
Dinh

2000
1500
1000
500
200
100
0 m

Masher/White Wing JANUARY–MARCH 1966

Operation Masher, a combined U.S., ARVN, and ROKA effort, began on January 28, 1966, and was the first of many "search-and-destroy" operations. An ominous sign, indicative of both the confusion at the very top over the nature of the war and the fragility of public support at home, was President Lyndon Johnson's insistence that the name be changed, because "Masher" was too crude a title for a "nation-building" operation and would have an adverse effect on public opinion.

On February 4, at Washington's insistence, the operation was renamed White Wing, but it had little to do with "nation-building." Like most search-and-destroy operations, it was first and foremost a combat operation. The mission was to locate and destroy enemy forces in the Bong Son Plain and surrounding areas in II Corps' Binh Dinh Province. In addition to local Viet Cong guerrillas, these forces included the 3rd NVA "Sao Vang" or "Yellow Flag" Division's 18th and 22nd NVA regiments and its 2nd Main Force VC Regiment.

While the ARVN Airborne Brigade, the 22nd ARVN Division, and the ROKA Capital Division conducted ground operations along Highway 1, Vietnam's main north-south coastal road, the U.S. Army's 1st Cavalry Division (Airmobile) would use its helicopter-borne forces to seek out the enemy further inland. Meanwhile, a 4,000-man U.S. Marine Corps amphibious landing in Quang Ngai Province, to the north of Bong Son, would sweep inland and link up with the Masher/White Wing forces in the northern An Lao Valley. The 3rd Brigade, 1st Cavalry Division (Airmobile) began Phase I of the operation on January 28, 1966, with an air assault into landing zones in the Bong Son Plain, where heavy contact was made with the 7th and 9th battalions of the NVA 22nd Regiment.

Phase II, an air assault into the An Lao Valley by the 1st Cavalry Division's 2nd Brigade, began on February 4 with the landing of four U.S. battalions on the mountains overlooking the valley. The three-day sweep that followed failed to make enemy contact, but Phase III, an air assault by the 3rd Brigade into the Kim Son or "Eagle's Claw" Valley, had better results.

Radiating outward from LZ Bird, U.S. forces made contact with the 93rd Battalion, 2nd VC Regiment, driving them from the area. In hard fighting at the "Iron Triangle" south of LZ Bird, the division's 2nd Brigade, aided by B-52 bomber strikes, also drove the enemy forces from the field. Phase IV, involving search-and-destroy operations in the Cay Giap Mountains between Bong Son and the South China Sea, was inconclusive, for the 3rd NVA Division had withdrawn from the area.

The 42-day Masher/White Wing operation ended on March 6, 1966. Some 1,342 enemy soldiers had been killed by troopers of the 1st Cavalry Division (Airmobile), at a cost of 228 U.S. troops killed and another 788 wounded. ARVN and ROKA forces had killed another 808 enemy soldiers. The 3rd NVA Division was pronounced destroyed, but as was true of other "destroyed" enemy units throughout the war, it soon rose again from the dead.

In one of the most dangerous tasks of the war, elements of the 1st Cavalry Division (Airmobile) launch an air assault on LZ 5, a mountain ridge in the Masher/White Wing area of operations. The CH-47 "Chinook" from which they emerge is a craft with a 115-mile range and the capacity to carry 44 men or a cargo of up to 10,366 pounds.

"As a drenching rain fell through the night, the Americans took cover behind the raised gravestones of an old cemetery. Working under a murderous hail of Communist fire, Sgt. Reid Pike, 23, of Albuquerque, N.M., calmly fashioned a transmitter from the parts of two damaged radios and managed to call for help. When a convoy of helicopters arrived the next morning, the men made a mad dash for the landing zone—all, that is, except the dozens of poncho-shrouded casualties who lay in the muddy ooze of shallow trenches."

—Newsweek,
February 14, 1966

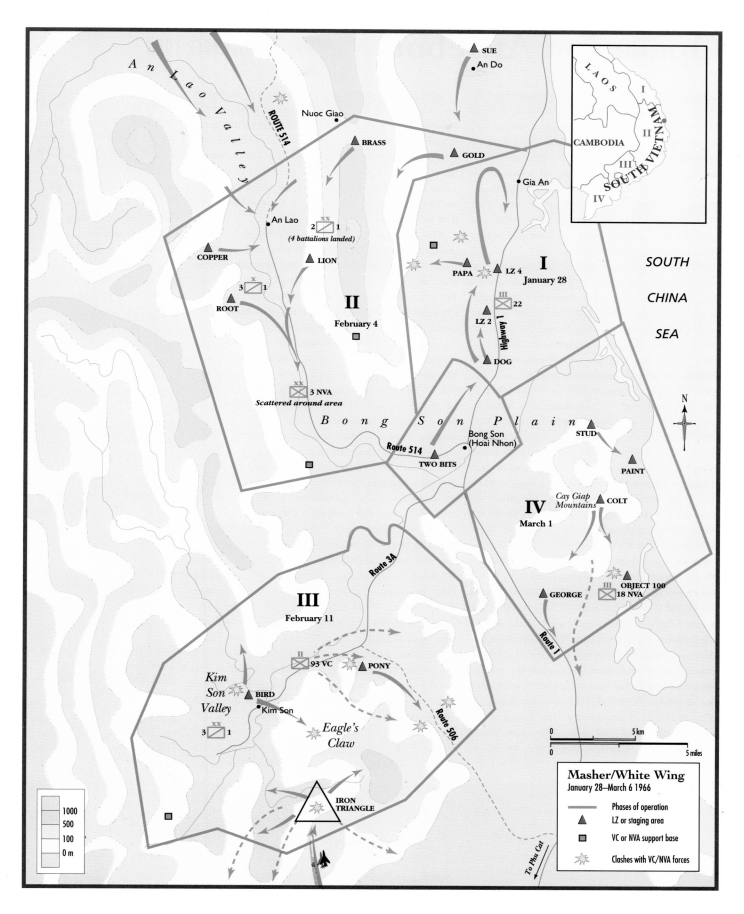

Masher/White Wing
January 28–March 6 1966

——— Phases of operation

▲ LZ or staging area

■ VC or NVA support base

✳ Clashes with VC/NVA forces

Operation Attleboro SEPTEMBER–NOVEMBER 1966

Operation Attleboro began on September 14, 1966, and was a search-and-destroy operation by the 196th Light Infantry Brigade, which had arrived in Vietnam the month before. Named after the Massachusetts town near where the brigade had been formed, Attleboro was intended as the first in a series of operations designed by the new commander, Brigadier General Edward H. deSaussure, to combat test his brigade against supposedly light opposition from local guerrilla forces.

For the first month and a half, in what was later labeled Phase I, the brigade maneuvered without significant enemy contact in the jungle areas along the edge of the Michelin Rubber Plantation northeast of its base camp at Tay Ninh, as well as north and west of the town of Dau Tieng (Tri Tam), where it established an artillery base and forward command post. But that changed dramatically on November 3, when the veteran 1st Battalion, 27th Infantry, attached to the 196th Brigade from the U.S. 25th Infantry Division, ran head-on into elements of the 9th Viet Cong Division in dense jungle about eight miles northwest of Dau Tieng. In Phase II of Attleboro, a major three-day battle ensued between the "Wolfhounds" (the 27th Infantry) and the 9th VC Division's 101st NVA Regiment and elements of its 271st, 272nd and 273rd VC regiments.

A strange anomaly of this battle is the fact that it was conducted throughout by a single infantry battalion commander, Major Guy S. Meloy, of the 1st Battalion, 27th Infantry, who at the height of the action had 11 rifle companies under his command. Brigadier General deSaussure (who was later relieved of command for his conduct of the operation) and the commanders of his 2nd Battalion, 1st Infantry, 3rd Battalion, 21st Infantry, and 4th Battalion, 31st Infantry, remained at the brigade advanced command post at Dau Tieng, releasing their rifle companies piecemeal to Major Meloy's command.

Meloy's ultimately brigade-sized force included his own three rifle companies, three rifle companies of the 2nd Battalion, 27th Infantry (the commander of which, Lieutenant William C. Barott, was killed while coming to his sister battalion's relief), three rifle companies of the 2nd Battalion, 1st Infantry, and one rifle company each from the 3rd Battalion, 21st Infantry and the 4th Battalion, 31st Infantry.

On November 7, Meloy was ordered to break contact, as the 1st Infantry Division took over the fight, launching Phase III of the operation. The most significant contact of this phase was by the 1st Infantry Division's 1st Battalion, 28th Infantry. On November 8th, near the hamlet of Ap Cha Do northeast of Major Meloy's earlier battle, the 1st Battalion under the command of Lieutenant Colonel Jack Whitted was attacked by the 272nd VC Regiment and the 101st NVA Regiment while still in its night defensive positions. A bitter four-hour fight ensued that left more than 300 enemy bodies on the battlefield. It was later discovered that the reason for the enemy's stiff resistance was that they were defending a mile-long base camp hidden in the jungle and containing one of the largest weapons caches found so far. It included more than 19,000 grenades, 1,135 pounds of explosives, and 400 Bangalore torpedoes.

By November 15, the enemy had broken contact and begun to withdraw across the border into sanctuaries in Cambodia, leaving the bodies of 1,106 of its soldiers on the battlefield, including four battalion commanders and five company commanders. Total U.S. losses were 155 killed in action and 494 wounded, including the author, who was wounded by an enemy claymore mine while serving as an operations officer of the 1st Battalion, 2nd Infantry, 1st Infantry Division. On November 24, Attleboro came to an end. But it was the precursor of things to come, for the battle convinced General William C. Westmoreland, the U.S. commander in Vietnam, that the usually elusive enemy would fight to protect its base areas. That thesis would soon be put to the test.

"Then the sun would go down and I could feel my stomach sinking. There goes the light. There goes one of your senses, the most important one. Life stops. There's no electricity. There's no technology. It's just hovels made out of corrugated tin and Coke boxes, cardboard, sticks, thatch. There's nothing else over there. The only technology you have is death: M–16s—black plastic rifles—grenades, pocket bombs, Claymores, M–79s, M–60s, mortars, jungle utilities, flak jackets, jungle boots, C4, radios and jet planes to drop the napalm. That was the only technology happening."

—U.S. soldier

Rushed in from training in the United States, members of the 196th Infantry Brigade begin a sweep against the Viet Cong in War Zone C. Within a month, the men had uncovered not only the 9th VC Division and the 101st NVA Regiment, but also a large enemy base complex.

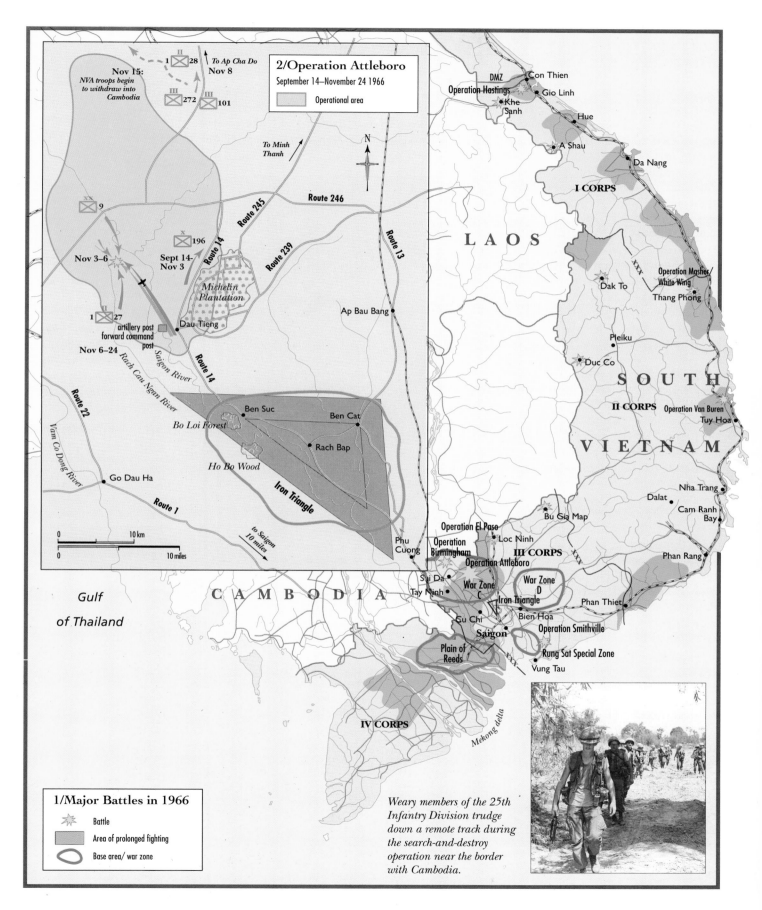

2/Operation Attleboro

September 14–November 24 1966

Operational area

Nov 15:
*NVA troops begin
to withdraw into
Cambodia*

1 | 28   *To Ap Cha Do*
            Nov 8

272   101

*To Minh
Thanh*

N

Route 245

Route 246

9

196

Nov 3–6

Route 14

Sept 14–
Nov 3

Route 239

Route 13

*Michelin
Plantation*

1 | 27

artillery post
forward command
post

Nov 6–24

Dau Tieng

Ap Bau Bang

LAOS

DMZ
Con Thien
Operation Hastings   Gio Linh
Khe
Sanh
Hue
A Shau
Da Nang

I CORPS

Dak To   XXX   Operation Masher/
                  White Wing
                  Thang Phong

Pleiku

Duc Co

SOUTH

II CORPS   Operation Van Buren
                  Tuy Hoa

VIETNAM

Saigon River

Rach Cau Ngan River

Route 22

Route 14

Route 1

Van Co Dong River

Go Dau Ha

0   10 km

0   10 miles

Ben Suc
Bo Loi Forest

Ben Cat

Rach Bap

Ho Bo Wood

Iron Triangle

to Saigon
10 miles

Nha Trang

Dalat

Cam Ranh
Bay

Bu Gia Map

Operation El Paso
Phu
Cuong   Operation
         Birmingham   Loc Ninh

Operation Attleboro   III CORPS

Sui Da   War Zone
Tay Ninh   C   War Zone
                  D
         Iron Triangle

Phan Rang

Gulf

of Thailand

C A M B O D I A

Cu Chi

Saigon

Bien Hoa

Operation Smithville

Plain of
Reeds

Rung Sat Special Zone

Vung Tau

Phan Thiet

IV CORPS

Mekong delta

1/Major Battles in 1966

✳ Battle

   Area of prolonged fighting

⬭ Base area/ war zone

*Weary members of the 25th
Infantry Division trudge
down a remote track during
the search-and-destroy
operation near the border
with Cambodia.*

Operation Bolo   JANUARY 1967

Operation Bolo was the code name for a U.S. Air Force fighter sweep over the Hanoi area against North Vietnamese MiG-21 interceptors on January 2, 1967. During the last four months of 1966, these Soviet-supplied aircraft, with a maximum speed of 1,385 miles per hour (Mach 2.1), had become an increasing threat in the air war over North Vietnam. Unlike the older MiG-15s and MiG-17s, which were armed only with 23mm and 37mm cannons, the MiG-21s were also armed with heat-seeking Atoll missiles. Guided behind U.S. strike forces by ground air defense radars, they would launch high-speed attacks on the U.S. bomber formations. Although only 10 U.S. aircraft had been downed, the MiG-21s had intercepted 192 U.S. fighter-bombers, causing 107 to jettison their bomb load before they reached their targets.

The threat of the MiG-21s was even more deadly because Washington had inanely forbidden attacks on the MiG airfields in the Hanoi area. Instead of allowing the enemy aircraft to be attacked on the ground, where they were most vulnerable, the rule was that they could only be attacked while in the air. A deception operation was therefore planned to lure them into the air, where F-4 Phantom fighters would be disguised to resemble the less maneuverable F-105 Thunderchief bombers that normally made the strikes.

The original plan was for 28 Phantoms from the 8th Tactical Fighter Wing at Ubon, Thailand, under the command of Colonel Robin Olds, to sweep in from the west over the airfields at Phuc Yen and Gia Lam while another 28 Phantoms from the 366th Tactical Fighter Wing at Da Nang in South Vietnam would approach from the east over the airfields at Kep and Cat Bi, creating a pincer movement which would cut off any MiG escape routes across the Chinese border.

On January 2, 1967, Colonel Olds took off from Ubon, leading his Wolfpack into the attack. Unfortunately overcast weather prevented the Da Nang force from reaching the target area. Initially slow to react, the MiG-21s finally took the bait and began to attack what they thought were heavily laden F-105 bombers. A furious 15-minute dogfight ensued before the MiGs broke contact. All 28 F-4 Phantoms returned safely to base, but the North Vietnamese had lost seven MiG-21s, one to the

Sidewinder air-to-air missiles of Colonel Olds. Almost half of their entire 16-aircraft inventory had gone down in flames. The United States had won its first major aerial victory of the Vietnam War.

"The AAA round blew a hole in my wing so big that when I was on the ground I could stand up with my shoulders through it ... As I approached Udorn with the EA-6 close by and two Jolly Green helicopters in tow, I was sure I wasn't going to make it. Seven miles out the engine quit, but I was able to dead-stick it into Udorn, still carrying the 28,500-pounders. I couldn't believe it. We rolled out and I had to pump open the canopy by hand as we had no hydraulic pressure left. Charlie and I literally kissed the ground when we got out!"

—Jesse Randall,
U.S. pilot

F-105 Thunderchiefs (left) were unmaneuverable in air-to-air combat. The F-4 Phantom, by comparison, (below) earned itself the nickname 'MiG master.' Both are seen here led by RB-66 Destroyers.

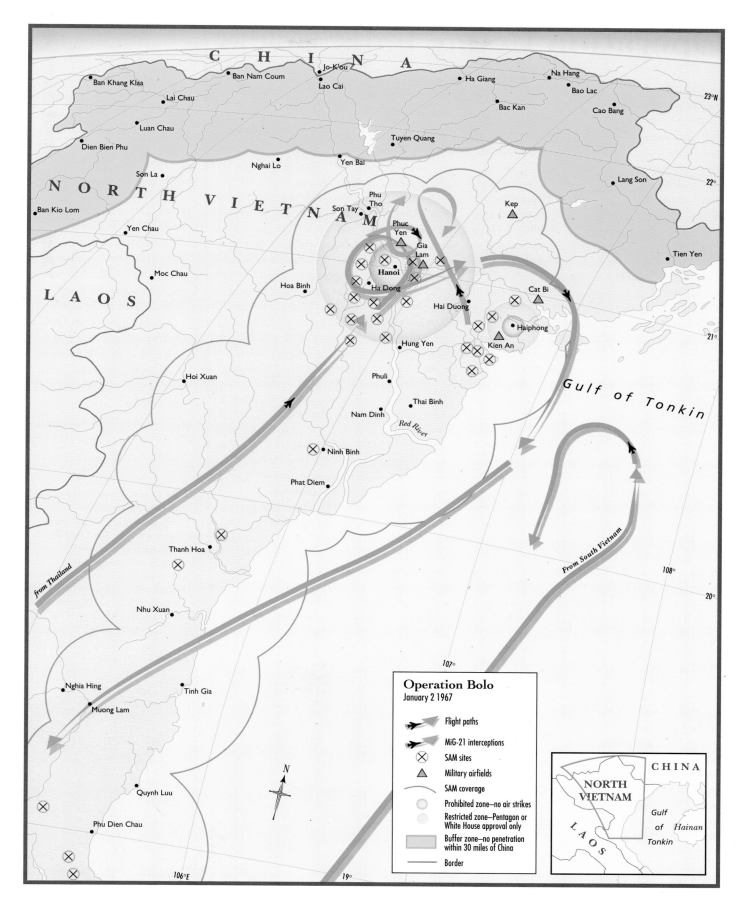

Operation Bolo
January 2 1967

Flight paths

MiG-21 interceptions

⊗ SAM sites

▲ Military airfields

SAM coverage

Prohibited zone—no air strikes

Restricted zone—Pentagon or
White House approval only

Buffer zone—no penetration
within 30 miles of China

Border

Operation Cedar Falls   JANUARY 1967

Based on the successful attempt in Operation Attleboro to force the enemy to stand and fight to protect their base areas, Operation Cedar Falls was designed to clear out the Viet Cong base area northwest of Saigon known as the "Iron Triangle." Even in the Viet Minh era, this was a well-fortified guerrilla base area honeycombed by tunnels. It provided a haven for terrorists in the Saigon area and was the headquarters for the VC Military Region IV. The 165th and 272nd VC regiments were also thought to be in the area, as well as the independent VC Main Force Phu Loi Battalion.

Under the command of the corps-level II Field Force Vietnam, Operation Cedar Falls would involve the U.S. 1st Infantry Division, 25th Infantry Division, 173rd Airborne Brigade, 196th Light Infantry Brigade, and the 11th Armored Cavalry Regiment. In addition, the 5th ARVN Division and the VNN 3rd Riverine Company and 30th River Assault Group would help to seal off the operational area.

It was planned as a classic "hammer and anvil" operation, with the ARVN and VNN forces, the 25th Infantry Division, and the 199th Light Infantry Brigade south of the Saigon River forming the "anvil," while the "hammer" would launch helicopter and ground assaults to crush the enemy. One peculiar aspect would be the total evacuation and razing of the village of Ben Suc, the reputed center of VC activity in the "Iron Triangle."

Cedar Falls began on January 8, 1967, with an air assault on the village of Ben Suc by the 2nd Brigade, 1st Infantry Division and the movement of the "anvil" forces into position. As they did so, 25th Infantry Division elements made contact with a battalion of the 165th VC Regiment—the only time in the entire operation when the VC chose to stand and fight. On January 9, the "hammer" began to descend. Task Force Deane, consisting of the 173rd Airborne Brigade and the 11th Armored Cavalry Regiment, attacked from the east while the 1st Infantry Division's 3rd Brigade launched a heliborne assault from the north. Except for isolated small unit actions, no major battles ensued. Contrary to expectations, VC Main Force units had not stood and fought but had slipped away into the jungle.

The 19-day operation ended on January 26, 1967. Friendly losses included 72 U.S. soldiers killed in action and 337 wounded, while ARVN forces suffered 11 casualties with 8 wounded. Enemy losses included 750 VC killed and 280 captured. Large quantities of arms and equipment were uncovered, including 23 mortars and machine guns, 590 rifles, 60,000 rounds of ammunition and 750 uniforms.

Cedar Falls was marked by several tactical innovations. One was the use of specially trained volunteers to explore the maze of tunnels that the VC had constructed throughout the area. These "tunnel rats" uncovered underground hospitals, supply caches, and headquarters. Helicopter loads of documents, records and plans were found, including maps and diagrams of U.S. billets in Saigon and plans for terrorist raids. Another innovation was the use of "Rome plows" to clear away vegetation along roads in order to prevent enemy ambushes as well as in the construction of landing zones for future operations. Rome plows (named after their manufacturer, the Rome Caterpillar Company in Georgia) had a specially configured dozer-blade developed for heavy duty land-clearing operations. During Cedar Falls, four square miles of jungle were cleared and many miles of road made passable.

Claims at the time that "the Iron Triangle is no more" proved illusory, for the VC soon moved back into the area. Whatever its military success, however, Cedar Falls was a public opinion disaster. The forced evacuation of the 5,987 residents of Ben Suc to refugee camps at Phu Loi and the total destruction of their village was widely and critically reported and became a rallying point for the antiwar movement.

"While the experience was an unpleasant one for some of the GIs, they did their best to make it as painless as possible for the uprooted. Before the evacuees were bundled on to barges and carts, they were permitted to collect their food and livestock and furniture to take along on the journey. But it was made clear that there would be no going home. Even as the last of the evicted still poked around their wood and thatched huts assembling their belongings, U.S. troops began to burn and bulldoze their villages to the ground."

—Newsweek
January 23, 1967

The Cu Chi tunnel complex near the Iron Triangle was a staggering feat of engineering which gave the Viet Cong the advantage of virtually impermeable subterranean fortresses from which to launch attacks. While U.S. Army records state that 525 tunnels were destroyed during Cedar Falls, this was merely the tip of the iceberg.

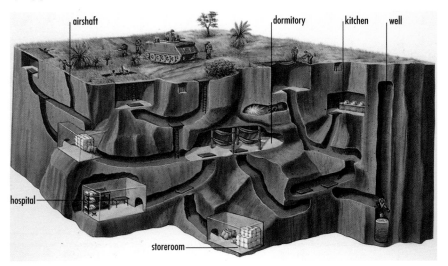

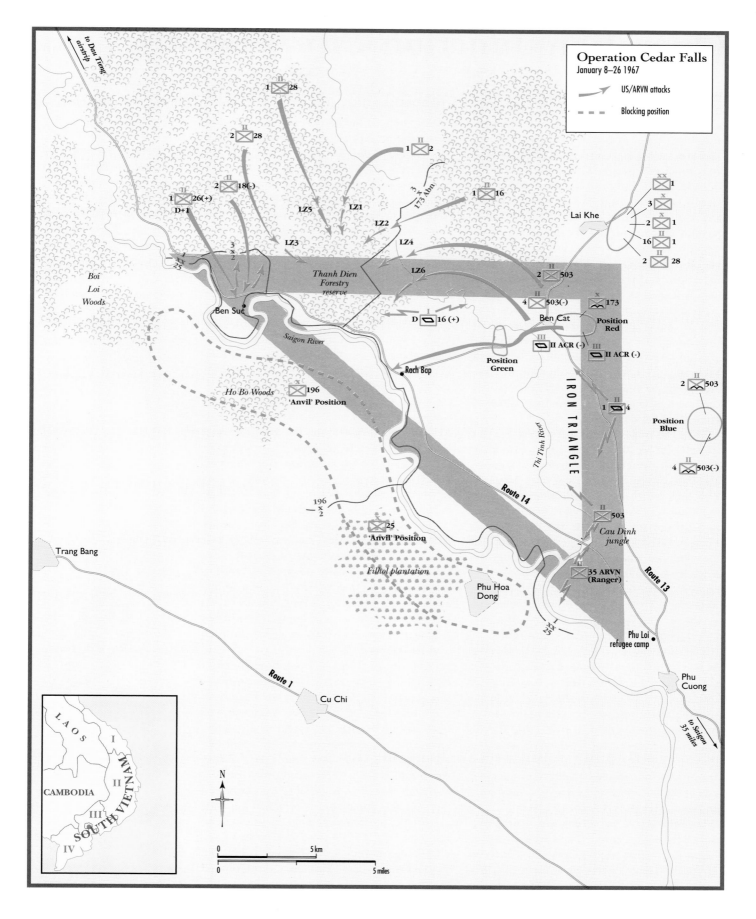

Operation Cedar Falls
January 8–26 1967

US/ARVN attacks

Blocking position

1 ⊠ 28

2 ⊠ 28

1 ⊠ 2

2 ⊠ 18(-)

1 ⊠ 26(+)
D+1

LZ5

LZ1

3 x 2
173 Abn

1 ⊠ 16

XX 1

3

2 ⊠ 1

16 ⊠ 1

2 ⊠ 28

Lai Khe

3 x 2

LZ3

LZ2

LZ4

1 xx 25

LZ6

Thanh Dien Forestry reserve

2 ⊠ 503

Boi Loi Woods

Ben Suc

Saigon River

D ▭ 16 (+)

4 ⊠ 503(-)

x 173

Ben Cat

Position Red

III II ACR (-)

III II ACR (-)

Rach Bap

Position Green

Thi Tinh River

2 ⊠ 503

Ho Bo Woods

x 196
'Anvil' Position

Position Blue

1 ▭ 4

4 ⊠ 503(-)

196 x 2

⊠ 25
'Anvil' Position

Filhol plantation

I R O N   T R I A N G L E

Route 14

⊠ 503

Cau Dinh jungle

Trang Bang

Phu Hoa Dong

35 ARVN
(Ranger)

Route 13

1 xx 25

Phu Loi
refugee camp

Route 1

Cu Chi

Phu Cuong

to Saigon
35 miles

N

L A O S

I

CAMBODIA

II

S O U T H   V I E T N A M

III

IV

0   5 km

0   5 miles

to Dau Tieng
airstrip

Operation Junction City FEBRUARY–MAY 1967

Junction City, a corps-level search-and-destroy operation in War Zone C, was the largest U.S. military offensive of the war. U.S. forces consisted of the 1st Infantry Division, with the attached 1st Brigade, 9th Infantry Division; the 25th Infantry Division, with the attached 3rd Brigade, 4th Infantry Division and 196th Light Infantry Brigade; the 173rd Airborne Brigade; and the 11th Armored Cavalry Regiment. South Vietnamese forces included Task Force Alpha's 1st and 5th Vietnamese Marine Corps battalions, TF Wallace's 35th ARVN Ranger Battalion, and the ARVN 3rd Battalion, 1st Cavalry Regiment.

The operation had three main objectives: to search out and destroy the 9th Viet Cong Division and 101st NVA Regiment based in the area; to destroy the Central Office for South Vietnam, the enemy's headquarters in the South; and to establish a Special Forces CIDG camp and airfield at Prek Klok from which to monitor enemy movement.

The area involved was to be cordoned by friendly forces, who would then close in to destroy the enemy forces, supply depots, and base camps caught in the trap. The U.S. 25th Infantry Division's 196th Infantry Brigade would use a heliborne assault to seal the northwestern portion, while its 3rd Brigade, 4th Infantry Division would move overland to seal the southwestern part. TF Wallace and the 1st Brigade, 1st Infantry Division would use helicopter assault to seal the northern portion while the 173rd Airborne Brigade sealed the northeast. The latter attack included the only parachute assault by U.S. forces in the war.

The southeastern portion would be secured by the 1st Infantry Division's 1st Squadron, 4th Cavalry and the 2nd Battalion, 2nd Infantry (Mechanized), while the 1st Brigade, 9th Infantry Division would secure the main supply routes into the operational area. Once the 40-mile cordon was complete, the 11th Armored Cavalry Regiment and the 2nd Brigade, 25th Infantry Division would close in from the open end of the horseshoe-shaped area, compressing and destroying the enemy before them.

On February 22 the cordon was secured with only light enemy contact, and friendly forces began their drive into the horseshoe, uncovering major supply caches but without real incident, except for battles with elements of the 101st NVA and 272nd VC regiments at Prek Klok on February 28 and March 10.

On March 18 the cordon forces were withdrawn and the operation concentrated on the construction of the CIDG camp and airfield, on securing Routes 246 and 244, and on interdicting enemy lines of supply and communication. Three major battles were fought during this phase, all initiated by the enemy. At Ap Bau Bang on March 19–20 a troop of the 3rd Squadron, 5th Cavalry was attacked in its overnight camp by the 2nd and 3rd Battalions of the 273rd VC Regiment, who were repulsed with terrible losses.

On March 21, Fire Support Base Gold near Suoi Tre, manned by the 2nd Battalion, 77th Artillery and the 3rd Battalion, 22nd Infantry, came under heavy enemy attack by the 273rd VC Regiment. The situation became so desperate that the artillery fired "beehive" rounds—a version of the canister grapeshot round, each containing 8,000 steel fleshettes—directly into the enemy ranks. Believing the fire base to be cut off from outside help, the VC troops were taken unawares by the tanks and armored personnel carriers of the 2nd Battalion, 22nd Infantry (Mechanized) and the 2nd Battalion, 34th Armor, and the regiment was decimated.

The final battle was at Ap Gu, where the 1st Battalion, 26th Infantry, commanded by Lieutenant Colonel Alexander M. Haig, had established a night defensive position at Landing Zone George. On April 1 this came under attack by all three battalions of the 271st VC Regiment and elements of the VC 70th Guards Regiment. The attacks were again beaten back with terrible losses.

Primarily a U.S. Army operation, Junction City involved major U.S. Air Force support. The outcome of the operation was mixed. All three regiments of the 9th VC Regiment had been engaged, with 2,728 Viet Cong troops killed and 34 captured. American losses included 282 killed and 1,576 wounded. A CIDG camp had been completed on May 14. But although forced to relocate temporarily to a safe haven in Cambodia, COSVN had not been captured and continued to operate throughout the rest of the war. Enemy activity in War Zone C had been disrupted, but Operation Junction City was not, as some claimed, a turning point in the war.

"One day during a fire fight, for the first time in my life, I heard the cries of the Vietnamese wounded, and I understood them. When somebody gets wounded, they call out for their mothers, their wives, their girlfriends. There I was listening to the VC cry for the same things. That's when the futility of the war really dawned on me."

—U.S. soldier

Arms and supplies are dropped for the 900 members of the 173rd Airborne Brigade sent into the Communist-riddled jungles of the Cambodian border regions in War Zone C to begin Operation Junction City, the first major U.S. combat parachute assault since the Korean War.

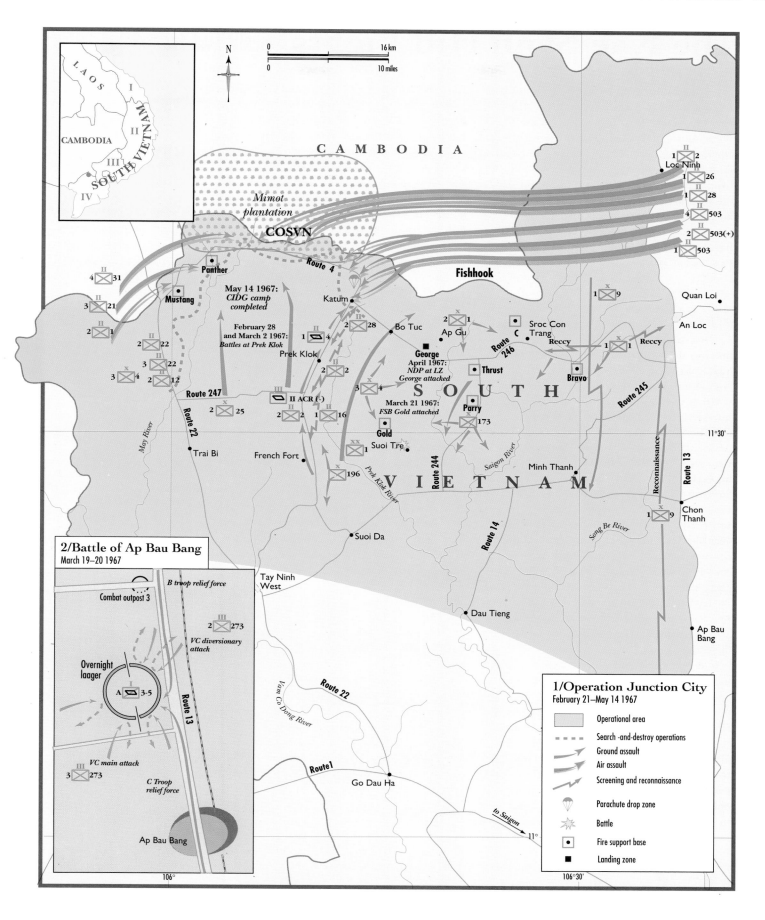

N

0 _____ 16 km
0 _____ 10 miles

LAOS
CAMBODIA
SOUTH VIETNAM
I
II
III
IV

C A M B O D I A

Mimot plantation

COSVN

Route 4

Fishhook

1 [II] 2
Loc Ninh
1 [XX] 26
1 [II] 28
4 [XX] 503
2 [II] 503(+)
1 [XX] 503

4 [II] 31

Panther

3 [II] 21

Mustang

2 [II] 1

May 14 1967:
CIDG camp completed

Katum

1 [X] 9

Quan Loi

An Loc

2 [II] 22

February 28 and March 2 1967:
Battles at Prek Klok

2 [II] 28

Bo Tuc

2 [X] 1
Ap Gu

Sroc Con Trang

1 [X] 1

Reccy   Reccy

C

3 [II] 22

1 [XX] 4

Prek Klok

George
April 1967:
NDP at LZ George attacked

Thrust

Bravo

3 [X] 4   2 [X] 12

1 [XX] 2

2 [III] 2

Route 247

2 [X] 25

III II ACR (-)

2 [XX] 2   1 [XX] 16

3 [X] 4

March 21 1967:
FSB Gold attacked

Parry
173

Route 245

Route 246

S O U T H

Route 244

Route 13

Trai Bi

French Fort

Gold
Suoi Tre

2 [XX] 1

1 [X] 196

Prek Klok River

V I E T N A M

Minh Thanh

11°30'

Reconnaissance

1 [X] 9
Chon Thanh

Suoi Da

Song Be River

Route 14

Saigon River

2/Battle of Ap Bau Bang
March 19–20 1967

Combat outpost 3

B troop relief force

2 [III] 273

VC diversionary attack

Overnight laager

A [I] 3-5

Route 13

VC main attack

3 [III] 273

C Troop relief force

Ap Bau Bang

Tay Ninh West

Dau Tieng

Ap Bau Bang

Vam Co Dong River

Route 22

Route 1

Go Dau Ha

to Saigon

11°

106°   106°30'

1/Operation Junction City
February 21–May 14 1967

Operational area

- - - - Search-and-destroy operations

⟶ Ground assault

⟶ Air assault

⟶ Screening and reconnaissance

⛱ Parachute drop zone

✸ Battle

•⃣ Fire support base

■ Landing zone

The Khe Sanh Hill Fights   APRIL–MAY 1967

Long before it came to worldwide attention during the 1968 siege, Khe Sanh had been of interest to both the U.S. military and the North Vietnamese Army. Located in the northwest corner of Quang Tri Province, in rugged mountainous terrain four miles from the Laotian border and 14 miles south of the DMZ, the Khe Sanh plateau overlooked Route 9, the main east–west artery in the area.

In August 1962, a U.S. Special Forces Civilian Irregular Defense Group camp had been constructed at what was to become the Marine combat base there, from which to monitor enemy infiltration down the nearby Ho Chi Minh Trail in Laos. In May 1964, they were joined by a Marine radio intelligence unit, which established an intercept station eight miles to the north, on Tiger Tooth Mountain, officially Hill 1015 (i.e. 1015 meters high), the highest terrain feature in northern I Corps.

When the site came under enemy attack in July 1964, the Marines were withdrawn, and it was almost two years before they reluctantly returned. This was at the insistence of General William C. Westmoreland, who had a special interest in Khe Sanh. He saw it as the logical jumping-off point for ground operations across Laos to cut the trail and isolate the southern battlefield, an operation both he and the Joint Chiefs of Staff in Washington had recommended several times to the president, without success. The Marines did not share his enthusiasm, and it was only after constant prodding that the 1st Battalion, 4th Marines were dispatched to Khe Sanh in April 1966. When a sweep of the area met no enemy resistance, they were withdrawn on May 1.

In September 1966, again at Westmoreland's urgings, the Marines returned, this time to open a combat base. One of their first acts was to call in the Seabees, Navy Construction Battalion 10, to expand and resurface the airstrip there. When the 1st Battalion, 3rd Marines moved into the base, the CIDG camp relocated to Lang Vei, six miles to the southwest. Patrolling out to the limits of their artillery coverage, the Marines still made little contact with the enemy, and leaving behind a single rifle company to garrison the base, the bulk of them withdrew in February 1967.

On April 24, 1967, a patrol from Company B, 1st Battalion, 9th Marines prematurely triggered an attempt by the 325C NVA Division to overrun the base. The Khe Sanh "Hill Fights" had begun. On April 25, the 3rd Battalion, 3rd Marines (3/3) were committed to the fight and began an assault on Hill 861, the main NVA avenue of attack. On April 26, they were reinforced by the 2nd Battalion, 3rd Marines (2/3). On April 28 the Marines launched a two-battalion assault to clear Hill 861 and continue the attack to seize Hill 881.

The enemy had withdrawn from Hill 861, but continued to put up stiff resistance on Hill 881, and it was not until May 5 that the hill was finally taken. The NVA 325C Division withdrew toward North Vietnam and Laos, and on May 11 the hill fights officially came to an end. The NVA had left 940 bodies on the battlefield, while U.S. losses stood at 155 killed and another 425 wounded.

While the Marine infantry had fought valiantly, "much of the credit for overwhelming the enemy force," said the official Marine history, "goes to the supporting arm." The fighter bombers of the 1st Marine Aircraft Wing had flown more than 1,100 sorties, expending more than 1,900 tons of bombs. In addition, 23 U.S. Air Force B-52 bomber strikes hit enemy troop concentrations and lines of supply. Artillery, including the Army's 175mm guns at Camp Carroll and the Rockpile 10 miles to the east, fired more than 25,000 rounds in support of the Marines at Khe Sanh.

"We got back. We was all out of breath. The first thing they did was, they started laughing. I'm looking at these nuts and then I'm laughing with them. That's when you find out that laughing at death is laughing that you made it alive. You faced it, dealt with it and survived. All of a sudden, it's a joke."

—U.S. soldier

Less than 10 miles from North Vietnam, Marines await evacuation from Hill 881. Driven from the interior of South Vietnam, General Giap instigated attacks in the DMZ area in the hope of regaining the initiative.

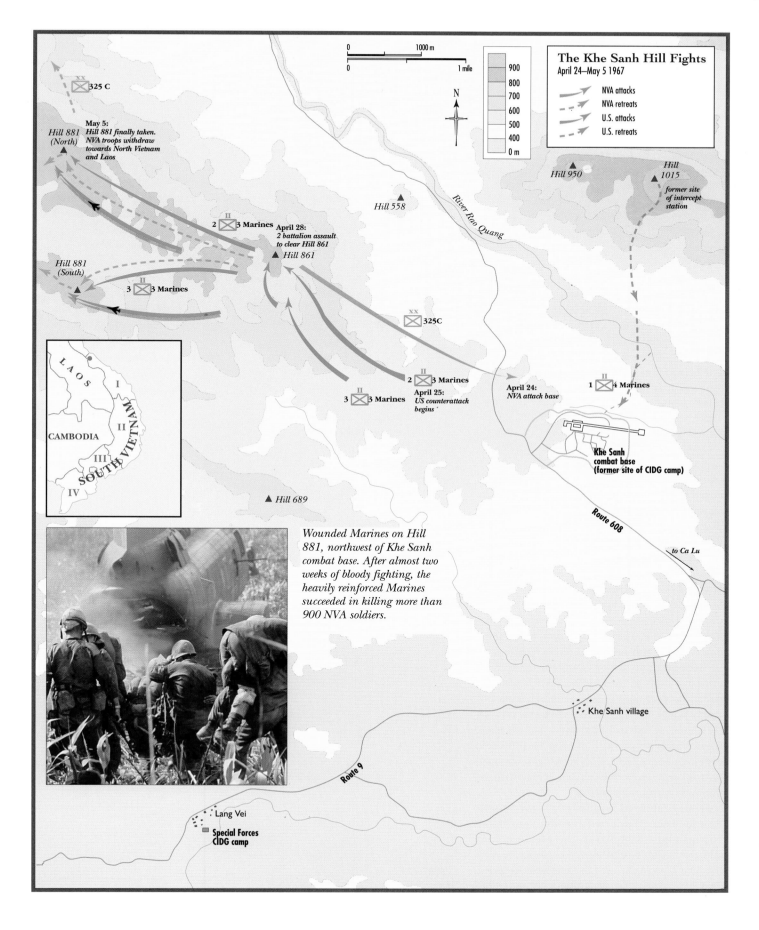

0   1000 m
0   1 mile

	900
	800
	700
	600
	500
	400
	0 m

N

The Khe Sanh Hill Fights
April 24–May 5 1967

NVA attacks
NVA retreats
U.S. attacks
U.S. retreats

XX 325 C

Hill 881 (North)

May 5:
*Hill 881 finally taken.
NVA troops withdraw
towards North Vietnam
and Laos*

Hill 950

Hill 1015

*former site
of intercept
station*

Hill 558

River Rao Quang

2 3 Marines

April 28:
*2 battalion assault
to clear Hill 861*

Hill 861

Hill 881 (South)

3 3 Marines

325C

2 3 Marines

3 3 Marines

April 25:
US counterattack begins

April 24:
NVA attack base

1 4 Marines

Khe Sanh
combat base
(former site of CIDG camp)

LAOS

I

CAMBODIA

II

SOUTH VIETNAM

III

IV

Hill 689

Route 608

to Ca Lu

Khe Sanh village

*Wounded Marines on Hill
881, northwest of Khe Sanh
combat base. After almost two
weeks of bloody fighting, the
heavily reinforced Marines
succeeded in killing more than
900 NVA soldiers.*

Route 9

Lang Vei

Special Forces
CIDG camp

Riverine Operations MAY 1967

The American equivalent of the French *dinas-saut* (Division navale d'assaut) forces in the First Indochina War was the U.S. Navy's River Patrol Force (Task Force 116). Its mission to deny the enemy the use of the 3,000 nautical miles of rivers, canals, and small streams in South Vietnam, including the Mekong delta and other inland waterways, began in January 1965 with Operation Game Warden.

In June 1967, the Mobile Riverine Force became operational, supplementing the River Patrol Force with a heavier combat capability. A joint U.S. Army and Navy operation, it consist-ed of the Navy's Riverine Assault Force (Task Force 117) and the 2nd Brigade of the Army's 9th Infantry Division, which constructed a base camp at Dong Tam (meaning "united hearts and minds") near My Tho in the Mekong delta. The brigade consisted of the 3rd and 4th battal-ions, 47th Infantry, the 3rd Battalion, 60th Infantry and the 3rd Battalion, 39th Artillery, which was equipped with floating firing plat-forms for its 105mm howitzers.

Operating in the Mekong delta in IV Corps and in the Rung Sat Special Zone (RSSZ) at the mouth of the Saigon River, the Mobile Riverine Force was often combined with South Viet-namese forces, including the ARVN 7th and 21st divisions, VNN riverine forces, and South Vietnamese Marine Corps units.

Task Force 117 was organized into four 400-man river assault squadrons, each with several armored troop carriers and five armored gun-boats, called Monitors after their American Civil War predecessors. These were armed with .50-caliber machine guns, 20mm and 40mm guns, and 81mm mortars, and were protected by bar and plate armor. The task force main-tained a mobile riverine base with self-pro-pelled barracks-ships and barracks-barges that could house two of the Army's three infantry battalions, as well as LSTs, repair facilities, and tugs. The base could move up to 150 miles within 24 hours and could launch combat oper-ations with its 5,000-man force within 30 minutes of dropping anchor.

From June 1967 to July 1968, the Mobile Riverine Force conducted a series of operations codenamed Coronado in the Mekong delta and the RSSZ. While no major battles ensued, the Viet Cong grip on the delta was loosened. The 263rd and 516th Main Force VC battalions

were pushed back from the population centers into the remote Plain of Reeds, and Highway 4, the main artery through the delta, was re-opened for farm to market traffic.

The Mobile Riverine Force would later play a major role in the U.S. Navy's Southeast Asia Lake, Ocean, River, and Delta (SEALORDS) operations between 1968 and 1971.

"Not since the Mississippi flotilla was deployed to fight the Civil War battles of Vicksburg and Shiloh had the U.S. Army found use for an assault force designed especially for river warfare. But the war in Vietnam has seen the revival of many tactics and weapons of earlier days, and last week a U.S. river-borne assault force went on the attack in the Mekong delta, its most important vehicle an unwieldy-looking craft that bears a striking resemblance to the ironclads of a century ago."

—Newsweek,
July 3, 1967

A U.S. Navy inshore patrol craft (PCF), or "Swift" boat, returns to its mobile riverine base after patrolling the waters of the Mekong delta.

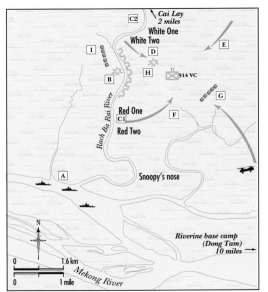

3/Operation Coronado V
September 15 1967

A	3rd Battalion, 60th Infantry and 11th River Assault Squadron proceed up Rach Ba Rai River
B	3rd Battalion attacked by VC
C1	Main section of convoy is forced back to Red One and Red Two beaches
C2	Remaining boat reaches White One beach
D	Main section of 3rd Battalion reach White One and White Two
E	5th Battalion, 60th Infantry link up with 3rd Battalion, 60th Infantry
F	3rd Battalion, 47th Infantry pushes north from Red One and Red Two
G	2nd Battalion, 60th Infantry takes up blocking position to the south-east
H	3rd Battalion, 60th Infantry encounters heavy resistance as it moves to link up with 5th Battalion, 60th Infantry
I	ARVN troops take up blocking positions on western bank of river

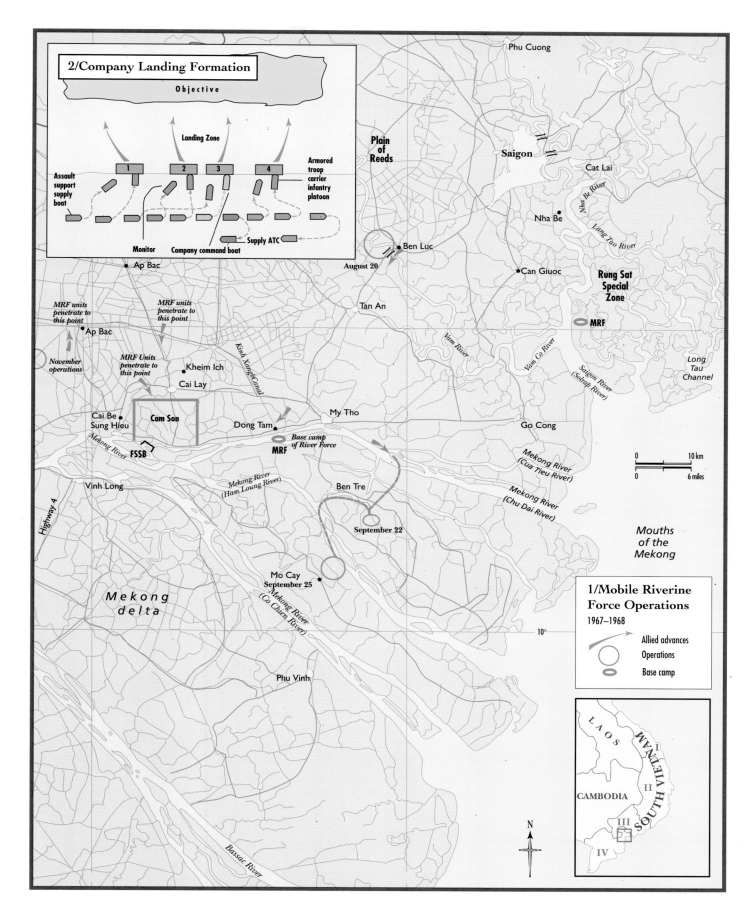

2/Company Landing Formation

Objective

Landing Zone

Assault support supply boat

Armored troop carrier infantry platoon

1   2   3   4

Monitor

Company command boat

Supply ATC

Phu Cuong

Plain of Reeds

Saigon

Cat Lai

Nha Be

Ben Luc

Can Giuoc

Rung Sat Special Zone

Tan An

MRF

Ap Bac

Long Tau Channel

MRF units penetrate to this point

MRF units penetrate to this point

Ap Bac

November operations

MRF Units penetrate to this point

Kheim Ich

Cai Lay

Kinh Xang Canal

Vam River

Vam Co River

Saigon River (Sohrab River)

Nha Be River

Vang Tao River

Cai Be
Sung Hieu

Cam Son

Dong Tam

My Tho

Go Cong

Mekong River

FSSB

MRF

Base camp of River Force

Mekong River (Cua Tieu River)

Mekong River (Chu Dai River)

Vinh Long

Mekong River (Ham Luong River)

Ben Tre

September 22

Mouths of the Mekong

Highway 4

Mekong delta

Mo Cay
September 25

Mekong River (Co Chien River)

10°

Phu Vinh

Bassac River

1/Mobile Riverine Force Operations

1967–1968

→ Allied advances

◯ Operations

⬭ Base camp

N

LAOS

CAMBODIA

SOUTH VIETNAM

I
II
III
IV

0   10 km
0   6 miles

CORDS MAY 1967

In the aftermath of Operation Junction City, it became obvious that conventional search-and-destroy operations were not the complete answer to the Vietnam War. While major enemy units had been pushed back from the main population areas, little had been done to extend the control of the South Vietnamese government (GVN), despite a number of "pacification" efforts. To remedy this situation, on May 9, 1967, President Lyndon B. Johnson appointed a civilian, Robert W. Komer, to the post of deputy commander of MACV, which carried the rank of ambassador.

Charged with overseeing the "other war," Komer created an entirely new organization called Civil Operations and Revolutionary Development Support (CORDS), which imposed a single unified management on the U.S. pacification effort and provided a single channel of advice to the GVN. Although outnumbered six to one by their military colleagues, the 1,000 U.S. civilians assigned to CORDS held most of the top jobs.

"Soldiers served directly under civilians and vice versa at all levels," Komer noted. "Personnel were drawn from all the military services, and from State, AID [Agency for International Development], CIA [Central Intelligence Agency], USIA [United States Information Agency], and the White House. A MACV general staff section was created under a civilian assistant chief of staff [and] four regional deputies for CORDS served under the U.S. corps level commanders. The cutting edge was unified civil-military advisory teams in all 250 districts and 44 provinces."

CORDS had two operating principles. The first was the long-term protection of the population from Viet Cong terror and intimidation. The second was assistance to the Saigon government in winning the "hearts and minds" of the people and in garnering their support. To that end, Komer was granted responsibility for the support and training of the Popular Forces, or village home guards, and the Regional Forces, or provincial militia, who the Americans had nicknamed "Ruff Puffs."

Komer also initiated the Hamlet Evaluation System, which attempted to measure the progress of the pacification effort. CORDS advisers had to rate the thousands of South Vietnamese villages against 18 factors. "In spite of its deficiencies," wrote Lieutenant General Phillip B. Davidson, the MACV chief of intelligence at the time, "as a general guide to the progress of pacification, it proved useful."

Komer was replaced in November 1968 by Ambassador William E. Colby, who later led the CIA from 1973 to 1976. To stress the need for more civilian involvement in the pacification effort, Colby changed the name of the organization to Civil Operations and *Rural* Development Support. He also expedited the training and equipping of the RF and the PF, as well as the newly created People's Self Defense Forces (PSDF), by distributing—with the approval of South Vietnamese president Nguyen Van Thieu—some 500,000 weapons to the countryside. By the end of 1969, the number of village-level PF troops had risen to 215,000 and the number of province-level RF troops had risen to 260,000. The PSDF had grown to include more than 400,000 armed villagers, and now surpassed in size the 400,000-man ARVN.

In June 1971, Colby was replaced by his deputy, George Jackson, who commanded CORDS until its dissolution in the Paris accords in January 1973. While the RF/PF and the PSDF were successful in operations against local VC guerrillas, who had practically disappeared from the battlefield after their abortive Tet uprising in 1968, they were no match for the tanks and heavy artillery of the cross-border NVA multi-division blitzkrieg that brought the war to a close in 1975.

CORDS was one of the most successful programs of the war, but, as Colby noted, "the rise in the antiwar movment after Tet 1968, and its increasing support by the American public [driven by] a feeling of frustration ... that the use of American military force in Vietnam had been ineffective, brutalizing, and costly in the blood of Americans and Vietnamese beyond any worthy objective" obscured that fact. CORDS' gradual post-Tet success "fatally lagged behind the American public's rapidly growing perception that the Vietnam enterprise was an exercise in futility."

A soldier stands guard in a South Vietnamese village. The level of protection afforded to rural communities fell dramatically during the Tet Offensive, as ARVN battalions shifted from pacification to urban fighting. By late 1968, however, the number of villages deemed "relatively secure" had risen from 60 to 76 percent.

"Armed with an organization, a working concept, and operating strategies, in the summer of 1967 Komer attacked the pacification problem head-on. But as so often happens, the Augean stable of pacification could not be cleaned overnight, even with a Hercules like 'Blowtorch' Komer doing the cleaning ... The CORDS organization of some 6,500 people had to be welded together and made operable—no small task."

—Lieutenant General Phillip B. Davidson

1/Summary of ARVN and VNMC Force Structure (Improvement and Modernization Program)

MAJOR ELEMENTS	end of June					
	68	69	70	71	72	73
INFANTRY						
Infantry Battalion	26	133	133	133	105¹	105
Infantry Regiment HQ	32	33	33	33	35	35
Infantry Division HQ	10	10	10	10	11	11
AIRBORNE						
Airborne Battalion	9	9	9	9	9	9
Airborne Brigade HQ	3	3	3	3	3	3
Airborne Division HQ	1	1	1	1	1	1
MARINE						
Battalion	6	6	9	9	9	9
Brigade HQ	2	2	3	3	3	3
Division HQ	-	-	1	1	1	1
RANGER						
Battalion	20	20	20	20	21	21
Border Defense Battalion	-	-	-	37	33	33
Ranger Group HQ	-	-	-	7	17	17
ARTILLERY						
105-mm Battalion	24	35	43	43	44	44
155-mm Battalion	6	12	15	15	15	15
175-mm Battalion	-	-	-	-	2	4
ADA Battalion	-	-	-	-	1	4
105-mm Section	-	-	-	100	176	176
ARMORED CAVALRY						
Cavalry Squadron (separate)	11	16	7	7	7	7
Cavalry Squadon (division)	-	-	10	10	11	11
Medium Tank Battalion	-	-	-	-	1	3
Armored Brigade HQ	-	2	2	3	4	4

MAJOR ELEMENTS	end of June					
	68	69	70	71	72	73
ENGINEER						
Combat Engineer Battalion (division)	10	10	10	10	11	12
Combat Engineer Battalion (separate)	13	13	12	12	12	12
Combat Engineer Group HQ	4	4	4	4	4	4
Engineer Battalion, Construction	8	10	13	17	17	17
Engineer Construction Group HQ	2	2	3	4	4	4
TRANSPORT COMPANIES						
Light Truck	21	30	31	31	32	30
Medium Truck	4	5	7	7	8	10
Medium Boat Group	1	5	5	5	5	5
Heavy Boat Group	-	-	1	1	1	1
REGIONAL FORCES						
Company	1050	1407	1645	1703	1669	1810
Group HQ	-	-	232	268	254	-
Battalion HQ	-	-	31	47	61	360
Sector Tactical Command Post	-	-	-	-	14	45
Boat Company	23	23	23	24	20	20
Weapon Platoon (separate)	-	44	43	38	24	-
Mechanical Platoon	47	50	50	50	50	50
POPULAR FORCES						
Rifle Platoon	4560	4861	6969	7560	7872	8186
MANEUVER BATTALION²	173	185	189	189	164	166
ARTILLERY BATTALION³	30	47	58	58	61	64

¹ No reduction in total companies. Converted from 4 battalions of three rifle companies per battalion to three battalions of 4 companies per battalion

² Includes Divisional Cavalry squadrons and Marine Corps battalions

³ Does not include Air defense artillery

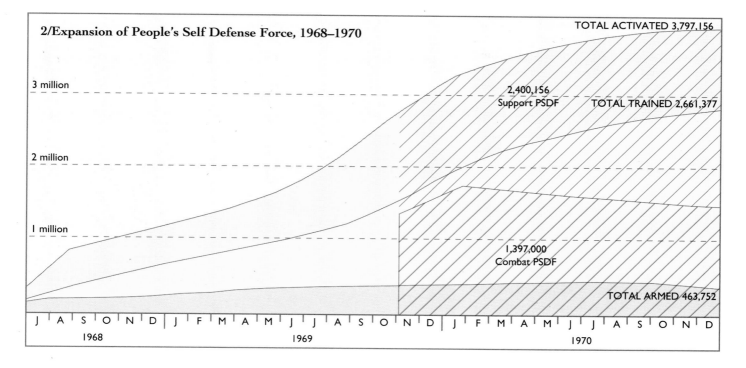

2/Expansion of People's Self Defense Force, 1968–1970

TOTAL ACTIVATED 3,797,156

2,400,156 Support PSDF   TOTAL TRAINED 2,661,377

1,397,000 Combat PSDF

TOTAL ARMED 463,752

3 million

2 million

1 million

J A S O N D	J F M A M J J A S O N D	J F M A M J J A S O N D
1968	1969	1970

The Siege of Con Thien SEPTEMBER–OCTOBER 1967

One of the hallmarks of the Vietnam War was its remarkable diversity. In 1967, for example, while Army and Navy forces in IV Corps were conducting riverine operations against elusive black-pajama-clad VC guerrillas in the marshes of the Mekong delta and Army forces in III Corps were engaged in search-and-destroy operations in the jungles of the Iron Triangle, the besieged Marines at the shell-cratered moonscape at Con Thien in I Corps were reliving the trench warfare of World War I.

Con Thien, which means "hill of angels" in Vietnamese, was located 14 miles inland from the South China Sea and two miles south of the DMZ between North and South Vietnam. On a hill rising about 520 feet above the flat countryside, the outpost offered excellent observation over one of the enemy's principal supply routes into South Vietnam. Con Thien was also the western anchor for the so-called McNamara Line of electronic sensors, under construction at that time.

Only large enough to accommodate a reinforced infantry battalion, the outpost came under ground attack in July 1967 by NVA forces operating out of the supposedly neutral DMZ area and by intense artillery fire. Intelligence estimated that the NVA had some 130 artillery pieces emplaced in well-fortified positions along the north bank of the Ben Hai River, which bisected the five-mile wide buffer zone. These included 152mm gun howitzers and 130mm guns with a 31,000-meter range that exceeded everything in the Marine arsenal.

Driven back by a series of Marine spoiling attacks in the DMZ area, the NVA tried to overrun Con Thien again in September. Held by the 3rd Battalion, 9th Marine Regiment, the outpost was attacked by elements of the 324B NVA Division. When the ground attack failed, the NVA began an intense artillery bombardment, which reached a peak during the week of September 19–27, when 3,077 mortar, artillery, and rocket rounds struck the outpost.

To counter this violent barrage, the 105mm, 155mm, and 8-inch howitzers and 155mm guns of the 11th, 12th, and 13th Marine artillery regiments and III Marine Amphibious Force artillery were reinforced by naval gunfire support from warships offshore and by the Army's 2nd Battalion, 94th Artillery and 8th Battalion, 4th Artillery, whose 175mm self-propelled guns

with their 32,700-meter range matched those of the NVA. During the 1967 artillery duel, the NVA fired 42,190 rounds, while U.S. forces replied with 281,110 rounds. This artillery support was augmented by massive air strikes by Air Force, Navy, and Marine tactical fighter bombers as well as Air Force B-52 strategic bombers with 60,000-pound bomb loads. In Operation Neutralize, 790 B-52 sorties were flown in support of Con Thien, and by October 31 the siege had been broken.

Con Thien was initially portrayed by the media as another Dien Bien Phu, but as General William C. Westmoreland wryly observed, "If comparable in any way to Dien Bien Phu, it was a Dien Bien Phu in reverse. The North Vietnamese lost well over 2,000 men, while Con Thien continued to stand as a barrier to enemy movement." NVA General Vo Nguyen Giap evidently did not see it that way, for four months later he would try again with the siege of the Marine base at Khe Sanh.

"Monsoon rains added to the misery. During the sweltering 100-degree plus days in the summer, the red dust, indigenous to Con Thien, clogged men's nostrils and throats. Now, with the arrival of the torrential downpours, the reddish dust became quagmires of knee-deep mud that could 'suck a Marine's boondockers off.' However the oozing mire did possess one advantage. When enemy shells buried in the mud less shrapnel would be dispersed."

—Al Hemingway,
A Place of Angels

A U.S. Air Force F-105 Thunderchief fires a deadly hail of rockets as it swoops over the rugged South Vietnamese countryside.

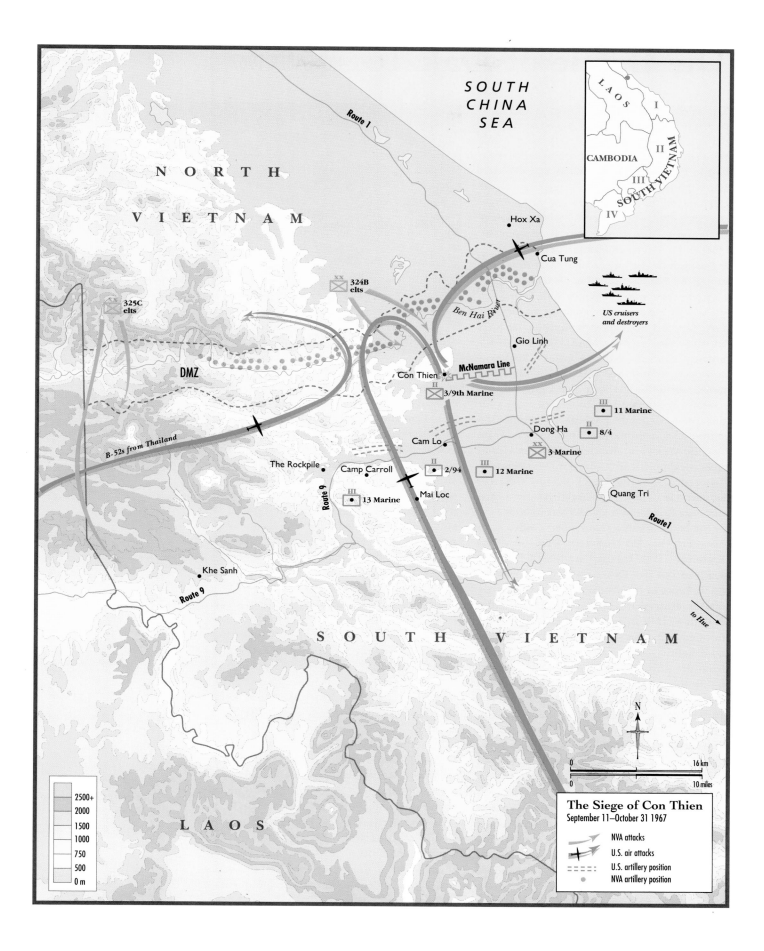

SOUTH
CHINA
SEA

NORTH
VIETNAM

Route 1

Hox Xa

LAOS

CAMBODIA

I

II

III

SOUTH VIETNAM

IV

Cua Tung

XX 324B
elts

XX 325C
elts

Ben Hai River

US cruisers
and destroyers

DMZ

Gio Linh

Con Thien

McNamara Line

B-52s from Thailand

XX 3/9th Marine

III 11 Marine

The Rockpile

Cam Lo

Dong Ha

II 8/4

XX 3 Marine

Route 9

Camp Carroll

II 2/94

III 12 Marine

III 13 Marine

Mai Loc

Quang Tri

Route 1

Khe Sanh

Route 9

S O U T H   V I E T N A M

to Hue

L A O S

N

2500+
2000
1500
1000
750
500
0 m

0   16 km
0   10 miles

The Siege of Con Thien
September 11–October 31 1967

→ NVA attacks
✈ U.S. air attacks
- - - U.S. artillery position
• NVA artillery position

The Battle of Dak To   NOVEMBER 1967

The NVA attack on Dak To in II Corps in November 1967 was the last of a series of "border battles" that began two months earlier with the siege of Con Thien in I Corps and continued in October with attacks on Song Be and Loc Ninh in III Corps. These attacks were part of Phase I of the *Tong Cong Kich–Tong Khoi Ngia* (General Offensive/General Uprising) strategy designed to lure U.S. forces away from the cities and into South Vietnam's periphery.

Located in the rugged mountainous area along the Laotian and Cambodian borders, where peaks rise to 6,000 feet, Dak To was the site of a U.S. Special Forces camp. In October 1967, intelligence reported that the 1st NVA Division, with its 24th, 32nd, 66th and 174th Infantry regiments and 40th Artillery Regiment had occupied the hills near Dak To and was preparing for an attack on that camp and the nearby camp at Ben Het. Instead of waiting for the assault, General Creighton W. Abrams, the acting U.S. commander in Vietnam while General William C. Westmoreland was conferring with political leaders in Washington, ordered a spoiling attack by the U.S. 4th Infantry Division, reinforced by the 173rd Airborne Brigade and six ARVN battalions.

The battle began on November 3 with a clash between the 4th Infantry Division's 3rd Battalion, 12th Infantry and NVA regulars south of Dak To. Other firefights followed, as the U.S. began to construct fire bases throughout the area. As the battle intensified, the 3rd Battalion, 12th Infantry assaulted the heavily fortified Hill 1338 south of Dak To, and after hard fighting, drove the 32nd NVA Regiment from the position. Similarly, after a four-day battle the ARVN 3rd and 9th Airborne battalions drove the NVA 24th Regiment from Hill 1416 to the northeast.

To cover their retreat the enemy committed their reserves, the 174th NVA Regiment, to a blocking position on Hill 875 to the southwest of Dak To. On November 19, the 2nd Battalion, 503rd Airborne Infantry (2/503) was ordered to take the hill, which the NVA had turned into a fortress. Stalled by the network of undergound tunnels, reinforced bunkers and fortified trench lines, the 2/503 was relieved on November 20 by the 4th Battalion, 503rd Airborne Infantry (4/503).

After hard fighting the hill was finally taken

on Thanksgiving Day, earning the unit the Presidential Unit Citation for bravery. The NVA broke contact and pulled back into its sanctuaries in Laos and Cambodia and the battle of Dak To officially ended on December 1. Enemy losses were put at 1,644 killed at a cost of 289 U.S. and 73 ARVN dead. As in earlier battles, this disparity reflected the intensity of U.S. fire support. But although U.S. artillery fired more than 170,000 rounds during the operation, MACV estimated that 70 percent of the enemy casualties were caused by air strikes. Tactical fighter bombers launched some 2,100 bomb, rocket, and napalm strikes while B-52 bombers flew an additional 228 sorties.

"Along with the gallantry and tenacity of our soldiers," said General Westmoreland, "our tremendously successful air logistic operation was the key to the victory." Air Force C-130 Hercules transports flew the 173rd Airborne Brigade to Dak To and delivered more than 5,000 tons of supplies during the battle, losing two C-130s on the airstrip to enemy fire in the process.

"The border battles were North Vietnamese failures," wrote Lieutenant General Phillip B. Davidson, MACV's chief of Intelligence. "The principal failure of [NVA General Vo Nguyen] Giap's diversionary battles was their inability to draw American units and command attention to the peripheries of South Vietnam. The strategic mobility of the Americans permitted them to move to the borders, smash Giap's attack, and redeploy back to the interior in a mobile reserve posture."

Amidst the chaos and paraphernalia of war, exhausted American troops converge on Hill 875, captured by paratroopers after some of the fiercest battles of the conflict.

"The thing that I can't forget about Nam was the smell of it. The smell. You smelled the napalm and you smelled the flesh burning. That will live with me to the end of my days. Nothing smells like Vietnam smells."

—U.S. soldier

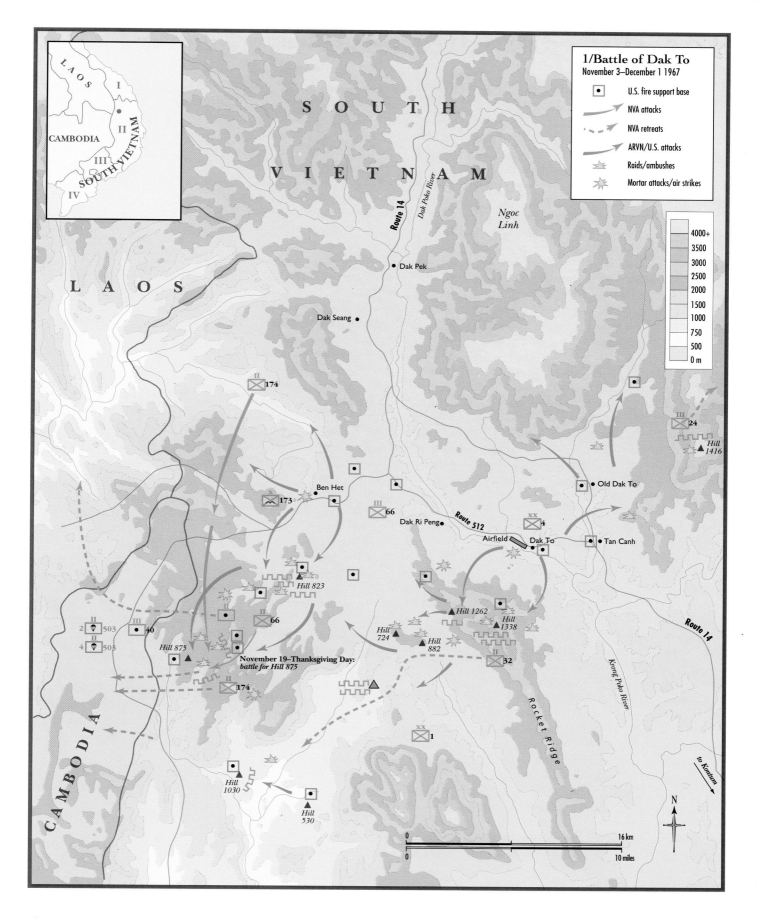

LAOS

CAMBODIA

SOUTH VIETNAM

I

II

III

IV

1/Battle of Dak To
November 3–December 1 1967

⊡ U.S. fire support base

NVA attacks

NVA retreats

ARVN/U.S. attacks

Raids/ambushes

Mortar attacks/air strikes

4000+
3500
3000
2500
2000
1500
1000
750
500
0 m

S O U T H

V I E T N A M

Ngoc Linh

Dak Poko River

Route 14

L A O S

Dak Pek

Dak Seang

174

Ben Het

173

66

Dak Ri Peng

Route 512

Old Dak To

4

Airfield   Dak To

Tan Canh

III
24
Hill 1416

Hill 823

66

2 503
4 503

40

Hill 875

174

November 19–Thanksgiving Day:
battle for Hill 875

Hill 1262

Hill 1338

Hill 724

Hill 882

32

1

Hill 1030

Hill 530

Krong Poko River

Rocket Ridge

Route 14

to Kontum

0   16 km
0   10 miles

N

C A M B O D I A

The 1968 Tet Offensive   JANUARY–MARCH 1968

The North Vietnamese 1968 Tet Offensive was the most decisive battle of the war. It put an end to the illusion that U.S. intervention could result in an independent South Vietnam free of Communist aggression and was the beginning of the end of U.S. involvement, despite the fact that the United States and its Vietnamese ally won decisively on the battlefield.

The Tet Offensive—officially Phase II of the TCK/TKN (*Tong Cong Kich/Tong Khoi Ngia*, or General Offensive/General Uprising) campaign that had begun with the "border wars" the previous September—was an overwhelming political and military defeat for North Vietnam, sounding the death knell for their Viet Cong guerrillas. In Communist theory the "General Uprising" had an almost mystical quality, marking the time when the people would rise up and throw off the yoke of their oppressors. The idea had been incorporated into North Vietnamese Communist Party dogma as early as 1947, and in 1967 the Politburo in Hanoi was convinced that the time was ripe.

It was deluding itself. No ARVN forces defected, and instead of flocking to the Communists, the South Vietnamese people fled to the protection of the allies. In the wake of the Tet Offensive, many Communist soldiers and units also defected to the allied side. These desertions reached a peak in 1969, when 47,087 Viet Cong guerrillas took advantage of the "Chieu Hoi" ("Open Arms") government amnesty program which had been instituted by President Diem in 1963.

Ordering their guerrillas to emerge from hiding, the VC and NVA forces in the South launched a countrywide assault on the cities of South Vietnam on the morning of January 31, 1968, taking advantage of the Tet (lunar New Year) ceasefire then in effect. A premature attack in II Corps on January 30 had put allied forces on alert, but no one anticipated the magnitude of the attack.

About 84,000 VC and NVA troops mounted simultaneous assaults on 36 of the 44 provincial capitals, 5 of the 6 autonomous cities, including Saigon and Hue, 64 of the 242 district capitals, and 50 hamlets. With many of the ARVN troops on holiday leave, the North Vietnamese enjoyed initial successes. Within days, however, most of the attacks in the smaller towns had been turned back. Heavy fighting continued

for a while in Kontum and Ban Me Thuot in II Corps and in Can Tho and Ben Tre in IV Corps, and protracted battles would rage in Saigon and Hue, but the attackers were unable to hold any of the cities, and the remnants of the VC and NVA forces withdrew in defeat.

In the first half of 1968 the Communists had lost an estimated 120,000 men, over half of their total strength when the Tet Offensive began. At the height of the battle, in January and February, 45,000 were killed and 5,800 captured in their fighting elements alone. The Viet Cong was practically annihilated, and the war was henceforth almost entirely an NVA affair. Some believe that the NVA deliberately sacrificed their southern brethren in order to lessen any postwar competition for power, like the Red Army in 1945, which instigated the Warsaw Uprising but held back while the Nazis slaughtered the Polish partisans.

Allied losses included 1,001 Americans and 2,082 South Vietnamese and allied troops. But despite this resounding military victory, the United States had suffered an irreversible political defeat. After Tet the U.S. focus was on disengagement rather than victory. Having supported the war for 31 months—the same length of time that they had supported the U.S. ground war in World War II—the American people began to run out of patience in October 1967. "Either win the damn thing or get out," was the prevailing sentiment.

The Tet Offensive three months later provided evidence that the U.S. government had no plans to do either. It did not begin to equal earlier military disasters, such as Pearl Harbor in 1941, the Battle of the Bulge in 1944, or the Korean War in 1950. But in each of these cases the president of the time had stepped in and rallied the American people, whereas in the wake of the Tet Offensive President Lyndon B. Johnson hid in the White House. While his troops had won on the battlefield, he had been psychologically defeated.

On March 31, 1968, President Johnson made a national television address in which he announced a unilateral halt to the bombing of North Vietnam except for the area north of the Demilitarized Zone, and in which he announced that he would not seek reelection. The United States had managed to snatch defeat from the jaws of victory.

Anguished South Vietnamese refugees flee across an improvised bridge over the Perfume River in Hue.

"The Viet Cong lost the best of a generation of resistance fighters, and after Tet increasing numbers of North Vietnamese had to be sent south to fill the ranks. The war became increasingly a conventional battle and less an insurgency. Because the people of the cities did not rise up against the foreigners and puppets at Tet—indeed they gave little support to the attack force—the Communist claim to moral and political authority in South Vietnam suffered a serious blow."

—Don Oberdorfer,
Tet!

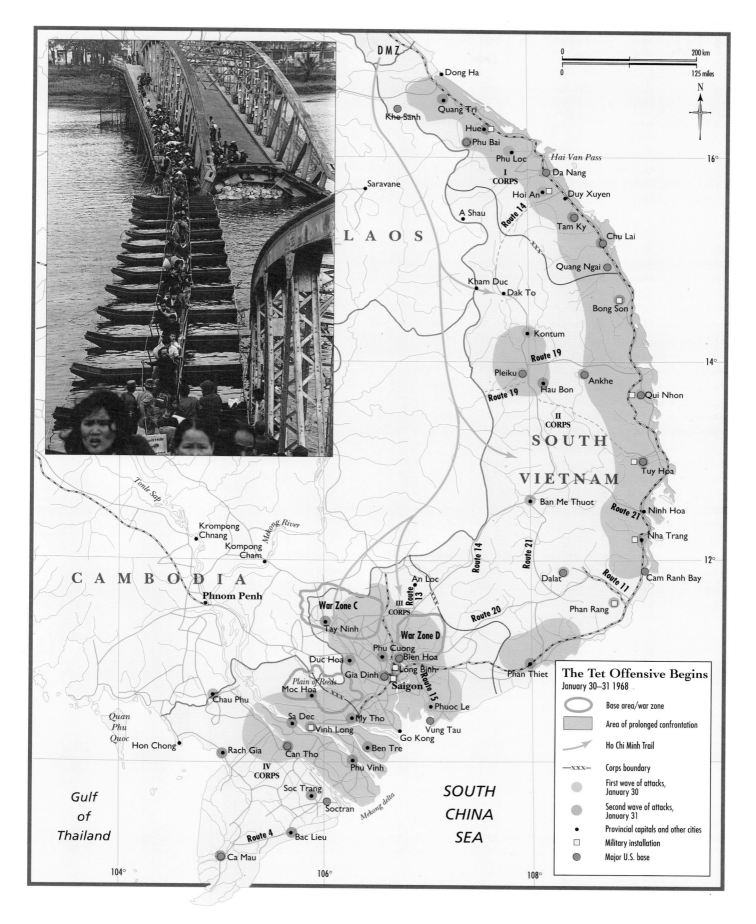

DMZ

Dong Ha

Khe Sanh   Quang Tri

Hue

Phu Bai

Phu Loc   *Hai Van Pass*   16°

I   Da Nang
CORPS

Saravane   Hoi An   Duy Xuyen

A Shau   Route 14   Tam Ky

LAOS   Chu Lai

Quang Ngai

Kham Duc   Dak To   Bong Son

Kontum

Route 19

Pleiku   Ankhe   14°

Route 19   Hau Bon   Qui Nhon

II
CORPS   SOUTH

VIETNAM   Tuy Hoa

Ban Me Thuot   Route 21   Ninh Hoa

Nha Trang

Route 14   Route 21   12°

CAMBODIA   Dalat   Route 11   Cam Ranh Bay

Krompong
Chnang   An Loc

Kompong
Cham   Route 20   Phan Rang

Phnom Penh   Route
13
III
CORPS

War Zone C

Tay Ninh   **War Zone D**

Phu Cuong
Duc Hoa   Bien Hoa   Phan Thiet
Gia Dinh   Long Binh
Plain of Reeds   **Saigon**   Route 15

Chau Phu   Moc Hoa   Phuoc Le

Quan   Sa Dec   My Tho   Vung Tau
Phu   Vinh Long   Go Kong
Quoc   Hon Chong

Rach Gia   Ben Tre
Can Tho
IV   Phu Vinh
CORPS

Gulf   Soc Trang
of
Thailand   Soctran   *Mekong delta*

Route 4   Bac Lieu   SOUTH
CHINA
Ca Mau   SEA

Tonle Sap   *Mekong River*

0   200 km
0   125 miles

N

The Tet Offensive Begins
January 30–31 1968

⬭   Base area/war zone

▨   Area of prolonged confrontation

➤   Ho Chi Minh Trail

—xxx—   Corps boundary

●   First wave of attacks,
January 30

●   Second wave of attacks,
January 31

•   Provincial capitals and other cities

□   Military installation

●   Major U.S. base

104°   106°   108°

The Battle for Saigon, Tet 1968   JANUARY–MARCH

Among the most vivid, and the most misleading, pictures of the Tet Offensive were the print and television shots of the fighting at the U.S. Embassy in downtown Saigon. At 2:45 A.M. on January 31, 1968, a 19-man platoon from the Viet Cong C-10 Sapper Battalion blew a hole in the embassy wall and entered the grounds. Although all were killed before they could enter the chancery building itself, pictures of that skirmish gave the false impression that Saigon had been overrun.

Although South Vietnam's capital was a main target of the Tet Offensive, it was never in danger of falling. The reason for this was the foresight of the "savior of Saigon," Lieutenant General Fred C. Weyand. The commander of II Field Force Vietnam, the corps-level headquarters at nearby Long Binh, which was responsible for Saigon's defenses, he had positioned his forces to repel the attack.

Weyand, who was the intelligence officer for General Joseph "Vinegar Joe" Stilwell in the China–Burma–India theater in World War II, had sensed early on that something was not right. On January 10, three weeks before the attack began, he asked for and received permission from General William C. Westmoreland to pull his combat forces back from the border areas to within the Saigon circle, a 28-mile zone surrounding the capital.

One of the largest corps-level units in the history of the U.S. military, II Field Force Vietnam had some 50 maneuver battalions (infantry and armor battalions and armored cavalry squadrons) under its command, including those of the U.S. 1st Infantry Division, 9th Infantry Division, 25th Infantry Division, 101st Airborne Division, 199th Light Infantry Brigade, and 11th Armored Cavalry Regiment. It also had operational control over the Australian, New Zealand, and Thai forces in the area and coordinated the efforts of the ARVN III and IV Corps, including their 5th, 7th, 9th, 18th, 21st, and 25th divisions.

Against this force, the Communists committed 35 battalions in the initial assault. Eleven battalions, mostly local VC units, were directed at the Capital Military Region, while the 5th VC Division attacked the supply depots, ammunition dumps, and II Field Force headquarters at Long Binh and the air base at nearby Bien Hoa (with 857,000 landings and takeoffs a year, the busiest airport in the world). The 7th NVA Division was responsible for blocking the roads to the north and northwest, while three VC battalions, the D16, the 267th, and a battalion from the 271st VC Regiment, attacked the airfield at Tan Son Nhut as well as the Military Assistance Command Vietnam and South Vietnamese Joint General Staff headquarters complexes there.

Within hours of the initial enemy assault General Weyand launched a 5,000-man counterattack, which included the helilifting of a platoon of the 101st Airborne Division's Charlie Company, 1st Battalion, 502nd Infantry to the roof of the embassy. His key decision, however, was to order the tanks and armored personnel carriers of the 25th Infantry Division's 3rd Squadron, 4th Cavalry at Cu Chi to move cross-country at all possible speed through the morning darkness to Tan Son Nhut and attack the enemy forces there on their flanks and rear.

Guided by flares dropped by the squadron commander, Lieutenant Colonel Glenn K. Otis, from his command-and-control helicopter, the "Three-Quarter Horse," slammed into the enemy attackers at 6:00 A.M. on February 1, and after hard fighting drove them from the battlefield. It was the decisive battle of the Tet Offensive. Given the fact that an enemy platoon inside the grounds of the U.S. Embassy had sent shock waves across the United States, the enemy capture of General Westmoreland's headquarters and the headquarters of the South Vietnamese military would have been catastrophic. Thanks to the foresight of General Weyand and the valor of the U.S. and South Vietnamese defenders, that never happened. Not only did the enemy attack at Tan Son Nhut fail, their assaults throughout the Saigon area failed as well. By February 3, the North Vietnamese were on the defensive.

On February 5 the cleanup operation of the Saigon area was turned over to the South Vietnamese military, which committed five Ranger battalions, five Marine battalions, and five Airborne battalions to the effort. By March 7, the battle for Saigon was over. The city was hit again in May by two NVA regiments during the enemy's so-called Mini-Tet offensive, but this time it was successfully defended by the South Vietnamese themselves.

"We fought from house to house and street to street. When we had to go inside a house we'd just shoot inside with our rifles and then the M-60. Then we had to go up into the house and make sure they were dead. We didn't have no flame-throwers. I didn't see no tanks in Saigon. They didn't have things like you see in the movies on TV about World War II. It surprised me. I was expecting for the tank to come up there and do the John Wayne type of things. We just had to shoot down the door, walk in and shoot the person down."

—A U.S. soldier, on fighting in the Cholon area

A Viet Cong guerrilla is taken into custody by American military policemen after the North Vietnamese attack on the U.S. Embassy and on South Vietnamese government buildings in Saigon.

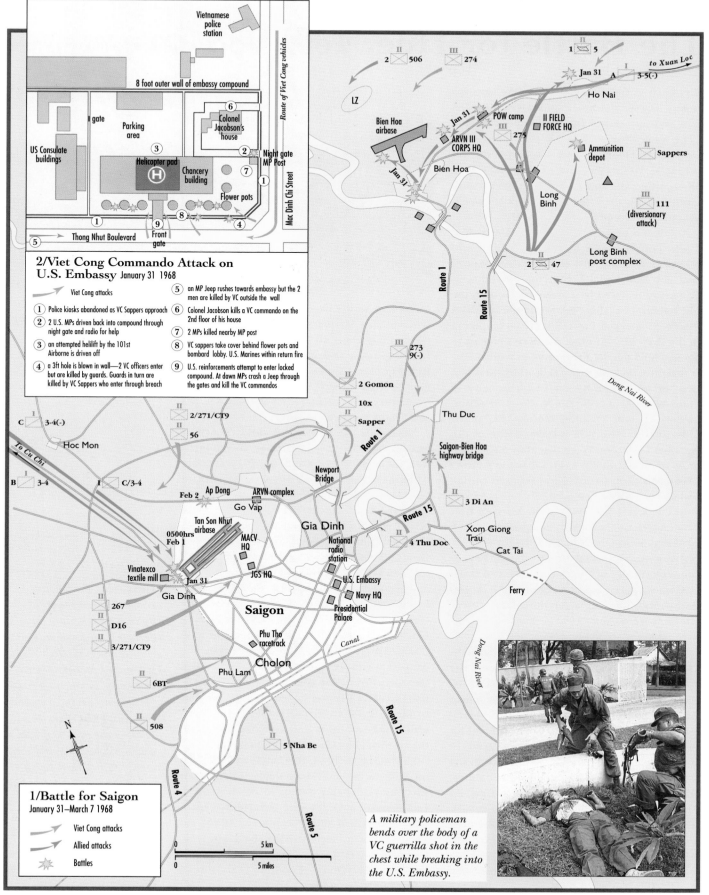

2/Viet Cong Commando Attack on U.S. Embassy January 31 1968

→ Viet Cong attacks

① Police kiosks abandoned as VC Sappers approach

② 2 U.S. MPs driven back into compound through night gate and radio for help

③ an attempted helilift by the 101st Airborne is driven off

④ a 3ft hole is blown in wall—2 VC officers enter but are killed by guards. Guards in turn are killed by VC Sappers who enter through breach

⑤ an MP Jeep rushes towards embassy but the 2 men are killed by VC outside the wall

⑥ Colonel Jacobson kills a VC commando on the 2nd floor of his house

⑦ 2 MPs killed nearby MP post

⑧ VC sappers take cover behind flower pots and bombard lobby. U.S. Marines within return fire

⑨ U.S. reinforcements attempt to enter locked compound. At dawn MPs crash a Jeep through the gates and kill the VC commandos

Embassy compound labels:
Vietnamese police station
8 foot outer wall of embassy compound
Route of Viet Cong vehicles
Colonel Jacobson's house
US Consulate buildings
Parking area
③
Helicopter pad (H)
Chancery building
② Night gate MP Post
⑦ ①
Flower pots
⑥
① ⑧ ⑨ ④
Front gate
⑤ Thong Nhut Boulevard
Mac Dinh Chi Street

1/Battle for Saigon
January 31–March 7 1968

→ Viet Cong attacks
→ Allied attacks
✳ Battles

N

0   5 km
0   5 miles

Map labels:
to Xuan Loc
2 506
274
1 5
Jan 31   A   3-5(-)
Ho Nai
LZ
Bien Hoa airbase
Jan 31   POW camp
II FIELD FORCE HQ
ARVN III CORPS HQ
275
Ammunition depot
Sappers
Bien Hoa
Long Binh
111 (diversionary attack)
Long Binh post complex
2   47
Jan 31
Dong Nai River
Route 1
Route 15
Thu Duc
Saigon-Bien Hoa highway bridge
273 9(-)
2 Gomon
10x
Sapper
Route 1
3 Di An
C   3-4(-)
2/271/CT9
56
Hoc Mon
B   3-4
C/3-4
Feb 2   Ap Dong
Go Vap
ARVN complex
Newport Bridge
Route 15
Xom Giong Trau
Cat Tai
Gia Dinh
4 Thu Doc
To Cu Chi
Tan Son Nhut airbase
0500hrs Feb 1
MACV HQ
JGS HQ
National radio station
U.S. Embassy
Navy HQ
Vinatexco textile mill
Jan 31
Gia Dinh
Saigon
Presidential Palace
267
D16
3/271/CT9
Phu Tho racetrack
Canal
Ferry
Dong Nai River
Cholon
6BT
Phu Lam
508
5 Nha Be
Route 4
Route 5
Route 15

A military policeman bends over the body of a VC guerrilla shot in the chest while breaking into the U.S. Embassy.

The Battle for Hue, Tet 1968 JANUARY–MARCH

The bitterest fighting of the Tet Offensive was not at Saigon, the new capital of South Vietnam, but at the old Imperial capital of Hue "The twenty-five day struggle for Hue was the longest and bloodiest ground action of the Tet offensive," said the *Washington Post*'s Don Oberdorfer, who witnessed it first-hand, "and, quite possibly, the longest and bloodiest single action of the Second Indochina War."

The battle began at 3:30 A.M. on January 31, 1968. The 6th NVA Regiment's 800th and 802nd battalions and the VC 12th Sapper Battalion launched a 122mm mortar and rocket barrage followed by a ground assault on the old Imperial Citadel. Meanwhile the 4th NVA Regiment attacked the U.S. MACV compound in the "New City" south of the river, which managed to hold out despite repeated assaults.

A lightly defended city that until then had been off-limits to U.S. combat forces, most of Hue was soon in NVA hands. "From dawn on January 31 until 5 A.M. on February 24," noted Oderdorfer, "the yellow-starred flag of the National Liberation Front flew atop the fortress gate of the Citadel, and a People's Army Command post occupied the restored throne room of the Nguyen emperors."

In the largest bloodbath of the Vietnam War, Communist cadres began a systematic roundup of Vietnamese government officials, military officers, Roman Catholic priests, and other "enemies of the people." The graves of 2,800 civilians who were marched off into the jungles and shot, bludgeoned, or buried alive were later uncovered, and 3,000 civilians were never accounted for.

The allied counterattack began immediately. Lieutenant General Ngo Quang Truong, the ARVN 1st Division commander, whose Black Panther reaction company had managed to hold on to the division headquarters compound in the Citadel, immediately ordered his 3rd Regiment, then on an operation north of the city, to come to his relief. Reinforced by the 2nd, 7th and 9th ARVN airborne battalions, they reached his headquarters in the Citadel's northeast corner on the evening of January 31. The next day General Truong began an attack to retake the entire Citadel and clear the north bank of the river.

At the request of the ARVN I Corps commander, U.S. forces were committed to clear the

A U.S. medical officer and his aides race across a battle–scarred terrain to evacuate a Marine wounded during the fierce street fighting that devastated much of the glorious city of Hue.

south bank of the river. On February 4, the 1st Battalion, 1st Marine Regiment, reinforced by the 2nd Battalion, 5th Marine Regiment, began fighting house-to-house to drive the enemy from the area. They were supported by naval gunfire from three U.S. Navy cruisers and five destroyers lying offshore. By February 9, the south bank had been cleared.

Meanwhile, on February 2, the U.S. Army's 3rd Brigade, 1st Cavalry Division (Airmobile), with the attached 1st Battalion, 501st Infantry from the 101st Airborne Division, established blocking positions to the west of the city to prevent NVA reinforcements, including the 304th NVA Division's 24th Regiment, the 325C NVA Division's 29th Regiment, and the 324B NVA Division's 99th Regiment, from entering Hue.

When 1st ARVN Division attacks north of the river stalled on February 12, they were reinforced by two VNMC (Vietnamese Marine Corps) battalions and the U.S. 1st Marine Division's 1st Battalion, 5th Marines. Intense house-to-house fighting—the Marines took one casualty for every yard gained—finally forced the enemy from the area, and on February 21 the 1st ARVN Division linked up with elements of the U.S. 1st Cavalry Division (Airmobile), which had launched a coordinated assault on the city from blocking positions to the west.

On March 2, 1968, the battle for Hue was officially at an end. More than 50 percent of the city had been damaged or destroyed. Communist casualties were estimated at more than 5,000 killed and 98 captured. ARVN and VNMC casualties included 384 killed and 1,830 wounded, while the U.S. Marines suffered 142 killed and 857 wounded and the U.S. Army 74 killed and 507 wounded.

"Gradually, the battling turned the once beautiful city into a nightmare. Hue's streets were littered with dead. A black–shirted Communist soldier sprawled dead in the middle of a road, still holding a hand grenade. A woman knelt in death by a wall in the corner of her garden. A child lay on the stairs, crushed by a fallen roof. Many of the bodies had turned black and begun to decompose, and rats gnawed at the exposed flesh."

Time,
February 16, 1968

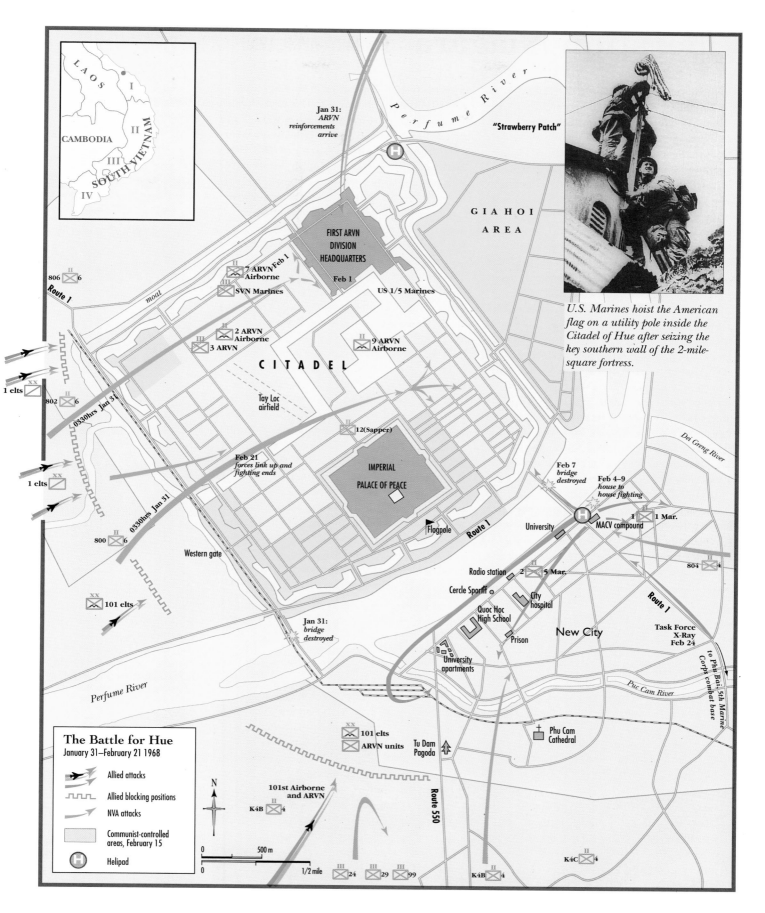

LAOS

CAMBODIA

SOUTH VIETNAM

I

II

III

IV

Perfume River

Jan 31:
*ARVN
reinforcements
arrive*

"Strawberry Patch"

GIA HOI
AREA

*U.S. Marines hoist the American
flag on a utility pole inside the
Citadel of Hue after seizing the
key southern wall of the 2-mile-
square fortress.*

FIRST ARVN
DIVISION
HEADQUARTERS

Feb 1

806   6

Route 1

moat

7 ARVN
Airborne   Feb 1

SVN Marines

US 1/5 Marines

2 ARVN
Airborne

3 ARVN

9 ARVN
Airborne

C I T A D E L

Tay Loc
airfield

1 elts

802   6

0330hrs Jan 31

12(Sapper)

Feb 21
*forces link up and
fighting ends*

IMPERIAL
PALACE OF PEACE

Dei Greng River

Feb 7
*bridge
destroyed*

Feb 4–9
*house to
house fighting*

1 elts

0330hrs Jan 31

800   6

Western gate

Flagpole

Route 1

University

MACV compound

1   1 Mar.

Radio station

2   5 Mar.

Cercle Sportif

City
hospital

Quoc Hoc
High School

Prison

New City

804   4

Route 1

Task Force
X-Ray
Feb 24

*to Phu Bai/5th Marine
Corps combat base*

101 elts

Jan 31:
*bridge
destroyed*

University
apartments

Perfume River

Puc Cam River

101 elts

ARVN units

Tu Dam
Pagoda

Phu Cam
Cathedral

The Battle for Hue
January 31–February 21 1968

→→ Allied attacks

⊓⊔⊓⊔ Allied blocking positions

→ NVA attacks

Communist-controlled
areas, February 15

Ⓗ Helipad

N

101st Airborne
and ARVN

K4B   4

Route 550

0   500 m

0   1/2 mile

K4B   4

24   29   99

K4C   4

Operation Niagara JANUARY–APRIL 1968

On January 5, 1968, as the enemy buildup in the Khe Sanh area became apparent, General William C. Westmoreland ordered his staff to plan a massive aerial bombardment program to counter the rapidly increasing threat. Called Operation Niagara, it was to be conducted in two phases. Niagara I would entail a comprehensive intelligence effort to locate the enemy, involving Marine, Navy, and Air Force strike, reconnaissance, and electronic warfare aircraft, as well as ground collection-gathering activities and electronic ground sensors. Niagara II was to consist of coordinated B-52 strategic bomber strikes on a round-the-clock basis.

On January 21, the enemy attack on Khe Sanh began, and Westmoreland ordered Niagara II into execution. Aerial bombardment and resupply became the heart of the defensive plan. The Air Force alone flew almost 1,400 reconnaissance missions, exposing slightly less than one million feet of film. Such high volume reconnaissance missions recommended an average of 150 targets a day. One such strike on February 15, eleven miles southwest of Khe Sanh, hit an enemy ammunition dump, setting off more than a thousand explosions and fires.

Completely cut off by road, Khe Sanh was totally dependent on aerial resupply. Between January 21 and April 8, the Air Force delivered 12,400 tons of supplies to the base. C-130 Hercules transports accounted for 90 percent of the total, making 496 parachute air drops and 273 landings, while C-123 Provider trans-ports made 105 drops and 179 landings and C-7 eight landings. Marine KC-130 tankers also delivered cargo during the early weeks, and throughout the siege Marine helicopters resupplied the hill positions around the base. Because of these airlifts, supply levels never became dangerously low.

The name Operation Niagara was derived from the steady fall of bombs on enemy positions in the area. More than 24,000 Air Force and Marine fighter bomber sorties were flown over the Khe Sanh area, as well as 2,700 B-52 bomber sorties, which dropped over 110,000 tons of bombs. During the height of the battle, heavy air attacks averaged 300 tactical sorties a day, with a three-ship B-52 cell arriving overhead every 90 minutes.

The B-52s did not normally bomb within two miles of friendly troops in order to avoid friendly fire casualties, but on February 26, after air observers detected extensive enemy bunker complexes within the buffer area around the Khe Sanh base, the B-52s, guided by ground radar, began bombing within one-sixth of a mile of the perimeter. According to the official Air Force account, B-52s flew 101 such close-in missions over the next month. In one instance, a prisoner-of-war reported that 75 percent of a 1,800-men regiment had been killed by a single B-52 strike. "The thing that broke their back basically was the fire of the B-52s," said General Westmoreland, when the siege was lifted on April 8.

"Without question the amount of firepower put on that piece of real estate exceeded anything that has ever been seen before in history by any foe and the enemy was hurt, his back was broken, by airpower."

—General William C. Westmoreland

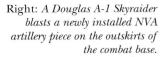

Left: *As a major NVA troop buildup below the DMZ becomes apparent, U.S. Marines, manning the fortified perimeter of Khe Sanh combat base, scan the surrounding countryside for signs of enemy activity.*

Right: *A Douglas A-1 Skyraider blasts a newly installed NVA artillery piece on the outskirts of the combat base.*

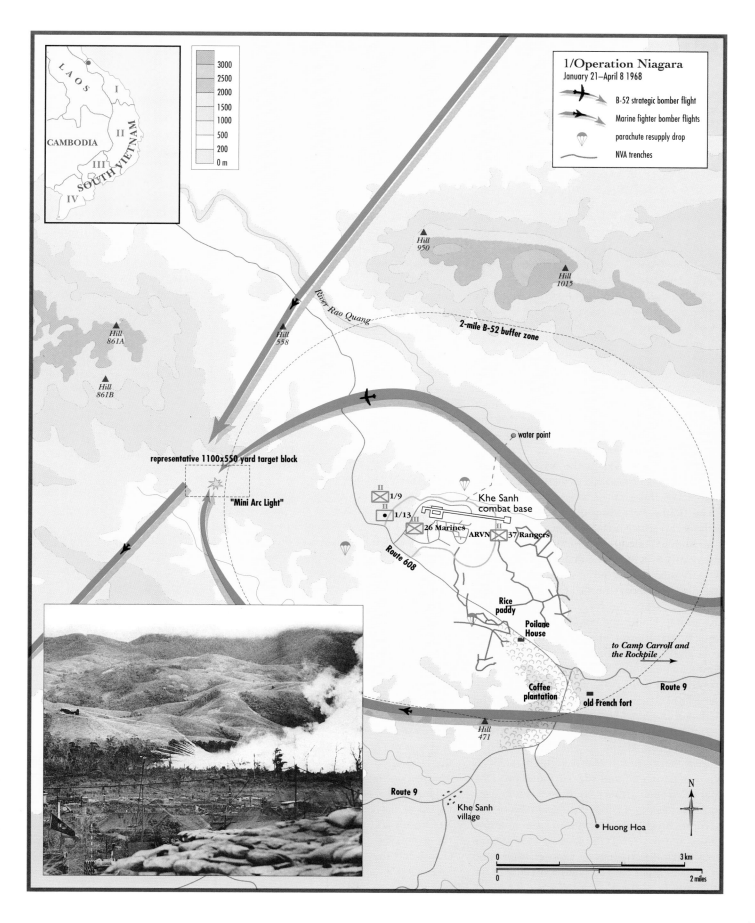

LAOS

I

CAMBODIA

II

III

SOUTH VIETNAM

IV

3000
2500
2000
1500
1000
500
200
0 m

1/Operation Niagara
January 21–April 8 1968

B-52 strategic bomber flight

Marine fighter bomber flights

parachute resupply drop

NVA trenches

Hill
950

Hill
1015

River Rao Quang

2-mile B-52 buffer zone

Hill
861A

Hill
558

Hill
861B

water point

representative 1100x550 yard target block

"Mini Arc Light"

1/9

1/13

Khe Sanh
combat base

26 Marines

ARVN

37 Rangers

Route 608

Rice
paddy

Poilane
House

to Camp Carroll and
the Rockpile

Coffee
plantation

old French fort

Route 9

Hill
471

Route 9

Khe Sanh
village

Huong Hoa

N

0   3 km

0   2 miles

The Siege of Khe Sanh   JANUARY–APRIL 1968

"I don't want any damn Dinbinfoo," President Lyndon B. Johnson told General Earle G. Wheeler, the chairman of the Joint Chiefs of Staff, as the 77-day siege of Khe Sanh by the NVA began on January 21, 1968. In an unprecedented move, Johnson asked for and received a written guarantee "signed in blood" from the JCS that the Marine outpost could hold out. Given the growing American public weariness with the war, the fall of Khe Sanh could indeed have been as catastrophic to Johnson's government as the fall of Dien Bien Phu had been to the French.

A Dien Bien Phu was precisely what the NVA commander, General Giap, had been trying to recreate, although after his defeat Giap claimed that Khe Sanh was just an attempt to divert U.S. attention away from the cities in preparation for the Tet Offensive. But postwar documents from Hanoi revealed that much more was at stake: Khe Sanh was to be a test of whether or not to proceed with Phase II of the TCK/TKN which began with the "border wars" the previous September.

If corp-sized attacks by the NVA across the Demilitarized Zone were not enough to provoke a U.S. invasion of North Vietnam, then Phase II (the Tet Offensive) could be ordered without threat to North Vietnam. The attacks at Khe Sanh and along the DMZ would also open a gap in U.S. defenses, so that during Phase III NVA regulars could pour south and provide the final spark for the General Uprising. In November 1967, the NVA began massing for the assault. Under the command of the corps-level Route 9 Front, the 40,000 troops in the area (half in the immediate vicinity of Khe Sanh) included the 304th "Delta" Division, the 325th "Gold Star" Division, and a regiment of the 324B Division. They were supported by the 68th and 164th Artillery regiments.

Defending Khe Sanh combat base was the 5,000-man 26th Marine Regiment reinforced by the 1st Battalion, 9th Marines, the 37th ARVN Ranger Battalion, and the 1st Battalion, 13th Marine Artillery. Direct fire support at the base was provided by 4.2-inch mortars, 105mm and 155mm howitzers, six 90mm gun medium tanks, and two ONTOS platoons with 106mm recoilless rifles. In general support from bases located 10 miles away at Camp Carroll and the Rockpile were the U.S. Army's 8th Battalion,

4th Artillery and its 2nd Battalion, 94th Artillery, whose 16 self-propelled 175mm guns, which had a range of 32,700 feet, were the only artillery weapons capable of firing at the North Vietnamese artillery emplacements in Laos. An attempt to move several of these guns to Khe Sanh in July 1967 had been turned back by an NVA ambush on Route 9, and from August all resupply was by air.

At Dien Bien Phu the French had conceded the surrounding hills to the enemy, whereas at Khe Sanh the Marines continued to outpost Hills 861 and 881, which had been seized in the hill fights the previous May, as well as Hills 558 and 950. The valley floor was therefore under constant surveillance. On January 21, 1968, several hundred 122mm rockets struck the base at Khe Sanh. An artillery and mortar attack detonated the Marine's ammunition dump, destroying much of their fuel supply.

On February 6, the 304th NVA Division's 66th Regiment, reinforced by 12 Russian-made PT-76 amphibious light tanks, overran the CIDG camp at Lang Vei. NVA rockets, artillery, and mortars continued to pound Khe Sanh while its infantry began a classic siege, constructing trenches, zigzag approaches, and parallels. On February 29, in the only serious ground assault of the siege, a battalion of the 304th NVA Division assaulted the ARVN 34th Ranger positions, only to be beaten back.

On April 1, the U.S. 1st Cavalry Division (Airmobile) launched Operation Pegasus to reopen Route 9. After meeting light enemy resistance, the head of the relief column, the 2nd Battalion, 7th Cavalry, linked up with the Marines on April 8, bringing the siege to an end. The Marines had suffered 199 killed and 830 wounded, while the Pegasus relief force had suffered 92 killed and 629 wounded. ARVN forces had lost 34 and 184 wounded. NVA losses are estimated at between 10,000 and 15,000, mostly to the Marine and Army artillery and to the 100,000 tons of bombs and rockets dropped during Operation Niagara.

The results of the battle were mixed. The failure of the United States to respond to the attack with an invasion of North Vietnam gave the green light for the Tet Offensive to go ahead, but the successful defense of the base forestalled the planned NVA cross-border invasion that was to follow.

"Coming over Khe Sanh, I looked down and it was one big round mountain with a jagged line around the top of it. That line was the trench line. The choppers could only go there when there was no incoming, but they had incoming five times a day. For the first time the reality of where I was and where I was going slapped me back worse than a bad nightmare. Now, I'm in a war. Oh, God, I could really die out here. Up until that point I never took it seriously. It was happening but it wasn't real. It was TV—hey, heroes and shit. No, I could really die in this place. I wasn't ready for that. It grabbed me and shook me every way but loose."

—U.S. Marine

A Marine CH-46 Sea Knight helicopter arrives to ferry dead and wounded "leathernecks" from Khe Sanh.

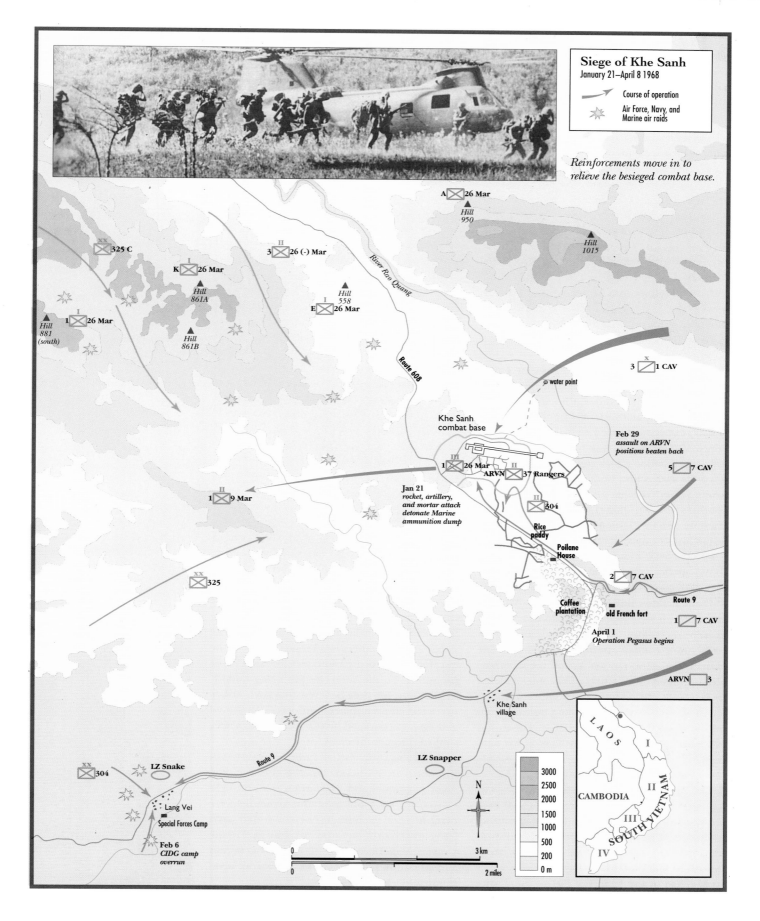

Siege of Khe Sanh
January 21–April 8 1968

→ Course of operation

✳ Air Force, Navy, and
   Marine air raids

*Reinforcements move in to
relieve the besieged combat base.*

A ⊠ 26 Mar
▲ *Hill 950*

▲ *Hill 1015*

XX ⊠ 325 C

3 ⊠ 26 (-) Mar

K I ⊠ 26 Mar

▲ *Hill 861A*

E I ⊠ 26 Mar

▲ *Hill 558*

River Rao Quang

Route 608

1 I ⊠ 26 Mar

▲ *Hill 881 (south)*

▲ *Hill 861B*

⦿ water point

3 X ⊠ 1 CAV

Khe Sanh
combat base

Feb 29
*assault on ARVN
positions beaten back*

1 III ⊠ 26 Mar
II ⊠ ARVN   II ⊠ 37 Rangers

5 ⊠ 7 CAV

*Jan 21
rocket, artillery,
and mortar attack
detonate Marine
ammunition dump*

II ⊠ 304

1 II ⊠ 9 Mar

Rice paddy

Poilane House

XX ⊠ 325

2 ⊠ 7 CAV

Coffee plantation

■ old French fort

Route 9

1 ⊠ 7 CAV

*April 1
Operation Pegasus begins*

ARVN ⊠ 3

Khe Sanh village

LZ Snapper

Route 9

XX ⊠ 304   ◯ LZ Snake

■ Lang Vei
Special Forces Camp

*Feb 6
CIDG camp
overrun*

N

0   3 km
0   2 miles

3000
2500
2000
1500
1000
500
200
0 m

LAOS
CAMBODIA
SOUTH VIETNAM
I
II
III
IV

The My Lai Massacre   MARCH 1968

The single worst atrocity in the history of the U.S. Army was the massacre on March 16, 1968, of between 300 and 400 innocent South Vietnamese civilians, including women and children, by soldiers of Charlie Company, 1st Battalion, 20th Infantry (C1/20) at My Lai hamlet in Quang Ngai Province. For many, the incident came to symbolize the war itself.

The assault began with a helicopter assault by elements of the American Division's 11th Infantry Brigade, including C 1/20, on Son My village in the northern part of II Corps. Estimated enemy strength in the province, which was a longtime Viet Cong stronghold, was 10,000–20,000 men, 2,000–3,000 of whom were assigned to local and main force Viet Cong units. A further 3,000–5,000 were local guerrillas, and 5,000 were cadres.

Charlie Company's objective was My Lai 4, one of several subhamlets of Son My village. The company commander, Captain Ernest L. Medina, anticipated a tough fight, for intelligence reports indicated that the 48th Local Force VC Battalion was based in the area. Although Medina's company had taken casualties from mines and booby traps, it had never been in direct combat with the enemy, and was spoiling for a fight. The company's First Platoon, led by Lieutenant William L. Calley, would lead the assault.

But when they landed there were no enemy forces in the area. With no provocation, an orgy of senseless killing ensured, led by Calley himself. It was cold-blooded murder. Women and children were raped and sodomized, houses were set ablaze, and the inhabitants were bayonetted as they attempted to escape. For hours the platoon ran amok, and the slaughter was only interrupted when a helicopter, piloted by Warrant Officer Hugh C. Thompson, landed to see what was going on. Telling his door gunners to shoot Calley if he interfered, Thompson evacuated as many of the civilians as his helicopter would hold. He was one of the only heroes of the day.

Thompson's account of the atrocities was ignored, and Medina, with no mention of civilian casualties, reported only that 69 Viet Cong soldiers had been killed. There it stood until March 1969, when a series of letters from Ronald Ridenhour, an American Division veteran who had heard rumors of the massacre, triggered an investigation. This was led by the Army Inspector General's Colonel William Wilson, and a formal board of inquiry was headed by Lieutenant General William R. Peers, who had commanded the 4th Infantry Division in Vietnam in from 1967 to 1968.

As a result of these investigations, the commander of the American Division at the time, Major General Samuel H. Koster, then serving as Superintendent of the U.S. Military Academy, was reduced in rank to brigadier general and censured for failing to investigate the atrocity when it happened. The 11th Infantry Brigade commander, Colonel Warren K. Henderson, was tried by court martial and acquitted. The battalion commander, Lieutenant Colonel Frank Barker, had been killed in action shortly after the incident, but Medina and Calley were brought to trial, along with two dozen other officers and non-commissioned officers. Calley was sentenced to life imprisonment for the murder of 22 unarmed civilians but the others were acquitted. Although Calley's sentence was upheld by the Court of Military Appeals, the Secretary of the Army reduced it to 10 years, and on November 9, 1974, Calley was paroled by President Richard M. Nixon and set free.

"The failure to bring justice to those who inflicted the atrocity casts grave doubts upon the efficacy of our justice system," said General Peers. Most veterans would have had Medina and Calley hung, drawn and quartered, and their remains displayed at the gates of the Infantry School at Fort Benning as an object lesson to all who entered. But the American public thought otherwise. To supporters of the war, Calley was being railroaded by the antiwar protesters. To the latter, he was being unfairly singled out, for they believed that such atrocities were commonplace, and were condoned and even encouraged by the Army itself. Calley slipped through the crack.

Crimes against civilians were certainly not unknown in Vietnam. During the war, 201 Army personnel and 77 Marines were brought to trial for such offenses. But atrocities were certainly not encouraged or condoned. At a 25-year retrospective on My Lai at Tulane University in December 1994, it was generally agreed that the incident at My Lai was an aberration and not the norm.

"Q: Did you obey your orders?
A: Yes, sir.
Q: What were your orders?
A: Kill anything that breathed."

—From the testimony of Salvadore LaMartina, member of Charlie Company

Top right: *Despite photographic evidence of the atrocities committed at My Lai, news of the massacre did not break until late 1969, when it shattered American visions of the war in Vietnam as a moral enterprise.*

Below: *Calley is escorted from the Army Disciplinary Barracks at Fort Leavenworth on November 8, 1974. Released on parole by the Secretary of the Army the following day, the former Charlie Company lieutenant went on to get married and work in his father's jewelry store.*

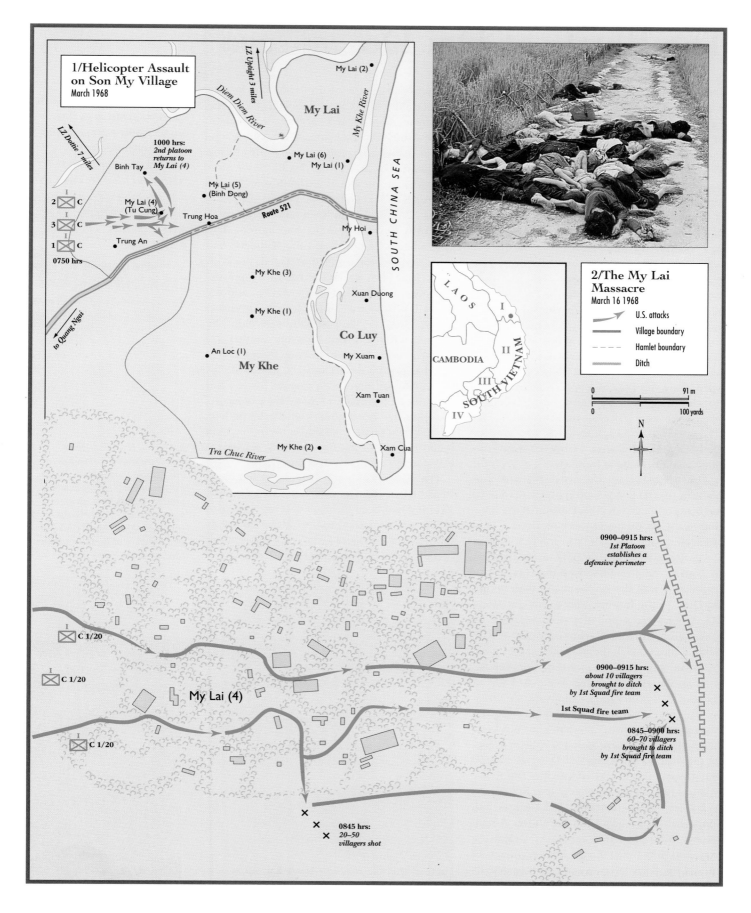

1/Helicopter Assault on Son My Village
March 1968

LZ Uptight 3 miles

Diem Diem River

My Lai (2)

My Lai

My Khe River

LZ Dottie 7 miles

1000 hrs:
2nd platoon returns to My Lai (4)

Binh Tay

My Lai (6)

My Lai (1)

2 ⊠ C

My Lai (4)
(Tu Cung)

My Lai (5)
(Binh Dong)

Trung Hoa

Route 521

SOUTH CHINA SEA

3 ⊠ C

1 ⊠ C

Trung An

0750 hrs

My Hoi

to Quang Ngai

My Khe (3)

Xuan Duong

My Khe (1)

Co Luy

An Loc (1)

My Xuam

My Khe

Xam Tuan

Xam Cua

Tra Chuc River

My Khe (2)

LAOS

CAMBODIA

SOUTH VIETNAM

I

II

III

IV

2/The My Lai Massacre
March 16 1968

⟶ U.S. attacks
━━ Village boundary
--- Hamlet boundary
∿∿ Ditch

0   91 m
0   100 yards

N

0900–0915 hrs:
1st Platoon establishes a defensive perimeter

I
⊠ C 1/20

I
⊠ C 1/20

0900–0915 hrs:
about 10 villagers brought to ditch by 1st Squad fire team

×
×

1st Squad fire team

×

0845–0900 hrs:
60–70 villagers brought to ditch by 1st Squad fire team

My Lai (4)

I
⊠ C 1/20

×
×

0845 hrs:
20–50 villagers shot

The Battle of Dai Do   APRIL–MAY 1968

The third phase of North Vietnam's *Tong Cong Kich/Tong Khoi Ngia* was to be the invasion of South Vietnam by NVA divisions poised north of the Demilitarized Zone. Although Phase I, the "border wars" of September–November 1967, had failed to draw U.S. units to the periphery and lay open the interior to attack, and although Phase II, the "General Uprising" that was to be triggered by the Tet Offensive, had failed to materialize, the North Vietnamese had not given up hope.

In May 1968, they launched what has been called their "Tet II" or "Mini Tet" offensive, striking 119 provincial and district capitals, military installations, and major cities, including Saigon. Unlike Tet I, which was primarily a Viet Cong uprising, Tet II was almost entirely an NVA affair. Most of the attacks were limited to mortar and rocket fire, but a major battle developed along the DMZ as the NVA attempted to do what they had failed to do at Khe Sanh—open an invasion corridor into the South. The first step was to crack the U.S. 3rd Marine Division DMZ defenses by overrunning the Marine combat base at Dong Ha.

The battle began on April 30, with the ambush of a U.S. Navy utility boat (LCU) by elements of the 320th NVA Division at the junction of the Bo Dieu and Cua Viet rivers. These rivers were vital logistics links for U.S. Marine forces deployed along the DMZ. From the Gulf of Tonkin, supplies flowed up the Cua Viet to its junction with the Bo Dieu, and then up the Bo Dieu to the Marine combat base at Dong Ha. From there supplies were transported by land and air to the Marine outposts at Khe Sanh, Camp Carroll, the Rockpile, and to numerous fire support bases, including Con Thien.

Since Battalion Landing Team 2/4 was in the area, it was ordered to eliminate the threat to the crucial waterway. Nicknamed "the Magnificent Bastards," the battalion was commanded by Lieutenant Colonel William Weise. At the abandoned villages of Dong Huan and Dai Do on the banks of the Bo Dieu, the Marines ran into heavy enemy fire. Reinforced by B Company, 1st Battalion, 3rd Marines, and supported by the boats of a Navy River Assault Group, Weise launched an attack to clear the area. Faced by the 48th and 52nd regiments of the 320th NVA Division, Weise was heavily outnumbered and forced to fall back to defensive positions north of the river. But he had stopped the enemy attack, and the NVA reinforcements were turned back by the "Gimlets" of the Army's 3rd Battalion, 21st Infantry, who occupied blocking positions at Nhi Ha to the northeast. On May 3, the 1st Battalion, 3rd Marine Regiment joined the battle, only to find that the NVA had fled.

The NVA attempt to open an invasion corridor into South Vietnam had failed. The "Magnificent Bastards" and the "Gimlets" had saved the day, for if they had failed, the NVA would have been free to overrun the major supply bases at Dong Ha and Quang Tri, and the entire DMZ defenses would have been undermined. However, the cost had been high. The Marines suffered 81 casualties and another 297 seriously wounded, while Army forces at Nhi Ha sustained 29 deaths and 130 wounded. But the enemy suffered even greater losses—not only did the NVA fail to achieve their objective, they also left 1,568 bodies on the battlefield, most of whom were killed by the more than 6,000 rounds of artillery and 27 air strikes called in by the American defenders.

The invasion of South Vietnam called for in Phase III of the General Offensive/General Uprising had been forestalled. It was four years before the NVA tried again with its Eastertide Offensive in 1972, and seven years before it succeeded with its 1975 Spring Offensive.

"I waited and watched those Marines about to go into battle. Some were standing watch, some readied equipment, some slept or rested, but all were quiet. No nervous jabbering, no false bravado, no whining, no melodramatics. They were professionals."

—2nd Lieutenant "Vic" Taylor, on "the Magnificent Bastards"

A Marine H-34 Sea Horse helicopter makes a one-wheeled landing on the Rockpile. Such hilltop outposts offered excellent vantage points from which to carry out surveillance of the jungle trails used by the NVA in its attempt to open an invasion corridor to the South.

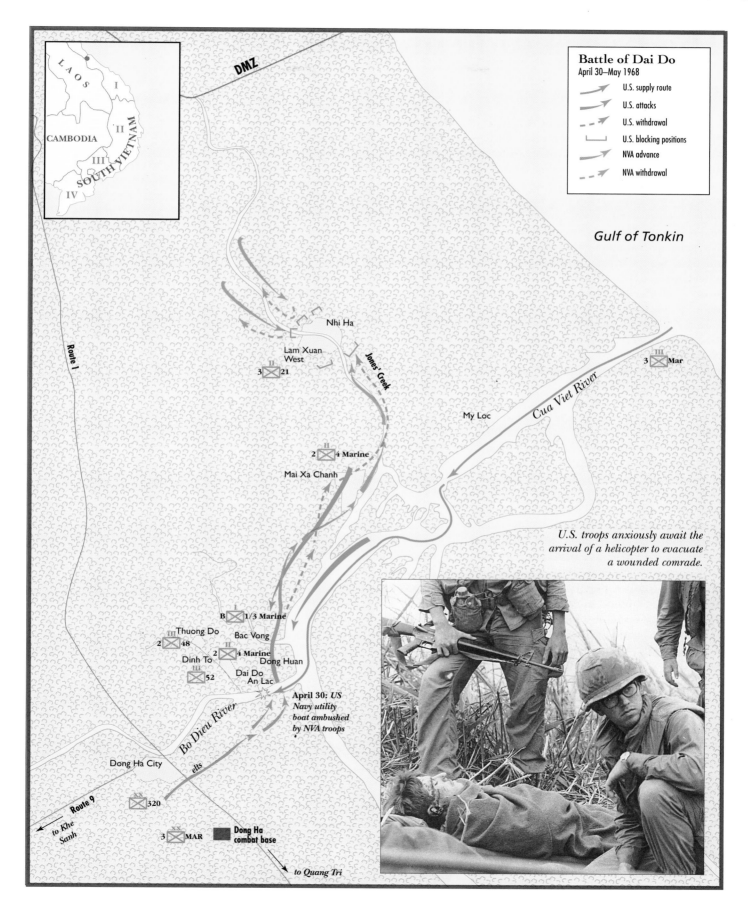

DMZ

Battle of Dai Do
April 30–May 1968

→ U.S. supply route
→ U.S. attacks
- - → U.S. withdrawal
⌐ U.S. blocking positions
→ NVA advance
- - → NVA withdrawal

LAOS

I

II

CAMBODIA

III

SOUTH VIETNAM

IV

Gulf of Tonkin

Route 1

Nhi Ha

Lam Xuan West

3 ⊠ 21

3 ⊠ Mar

Jones' Creek

Cua Viet River

My Loc

2 ⊠ 4 Marine

Mai Xa Chanh

U.S. troops anxiously await the arrival of a helicopter to evacuate a wounded comrade.

B ⊠ 1/3 Marine

Thuong Do   Bac Vong

2 ⊠ 48

Dinh To   2 ⊠ 4 Marine   Dong Huan

⊠ 52   Dai Do   An Lac

Bo Dieu River   April 30: US Navy utility boat ambushed by NVA troops

elts

Dong Ha City

Route 9   ⊠ 320

to Khe Sanh

3 ⊠ MAR   ■ Dong Ha combat base

to Quang Tri

The Evacuation of Kham Duc   MAY 1968

Besides the battle of Dai Do, the major engagement of the Communist "Mini Tet" offensive in May 1968 was the NVA siege of the Special Forces Civilian Irregular Defense Group camp at Kham Duc near the Laotian border in Quang Tin Province. Opened in September 1963 for border surveillance, it was the only CIDG border camp left in I Corps after the fall of the camp at Lang Vei, near Khe Sanh Marine Combat Base, in February 1968.

Totally inaccessible by road, Kham Duc was originally the site of a hunting lodge for South Vietnamese president Ngo Dinh Diem, who had a 6,000-foot all-weather paved airfield built there. Five miles away was the old French outpost of Ngok Tavak, manned by the 11th Mobile Strike Force with eight U.S. and three Australian advisers, as well as two 105mm howitzers of the U.S. Battery D, 2nd Battalion, 12th Marine Regiment.

On May 10, the outpost was attacked by an NVA battalion. After hard fighting it was abandoned, and survivors were evacuated by helicopter. The NVA then turned their attention to the main camp at Kham Duc. After a prolonged mortar attack, the 2nd NVA Division's 1st VC Regiment began a ground assault on May 12. The camp was reinforced by elements of the U.S. American Division's 2nd Battalion, 1st Infantry and 1st Battalion, 46th Infantry, as well as the five 105mm howitzers of Battery A, 3rd Battalion, 82nd Artillery. Fighting was intense, but when the NVA seized the surrounding high ground and brought the airfield under fire, the decision was made to withdraw.

The task of evacuation was given to the 7th U.S. Air Force, 834th Division, which controlled all U.S. airlift in South Vietnam. Its C-123 Provider and C-130 Hercules transports had previously kept the camp supplied. In the four weeks before the siege, the airlifters had brought in 400 tons of supplies. When it began, they brought in 1,500 reinforcements, including 900 from the American Division. Now the operation had to be reversed. The Army's CH-47 Chinook helicopters that were to begin the evacuation were driven off by ground fire and the task was turned over to the Air Force.

The fixed-wing evacuation began on May 12, and although the airstrip was under heavy fire, the C-130s began to land and take on passengers. One aircraft was shot down as it took off,

killing all on board, including 200 Vietnamese dependents of the camp's defenders. Another was destroyed on the airstrip by enemy fire. But the airlifters kept coming, and they were joined by Army helicopters taking advantage of the deadly suppressive fire laid down on the surrounding hills by Air Force tactical fighters.

Through a mixup in orders, three Air Force combat air controllers were brought into Kham Duc just as the evacuation was complete. Taking cover in a culvert near the airstrip, they held off the NVA with M-16 rifle fire. Although Kham Duc was now in enemy hands, a C-123 Provider, flown by Lieutenant Colonel Joe M. Jackson, landed on the abandoned strip and under intense enemy fire rescued the men from almost certain death. "We were dead," said one, "and all of a sudden we were alive!" Jackson was later awarded the Medal of Honor, becoming the only airlifter of the war to receive the nation's highest award. Although two C-130s were destroyed, the airlifters brought out 500 of the camp's defenders, nearly all in the last few minutes before the camp was overrun.

U.S. losses at Kham Duc included 24 killed, 26 missing in action, and 133 wounded, while the enemy lost an estimated 345 killed and wounded. But the greatest loss was the loss of the ground surveillance capacity over the upper reaches of the Ho Chi Minh Trail in Laos. One by one, beginning with the 1965 abandonment of the camps at Ta Ko, A Ro, Aloui, and Ta Bat, followed by the fall of the camp in the A Shau Valley in 1966, and ending with the fall of Kham Duc in May 1968, all the border surveillance camps had been taken out of action.

"The pilot saw no one left on the ground, so he took off. We figured no one would come back and we had two choices: either be taken prisoner or fight it out. There was no doubt about it. We had eleven magazines among us and were going to take as many of them with us as we could."

—Technical Sergeant Mort Freedman, on seeing the last Provider take off

The Lockheed C-130 Hercules was the fixed-wing workhorse of the war. Providing airlift capability whenever necessary, it played a vital role in the evacuation of both Kham Duc and Saigon.

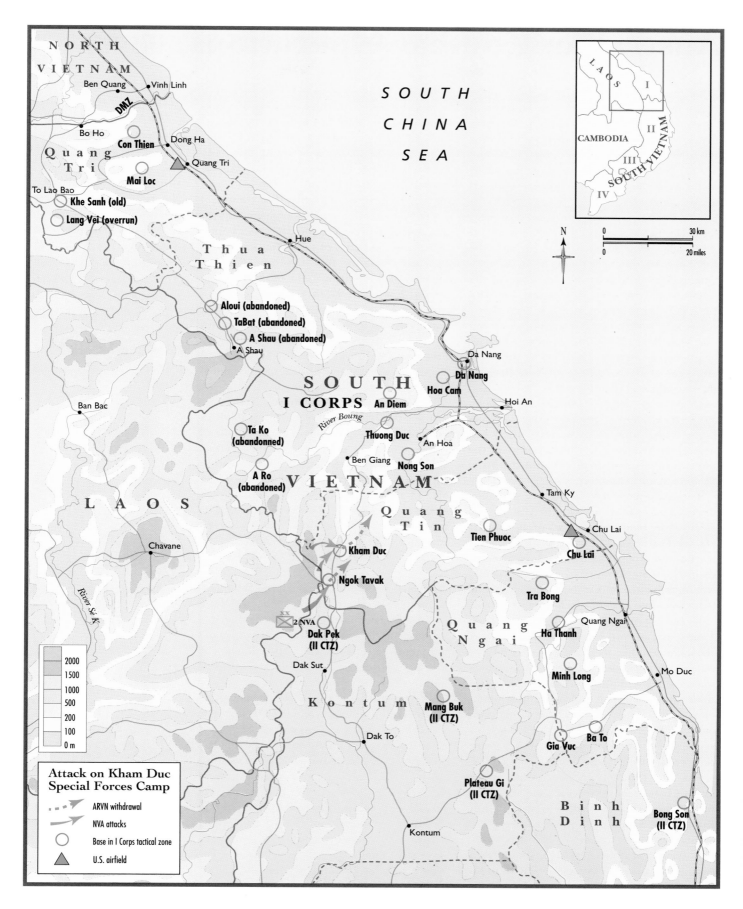

NORTH
VIETNAM

Ben Quang   •Vinh Linh
•   DMZ
Bo Ho   •
Con Thien   •Dong Ha
Q u a n g
T r i   ▲•Quang Tri
Mai Loc
•To Lao Bao
○ **Khe Sanh (old)**
○ **Lang Vei (overrun)**

SOUTH
CHINA
SEA

T h u a
T h i e n   •Hue

⊗ **Aloui (abandoned)**
⊗ **TaBat (abandoned)**
○ **A Shau (abandoned)**
•A Shau

Da Nang•
○   ⊘**Da Nang**
S O U T H   **Hoa Cam**
I CORPS   ○
•Ban Bac   **An Diem**   Hoi An•
                River Boung   ○
○ **Ta Ko**   ○
(abandonned)   **Thuong Duc**   •An Hoa
            •Ben Giang   ○
○ **A Ro**   **Nong Son**
(abandoned)   V I E T N A M
                •Tam Ky
            Q u a n g
            T i n   ▲•Chu Lai
            ○ **Tien Phuoc**   **Chu Lai**
    Kham Duc
    Ngok Tavak   ○ **Tra Bong**

L A O S   •Quang Ngai
•Chavane   ⊠ 2 NVA   Q u a n g   ○
            Dak Pek   N g a i   **Ha Thanh**
            (II CTZ)
River Sé K   •Dak Sut   •Mo Duc
                    ○ **Minh Long**
        K o n t u m   ○ **Mang Buk**
                    (II CTZ)   ○ ○ **Ba To**
            •Dak To   **Gia Vuc**
                ○ **Plateau Gi**
                (II CTZ)   B i n h
                            D i n h   ○ **Bong Son**
        •Kontum   **(II CTZ)**

Inset map:
LAOS   I
CAMBODIA   II
    III
SOUTH VIETNAM
IV

N

0 _____ 30 km
0 _____ 20 miles

Elevation scale:
2000
1500
1000
500
200
100
0 m

**Attack on Kham Duc
Special Forces Camp**

- - - ▶   ARVN withdrawal
——▶   NVA attacks
○   Base in I Corps tactical zone
▲   U.S. airfield

Australian Combat Operations 1965–1971

"The Queen has been graciously pleased on the advice of Her Majesty's Australian Ministers to approve the posthumous award of the Victoria Cross to Warrant Officer Class II Kevin Arthur Wheatley," read the *London Gazette* on December 15, 1966. It was the first of four announcements of the award of the British Commonwealth's highest medal for bravery by Queen Elizabeth II to members of the Australian Army for service in Vietnam.

Wheatley, who had served as an adviser at the U.S. Special Forces CIDG camp at Tra Bong in Quang Ngai Province, was a member of the Australian Army Training Team Vietnam (AATTV) that had been serving in the country since May 1962. The 1st Battalion, Royal Australian Regiment (RAR) also served farly on in the hostilities, from May 1965 to May 1966, alongside the U.S. 173rd Airborne Brigade then headquartered at Bien Hoa air base. Also serving alongside the 173rd Airborne were an armored cavalry troop from the Prince of Wales Light Horse, the 105th Battery, 4th Royal Australian Artillery, the 161st Battery of the Royal New Zealand Artillery, and the 161st Flight of Sioux helicopters.

Royal Australian Navy destroyers, including the HMAS *Hobart*, served with the U.S. Seventh Fleet's shore bombardment task group and the Market Time coastal surveillance force, while the Royal Australian Air Force (RAAF) deployed its No. 9 Squadron of Iroquois helicopters, No. 35 Squadron of Caribou transports, and No. 2 Squadron of Canberra bombers.

The largest Australian contingent was the 1st Australian Task Force (ATF). Formed in April 1966, it established its headquarters in the Nui Dat rubber plantation in Phuoc Tuy Province, some 35 miles southeast of Saigon. The province, which was their primary area of operations, included Route 15, the main supply route between Saigon and the port of Vung Tau, where the Australians established a logistics center of their own.

The 1st ATF consisted of two (later three) infantry battalions of the RAR (and, after 1967, two rifle companies from the 1st Battalion, Royal New Zealand Regiment) as well as artillery and other support units. Instead of the U.S. system of individual replacement, the Australians rotated whole units, and all of the then nine RAR battalions served at least one tour in Vietnam. At its peak strength, the ATF included 8,300 men, three-quarters of whom were in combat units. Enemy forces in the area included local guerrillas, the 5th VC Division's 274th and 275th regiments and the D445 Provincial Mobile Battalion. Before the Australians arrived, the VC had cut Route 15, and most of the province was under their control.

The ATF fought a number of major engagements in Phuoc Tuy Province, the most important being the battle of Long Tan on August 18, 1966, where the 108 "diggers" (Australian soldiers) of D Company of the 6th RAR fought off the 2,500-man 275th VC Regiment reinforced by the independent D445 VC Main Force Battalion. The battle set such a standard of valor that D Company was awarded the U.S. Presidential Unit Citation for bravery, and August 18 was designated Australian National Day for Vietnam veterans.

Later, during the NVA "Mini-Tet" Offensive in 1968, the 1st and 3rd battalions of the RAR established fire support bases (FSB) Coral and Balmoral north of Saigon, outside their normal area of operations, to block the NVA invasion corridor between War Zone D and Saigon. On May 13, the 1st RAR at FSB Coral was attacked by the 2nd Battalion, 141st NVA Regiment. The attack was beaten back, but on May 16 the NVA tried again with the other two battalions of the 141st NVA Regiment, the 267th and 275th infiltration groups, the C-17 Recoilless Rifle Company and the C-18 Antiaircraft Company. Again they were beaten back, leaving 600 dead. On May 28, the 165th NVA Regiment launched an attack on the 3rd RAR at FSB Balmoral, and were repulsed yet again with terrible losses. The invasion corridor had been blocked, and the Mini Tet Offensive soon fizzled out.

The 1st Australian Task Force, including the New Zealand contingent, withdrew from Phuoc Tuy Province in late 1971 as part of the general allied withdrawal from the war. A small military advisory group remained in the area until December 1972. In the course of its 10-year involvement in Vietnam, Australia sent 47,424 military personnel to Vietnam, including 17,412 national servicemen (draftees). During the course of the war the force suffered a total of 494 killed and 2,368 wounded in action. The New Zealander contingent suffered 35 killed and 135 injured.

"I thought of the Vietnamese (ARVN) as soldiers who had been fighting for years, since World War II. We didn't scorn them but had sympathy for them ... I saw American troops only in passing. I recall one most unprofessional group of conscripts ... in the bush trying to draw enemy fire. They had cigarette packets in their helmet bands, wore white T-shirts, and were by our standards pretty slack."

—a New Zealand infantryman

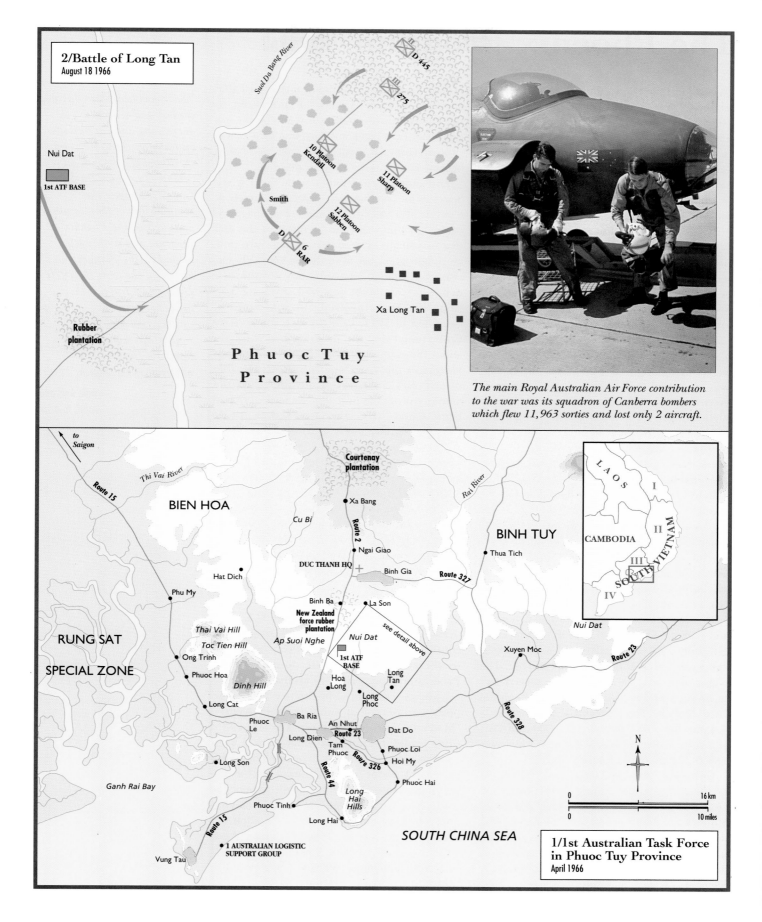

2/Battle of Long Tan
August 18 1966

Nui Dat

1st ATF BASE

Suoi Da Bang River

II D 445

III 275

10 Platoon Kendall

11 Platoon Sharp

Smith

12 Platoon Sabben

D 6 RAR

Rubber plantation

Xa Long Tan

P h u o c T u y P r o v i n c e

The main Royal Australian Air Force contribution to the war was its squadron of Canberra bombers which flew 11,963 sorties and lost only 2 aircraft.

to Saigon

Courtenay plantation

Thi Vai River

Route 15

BIEN HOA

Cu Bi

Xa Bang

Route 2

Ngai Giao

DUC THANH HQ

Binh Gia

Rai River

BINH TUY

Thua Tich

Route 327

Hat Dich

Phu My

Binh Ba

La Son

New Zealand force rubber plantation

Nui Dat

see detail above

Thai Vai Hill

Toc Tien Hill

Ap Suoi Nghe

Nui Dat

1st ATF BASE

Long Tan

Xuyen Moc

Route 23

RUNG SAT

Ong Trinh

SPECIAL ZONE

Phuoc Hoa

Dinh Hill

Long Cat

Hoa Long

Long Phoc

Route 328

Ba Ria

An Nhut

Dat Do

Phuoc Le

Route 23

Long Dien

Tam Phuoc

Phuoc Loi

Hoi My

Route 326

Long Son

Route 44

Phuoc Hai

Ganh Rai Bay

Long Hai Hills

Phuoc Tinh

Route 15

Long Hai

SOUTH CHINA SEA

Vung Tau

• **1 AUSTRALIAN LOGISTIC SUPPORT GROUP**

N

LAOS
I
CAMBODIA
II
III
SOUTH VIETNAM
IV

Nui Dat

0 — 16 km
0 — 10 miles

1/1st Australian Task Force in Phuoc Tuy Province
April 1966

The Phoenix Program   JULY 1968

"A revolution is not a dinner party, or writing an essay, or painting a picture, or doing embroidery; it cannot be so refined, so leisurely and gentle, so temperate, kind, courteous, restrained and magnanimous," said Chinese Communist leader Mao Zedong in 1927. "A revolution is an insurrection, an act of violence by which one class overthrows another." An essential part of that revolution was terror.

North Vietnam Politburo member, Truong Chinh (an alias meaning "Long March," a tribute to Maoist strategy) was instrumental in incorporating terror into North Vietnam's policy of *Dau tranh chinh tri* or political struggle. From 1957 to 1972, 36,725 village chiefs, government officials, and members of anti-communist civic or religious groups in the South were assassinated by VC terror squads. Another aspect of Communist strategy was the formation of parallel "revolutionary" governments at every level to subvert the government of South Vietnam. This 70,000-strong "Viet Cong Infrastructure," or VCI, was the heart of the revolutionary movement in the South.

Neutralizing the VCI was a primary mission of CORDS, the organization formed in 1967 to fight the "other war." One of its first acts was to establish a program to gather intelligence on the VCI. ICEX (Intelligence Coordination and Evaluation) combined the U.S. intelligence collection agencies of MACV and the CIA, with Government of Vietnam (GVN) intelligence assets, including their Central Intelligence Organization, Special Branch, and police.

These joint committees at provincial, district, and national level would identify VCI in three categories. "A" were leaders, "B" were those in key positions, and "C" were rank-and-file. The names of those in "A" and "B" were turned over to military officials (including the Regional Force/Popular Force provincial and local militia), the National Police, or the 4,000-man PRU (Provisional Reconnaissance units), which was specifically organized for that task.

Until the 1968 Tet Offensive, ICEX was mired in turf battles among the various agencies. But the shock of that attack prompted South Vietnamese president Thieu to issue a decree on July 1, establishing the *Phung Hoang* plan to coordinate government efforts to destroy the VCI, defined as all non-military members of the Communist movement. *Phung*

Hoang was a legendary Vietnamese bird that appeared in times of peace and prosperity. As the closest approximation for Americans was the phoenix, a legendary Egyptian bird that is reborn from its own ashes, the operation became known as the Phoenix program.

Enormously controversial in the United States as an "assassination program," largely as a result of a North Vietnamese propaganda campaign that made no mention of the fact that assassinations were part of their own policy, the program was nevertheless generally successful. Although assassinations were forbidden, some no doubt occurred, given the passions of those involved. In testimony to Congress in 1971, CORDS director William Colby stated that the program had "brought about the capture of some 28,978 Communist leaders in the Viet Cong Infrastructure, that some 17,717 had taken advantage of the amnesty program, and that some 20,587 had been killed." He emphasized that "those killings occurred mostly in combat situations," and that "some 87.6 percent of those killed were killed by regular or paramilitary forces, and only 12.4 by police or irregular forces."

The momentum of the program came to an end with the 1972 NVA Eastertide Offensive, when pacification efforts had to be suspended to counter the attack. Ironically, it can be argued that the success of the program caused the NVA to launch that attack, turning from guerrilla war to a conventional cross-border attack by their regular forces. In any event, the program officially ended with the U.S. withdrawal in March 1973. Although plagued by South Vietnamese government corruption and inefficiency, there is little doubt that the Phoenix program seriously hurt the VCI.

This was confirmed by Stanley Karnow in postwar conversations with Communist leaders: "Madame Nguyen Thi Binh, a veteran Viet Cong leader, told me that Phoenix had been 'very dangerous,' adding: 'We never feared a division of troops but the infiltration of a couple of guys into our ranks caused tremendous difficulties for us.' Nguyen Co Thach, Vietnam's foreign minister from 1975, admitted that the Phoenix effort 'wiped out many of our bases' in South Vietnam, compelling numbers of North Vietnamese and Viet Cong troops to retreat to sanctuaries in Cambodia."

"Search-and-destroy tactics, cordon-and-search operations, limited nation-building by the GVN, and the Phoenix program all combined to doom the Viet Cong ... Despite the combination of shortcomings and success, the Phoenix program was simply left behind by the changing nature of the war. By 1970 Hanoi had dropped the facade of internal insurrection and concentrated on building toward a conventional invasion of the South."

—Dale Andradé,
Ashes to Ashes

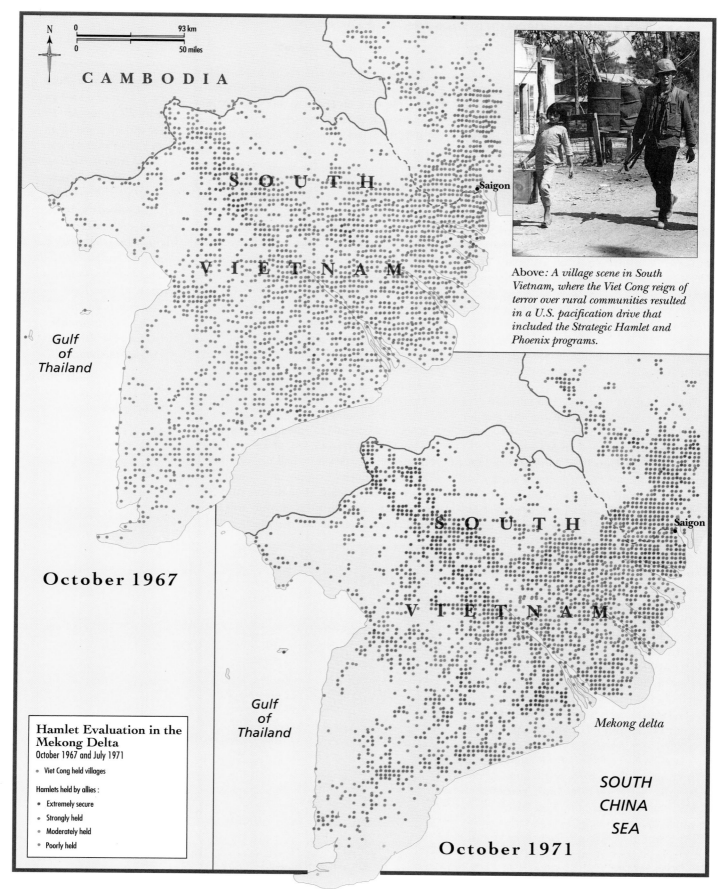

N

0   93 km

0   50 miles

CAMBODIA

SOUTH

VIETNAM

Gulf
of
Thailand

Saigon

Above: *A village scene in South
Vietnam, where the Viet Cong reign of
terror over rural communities resulted
in a U.S. pacification drive that
included the Strategic Hamlet and
Phoenix programs.*

October 1967

SOUTH

VIETNAM

Gulf
of
Thailand

Saigon

Mekong delta

SOUTH

CHINA

SEA

October 1971

**Hamlet Evaluation in the
Mekong Delta**
October 1967 and July 1971

• Viet Cong held villages

Hamlets held by allies :

• Extremely secure

• Strongly held

• Moderately held

• Poorly held

Sealords   DECEMBER 1968

Although Vietnam is thought of as a land and air war, U.S. Navy surface warships played a major role in the hostilities. Their role included the bombardment of enemy positions along the North Vietnamese coast, the naval gunfire support of friendly ground forces ashore, the Market Time interdiction of enemy sea lines of supply, and the Sealords construction of infiltration barriers in the Mekong delta.

From May 1965, the U.S. Seventh Fleet's Task Group 70.8, including cruisers, destroyers, and, at times, the battleship U.S.S. *New Jersey*, ranged the entire coast of Vietnam. From October 1966 to October 1968, in Operation Rolling Thunder, U.S. Navy warships, plus a Royal Australian Navy destroyer, bombarded the North Vietnamese coast. Twenty-nine ships were struck by coastal counterbattery fire, and 5 sailors were killed and 26 wounded. No warships were sunk but 19 had to withdraw from the gunline for repairs.

During and after the 1968 Tet Offensive, the Task Group had 22 warships on the gunline firing in support of allied forces in I Corps. From September 1968 to March 1969, the U.S.S. *New Jersey* alone fired 3,615 16-inch shells and nearly 11,000 5-inch shells in support of U.S. 3rd Marine Division operations in the DMZ. In May 1972, as part of Operation Linebacker I, Task Group 70.9 bombarded targets near Haiphong and along the coast of North Vietnam, firing more than 110,000 rounds. One destroyer was hit by an enemy MiG air attack and 16 were hit by enemy shore batteries, but again none were sunk.

The largest naval operation of the war was Operation Sealord, an acronym for Southeast Asia Lake, Ocean, and Delta Strategy. Designated Task Force 194, it combined 586 U.S. Navy vessels, including the warships of the Coastal Surveillance Force and the gunboats of the River Patrol Force and the Mobile Riverine Assault Force, with 655 VNN (South Vietnamese Navy) warships and gunboats. The aim was to cut enemy supply lines from Cambodia and disrupt enemy base areas in the Mekong delta and other waterways. Beginning in October 1968, the two-year campaign involved the creation of a series of barriers to form an interdiction line that would stretch from the Gulf of Thailand, through the Mekong delta, to the city of Saigon.

The first barrier was established in November with the opening of two canals between Rach Gia on the Gulf of Thailand and Long Xuyen on the Bassac River. The second barrier was created later that month when gunboats opened the waterway between Ha Tien on the Gulf and Chau Duc on the upper Bassac. With the "Giant Slingshot" operation in December, the third barrier was established when, after hard fighting, the Vam Co Dong and Vam Co Tay rivers on either side of the "Parrot's Beak" (a Cambodian salient thrusting into South Vietnam) were secured from enemy control.

The barrier system was completed in January 1969 when patrol sectors were established westward from the Vam Co Tay River to the Mekong River. A waterway interdiction barrier then extended from Tay Ninh City north of Saigon to the Gulf of Thailand. The U.S. Navy's role in Sealords ended in April 1971, when the operation was turned over to the VNN.

The four barrier operations succeeded in capturing 300 enemy soldiers and killing another 3,000 at a cost of 186 allied personnel killed and another 1,451 wounded. More meaningful is the effect that Sealords had on interdicting the enemy's lines of supply and communication. It is significant that during the NVA Eastertide invasion in 1972, the only area of the country not hit was the Mekong delta.

A U.S. Navy SEAL (Sea, Air, Land) team member checks out a Viet Cong bunker during the destruction of a canalside enemy base in the Mekong delta.

"From the moment New Jersey *arrived on the gun line on 29 September 1968, there was no doubt in any man's mind that we were going to bash the hell out of some North Vietnamese. I can tell you, after talking to ground-pounders who saw the ship at work, that no sight of the entire war was as impressive as our battleship letting loose with its main battery of nine 16-inch guns. ... there was nothing— nothing —which could withstand the penetrating force and the impact."*

—Robert F. Dorr

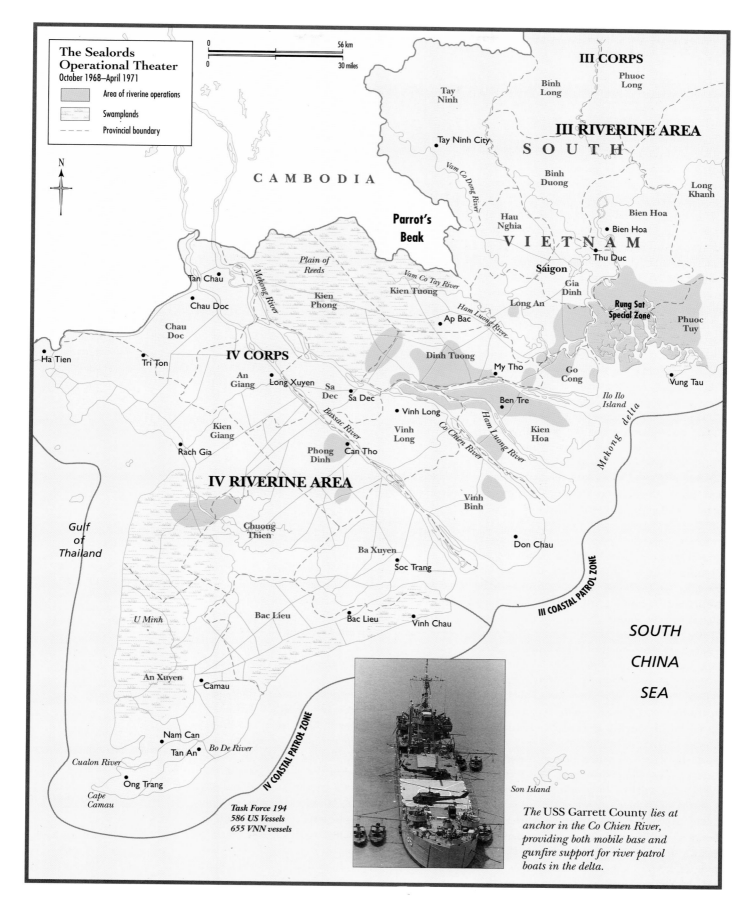

The Sealords
Operational Theater
October 1968–April 1971

Area of riverine operations

Swamplands

--- Provincial boundary

N

0 .... 56 km
0 .... 30 miles

CAMBODIA

III CORPS

Tay Ninh

Binh Long

Phuoc Long

Tay Ninh City

III RIVERINE AREA
S O U T H

Binh Duong

Long Khanh

Parrot's Beak

Vam Co Dong River

Hau Nghia

Bien Hoa

Bien Hoa

Plain of Reeds

V I E T N A M

Thu Duc

Tan Chau

Mekong River

Kien Phong

Vam Co Tay River

Kien Tuong

Saigon

Gia Dinh

Chau Doc

Long An

Rung Sat Special Zone

Phuoc Tuy

Chau Doc

Ham Luong River

Ap Bac

Ha Tien

IV CORPS

Dinh Tuong

My Tho

Go Cong

Vung Tau

Tri Ton

An Giang

Long Xuyen

Sa Dec

Ben Tre

Ilo Ilo Island

Sa Dec

Vinh Long

Mekong delta

Bassac River

Vinh Long

Kien Hoa

Kien Giang

Phong Dinh

Can Tho

Co Chien River

Ham Luong River

Rach Gia

IV RIVERINE AREA

Vinh Binh

Gulf of Thailand

Chuong Thien

Don Chau

III COASTAL PATROL ZONE

Ba Xuyen

Soc Trang

SOUTH

CHINA

U Minh

Bac Lieu

Bac Lieu

Vinh Chau

SEA

An Xuyen

Camau

IV COASTAL PATROL ZONE

Nam Can

Tan An   *Bo De River*

Cualon River

Ong Trang

Son Island

Cape Camau

Task Force 194
586 US Vessels
655 VNN vessels

The USS Garrett County lies at anchor in the Co Chien River, providing both mobile base and gunfire support for river patrol boats in the delta.

Hamburger Hill   MAY 1969

"Hamburger Hill," or, more properly, Ap Bia Mountain or Hill 937, was the graphic nickname given by soldiers to the site of a deadly 10-day battle in May 1969. The battle spelled finish to large-scale U.S. Army and Marine Corps offensive engagements in the war and was the culmination of major U.S. ground combat operations in Vietnam.

Hamburger Hill formed part of Operation Apache Snow, which was designed to keep pressure on NVA units located in the A Shau Valley, in southwestern Thua Thien Province, and to prevent the NVA from using it as a staging area to mount attacks on Hue and the coastal provinces. The A Shau Valley, in rugged country along the Laotian border, was the site of Base Area 611, a terminus of the Ho Chi Minh Trail. Dewey Canyon, an earlier operation by the U.S. 9th Marine Regiment, had revealed that the NVA had constructed major roads in the area, and as many as 1,000 trucks were moving supplies into the base camps there.

The task of destroying the NVA 29th Regiment, which was in the A Shau Valley at this time, was given to the 3rd Brigade, 101st Airborne Division, which launched a helicopter assault into the area on May 10, 1969. For the next week the brigade's 3rd Battalion, 187th Infantry, struggled to take Hill 937.

When it became obvious that the task would be too much for that battalion alone, the 3rd Brigade's 2nd Battalion, 502nd Infantry, was brought into the battle from the northeast. The ARVN 2nd Battalion, 3rd Infantry Regiment, attacked from the southeast, and two companies of the brigade's 2nd Battalion, 506th Infantry reinforced the 3rd Battalion, 187th Infantry. On May 20, 1969, Hill 937 finally fell to that combined U.S. and ARVN assault.

Forty-six American soldiers were killed in the operation, and a further 400 were wounded. Earlier in the war those casualties would have provoked little public attention—543 Americans were killed in action during the week of February 10–17, 1968 alone, and a further 2,547 wounded, without causing an outcry.

But American patience with the war had finally run out. Massachusetts senator Edward Kennedy condemned the operation as "senseless and irresponsible," and the June 27, 1969, issue of *Life* displayed the photographs of the 241 servicemen killed in Vietnam the previous

week, including those who had died in the assault on Hill 937. One of the captions, taken from a letter written by a soldier who took part in that assault, read "You may not be able to read this. I am writing in a hurry. I see death coming up the hill." Many readers undoubtedly thought that all those pictured had died at Hamburger Hill.

When U.S. forces pulled back to their base camps after the battle and abandoned Hill 937 to the enemy—as had always been the intention—the American people were further outraged. In a reaction remarkably similar to the restrictions imposed in the closing days of the Korean War, General Creighton Abrams, the commander of U.S. Military Assistance Command Vietnam, was ordered by Washington to avoid such large-scale battles in the future. From then on, America military efforts would concentrate on "Vietnamization" rather than on ground combat operations.

A wounded U.S. paratrooper is rushed to safety during the fierce battle to wrest the strategically located peak from the hands of the Communists.

"No matter how tough the job is, the American soldier gets the job done. He might hate the hell out of it, but he never quits. In Hamburger Hill, they might have grumbled, but my God they were there when the chips were down. They eventually went up that hill and took it!"

—Colonel Joseph B. Conmy, Jr., Commander of 3rd Brigade, 101st Airborne Division

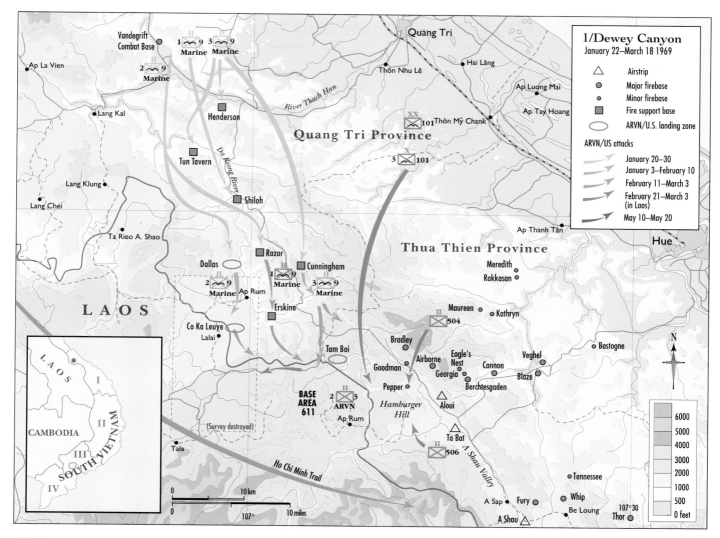

Vandegrift
Combat Base

Ap La Vien

1 〰 9
Marine

3 〰 9
Marine

2 〰 9
Marine

Lang Kal

Henderson

Quang Tri

Thôn Nhu Lê

Hai Lãng

Ap Luong Mai

Ap Tay Hoang

River Thach Han

XX
101 Thôn Mỹ Chank

Quang Tri Province

X
3 〰 101

Tun Tavern

Lang Klung

Lang Chei

Da Krong River

Shiloh

Ta Rieo A. Shao

Ap Thanh Tân

Thua Thien Province

Hue

Razor

Dallas

2 〰 9
Marine

Ap Rum

1 〰 9
Marine

Cunningham

3 〰 9
Marine

Meredith
Rakkasan

L A O S

Erskine

Co Ka Leuye
Lalai

Tam Boi

Maureen

Kathryn

504

Bradley

Airborne

Eagle's
Nest

Veghel

Bastogne

Goodman

Georgia

Cannon

Blaze

Pepper

Berchtesgaden

N

**BASE
AREA
611**

2 〰 3
ARVN

Ap Rum

*Hamburger
Hill*

Aloui

(Survey destroyed)

Tala

Ta Bat

506

A Shau Valley

Tennessee

Ho Chi Minh Trail

A Sap   Fury

Whip

Be Loung

A Shau

Thor

107°   107°30

1/Dewey Canyon
January 22–March 18 1969

△ Airstrip
● Major firebase
• Minor firebase
■ Fire support base
⬭ ARVN/U.S. landing zone

ARVN/US attacks
→ January 20–30
→ January 3–February 10
→ February 11–March 3
→ February 21–March 3
    (in Laos)
→ May 10–May 20

6000
5000
4000
3000
2000
1000
500
0 feet

Inset map:
LAOS
CAMBODIA
SOUTH VIETNAM
I
II
III
IV

0   10 km
0   10 miles

*Paratroopers arrive to reinforce the beleaguered U.S.
forces, engaged for more than a week in bitter
fighting around the 3,000-foot peak.*

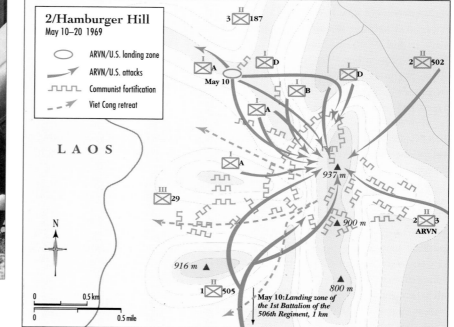

2/Hamburger Hill
May 10–20 1969

⬭ ARVN/U.S. landing zone
→ ARVN/U.S. attacks
⌐⌐⌐ Communist fortification
⇠ Viet Cong retreat

3 187

L A O S

A   D

May 10

D

B

2 502

A

A

III
29

937 m

▲ 900 m

2 3
ARVN

916 m ▲

▲ 800 m

1 505

May 10: *Landing zone
of the 1st Battalion of the
506th Regiment, 1 km*

N

0   0.5 km
0   0.5 mile

Korean Combat Operations   1965–1973

"The kind of war that we have here can be compared to an orchestra," said General Creighton Abrams, the U.S. commander in Vietnam. "It is sometimes appropriate to emphasize the drums, or the trumpets, or the bassoon, or even the flute. The Vietnamese, to a degree, realize this and do it. The Koreans on the other hand, play one instrument—the bass drum."

Abrams' remarks were meant both to sound a note of caution as to the sometimes heavy-handed methods of the Koreans, and to pay tribute to their fighting abilities, for the Republic of Korea (ROK) Army area of operations, extending along the II Corps coastline, from Phan Rang, south of Cam Ranh Bay, to Qui Nhon farther north, was one of the country's most secure areas. "Where ROKs are," said their commander, Lieutenant General Chae Myung Chin, "it is 100 percent secure."

The 50,000-strong Korean force was the largest of the allied contingents to serve in Vietnam, and the last to depart. The ROK Marine Corps' 2nd (Blue Dragon) Brigade landed in Vietnam in September 1965, and, after a brief stay in II Corps, was sent north to I Corps to operate with the U.S. III Marine Amphibious Force (III MAF). Establishing a base camp on the Batangan Peninsula southwest of the airfield at Chu Lai, and later at Hoi An, south of Da Nang, the 2nd ROK Marine Brigade remained with III MAF until its return to Korea in February 1972.

Meanwhile, the ROK Capital (Tiger) Division's lead elements began to land in Qui Nhon in September 1965, and by April 1966, its three regiments and supporting artillery were in place. In September 1966, the 9th (White Horse) Division arrived and established a base at Ninh Hoa, near the major port at Cam Ranh Bay. ROK Forces Vietnam Field Command established a corps-level headquarters at Nha Trang, near U.S. I Field Force headquarters. The primary area of responsibility of its two Army divisions was the central coastal area of II Corps, from the airbase at Phan Rang to the port of Qui Nhon. Their mission, which was to provide security for ports and logistical supply depots in the area and to keep the hundreds of miles of road between the depots and the U.S. air bases open, was mainly defensive.

But that did not rule out offensive operations. In addition to small-unit cordon and search operations in their local areas, ROK forces conducted large-scale operations against the NVA in their area. In July 1967, for example, the Capital and 9th divisions launched a preemptive attack on the 95th NVA Regiment in Phu Yen Province, driving it from the area and killing 638 enemy troops.

In 1969, the ROK mission was shifted to that of pacification. It was a mission they did not relish, believing that their job was to pursue the enemy, not "win hearts and minds." But like it or not, small unit operations in support of pacification were the rule throughout the rest of their stay. An exception was an operation by elements of the ROK Tiger Division, during the NVA Eastertide Offensive of 1972, to clear Ankhe Pass on Route 19 between Qui Nhon and Pleiku. A battalion of the NVA 3rd Gold Star Division had cut the road, blocking the movement of vitally needed supplies for the battle then raging at Kontum.

On April 2, ROK forces, supported by U.S. air strikes, began an assault on the NVA positions. After hard fighting, including a mounted assault by flamethrowing M-113 armored personnel carriers from their reconnaissance company, the pass was opened on April 22. The Koreans claimed to have killed 705 enemy soldiers, with a loss of only 51 ROK troops.

ROK Army forces, the final elements of which departed on March 16, 1973, were among the last allied troops to leave Vietnam. The ROK military had lost 4,407 soldiers and Marines during its stay, but had accomplished its mission. And it was its enemies who paid it the greatest compliment. According to historian Dale Andradé, one captured Viet Cong document warned that "contact with the Koreans is to be avoided unless victory is 100 percent certain." The bass drum had evidently attracted the attention of the Viet Cong.

"The Koreans have a formidable reputation, it is universally agreed. Their tactics, according to both Vietnamese and Americans, go like this: When they are shot at, or when a mine explodes among their soldiers, they march into the nearest hamlet and make an example of the first Vietnamese they find. The lesson is simple: if you allow someone to shoot at us or plant mines in our path, this is what happens to you. This strategy obviously helps the Koreans protect themselves, but it does little towards winning the hearts and minds of the people."

—Newsweek, 1966

A South Korean weapons platoon wades through a stream in Vietnam. Entering the conflict with weaponry which was only marginally better than that of the South Vietnamese, the Korean contingent slowly acquired more sophisticated American arms.

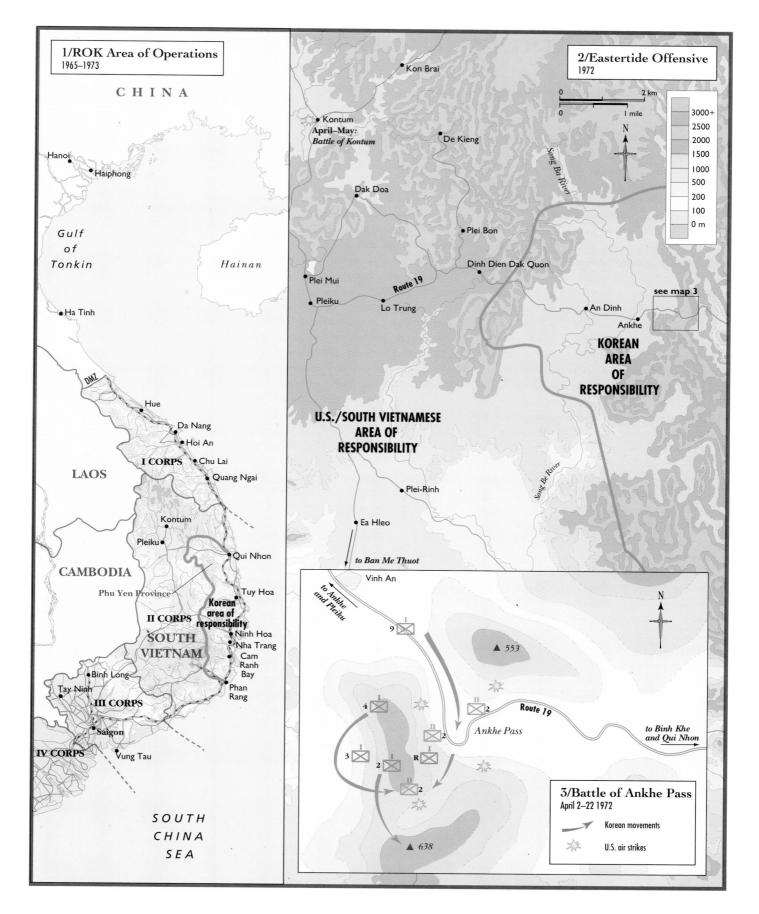

1/ROK Area of Operations
1965–1973

CHINA

Hanoi
Haiphong

*Gulf
of
Tonkin*

Hainan

Ha Tinh

DMZ

Hue
Da Nang
Hoi An
I CORPS
LAOS
Chu Lai
Quang Ngai

Kontum
Pleiku
CAMBODIA
Qui Nhon

Phu Yen Province
Tuy Hoa
II CORPS
Korean area of responsibility
SOUTH VIETNAM
Ninh Hoa
Nha Trang
Cam Ranh Bay
Binh Long
Tay Ninh
III CORPS
Phan Rang
Saigon
IV CORPS
Vung Tau

*SOUTH
CHINA
SEA*

2/Eastertide Offensive
1972

Kon Brai

Kontum
April–May:
Battle of Kontum
De Kieng

Dak Doa

Plei Bon

Dinh Dien Dak Quon

Plei Mui
Route 19
Pleiku
Lo Trung
An Dinh
Ankhe
see map 3

**KOREAN
AREA
OF
RESPONSIBILITY**

**U.S./SOUTH VIETNAMESE
AREA OF
RESPONSIBILITY**

Plei-Rinh

Ea Hleo

to Ban Me Thuot

Song Ba River
Song Be River

0 2 km
0 1 mile
3000+ 2500 2000 1500 1000 500 200 100 0 m
N

Vinh An
*to Ankhe
and Pleiku*
9
▲ 553
4
Route 19
Ankhe Pass
*to Binh Khe
and Qui Nhon*
3
2 R
2
▲ 638
N

3/Battle of Ankhe Pass
April 2–22 1972
→ Korean movements
✳ U.S. air strikes

The Cambodian Incursion APRIL–MAY 1970

"This is not an invasion of Cambodia," said President Nixon in a televised address to the American people on April 30, 1970, as he announced that U.S. and South Vietnamese forces had begun a cross-border incursion. "We take this action not for the purpose of expanding the war into Cambodia but for the purpose of ending the war in Vietnam and winning the just peace we all desire."

On March 18, 1969, Nixon had authorized Operation Menu, the "secret" bombing of Cambodia to forestall enemy attempts to take advantage of the U.S. troop withdrawals scheduled to begin that July. From the start the VC and NVA had used the border areas of "neutral" Cambodia as sanctuaries for their combat forces and supply depots, and their logistical lifeline ran through Cambodia. Their base areas in northeast Cambodia were fed by the Ho Chi Minh Trail, which ran from North Vietnam through Laos and into Cambodia. Southern base areas were supplied by the Sihanouk Trail, which ran from Kompong Som or Sihanoukville on the Gulf of Thailand. COSVN, the headquarters for all enemy operations in the South, was thought to be located in the border area.

With the tacit approval of Prince Norodom Sihanouk, then Cambodia's head of state, who reestablished diplomatic relations with the United States a month after the bombing began, Operation Menu concentrated on these border supply areas. But when Prince Sihanouk was deposed in March 1970 by his prime minister, General Lon Nol, the American bombing campaign began to include the support of Cambodian Army operations against its own Khmer Rouge guerrillas.

Neither the COSVN headquarters nor the supply depots were seriously damaged. Worse, the bombing triggered a move by the NVA to attack westward into Cambodia from their bases along the border. The capital, Phnom Penh, was threatened, and if it fell, all of Cambodia would become a vast NVA base area. In response to this threat, as well as to buy time for the Vietnamization of the war and the withdrawal of U.S. troops, President Nixon authorized a limited U.S. "incursion" into neighboring Cambodia.

In III Corps, where the enemy threat was greatest, the operation would involve a combined U.S./ARVN attack on the "Parrot's Beak" and "Fishhook" areas of Cambodia to destroy base areas there. On May 1, a 15,000-man force, including the U.S. 11th Armored Cavalry Regiment and elements of the 1st Cavalry Division (Airmobile), enveloped the Fishhook area, only to find that the enemy had abandoned the base camp and fled westward. An 8,700-man ARVN task force and elements of the U.S. 25th Infantry Division also enveloped the base areas in the Parrot's Beak, and after two days of stiff resistance, the enemy fled. The allies captured 23,000 individual weapons, 2,500 crew-served weapons (machine guns and mortars), over 16 million rounds of small-arms ammunition, and 143,000 rounds of mortar and recoilless rifle ammunition.

In II Corps, west of Pleiku, the U.S. 4th Infantry Division and elements of the 101st Airborne Division, along with the 22nd ARVN Division, also conducted raids into Cambodia to destroy enemy base areas and disrupt the Ho Chi Minh Trail. Staging out of the U.S. Special Forces camp at Plei D'Jereng, on the Cambodian border, the U.S. forces launched helicopter assaults into Cambodia, only to find that the NVA there had fled as well. In mid-May the U.S. forces withdrew and the operation was turned over to the South Vietnamese. Likewise, in III Corps the U.S. forces withdrew from Cambodia on June 30, leaving the ARVN forces to mop up. Some 11,000 NVA and VC forces had been killed and another 2,500 captured, at a cost of 976 allied forces killed, including 338 Americans, and 4,534 wounded, including 1,525 Americans.

From a military point of view, the incursion was a success. The pressure on Lon Nol had been relieved and the NVA offensive had been set back for two years, lessening the dangers to the U.S. withdrawal. As President Nixon said on June 30, "We have bought time for the South Vietnamese to strengthen themselves against the enemy." But this success came at a political price, inflaming the antiwar movement and increasing congressional opposition. On June 24, 1970, the Senate repealed the Gulf of Tonkin Resolution, which had been the original basis for intervention. Nixon, like Johnson before him, turned to his constitutional authority as commander-in-chief as the legal basis to continue the war.

"Calmly and methodically, but disconnected, like you're watching yourself do it— Clint Eastwood would have been proud of me—I moved my M-16 … The guy fired and I fired back on top of him, emptied eight or nine rounds right back at him … I knew that I had really blasted somebody for the first time. The gurgling went on for thirty or forty seconds, a retching scream for a long time. I felt strange. The consequences of pulling the trigger came home to me the next day when I found blood, hair and tissue all over this one tombstone."

—U.S. soldier

In a joint Cambodian/ARVN operation to reopen supply routes in the stricken land, South Vietnamese UH-1 Huey helicopters land on a Cambodian highway to pick up South Vietnamese Marines.

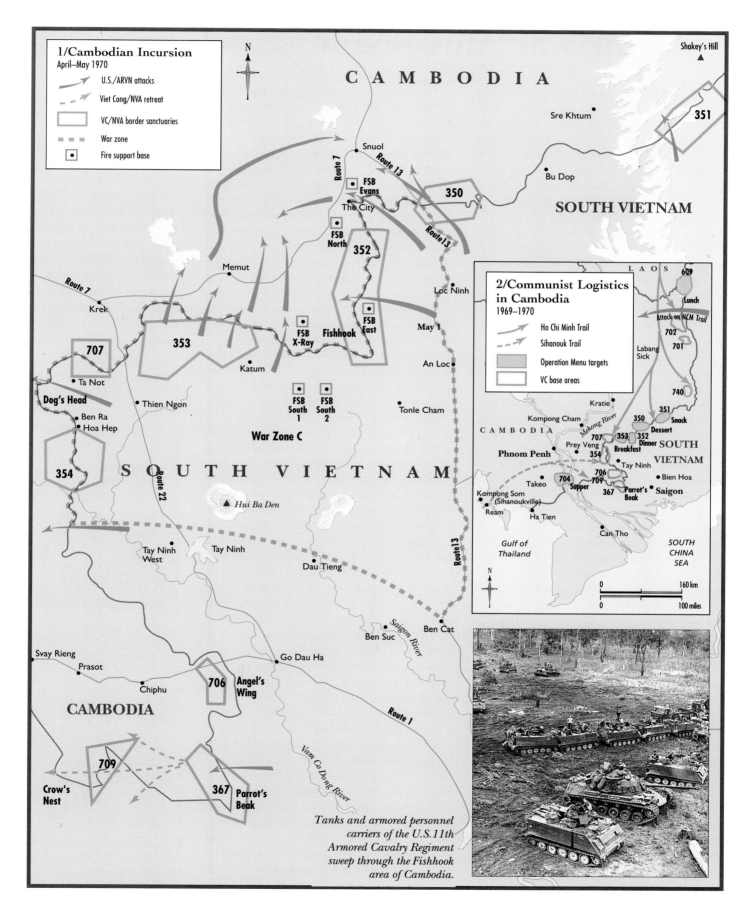

1/Cambodian Incursion
April–May 1970

- → U.S./ARVN attacks
- ⇢ Viet Cong/NVA retreat
- ▭ VC/NVA border sanctuaries
- ▪▪▪ War zone
- ⊡ Fire support base

CAMBODIA

Shakey's Hill ▲

Sre Khtum

351

Snuol

Route 7

Route 13

⊡ FSB Evans

Bu Dop

350

The City

SOUTH VIETNAM

⊡ FSB North

Route 13

352

Memut

Loc Ninh

Route 7

Krek

⊡ FSB X-Ray

Fishhook

⊡ FSB East

May 1

353

707

• Ta Not

Katum

An Loc •

Dog's Head

• Thien Ngon

⊡ FSB South 1   ⊡ FSB South 2

Tonle Cham •

• Ben Ra
• Hoa Hep

354

Route 22

War Zone C

SOUTH VIETNAM

▲ Hui Ba Den

2/Communist Logistics in Cambodia
1969–1970

- → Ho Chi Minh Trail
- ⇢ Sihanouk Trail
- ▓ Operation Menu targets
- ▭ VC base areas

LAOS

609

Lunch

Attack on HCM Trail

702

701

Labang Sick

740

Kratie •

351

Kompong Cham •

350

Snack

CAMBODIA

Mekong River

707

353

352

Dessert

Dinner

Prey Veng •

354

SOUTH VIETNAM

Phnom Penh

Breakfast

Tay Ninh •

• Bien Hoa

• Takeo

704

706

709

Supper

367

Parrot's Beak

Saigon

Kompong Som (Sihanoukville) •

• Ream

• Ha Tien

Can Tho •

Gulf of Thailand

SOUTH CHINA SEA

N
↓

0 ___ 160 km
0 ___ 100 miles

Tay Ninh West

Tay Ninh

Dau Tieng

Route 13

Ben Cat

Svay Rieng

Prasot •

Go Dau Ha

Saigon River

Ben Suc

Chiphu •

706

Angel's Wing

Route 1

CAMBODIA

Vam Co Dong River

709

367

Parrot's Beak

Crow's Nest

Tanks and armored personnel carriers of the U.S. 11th Armored Cavalry Regiment sweep through the Fishhook area of Cambodia.

The Antiwar Movement   DECEMBER 1967–MARCH 1972

"Friends, in struggling hard to make the United States Government stop its aggression in Vietnam, you are defending justice and, at the same time, you are giving us your support," said Ho Chi Minh in his New Year greeting to the American antiwar movement in December 1967. "We enjoy the support of brothers and friends on the five continents. We shall win, and so will you."

Until it became impolitic to do so in the wake of the boat people, the reeducation camps, and the shift in public attitudes toward Vietnam veterans, the American antiwar movement used to brag that Ho Chi Minh was right, that through their efforts he had indeed won the Vietnam War on the streets of Washington. But on closer examination the conventional wisdom that the antiwar movement ended the war, like so much conventional wisdom about the Vietnam War, has turned out to be wrong.

The antiwar movement was much more than large student demonstrations with antiwar placards and enemy flags. It ranged from protestors such as the late political scientist Dr. Hans Morgenthau, who disapproved of anything that diverted America from its main interests in Europe, to a tiny band of traitors who provided information on American POWs to their North Vietnamese torturers. But the vast majority of people involved were between these extremes. They included those genuinely opposed to U.S. intervention abroad and those appalled by the suffering, as well as students liable for conscription in a war which they neither approved of nor understood.

The number of antiwar protestors was impressive. In early 1965, 20,000 demonstrators came to Washington, and as the war progressed, this number grew. In April 1967, 100,000 protestors gathered in New York and 20,000 in San Francisco. A "March on the Pentagon" on October 21, 1967, drew 50,000 demonstrators, and a rally in New York in April 1968 drew 200,000 protestors. The Democratic National Convention in Chicago in August 1968 was marked by widely televised clashes between protestors and police. In October 1969, the National Moratorium drew large crowds to Washington, D.C., and to other cities, and on November 15, 1969, the New Mobilization Committee to End the War in Vietnam drew 250,000 demonstrators to Washington.

The Cambodian incursion in April 1970 touched off widespread student rioting, and on May 4, four students were killed at Kent State University after the burning of the ROTC building there. Demonstrations and riots continued until the U.S. withdrawal in March 1973. But did the antiwar movement cause the withdrawal, or was such reasoning a case of *post hoc ergo propter hoc*, the logical fallacy of "after this, therefore because of it"? Postwar analysis has favored the latter explanation. Protestors saw the fact that 30,000 Americans fled to Canada to avoid the draft as evidence of the bankruptcy of U.S. policy. But it was later revealed that more than 40,000 Canadian had come south to voluntarily serve in the U.S. military.

In a Smithsonian Institution conference in 1983, Rochester University professor John Mueller's study of public opinion revealed that the protest movement was "actually somewhat counterproductive in its attempts to influence public opinion—that is, the war might have been somewhat more unpopular had the protest not existed [since] the Vietnam protest movement generated negative feelings among the American people to an all but unprecedented degree ... Opposition to the war became associated with violent disruption, stink bombs, desecration of the flag, profanity, and contempt for American values." He pointed out that the presidental "peace" candidates, Hubert Humphrey in 1968 and George McGovern in 1972, were both soundly defeated at the polls, the latter by the greatest margin in modern times. Even the "protest vote" for Eugene McCarthy at the New Hampshire primaries in 1968 turned out to consist of people favoring a more vigorous prosecution of the war.

One of the great mistakes of the movement was to denigrate the soldiers rather than the politicians responsible for U.S. involvement. At a 1985 conference at the State University of New York at Stonybrook an activist said that he had protested in order to "bring the boys home safely." A young student asked, "When you were calling them baby killers and spitting at them and throwing rocks at them, was that just your way of saying 'Glad to see you'?" It was obvious that the moral high ground the protestors had occupied during the war had eroded, and with the outpouring of public support for the Gulf War, it disappeared completely.

"A feeling is widely and strongly held that 'the Establishment' is out of its mind. The feeling is that we are trying to impose some U.S. image on distant peoples we cannot understand ... and we are carrying the thing to absurd lengths. Related to this feeling is the increased polarization that is taking place in the United States with seeds of the worst split in our people for more than a century."

—Note to Defense Secretary McNamara from his deputy John McNaughton, May 1967

Above: *An American antiwar poster parodies the World War II Uncle Sam poster, "I Want You for U.S. Army."*

Right: *Brandishing Viet Cong and U.S. flags, demonstrators throng Pennsylvania Avenue in Washington, D.C.*

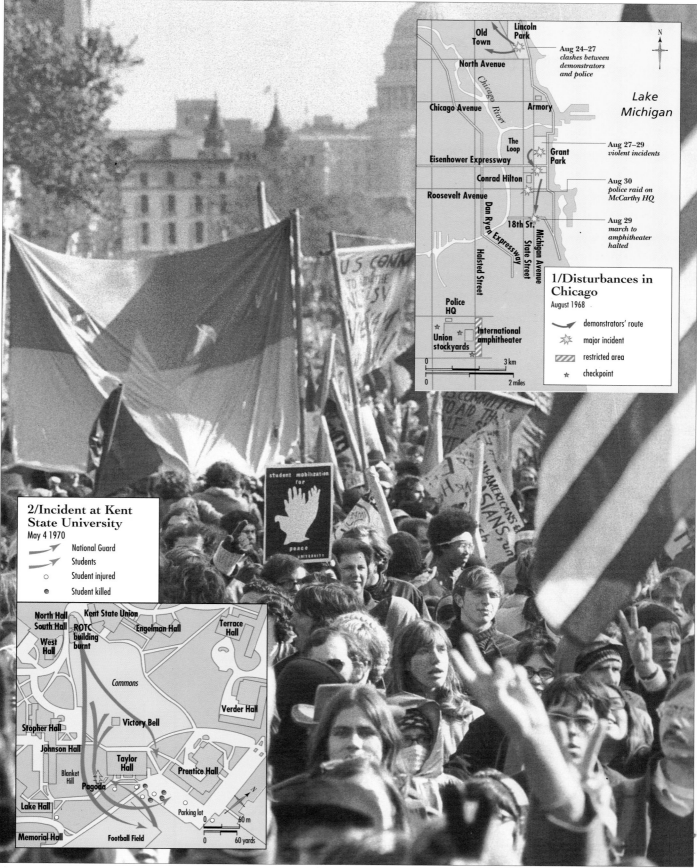

1/Disturbances in Chicago
August 1968

Aug 24–27
clashes between demonstrators and police

Aug 27–29
violent incidents

Aug 30
police raid on McCarthy HQ

Aug 29
march to amphitheater halted

Old Town
Lincoln Park
North Avenue
Chicago Avenue
Armory
Lake Michigan
Chicago River
The Loop
Eisenhower Expressway
Grant Park
Conrad Hilton
Roosevelt Avenue
Dan Ryan Expressway
18th St.
Michigan Avenue
State Street
Halsted Street
Police HQ
Union stockyards
International amphitheater

0 ———— 3 km
0 ———— 2 miles

→ demonstrators' route
✶ major incident
▨ restricted area
★ checkpoint

2/Incident at Kent State University
May 4 1970

→ National Guard
→ Students
○ Student injured
● Student killed

North Hall
South Hall
West Hall
Kent State Union
ROTC building burnt
Engelman Hall
Terrace Hall
Commons
Verder Hall
Stopher Hall
Victory Bell
Johnson Hall
Taylor Hall
Prentice Hall
Blanket Hill
Pagoda
Lake Hall
Parking lot
Memorial Hall
Football Field

0 ———— 60 m
0 ———— 60 yards

Part VI: Vietnamization

The very word "Vietnamization" reveals how little the true nature of the Second Indochina War was understood. The reality is that the war was "Vietnamized" from the start, but the limited-war theorists and counterinsurgency gurus so obfuscated the conflict that, to this day, many believe that the Vietnam War was between the United States and North Vietnam, rather than between North Vietnam and South Vietnam.

The advocates of counterinsurgency established the image in the public mind of a struggle between U.S. military forces and black-pajama-clad peasant guerrillas, where the objective was not to defeat the enemy but to win hearts and minds. The misperception was thus fostered that Vietnam was not a real war but an extended pacification campaign.

A prime example of this misperception was the reaction to an American officer's statement during the 1968 Tet Offensive that Ben Tre in the Mekong delta "had to be destroyed in order to save it." Dale Minor wrote in *The Information War* that "the corruption of language, of vision, and of sensibility which has arisen like a poisonous ground fog from the Vietnam war sometimes produces its own parody. Perhaps the most well known was the explanation for the leveling of Ben Tre during the Tet Offensive." But the real "corruption of language, of vision, and of sensibility" was in the reaction to that cliché, for judged in terms of war it was merely a statement of the obvious. The Allies could have used those words to describe the leveling of St. Lô during the Normandy campaign in 1944, and the Russians could certainly have said the same about Stalingrad.

In a country where war had become the norm, Saigon townspeople go about their daily business heedless of South Vietnamese troops setting up a roadside machine gun patrol.

Closer to home, as Dave Palmer notes in *The Way of the Fox*, during the American Revolution the Continental Congress ordered that "if General Washington and his council of war should be of the opinion that a successful attack may be made on the [British] troops in Boston, he [may] do it in any manner he may think expedient, notwithstanding the town and the property in it may thereby be destroyed." General William Tecumseh Sherman would no doubt describe his burning of Atlanta during the Civil War as "destroying it in order to save it for the Union."

A further example of how this false presentation of the struggle as an exercise in nation-building rather than a war helped to undermine public support was revealed by the *Washington Post* war correspondent Don Oberdorfer. In *Tet!*, Oberdorfer tells of the visit of then CBS anchorman Walter Cronkite to Hue in 1968, when the battle for the city was still raging. The more Cronkite, a World War II war correspondent, looked, "the more it reminded him of Europe in World War II and the less relevant it seemed to the original conception of a struggle to build a nation."

Spending the evening at the MACV-Forward headquarters at Phu Bai, Cronkite watched deputy MACV commander General Creighton Abrams and his staff "mulling the deployment of task forces and separate battalions, speaking of pincer movements, blocking forces and air strikes and drawing blue arrows on the battle maps. 'It was sickening to me,' Cronkite recalled later. 'They were talking strategy and tactics with no consideration of the bigger job of pacifying and restoring the country. This had come to be a total war, not a counterinsurgency effort to get the North Vietnamese out so we could support the indigenous effort. This was a World War II battlefield.' Earlier he had been told that the United States was trying to build a nation while fighting a war on foreign soil, instead of fighting and destroying and rebuilding later as in World War II."

The North Vietnamese were obviously not in on the party line. With their multi-division cross-border invasion, they thought they were fighting an old-fashioned war of conquest. But instead of blaming them,

Cronkite blamed the U.S. military for believing that turning back the enemy attack was a more immediate and "bigger job" than "pacifying and restoring the country." He did not explain how he would do the latter without first accomplishing the former. Disillusioned by battlefield realities, Cronkite turned against the Vietnam War. Claiming that the Tet Offensive was a draw, he called for a negotiated settlement, "not as victors but as an honorable people who lived up to their pledge to defend democracy, and did the best they could." President Johnson said, "If I've lost Cronkite, I've lost middle America."

It was a damaging wound, but the tragedy was that it was largely self-inflicted. Vietnam never was the test case for counterinsurgency that Kennedy claimed it to be, and as the North Vietnamese now freely admit, the National

The tanks and personnel carriers of the 11th Armored Cavalry Regiment take part in the 1970 "incursion" into Cambodia, ordered by Nixon in response to the NVA advance on Phnom Penh and in order to buy time for Vietnamization.

Liberation Front, so beloved by those who believed the war was an internal South Vietnamese affair, was a manufactured mirage from the start. For both sides, the struggle for Vietnam was a total war for national survival.

A comparison with the Korean War reveals the effect that delusions of nation-building had on the conduct of the war. Both wars were an outgrowth of the Cold War, and both Communist North Korea and Communist North Vietnam received military aid from China and the Soviet Union. This imposed severe limitations on how the war could be fought. In both cases the United States became involved in order to blunt what was seen as an attempt by the Soviet Union and China to expand Communism by force of arms. But at the same time, the fear of becoming involved in a war with the Soviet Union or China inhibited these efforts. As Henry Kissinger put it, "Our perception of the global challenge at the same time tempted us to distant enterprises and prevented us from meeting them conclusively." As a result, although it was not apparent at the time, both wars were fought on the strategic defensive, rather than on the strategic offen-

sive as in World War II, where the objective was to destroy the enemy's armed forces and occupy his territory so as to break his will to resist.

Military victory is not possible on the strategic defensive. The best possible battlefield outcome is stalemate, with the war terminated by political negotiations. In Korea, stalemate was reached after the Chinese Spring Offensive in April 1951, and two years of vicious outpost battles continued until the Korean Armistice of 1953. The same thing happened in the wake of the Tet Offensive. Again the battlefield was stalemated, but as historian Ronald Spector points out in *After Tet*, it took another year of bitter fighting before the United States finally realized this. It was not until 1972, with their ill-fated Eastertide Offensive, that the North Vietnamese realized it as well. Both wars were coalition efforts, with the United States assisting a beleaguered ally. At the end

Refugees from the Cholon suburb of Saigon take up temporary residence in a truck a short distance from their blazing homes. As millions flee in the Communist onslaught, schools, churches, pagodas, and abandoned vehicles are transformed into makeshift shelters.

of the war in Korea, United Nations Command troop strength stood at 590,911 Republic of Korea forces, 302,483 U.S. forces, and 39,145 troops from other UN countries, including most of the NATO nations. In Vietnam, by comparison, the South Vietnamese had 1,100,000 men under arms at the time of the U.S. withdrawal in 1973. U.S. troop strength peaked at 543,400 in April 1969, and the "Free World Military Forces" from Australia, New Zealand, South Korea, and Thailand peaked at 68,889.

The crucial difference between the two wars was the military relationships that developed between the United States and its allies. In both cases there was a U.S. military advisory group in the country when hostilities began. The Korean Military Advisory Group (KMAG) had been formed in 1949 as a successor to provisional military advisory groups dating back to 1946. In Vietnam, MACV had been formed in 1962 as the successor to MAAG–Vietnam and its predecessor, MAAG–Indochina, which dated back to September 1950. When the war started in Korea, the Eighth U.S. Army took control of KMAG, which it super-

vised as one of its several subordinate commands. While the Eighth U.S. Army concentrated its attention on the external North Korean and later the Chinese enemy, KMAG devoted itself to advising the Korean military. From 470 personnel in July 1950, it grew to 1,308 before the war was over. When the Korean War began, the Republic of Korea Army (ROKA) consisted of eight poorly equipped infantry divisions, most of which were literally decimated by the opening North Korean Army offensive. Things were so bad in those early days that cynics said that KMAG stood for "Kiss My Ass Goodbye." But instead of pushing ROKA to one side, as would be done with South Vietnamese forces in the Vietnam War, the United States decided to continue to train and develop ROKA forces on the battlefield.

When the war ended, ROKA had 590,911 men under arms and 16 well-trained, well-equipped, and battle-hardened divisions in the field. Because "Koreanization" had been U.S. policy from the beginning there

Women grieve for South Vietnamese victims of the Viet Cong after the discovery of hundreds of bodies in mass graves outside the city of Hue.

was no need for the equivalent of "Vietnamization." By comparison, MACV remained the U.S. military headquarters throughout the involvement in Vietnam. When the major U.S. troop buildup began in 1965, MACV remained in Saigon rather than move to the field near its combat units, as the Eighth U.S. Army did in Korea. Although more U.S. ground combat corps and divisions were deployed to Vietnam than to Korea, no field army headquarters was ever established.

Before the U.S. troop buildup, MACV was exclusively occupied with building up the South Vietnamese military. After 1965, its attention was almost entirely directed to U.S. military operations. The advisory effort, and the South Vietnamese military, were shunted aside and largely ignored. Unlike the ROKA units, which were under Eighth U.S. Army command and operated with it in the field, South Vietnamese military units were left under South Vietnamese command and rarely operated with U.S. military forces. "I consistently resisted suggestions

that a single, combined command could more effectively prosecute the war," said General Westmoreland in his *Report on the War.* "I believed that subordinating the Vietnamese forces to U.S. control would stifle the growth of leadership and acceptance of responsibility essential to the development of Vietnamese Armed Forces capable of defending their country. Moreover, such a step would be counter to our basic objective of assisting Vietnam in a time of emergency and of leaving a strong, independent country at the time of our withdrawal."

But the opposite proved true. After the war, when South Vietnamese military and civilian leaders were asked about strategic planning, they made it clear that "there was little strategic planning; that, in fact, Saigon, which had no strategy of its own when the Americans

Local men and boys flock to see the wreckage of a U.S. B-52 shot down over Hanoi. Roundly denounced both at home and abroad, Operation Linebacker II was successful in its aim of forcing the North Vietnamese back to the negotiating table.

were in the country, also failed to develop a real strategy after they left." One reason for this, said Colonel Hoang Ngoc Lung, former JGS chief of intelligence, was that "the South's national goals and strategy were based on the assumption that full American support would be available until proven unnecessary. This assistance was perceived as being part of the U.S. strategy which followed the end of World War II with respect to the containment of Communism in Asia as well as in Europe."

This proved to be a faulty assumption. In the aftermath of the Tet Offensive, the United States gave up on the idea of victory in Vietnam. As his Marine regimental commander told Lieutenant Colonel Bernard Trainor when he took command of an infantry battalion in 1969, "We're no longer here to win, we're merely 'campaigning,' so keep the casualties down."

That was Washington's attitude as well. "Vietnamization" was the brainchild of Nixon's defense secretary Melvin Laird, a "total politician," in Lieutenant General Phillip Davidson's words, who "saw the war pragmatically as a losing proposition" and to whom "Vietnamization offered a way to get the United States, the Republican Party, Richard Nixon, and most important, Melvin Laird, out of the Vietnamese quagmire. Whether it would work or not was secondary. It was an exit." *Commentary* editor Norman Podhoretz saw this in a larger context. In a March 1980 article, he argued that Vietnamization was actually "the model or paradigm of a new strategy of retreat." Just as President Kennedy saw Vietnam as the test case for the counterinsurgency doctrine, so the country was to be "the paradigmatic testing-ground" for the Nixon Doctrine, a new strategy of containment through surrogate power. Announced on July 25, 1969, the doctrine said that while the United States would keep its

Despite the provisions of the Paris accords, the South Vietnamese military, members of which are seen here in a helicopter evacuation from Tuy Hoa, were left virtually defenseless in the face of the North Vietnamese aggressors.

treaty commitments, would provide a nuclear shield, and would continue to provide military and economic assistance as appropriate, it would "look to the nation directly threatened to assume the primary responsibility of providing the manpower for its defense."

The irony was that the Nixon Doctrine described almost exactly the relationship between North Vietnam and its Soviet and Chinese allies, who had provided a nuclear shield that effectively deterred a U.S. invasion of North Vietnam, as well as massive amounts of military aid and assistance. As Bui Diem, the former South Vietnamese ambassador to the United States, commented, the fact that the Chinese had left the actual fighting to the North Vietnamese gave the latter an advantage. "American support, even when it was militarily effective, was not an unmixed blessing … The enemy, of course, even though he was maneuvered between Moscow and Peking and therefore may have seemed to possess a modicum of independence, was solidly dependent on foreign troops in his ranks, and his allies … disguised their influence quite effectively, whereas the United States did not."

But Colonel Lung pointed out that the greatest failing of Vietnamization was that the South Vietnamese had

Henry Kissinger is congratulated by President Nixon after the announcement that Kissinger and North Vietnam's Le Duc Tho have jointly received the 1973 Nobel Peace Prize for their role in the Vietnamese peace negotiations.

"missed the vital point: a new strategy had been announced by the Americans. Vietnamization was more than a modernization and expansion of the RVNAF; it was essentially a strategy that would require the Vietnamese to survive with greatly reduced American participation. Had [South Vietnamese] President Thieu and the Joint General Staff fully realized that fact, perhaps they would have begun then to build a strategy to cope with it. Instead the RVNAF made no adjustments in doctrine, organization or training to compensate for the departure of American troops and firepower."

Paradoxically, the most trenchant critique of the concept of Vietnamization was provided by Chinese Marshal Lin Biao in his 1965 article "Long Live the Victory of People's War. The article set out the threat of the "people's war," the Chinese variant of the "wars of national liberation" that the United States had originally intervened in Vietnam to counter. His powerful indictment of foreign aid applies not only to fighting a people's war but to defeating one as well. "The victory of the anti-Fascist War [World War II] was the result of the common struggle of the people of the world … The common victory was won by all the peoples, who gave one another support and encouragement. Yet each country was, above all, liberated as a result of its own people's efforts.

"In order to make a revolution and to fight a people's war and be victorious," continued Lin Biao, "it is imperative to adhere to the policy of self-reliance, rely on the strength of the masses in one's own country and prepare to carry on the fight independently even when material aid from outside is cut off. If one does not operate by one's own efforts, does not independently ponder and solve the problems of the revolution in one's country, and does not rely on the strength of the masses but leans wholly on foreign aid … no victory can be won, or be consolidated even if it is won."

Right: Two blind Montagnard children are led to safety by a South Vietnamese paratrooper in the mass exodus from South Vietnam.

Republic of Vietnam Armed Forces 1955–1975

President Nixon's announcement of the "Vietnamization" of the war on June 8, 1969, was greeted with bemusement by the South Vietnamese military or Republic of Vietnam Armed Forces, who had been fighting long before the Americans arrived on the scene. The RVNAF was established when the Republic of Vietnam was founded on October 26, 1955, and had its origins in the Vietnamese National Army, formed by the French in July 1949. Armed and equipped by MAAG–Vietnam and its successor, MACV, it had over a million men under arms by the U.S. withdrawal in 1973.

The RVNAF had five components: the Army of the Republic of Vietnam (ARVN), the Vietnamese Air Force (VNAF), the Vietnamese Navy (VNN) the Vietnamese Marine Corps (VNMC), and the territorial Regional Forces (RF) and Popular Forces (PF). The ARVN consisted of the I, II, III, and IV Corps, which were organized into 12 divisions. The Airborne Division, based in Saigon, was the Joint General Staff general reserve and was deployed where needed. The 1st, 2nd, and 3rd ARVN divisions were stationed in I Corps, the 22nd and 23rd divisions in II Corps, the 5th, 18th, and 25th divisions in III Corps, and the 7th, 9th, and 21st divisions in IV Corps.

Including non-divisional units, the ARVN comprised 105 light infantry battalions, 9 airborne infantry battalions, 21 ranger battalions, and 33 border defense battalions. In addition to these regular forces, territorial forces included 1,810 RF companies and 8,146 PF platoons. Artillery support included 44 battalions of 105mm howitzers, 15 battalions of 155mm howitzers, 4 battalions of 175mm guns, and 176 separate 105mm howitzer sections attached to RF and PF units. Armor units included 11 divisional armored cavalry squadrons and 3 tank battalions equipped with 90mm-gun M48 tanks.

With over 2,000 aircraft, the VNAF was the fourth largest air force in the world. Its 16 fighter bomber squadrons included A-1 fighter bombers, F-5 jet fighters, and A-37 jet fighter bombers. The 3 airlift squadrons included C-7 Caribou and C-130 Hercules transports. In addition to reconnaissance, liaison, and special mission squadrons, the VNAF included 17 squadrons of UH-1 Huey helicopters and 4 squadrons of CH-47 Chinook helicopters.

Most of the VNN's 1,500 ships were river patrol boats and other small craft, but the force also included ocean-going submarine chasers, minesweepers and former U.S. Coast Guard cutters. The VNMC, a separate service after 1965, was organized as a division and included the 147th, 258th, and 369th Marine brigades. Like the Airborne Division, it was part of the JGS reserve and was deployed nationwide to meet local emergencies.

The RVNAF had some capable generals, but the caliber of its senior leaders was poor. The force was riven by political differences, cowed by the NVA, who had defeated them in the First Indochina War, and undermined by the Americans. One ARVN staff officer, asked what mistakes the Americans made in preparing the South Vietnamese to fight, replied, "when American troops came to Vietnam, they try to do everything. And make the Vietnamese lose the initiative … So the Vietnamese don't rely on themselves, they rely on the American."

One of the great canards of the war was that the RVNAF would not fight. That North Vietnam was held at bay for more than six years before the Americans arrived and for three years after the last U.S. ground forces left is evidence that they would and did fight for their country. Although not widely reported, the RVNAF took four times as many casualties as the Americans. Not counting the final offensive, for which statistics are not available, the RVNAF suffered 223,748 killed and 570,000 wounded in the defense of their country. U.S. casualties include 47,244 killed in action, 10,446 dead from non-hostile causes, and 153,329 seriously wounded.

As Major General Homer Smith, the highest ranking U.S. officer in Vietnam at the time, pointed out, the collapse of South Vietnam in 1975 was caused not by cowardice but by the "family syndrome." The fact that the ARVN had their families with them on their battle positions made for great stability on local operations, when the soldiers fought to protect their wives and children, but it was a disaster during the withdrawal from the Central Highlands and the northern provinces in March 1975, when soldiers left their units to take care of their families, causing whole divisions to fall apart. When their families were safe, however, they fought valiantly. During the final NVA blitzkrieg, not one ARVN unit surrendered to the enemy.

"It was not so many months ago that General William Westmoreland felt obliged to pass the word down the U.S. chain of command: if you can't say something good about the ARVN, don't say anything at all. The resulting silence was almost as damaging to the ARVN as the heavy shellfire of criticism it replaced. Of late, however, the ARVN has been doing some pretty effective firing of its own on the battlefields. Its performance has enabled U.S. officers to talk about the ARVN again, this time in terms of results and performances from the DMZ to the Delta, including victories in 37 of the ARVN's last 45 major contacts with the Communists."

—New York Times, 1968

In a respite from the bloody battles raging throughout his land, a South Vietnamese soldier shares a joke with a Vietnamese woman.

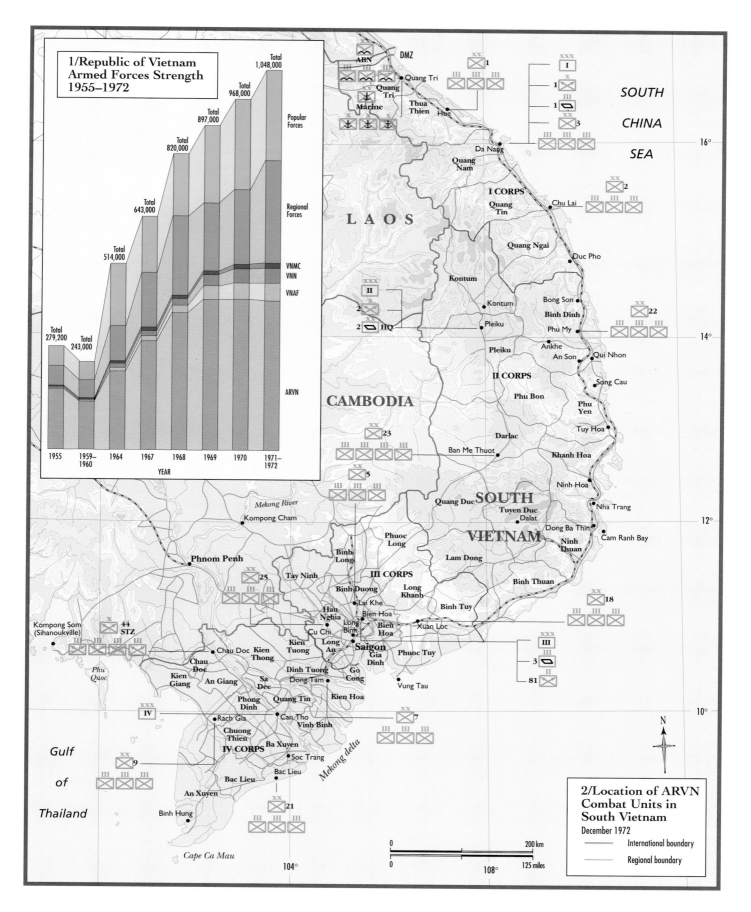

1/Republic of Vietnam Armed Forces Strength 1955–1972

Total 243,000 — 1955; Total 279,200 — 1959–1960; Total 514,000 — 1964; Total 643,000 — 1967; Total 820,000 — 1968; Total 897,000 — 1969; Total 968,000 — 1970; Total 1,048,000 — 1971–1972

Popular Forces; Regional Forces; VNMC; VNN; VNAF; ARVN

YEAR

2/Location of ARVN Combat Units in South Vietnam

December 1972

International boundary

Regional boundary

The U.S. Ground Force Withdrawal 1969–1973

One of the most pernicious myths of the Vietnam War is that U.S. forces were, in the words of one Asian diplomat in Beijing in 1990, "beaten like a wet rat" and forced to flee for their lives. It was not military pressure by the VC and the NVA that caused the U.S. withdrawal, but political pressure at home.

Shortly after taking office, President Nixon bowed to public sentiment and made a radical change in U.S. military policy. "I have decided to order the immediate redeployment from Vietnam of the divisional equivalent of approximately 25,000 men," he said at a press conference with South Vietnamese president Nguyen Van Thieu at Midway Island on June 8, 1969. "Vietnamization" was the new strategy, and it would be implemented in three phases. First, ground combat responsibility was to be turned over to the Republic of Vietnam Armed Forces, with the United States continuing to provide air, naval, and logistic support. Second, with the help of massive U.S. aid, the RVNAF would develop its own combat support capability in order to achieve self-reliance. Finally, the U.S. role would become strictly advisory.

The U.S. ground force troop withdrawal was executed in 14 increments. In the first increment, from July 1 to August 31, 1969, the 9th Infantry Division in the Mekong delta in IV Corps, minus one brigade, returned to the United States. The second increment, from September 18 to December 15, 1969, saw the return of the 3rd Marine Division, based along the DMZ, to its base in Okinawa, and the return of the 3rd Brigade, 82nd Airborne Division, to its parent division at Fort Bragg.

As secret peace talks began in Paris, and on the eve of the Cambodian incursion, the third increment, from February 1 to April 15, 1970, involved the withdrawal of the 1st Infantry Division from III Corps, and the 3rd Brigade, 4th Infantry Division, from the Central Highlands in II Corps. During the fourth increment, from July 1 to October 15, 1970, the remaining brigade from the 9th Infantry Division was withdrawn, as well as the 199th Light Infantry Brigade from III Corps. In the fifth increment, from October 16 to December 31, 1970, the rest of the 4th Infantry Division left II Corps and the 25th Infantry Division, minus one brigade, withdrew from III Corps.

The sixth increment, from January 1 to April 30, 1971, saw the largest single reduction, when the III Marine Amphibious Force HQ and the 1st Marine Division left Vietnam, ending the Marine presence. The corps-level I Field Force Vietnam was disbanded and 41,848 Army forces left III Corps, including the 1st Cavalry Division (Airmobile) minus one brigade, the 11th Armored Cavalry Regiment, and the remaining brigade from the 25th Infantry Division.

The corps-level II Field Force Vietnam was disestablished, and one air cavalry squadron and three infantry battalions departed during the seventh increment, from May 1 to June 30, 1971. The 173rd Airborne Brigade from II Corps left during the eighth increment, from July 1 to November 30, 1971. During the ninth increment, from September 1 to November 30, 1971, the Americal Division left I Corps. In the tenth increment, from December 1, 1971, to January 31, 1972, after supporting RVNAF operations in Lam Son 719, the 101st Airborne Division was withdrawn from I Corps. It had been the last division-sized unit in the country.

The withdrawals continued through the NVA Eastertide Offensive in 1972, with 2 cavalry squadrons, 5 infantry battalions and 4 air cavalry squadrons departing during the eleventh increment, from February 1 to April 30, 1972. Even as fighting continued, the last of the brigade-sized units, the 3rd Brigade, 1st Cavalry Division (Airmobile), and the 196th Infantry Brigade, were withdrawn during the twelfth increment, from May 1 to June 30, 1972. XXIV Corps was deactivated during the thirteenth increment, from May 1 to August 31, 1972, and the last infantry battalion, the 3rd Battalion, 21st Infantry, was withdrawn. The fourteenth increment, from September 1 to November 30, 1972, saw the departure of various units, leaving a residual Army presence of 16,000 administrative, support, and advisory personnel.

The U.S. Army was not defeated during the NVA final offensive in the spring of 1975 for one simple reason—having withdrawn in good military order almost three years earlier, they were not there to be defeated. But that does not mean that the United States had not lost the war. "You know you never beat us on the battlefield," I told my NVA counterpart on the Four Power Joint Military Team in Hanoi one week before the fall of Saigon. "That may be so," he replied, "but it is also irrelevant."

"There was something unresolved, in that I wanted to stay and get back at the VC for all my friends. There was a constant process of rerunning the mental tapes of your friends who had gotten killed. Never left my mind. I wanted to kill. I couldn't get it out of my mind. But suddenly I had a chance to stay alive. It was an alternative that I hadn't considered."

—U.S. soldier

A happy G.I. prepares to board a troop carrier at Phu Bai airport as the 196th Infantry Brigade leave Vietnam on June 19, 1972.

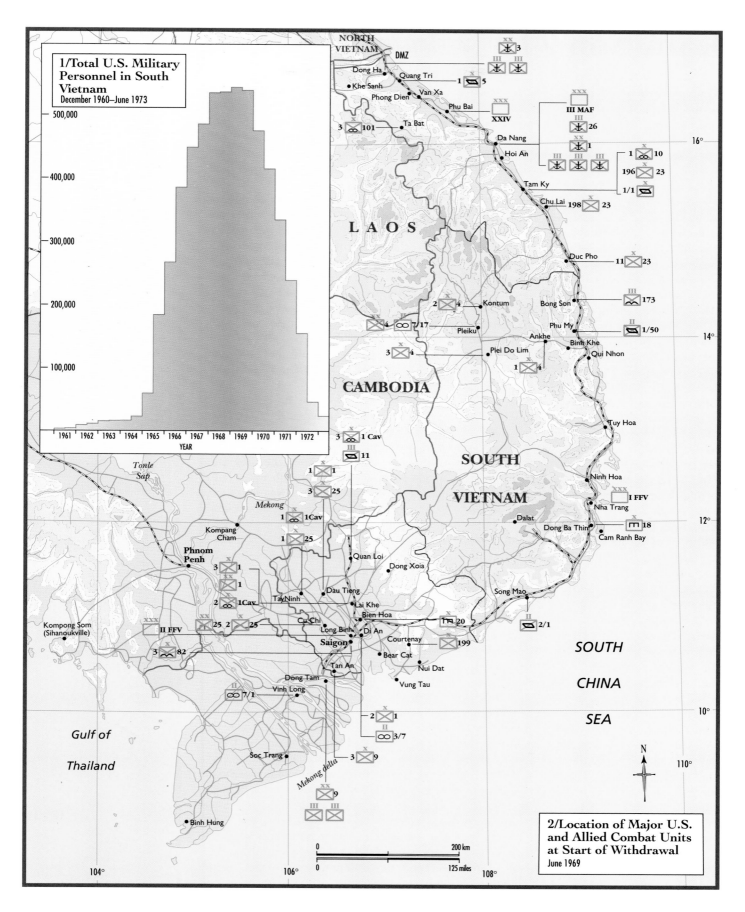

1/Total U.S. Military Personnel in South Vietnam
December 1960–June 1973

500,000
400,000
300,000
200,000
100,000

1961 1962 1963 1964 1965 1966 1967 1968 1969 1970 1971 1972
YEAR

NORTH VIETNAM
DMZ

Dong Ha
Khe Sanh
Quang Tri
Van Xa
Phong Dien
Phu Bai
Ta Bat

3 ∞ 101

XX 3
III III
X 1 5

XXX XXXX
XXIV III MAF

26
1

Da Nang
Hoi An

1 ∞ 10
196 23
1/1
198 23

LAOS

Tam Ky
Chu Lai

Duc Pho 11 23

Bong Son 173

Kontum 2 4

Phu My
Ankhe
Binh Khe
Qui Nhon

1/50

7/17
Pleiku
3 4
Plei Do Lim
1 4

CAMBODIA

Tuy Hoa

SOUTH

VIETNAM

Ninh Hoa

I FFV
Nha Trang
Dalat
Dong Ba Thin
Cam Ranh Bay
18

3 ∞ 1 Cav
11

1 1
3 25

Tonle Sap

Mekong

1 ∞ 1Cav

Kompang Cham

1 25

Phnom Penh

3 1
1
2 ∞ 1Cav

Quan Loi
Dong Xoia

Song Mao 2/1

TayNinh
Dau Tieng
Lai Khe
Bien Hoa
Cu Chi
Long Binh
Di An
Saigon

20

Kompong Som (Sihanoukville)

II FFV
25 2 25

Courtenay 199

3 82

Tan An
Bear Cat
Nui Dat
Vung Tau

Dong Tam
Vinh Long
∞ 7/1

2 1
3/7

SOUTH

CHINA

SEA

Soc Trang
3 9

N

Mekong delta

9

Binh Hung

0   200 km
0   125 miles

2/Location of Major U.S. and Allied Combat Units at Start of Withdrawal
June 1969

Gulf of Thailand

16°
14°
12°
10°
110°

104°   106°   108°

Lam Son 719   JANUARY–APRIL 1971

Conceived as a counterpart to the Cambodian incursion, which disrupted North Vietnamese supply lines and destroyed their base areas in the Cambodian border regions, Lam Son 719 was designed to repeat that success in Laos and to test the effectiveness of "Vietnamization." But major differences between the Cambodian incursion and the Laotian invasion would prove to be critical.

In reaction to the Cambodian incursion, the December 1970 Cooper–Church Amendment to the defense appropriations bill forbade the introduction of U.S. ground troops into Laos, and U.S. advisers could not accompany the ARVN forces to which they were attached. While the U.S. Seventh Fleet, with the 31st Marine Amphibious Unit on board, staged an amphibious feint off the port of Vinh, the only direct U.S. support permitted was long-range cross-border artillery fire, helicopter lift, and helicopter and fixed-wing air strikes.

Unlike previous attacks on Communist base areas where the enemy chose not to make a stand, the Laotian base areas were critical to the NVA prosecution of the war. "The Ho Chi Minh Trail was in 1971 the *only* means of supplying the entire enemy force in South Vietnam, southern Laos, and Cambodia," noted Lieutenant General Phillip B. Davidson. "If the ARVN could cut the trail … they would deal a devastating blow to all Communist operations in South Vietnam … The North Vietnamese had to oppose Lam Son 719 with every resource they could bring to bear."

Lam Son 719 consisted of four phases. On January 30, the U.S. 1st Brigade (Mechanized), 5th Infantry Division, and the 101st Airborne Division (Airmobile) would reopen Route 9 to the old Khe Sanh Marine base, which would serve as both a logistics and fire support base and a jumping-off place for ARVN heliborne assaults into Laos. In Phase II, scheduled for February 8, the ARVN would launch a three-pronged attack to seize the town of Tchepone and Base Area 604. The ARVN Airborne Division and the 1st Armored Brigade would launch the main attack astride Route 9 to Aloui, from where they would launch an assault on Tchepone, 15 miles away.

South of Route 9 the 1st ARVN Division, less its 2nd Regiment, would move overland to provide flank security while an ARVN Ranger

Group established a base at Tabat to guard the northern flank. A Vietnamese Marine Corps brigade would remain in reserve at Khe Sanh. Phase III was to be the razing of Base Area 604 and Phase IV was to be the destruction of Base Area 611. After 90 days the forces would return to South Vietnam.

The ARVN forces seized Aloui on February 10, but instead of continuing the momentum of the attack they froze in place, reportedly on the secret orders of President Nguyen Van Thieu. This decision virtually guaranteed even heavier casualties, for it gave the enemy time to concentrate the defending forces. By February 18, the NVA 70B Corps, supported by T-34 and T-54 medium tanks, heavy artillery, and antiaircraft guns, began closing in, with its 308th Division on the northern flank, its 2nd Division on the west, and its 304th and 324B divisions on the south.

Outnumbered from the start, the ARVN 17,000-man force originally faced 22,000 North Vietnamese combat and logistical troops. By the end of the operation the ARVN force, which was now down to 8,000 effectives, faced 40,000 NVA regulars. Although two infantry battalions of the ARVN 2nd Regiment were helilifted from Khe Sanh into the now deserted village of Tchepone on March 6, it was a meaningless gesture. Withdrawing from Tchepone on March 8, the ARVN invasion force now had to extricate itself from certain disaster. Supported by massive air strikes, the remnants of the invasion force fought their way back to South Vietnam.

Lam Son 719 officially came to an end on April 6. Losses were appalling. The South Vietnamese suffered 7,682 casualties—almost half of their force—including 1,764 killed in action. The United States lost 108 helicopters and another 618 were damaged, and suffered 1,402 casualties, including 215 killed. Enemy losses, most of which resulted from U.S air strikes, were estimated at 20,000.

On April 7, 1971, in a televised report to the nation, President Nixon announced, "Tonight I can report that Vietnamization has succeeded." The truth was exactly the opposite. But in war nothing is ever final, and a year later these same demoralized ARVN forces had their revenge, this time sending the NVA reeling back in defeat.

"To the modern American cavalryman of the air, the plunge into Laos has been something like an old-time charge on horseback: admirably heroic, stunningly effective—and terribly costly. For four weeks now, American helicopter pilots have flown through some of the heaviest flak in the history of the Indochinese war … The customary bravado of the American chopper pilot [is] beginning to wear a bit thin."

—Newsweek, March 15, 1971

A South Vietnamese soldier drags a crate of supplies from one of the many North Vietnamese bunkers discovered along the Ho Chi Minh Trail. The bunkers contained caches of arms, gasoline, and uniforms.

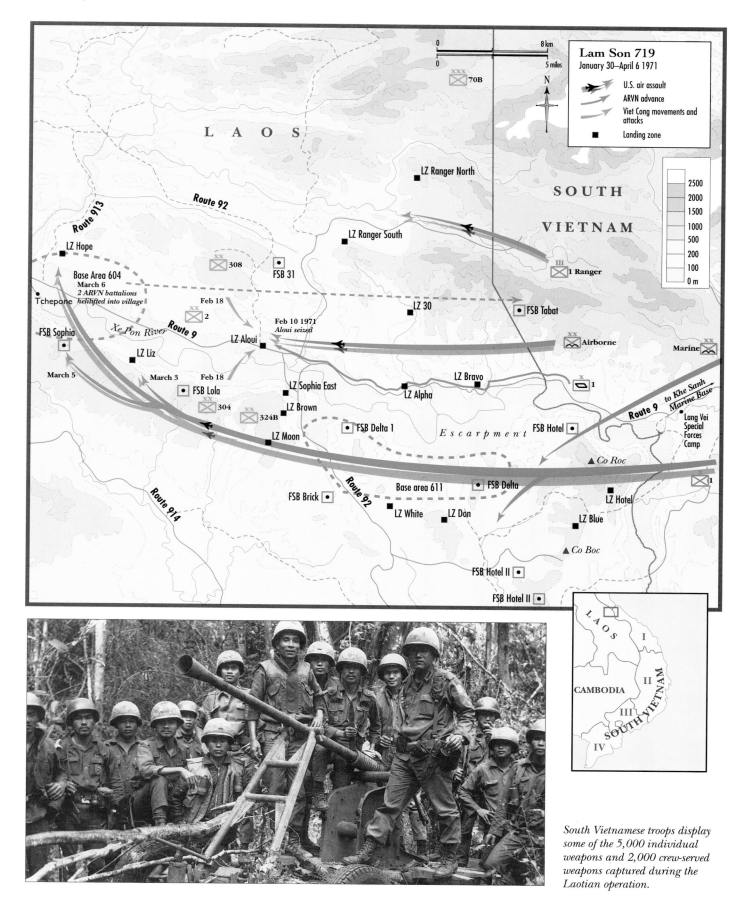

Lam Son 719
January 30–April 6 1971

→ U.S. air assault
→ ARVN advance
→ Viet Cong movements and attacks
■ Landing zone

2500
2000
1500
1000
500
200
100
0 m

L A O S

SOUTH

VIETNAM

LZ Ranger North

Route 92

Route 913

LZ Hope

Base Area 604
March 6
*2 ARVN battalions
helilifted into village*

Tchepone

Xe Pon River

FSB Sophia

March 5

LZ Liz

March 3

Feb 18

FSB Lola

304

324B

LZ Moon

Route 914

Route 92

FSB Brick

308

FSB 31

Feb 18
2

Route 9

LZ Aloui

Feb 10 1971
Aloui seized

LZ Sophia East

LZ Brown

FSB Delta 1

LZ White

Base area 611

LZ Ranger South

LZ 30

FSB Tabat

Airborne

LZ Bravo

LZ Alpha

Escarpment

FSB Hotel

LZ Don

FSB Delta

1 Ranger

Marine

1

Route 9   to Khe Sanh
            Marine Base

Lang Vei
Special
Forces
Camp

▲ Co Roc

LZ Hotel

LZ Blue

1

▲ Co Boc

FSB Hotel II

FSB Hotel II

70B

L A O S

I

CAMBODIA

II

III

SOUTH VIETNAM

IV

*South Vietnamese troops display
some of the 5,000 individual
weapons and 2,000 crew-served
weapons captured during the
Laotian operation.*

Eastertide: Quang Tri   MARCH–SEPTEMBER 1972

The NVA Eastertide Offensive in 1972 was a debacle which would cost General Vo Nguyen Giap his job and set back North Vietnam's conquest of South Vietnam for another three years. The largest Communist military offensive since Chinese intervention in the Korean War two decades earlier, it began on Maundy Thursday, March 30, 1972. It was a go-for-broke operation involving virtually every combat unit in the NVA, the equivalent of 20 divisions. More than 125,000 men were involved, divided into 14 divisions and 26 separate regiments supported by tanks and heavy artillery.

The object of the Eastertide Offensive was simple—the military conquest of South Vietnam. To accomplish this, the NVA would first destroy the ARVN defenders by a three-pronged, coordinated multi-division attack at Quang Tri in the north, Kontum in the center and An Loc in the south.

Several factors were taken into account when the decision to launch the attack was made. First, almost all U.S. ground forces had been withdrawn, and in the spring of 1972 only two combat brigades remained in the country. Second, after the rout of the South Vietnamese forces during their Laotian invasion the year before, it was assumed that the ARVN would crumble under the weight of the NVA attack. Third, the North Vietnamese Politburo thought it important to attack while there was still a residual U.S. presence in Vietnam so as to inflict a humiliating defeat on President Richard Nixon in an election year, a defeat which would force him from office and thereby destroy American war policies.

On March 30, under cover of an artillery barrage from their 130mm gun howitzers in the so-called Demilitarized Zone that outranged the 105mm and 155mm howitzers of the ARVN defenders by some 10,000 meters, the NVA corps-level B-5 Front hit the green 3rd ARVN Division head on. The odds in their favor were overwhelming. The B-5 Front consisted of the 304th and 308th NVA divisions, three separate infantry regiments, two tank regiments, and four artillery regiments. In reserve were the 325th and 320th NVA divisions along the DMZ and the 312th Division to the east in nearby Laos. Farther to the south, opposite Hue, was the 324B NVA Division.

By April 1, the NVA had driven the 3rd ARVN Division from their initial defensive positions. As they attempted to regroup further south, the division's 57th Regiment broke, and its 56th Regiment, holding the firebase at Camp Carroll, surrendered to the enemy. A new defensive line was established around the city of Quang Tri, and the 3rd ARVN Division commander, Brigadier General Vu Van Giai, was reinforced by two marine brigades, four ranger groups, and one armored brigade.

On April 23, reinforced by elements of the 325th NVA Division, the enemy resumed the attack, compressing the ARVN defenders into Quang Tri City. On May 1, under heavy artillery fire, mass panic set in and Quang Tri was abandoned to the enemy. The 3rd ARVN Division had ceased to exist.

With Hue now threatened, South Vietnamese president Nguyen Van Thieu fired the I Corps commander, Lieutenant General Hoang Xuan Lam, and replaced him with Lieutenant General Ngo Quang Truong, the best general in the South Vietnamese military. Arriving in Hue on May 2, Truong immediately took charge. The Marine Division would defend Hue on the north and northwest, and the 1st ARVN Division would man the defenses to the west. The enemy advance had been checked, and on June 28, General Truong, reinforced by the Airborne Division, launched a counteroffensive to retake Quang Tri Province.

Assisted by Major General Frederick J. Kroesen, the senior U.S. adviser in I Corps (who would later serve as Army Vice Chief of Staff) and supported by massive U.S. firepower, including strikes by B-52 bombers and naval gunfire support from U.S. warships laying offshore, the counterattack moved slowly northward, routing the six opposing NVA divisions, and retaking Quang Tri City on September 16. Many of the firebases along the DMZ were recaptured, and by the end of October the situation in I Corps had been stabilized.

The South Vietnamese flag has finally been raised on the Citadel at Quang Tri (right), after months of heavy fighting, while on the east wall of the Citadel (far right), a South Vietnamese Marine mans his M-79 grenade launcher.

"Pigs sniffing around the corpses of North Vietnamese soldiers were the only things moving today in this battered town in the middle of the North Vietnamese offensive below the Demilitarized Zone. Overhead, rockets sped southward and shells north … Dong Ha, until four days ago a prosperous town of 18,000, is considered to be 'holding out.' But no humans move inside it. Any who do are killed by the marines on the south bank of the river."

—New York Times,
April 4, 1972

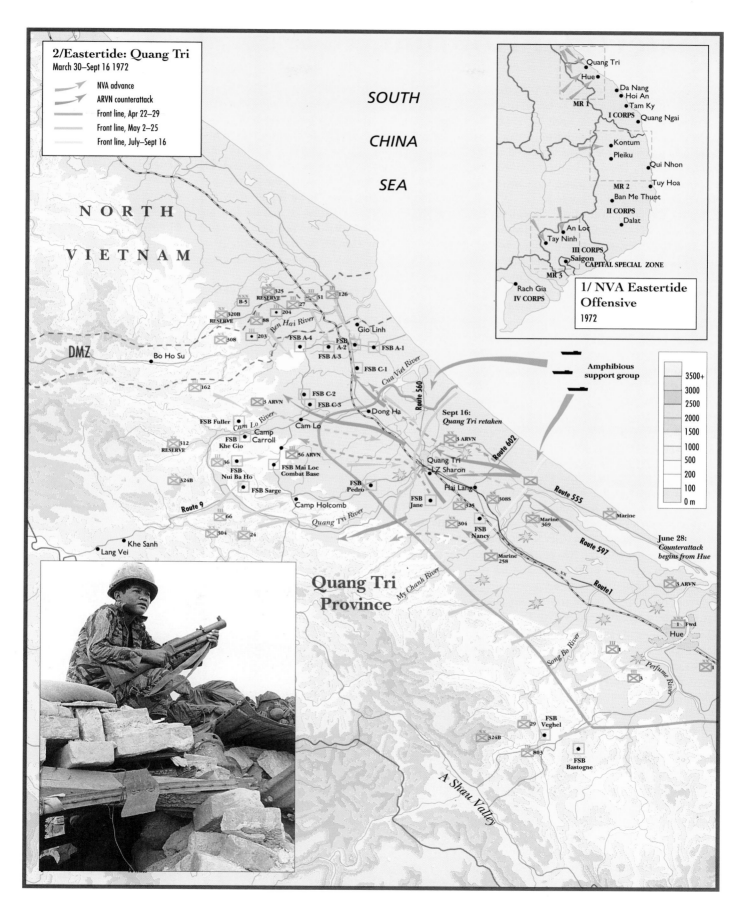

2/Eastertide: Quang Tri
March 30–Sept 16 1972

→ NVA advance
→ ARVN counterattack
— Front line, Apr 22–29
— Front line, May 2–25
— Front line, July–Sept 16

SOUTH

CHINA

SEA

NORTH

VIETNAM

DMZ

Ben Hai River

RESERVE
B-5
320B
RESERVE
308
204
88
203
325
27
31
126
Gio Linh
FSB A-4
FSB A-2
FSB A-3
FSB A-1
FSB C-1
Cua Viet River
162
FSB C-2
FSB C-3
Dong Ha
3 ARVN
Cam Lo River
FSB Fuller
312
RESERVE
FSB
Khe Gio
Camp
Carroll
Cam Lo
Route 560
36
FSB
Nui Ba Ho
56 ARVN
FSB Mai Loc
Combat Base
324B
FSB Sarge
Camp Holcomb
FSB
Pedro
Quang Tri River
Route 9
66
304
24
Khe Sanh
Lang Vei
FSB
Jane
325
304
FSB
Nancy
Marine
258

Sept 16:
Quang Tri retaken
3 ARVN
Quang Tri
LZ Sharon
Hai Lang
308S
Marine
369
Route 602
Route 555
Marine
Route 597
Route 1
June 28:
*Counterattack
begins from Hue*
3 ARVN

Amphibious
support group

3500+
3000
2500
2000
1500
1000
500
200
100
0 m

**Quang Tri
Province**
My Chanh River
Song Bo River
Perfume River
1 Fwd
Hue
1
1
3
FSB
Veghel
29
324B
803
FSB
Bastogne
A Shau Valley

Quang Tri
Hue
Da Nang
Hoi An
Tam Ky
Quang Ngai
MR 1
I CORPS
Kontum
Pleiku
Qui Nhon
Tuy Hoa
MR 2
Ban Me Thuot
II CORPS
Dalat
An Loc
Tay Ninh
III CORPS
Saigon CAPITAL SPECIAL ZONE
MR 3
Rach Gia
IV CORPS

**1/ NVA Eastertide
Offensive**
1972

Bo Ho Su

Eastertide: Kontum   APRIL–MAY 1972

The second prong of the NVA Eastertide Offensive was the attack on Kontum in central Vietnam, which began on April 12, 1972. The NVA objective was the same objective as in November 1965, which was thwarted at the battle of the Ia Drang—an attack across the Central Highlands to cut South Vietnam in two. This time they almost succeeded.

Under the command of the corps-level B-3 Front, the NVA committed three divisions to the assault. Advancing eastward from base areas in Laos and Cambodia, the 2nd and 320th NVA divisions, supported by a tank regiment and several artillery regiments, moved on Kontum, while the 3rd NVA Division operated in the coastal area along the South China Sea. In the Kontum area, the ARVN had the 22nd Division's 42nd Regiment at Tan Canh and its 47th Regiment at Dak To, reinforced by two armored cavalry squadrons and, initially, the ARVN Airborne Division. Along the coast were the 22nd Division's 40th and 41st regiments while farther south, near Ban Me Thuot, was the 23rd Division.

By April 15 the bases at Dak To and Tan Canh were surrounded, and the outposts on "Rocket Ridge," to the west of Kontum, were overrun. Artillery fire intensified and on April 23, the NVA 2nd Division launched a tank-led attack on Tan Canh. The ARVN 42nd Regiment was routed and the ARVN 22nd Division commander, Colonel Le Duc Dat, and his staff disappeared when their headquarters were overrun, never to be heard from again. A similar disaster struck the ARVN 47th Regiment at Dak To, whose members abandoned 30 artillery pieces as they fled for their lives. In the midst of the fight the Airborne Division had been withdrawn to reinforce I Corps, and by May 4, Kontum was virtually defenseless. To make matters worse, the 3rd NVA Division on the coast had cut Highway 1, the main north–south supply route, and had driven the ARVN 40th and 41st regiments from their bases. The division of South Vietnam was imminent.

All that stood in the way was the capture of Kontum. Seeing the danger, South Vietnamese president Nguyen Van Thieu fired the II Corps commander, Lieutenant General Ngo Dzu, and replaced him with a competent military professional, Major General Nguyen Van Toan. The 23rd ARVN Division commander, Colonel Ly

Tong Ba, was brought up from Ban Me Thuot to take charge of the battle. Like General Truong in I Corps, Ba proved to be the man for the job. Bringing in his own three regiments, he reorganized Kontum's defenses just in time to turn back an NVA five-regiment attack on May 14. For the next two weeks the enemy continued the attack, only to be repulsed by the ARVN defenders supported by massive U.S. air strikes and TOW-missile-equipped antitank helicopters. On May 28, the tide of battle shifted and Ba ordered a house-to-house counterattack to clear the enemy from the city.

On May 30, President Thieu flew to Kontum to pin a general's star on Colonel Ba. The defense of Kontum had been assured and the threat to cut South Vietnam in two had once again been thwarted. In July the reconstituted 22nd ARVN Division recaptured the coastal towns, bringing the Eastertide Offensive in central Vietnam to an end. As Dale Andradé noted in *Trial by Fire*, "Far from cutting South Vietnam in two [the NVA] did not capture a single province capital, and failed to decisively defeat any major South Vietnamese combat unit."

One tragic consequence of the battle was the death of John Paul Vann, the U.S. senior adviser in II Corps, who many credit with stiffening the ARVN defenses at Kontum. Vann first came to public attention after the battle of Ap Bac in 1963, where Colonel (then Captain) Ba was a participant, and saw his protegé promoted to Brigadier General before being killed in a helicopter crash near Pleiku on June 9.

> *"Every GI in the country remembered where he was, that cool misty morning when the NVA punched ... Specialist Six William Ferrand, advising an ARVN battalion on April 2, watched enemy troops gaining momentum in the forested and rugged highlands north of Pleiku ... Soon, the NVA were so close and so densely packed that it was like a shooting gallery. Ferrand shouldered an M16, popped off single shots, and saw one of them blow a man's head off. He and his comrades prudently began to withdraw."*
>
> —Robert F. Dorr

An NVA antiaircraft unit goes into action as the battle around Kontum enters its sixth week. As the Eastertide Offensive raged on, Radio Hanoi claimed that the NVA had killed or wounded more than 90,000 South Vietnamese troops and civilians.

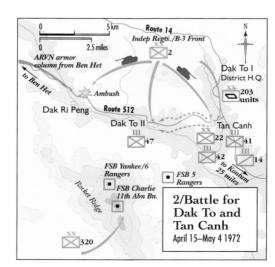

2/Battle for Dak To and Tan Canh
April 15–May 4 1972

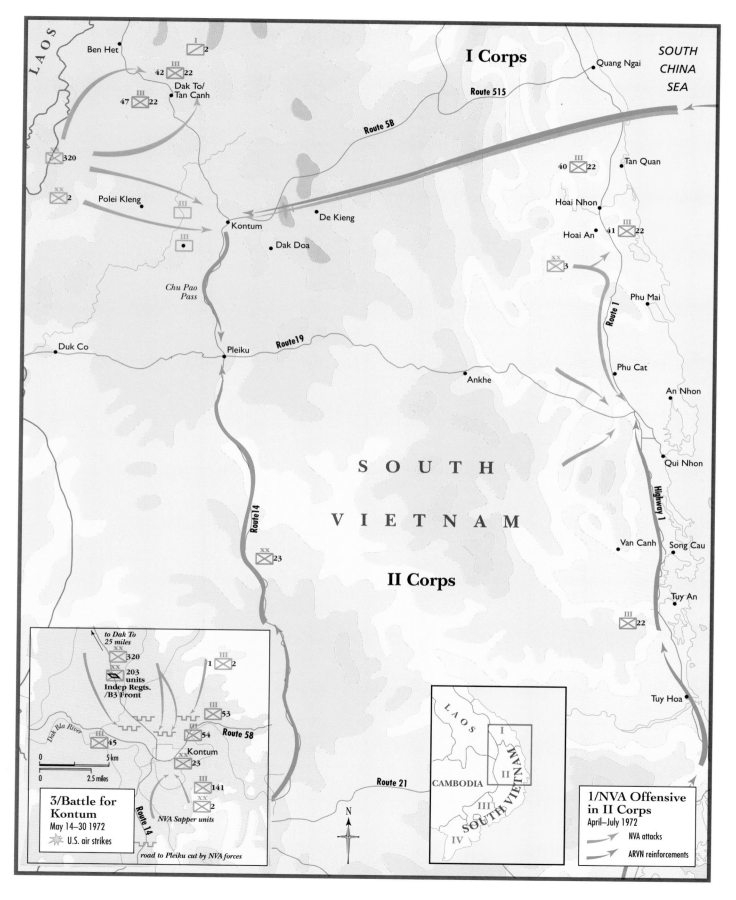

I Corps

SOUTH
CHINA
SEA

Route 515

Route 5B

S O U T H

V I E T N A M

II Corps

**3/Battle for
Kontum**
May 14–30 1972

✸ U.S. air strikes

to Dak To
25 miles

203 units
Indep Regts.
/B3 Front

Dak Bla River

Route 58

Kontum

NVA Sapper units

road to Pleiku cut by NVA forces

Route 14

0   5 km

0   2.5 miles

N

LAOS

CAMBODIA

Route 21

SOUTH VIETNAM

I

II

III

IV

**1/NVA Offensive
in II Corps**
April–July 1972

➤ NVA attacks

➤ ARVN reinforcements

Eastertide: An Loc APRIL–JULY 1972

The third prong of the NVA Eastertide Offensive was directed at An Loc, 75 miles north of Saigon. On April 2, 1972, the corps-level B-2 Front began its attack with a feint along the Cambodian border west of Tay Ninh by its 24th NVA Separate Infantry Regiment. Consisting of the so-called Viet Cong 5th, 7th and 9th divisions, now manned almost entirely by NVA regulars, the B-2 Front's objective was to seize An Loc as the seat of its "Provisional Revolutionary Government of South Vietnam," the new title of the Viet Cong.

Moving from its bases in Cambodia, the 5th VC Division would attack Loc Ninh, 10 miles north of An Loc. The 9th Division would seize An Loc itself, and the 7th Division would block Highway 13 south of An Loc to prevent ARVN reinforcements from reaching the town. An Loc was defended by elements of the 5th ARVN Division, reinforced by a two battalion task force, TF 52, from the 18th ARVN Division which was outposting the road between An Loc and Loc Ninh. Elsewhere in the III Corps area was the remainder of the 18th ARVN Division and the 25th ARVN Division.

The 5th VC Division, supported by 25 medium tanks, overran Loc Ninh on April 6, after two days of hard fighting. Ordered to withdraw, TF 52 was cut to pieces and only a few survivors made it to An Loc. On April 7, the 5th VC Division overran the airfield at Quan Loi, cutting off airlanded resupply to An Loc. With the land supply route to the South cut by the 7th VC Division, the city could only be resupplied by airdrop and helicopter.

It was the inadequacy of the NVA supply lines that helped to save An Loc. Instead of launching its attack from the west when the 5th VC Division attacked from the north, the 9th Division stalled for a week, waiting for its supplies. Taking advantage of the lull, President Nguyen Van Thieu ordered the 21st ARVN Division and the 1st Airborne Brigade to reinforce the defenders. The 21st ARVN Division engaged the 7th VC Division road block at Chon Thanh and the 1st Airborne Brigade established positions at "Windy Hill" two miles southeast of the city. The 5th ARVN Division moved two battalions into the town itself, raising the strength there to 3,000 men.

Under heavy U.S. air attack, the 9th VC Division finally launched its assault on April 19,

seizing the northern part of An Loc before stalling on April 23. On May 11, the attack was resumed by the 5th VC Division under cover of a 7,000-round artillery barrage, but it again failed, due to the tenacity of the ARVN defenders and to awesome U.S. air support. The air strikes were planned by the senior adviser to III Corps, Major General James F. Hollingsworth, who—like John Paul Vann in II Corps—was credited with stiffening the backbone of the ARVN. A former assistant commander of the U.S. 1st Infantry Division, which had operated in the same area six years previously, Hollingsworth's watchword was "Kill Cong!" "You hold, and I'll do the killing," he told his ARVN counterparts as 30 B-52 strikes hit the massed enemy ranks with devastating results.

The NVA tried again on May 12 and 14, but the steam had gone out of their offensive. ARVN counterattacks cleared the city of the remaining NVA attackers and on July 11 the 95-day siege of An Loc was officially at an end. All three prongs of the NVA Eastertide Offensive had not only been blunted but turned back with terrible losses. The NVA took more than 100,000 casualties in its 200,000-man invasion force, and lost more than 50 percent of its tanks and heavy artillery. North Vietnamese plans for the conquest of South Vietnam were set back another three years, and the NVA commander, General Vo Nguyen Giap, was quietly eased out of power, to be replaced by his deputy, General Van Tien Dung, who led the final offensive in 1975. "Giap's ouster was not surprising," noted Dale Andradé, "considering that his strategy was flawed from its inception. He attacked on three fronts, and so lacked the strength to prevail on any one of them."

While the NVA gained half of the northern provinces of Quang Tri, Thua Thien, Quang Nam and Quang Tin, thereby expanding their supply corridors to the South, by their own accounts this territory was merely "rubber trees and bricks." Instead of the provincial capital of An Loc, they had to settle for the village of Loc Ninh as their capital. For the allies, this test of Vietnamization was much more encouraging than Lam Son 719 a year earlier, proving that when competently led, ARVN forces fought well against overwhelming odds. But they remained heavily dependent on U.S. advisers and even more so on U.S. airpower.

"Quang Tri City could not have been retaken nor could ARVN forces have held Kontum and An Loc, had it not been for the support provided by the U.S. Air Force."

—Lieutenant General Ngo Quang Truong

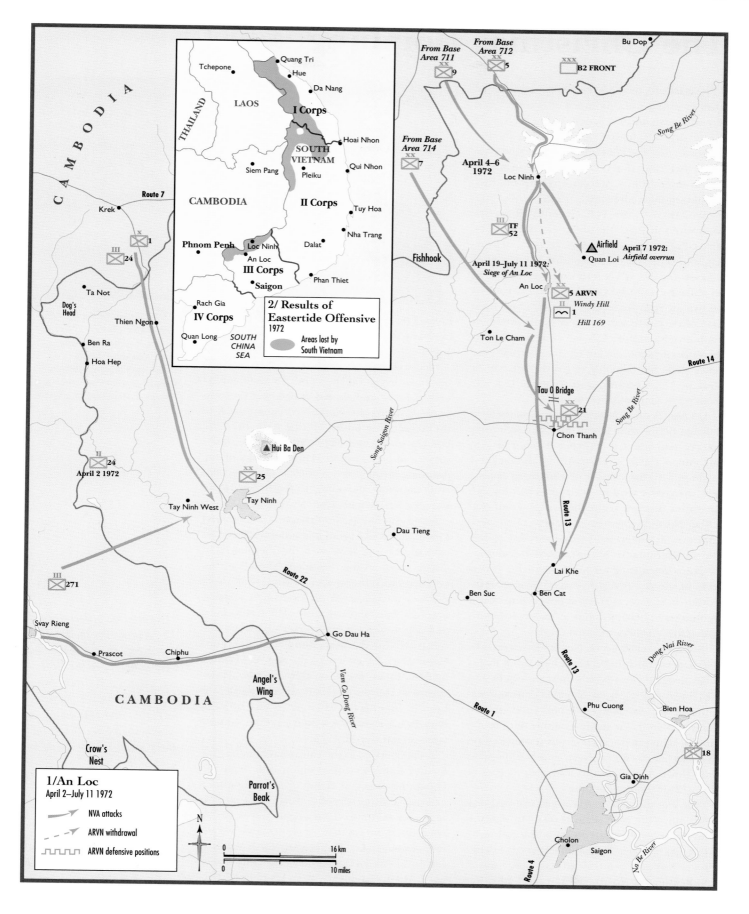

2/ Results of Eastertide Offensive
1972

⬮ Areas lost by South Vietnam

1/An Loc
April 2–July 11 1972

➤ NVA attacks

⤏ ARVN withdrawal

〰〰 ARVN defensive positions

The Christmas Bombing   DECEMBER 1972

"The bastards have never been bombed like they're going to be bombed this time," said President Nixon in reaction to the NVA 1972 Eastertide Offensive. This was hardly the response that the Politburo had bargained on. Believing that the U.S. antiwar movement would severely limit American retaliation, they misjudged their adversary.

On April 2, the U.S. Seventh Fleet was authorized to strike the area near the DMZ by air and sea, and some 20 U.S. cruisers, destroyers, and other warships provided naval gunfire support for the ARVN forces ashore. The carrier strike force in the Gulf of Tonkin expanded to five aircraft carriers, the largest concentration of the entire war. On April 4, the president authorized a massive U.S. air campaign to turn back the invasion, including, for the first time since 1968, the bombing of North Vietnam. At Quang Tri, Kontum, and An Loc, U.S. air power played a decisive role.

On May 9, all of North Vietnam except for a 30-mile buffer zone along the Chinese border and certain sensitive targets was open to U.S. air and sea attack. Operation Linebacker I opened with the mining of Haiphong harbor with magnetic-acoustic sea mines by nine A-6 Intruder aircraft from the U.S.S. *Coral Sea.* Other North Vietnamese ports were mined too, and no large merchant ships entered or left North Vietnamese harbors until December. This was devastating for North Vietnam, 85 percent of whose war supplies came by sea. Meanwhile, U.S. Navy surface action groups fired more than 110,000 rounds at enemy locations along the North Vietnamese coast.

But the main attack on North Vietnam was by air. Operation Linebacker I had three major objectives: to close North Vietnam's land and rail lines of supply from China, to destroy stockpiles of oil, war materials, and food, and to interdict North Vietnamese supply lines to the South. When the operation was terminated on October 22, Air Force, Navy, and Marine pilots had flown 40,000 sorties and dropped more than 125,000 tons of bombs.

The bombing halt was a gesture of good faith, since the NVA seemed ready to sign formal peace agreements in Paris the following week. On October 26, National Security Adviser Henry Kissinger announced that peace was at hand. But the North Vietnamese had other

ideas. On December 13, the peace talks collapsed again, and the next day, Nixon ordered a resumption of the bombing.

Linebacker II, better known as the Christmas bombing, began on December 18. Condemned both at home and abroad, it had only one purpose—to bring the North Vietnamese back to the negotiating table. To that end, 742 B-52 bomber sorties and 640 fighter bomber sorties struck the area around Hanoi and Haiphong, dropping 20,000 tons of bombs. Twenty-six aircraft were lost, including 15 B-52s, but Hanoi was rendered defenseless.

Some Air Force members still believe that Linebacker II was proof that an unrestricted air campaign could have won the Vietnam War. Others contend that President Nixon's earlier openings to Moscow and Beijing, which split the Soviet/Chinese–North Vietnamese alliance, may have been more decisive. The result "owed as much to Nixon's superpower diplomacy as it did to Nixon the Mad Bomber," concluded Major Mark Clodfelter of the Air War College in 1990. In any event, on December 26, Hanoi agreed to resume negotiations, and on December 29, Linebacker II came to an end. The Paris Peace Treaty was signed less than a month later, on January 23, 1973.

A sad epilogue to the Christmas bombing was Stanley Karnow's conversation with Tran Duy Hung, the mayor of Hanoi: "American antiwar activists visiting the city during the attacks urged the mayor to claim a death toll of 10,000. He refused, saying that his government's credibility was at stake. The official North Vietnamese figure for civilian casualties for the period was 1,318 in Hanoi and 305 in Haiphong."

NVA troops guard the Gulf of Tonkin after President Nixon's decision to mine Haiphong harbor and other North Vietnamese ports in a gesture intended to underline continued U.S. involvement in the conflict.

"The briefing officer opened the curtain over the briefing board, and there it was—we were not going home. Not yet, anyway. We were going North. Our targets were to be Hanoi and Haiphong, North Vietnam. At last the B-52 bomber force would be used in the role it had been designed for. The goal for this new operation was to destroy the war-making capability of the enemy."

—From *The View from the Rock,* USAF

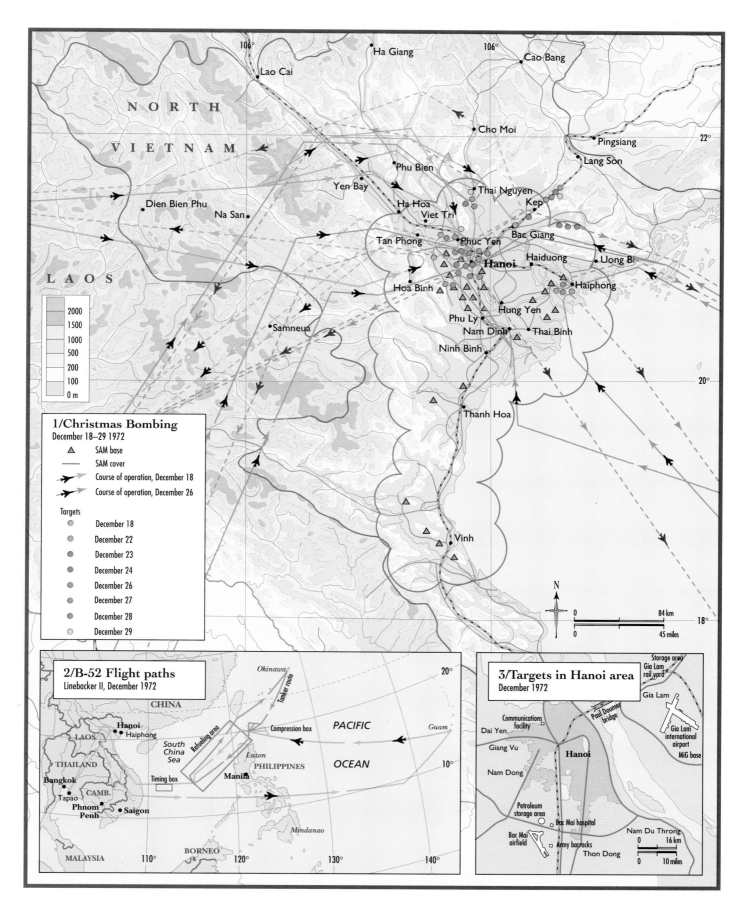

NORTH
VIETNAM

LAOS

Ha Giang
Cao Bang
Lao Cai
Cho Moi
Pingsiang
Lang Son
Phu Bien
Yen Bay
Thai Nguyen
Kep
Ha Hoa
Viet Tri
Dien Bien Phu
Na San
Tan Phong
Phuc Yen
Bac Giang
Haiduong
Uong Bi
Hanoi
Hoa Binh
Haiphong
Hung Yen
Phu Ly
Nam Dinh
Thai Binh
Samneua
Ninh Binh
Thanh Hoa
Vinh

106°
106°
22°
20°
18°

2000
1500
1000
500
200
100
0 m

1/Christmas Bombing
December 18–29 1972

▲ SAM base
— SAM cover
➤ Course of operation, December 18
➤ Course of operation, December 26

Targets
December 18
December 22
December 23
December 24
December 26
December 27
December 28
December 29

N

0 ——— 84 km
0 ——— 45 miles

2/B-52 Flight paths
Linebacker II, December 1972

Okinawa
CHINA
Hanoi
Haiphong
LAOS
THAILAND
Bangkok
Tapao
CAMB.
Phnom Penh
Saigon
South China Sea
Tanker route
Refueling area
Compression box
Timing box
Luzon
PHILIPPINES
Manila
Mindanao
BORNEO
MALAYSIA
PACIFIC
OCEAN
Guam

20°
10°
110°
120°
130°
140°

3/Targets in Hanoi area
December 1972

Storage area
Gia Lam rail yard
Gia Lam
Paul Doumer bridge
Gia Lam international airport
MiG base
Communications facility
Dai Yen
Giang Vu
Hanoi
Nam Dong
Petroleum storage area
Bac Mai hospital
Bac Mai airfield
Army barracks
Thon Dong
Nam Du Throng

0 ——— 16 km
0 ——— 10 miles

The Paris Peace Accords   JANUARY 1973

The "Agreement on Ending the War and Restoring the Peace in Vietnam" or Paris peace accords was signed on January 27, 1973, by the United States, the Republic of Vietnam (South Vietnam), the Democratic Republic of Vietnam (North Vietnam) and the Provisional Revolutionary Government of South Vietnam (Viet Cong). It had its beginnings on May 13, 1968, when the Vietnam peace talks began.

It was not until January 1969, however, that talks began in earnest after "peace candidate" Hubert Humphrey was defeated and the North Vietnamese found themselves dealing with Nixon. A further breakthrough occurred when the North Vietnamese–Soviet–Chinese alliance was weakened by Nixon's opening to China in 1971, the 1972 Moscow summit, and the defeat of the NVA Eastertide Offensive.

The North Vietnamese agreed to drop their demands for a coalition government in the South and the U.S. dropped its insistence on a total NVA withdrawal. When talks again broke down in December 1972, the 11-day Christmas bombing brought the North Vietnamese back to the negotiating table.

The South Vietnamese government correctly saw the agreement as a potential disaster, since it left 13 NVA divisions and 75 regiments—an estimated 160,000 troops—in the South. On October 22, 1972, National Security Adviser Henry Kissinger presented South Vietnamese president Nguyen Van Thieu with a copy of the agreement. According to Arnold Isaacs, Thieu wept, saying that the loss of South Vietnam would mean little to America, which had its own strategies to pursue with Moscow and Beijing, whereas "for South Vietnam the nature of the agreement was a matter of survival. The bargain that had been struck was 'tantamount to surrender.'" To induce Thieu to agree to the settlement, the United States promised "swift and severe retaliatory action" if the agreements were broken, but these promises proved to be just so many empty words.

On paper the agreement had something for everyone. For America, the most important part was Article 2: "A ceasefire shall be observed throughout South Vietnam as of 24:00 hours G.M.T. on January 27, 1973. At the same hour the United States will stop all its military activities against the territory of the Democratic Republic of Vietnam by ground, air, and naval

forces, wherever they may be based." Article 4 read, "The United States will not continue its military involvement or intervene in the internal affairs of South Vietnam." Article 5 stated that "within sixty days of the signing of this Agreement there will be a total withdrawal from South Vietnam of troops, military advisers, and military personnel." Article 6 read, "The dismantlement of all military bases in South Vietnam of the United States will be completed within sixty days." The most emotional aspect of the Agreement was Article 8: "The return of all captured military personnel and foreign civilians shall be carried out simultaneously with and completed not later than the same day as the troop withdrawal. The parties shall help each other to get information about those military personnel and civilians considered still missing in action."

For South Vietnam, the key provision was Article 15 which decreed that "the reunification of Vietnam shall be carried out step-by-step through peaceful means, without coercion." For North Vietnam the key provision was Article 21, which committed the United States to "contribute to healing the wounds of war and to postwar reconstruction of the Democratic Republic of Vietnam."

But as French president Charles de Gaulle once remarked, "Treaties are like young girls. They last while they last." In less than two years, the Agreement on Ending the war had become a worthless piece of paper.

"The last American soldiers in South Vietnam received the news today that the war was finally ending for them with emotions that ranged from elation and relief to disappointment, anger and resentment. For some who had grown fond of the special lifestyle here, there was a sense of loss. And there were some young men who had lived with the war more than half their lives, who had been crushed when their hopes for peace were shattered late last year and simply refused to believe when they heard President Nixon announce the agreement to stop shooting at 8 A.M. Sunday, Saigon time."

—New York Times, January 25, 1973

Operation Homecoming saw the return of 591 American POWs by March 1973. Despite Nixon's assertion that all POWs had now been freed, 2,413 men have never been accounted for.

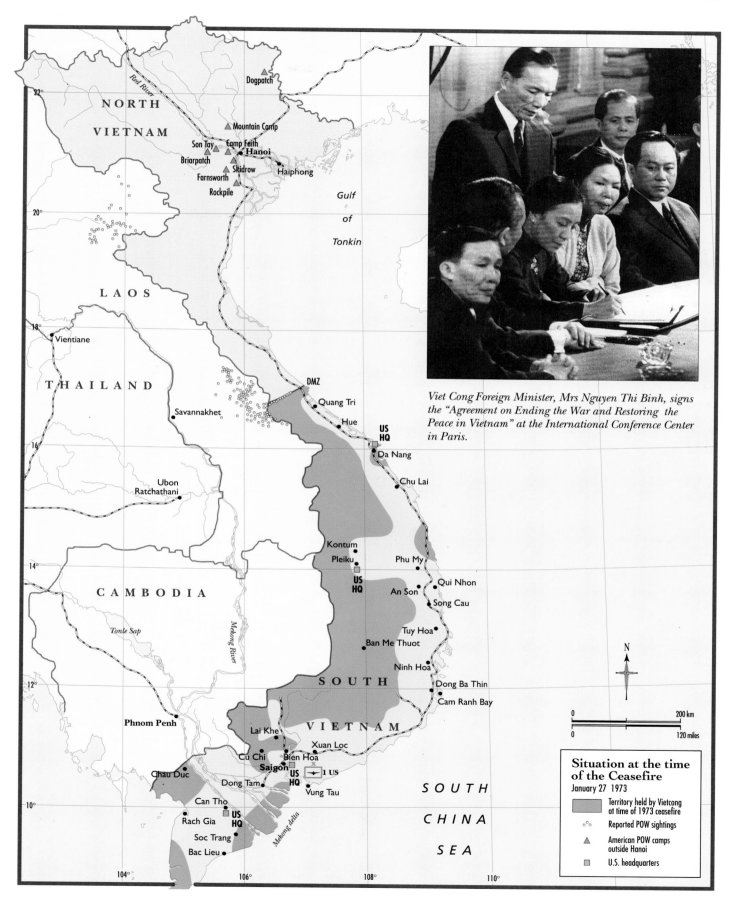

NORTH

VIETNAM

Red River

Dogpatch

Mountain Camp

Son Tay
Camp Faith
Briarpatch
Hanoi
Skidrow
Farnsworth
Haiphong
Rockpile

LAOS

Gulf

of

Tonkin

22°

20°

18°   Vientiane

THAILAND

Savannakhet

16°

DMZ
Quang Tri
Hue
US
HQ
Da Nang

Ubon
Ratchathani

Chu Lai

Kontum
Pleiku   Phu My
US   Qui Nhon
HQ   An Son
Song Cau

14°

CAMBODIA

Tonle Sap

Tuy Hoa

Mekong River

Ban Me Thuot

Ninh Hoa

SOUTH

Dong Ba Thin
Cam Ranh Bay

12°

Phnom Penh

Lai Khe   VIETNAM
Xuan Loc
Cu Chi   Bien Hoa
Saigon   X   1 US
Chau Duc   US
HQ
Dong Tam
Vung Tau

SOUTH

Viet Cong Foreign Minister, Mrs Nguyen Thi Binh, signs
the "Agreement on Ending the War and Restoring the
Peace in Vietnam" at the International Conference Center
in Paris.

N

0   200 km
0   120 miles

Can Tho   CHINA
Rach Gia   US
HQ   SEA
Soc Trang
Bac Lieu

10°

Mekong delta

104°   106°   108°   110°

**Situation at the time
of the Ceasefire**
January 27 1973

▨   Territory held by Vietcong
at time of 1973 ceasefire
ᵒᵒₒ   Reported POW sightings
▲   American POW camps
outside Hanoi
▨   U.S. headquarters

Part VII: The Final Offensive

"If Robert McNamara wasn't smart enough to win in Vietnam, why should we now accept his view that the war was unwinnable?" asked a reader in a letter to the editor in the June 12, 1995, issue of *The New Yorker*. "Like all complex human endeavors, the war did not have a pre-ordained outcome, but depended on several factors, including effective leadership."

Analyzing the leadership of the Vietnam War in a review of McNamara's memoirs in the June 1995 issue of *Army*, General Frederick J. Kroesen, who commanded the Americal Division in Vietnam and later served as Army vice chief of staff, noted that "at no time does he mention the winning of wars; hence, despite President John F. Kennedy's intent to ensure success and President Lyndon B. Johnson's simple, emphatic 'Win the War' dictum, the Defense Department never produced or even addressed a plan to do so. Instead, all planning was designed to foment a negotiated settlement ... The Joint Chiefs of Staff and General William C. Westmoreland, our commander in Vietnam, who offered some military thoughts on the matter, were ignored, overruled, or considered irrelevant."

What were these thoughts? Colonel Hoang Ngoc Lung wrote that "when U.S. forces started pouring into the South [in 1965], the Minister of Defense, General Cao Van Vien, wrote a paper entitled 'The Strategy of Isolation,' in which he likened the task of stopping infiltration to that of turning off the faucet of a water tank. General Vien advocated turning off the faucet through

A South Vietnamese soldier remains on the alert as civilians take cover beneath their conical hats during a North Vietnamese mortar bombardment at Que Son.

the isolation of North Vietnam. He would fortify a zone along the 17th parallel [the DMZ] from Dong Ha to Savannakhet and follow this with a landing operation at Vinh or Ha Tinh, just north of the 18th parallel, cutting off the North's front from its rear." General Vien later published this paper in the April 1972 edition of *Military Review*, the professional journal of the U.S. Army, adding the all too prescient conclusion that "in her alliance with the United States, Vietnam was hamstrung in her action, causing her strategy to be confined to the defensive."

In August 1965, a concept paralleling General Vien's plan was proposed by the U.S. Joint Chiefs of Staff. Their plan would deny North Vietnam "the physical capability to move men and supplies through the Lao corridor, down the coastline, across the DMZ, and through Cambodia … by land, naval and air actions." But, as Herbert Y. Schandler noted in *The Unmaking of a President*, "The plan was neither approved or rejected by the Secretary of Defense or the President."

General Westmoreland favored such a plan. As he relates in *A Soldier Reports*, in April 1967 he recommended a limited reserve call-up, which he felt was particularly justifiable if he "could get authority for a drive into Laos and possibly Cambodia and for an amphibious hook north of the DMZ." The plan ultimately foundered, Westmoreland said, on President Johnson's unwillingness to mobilize the reserves, as did a subsequent plan in the spring of 1968, for which the 1967 buildup of the Marine combat base at Khe Sanh was a prelude. "When the President began to search for the elusive point at which the costs of Vietnam would become unacceptable to the American people," Schandler noted, "he always settled on mobilization."

But in his perceptive analysis *The Key to Failure: Laos and the Vietnam War*, Norman Hannah singled out the "tacit agreement" reached in 1962 by Ambassador Averill Harriman, then assistant secretary of state for Far Eastern affairs, and Roger Hilsman, the director of the State Department's Bureau of Intelligence and Research, as the real villain of the piece. The tacit agreement, said Hannah, "was the American way of rationalizing our acceptance of the Communist reversal of the neutraliza-

tion of Laos" that had been agreed to at the 1962 Geneva accords. In order to protect the facade of that agreement, negotiated by Harriman himself, the United States would turn a blind eye when the Communists "circumspectively" used the infiltration routes through the Laotian panhandle. As Hilsman explained, "by 'circumspectively' we meant that they would continue to use the trails for infiltrating men on foot, cadres equipped with their own arms and whatever other heavier equipment they could carry … But we also meant that they would probably not make any blatant or obvious effort to turn trails into roads or to improve the roads except at places … where they could get away with it without being seen."

But Hilsman was deluding himself. The North Vietnamese had been working since 1959 to turn the Ho Chi Minh Trail through Laos into their supply lifeline for

The North Vietnamese dramatized the conflict in Vietnam in a series of colorful stamps in which heroic and grim-faced figures can be seen shooting down countless U.S. fighter bombers.

the war in the South, and it became a logistic superhighway that was ultimately their key to victory.

"North Vietnam had an Indochina strategy in which eastern Laos … was an instrument in bringing about Hanoi's conquest of South Vietnam," Hannah emphasizes. "The United States believed the opposite. Instead of using Laos as an instrument in the defense of South Vietnam, we told ourselves we had separated and 'postponed' the Laos problem pending a solution in South Vietnam which was to be achieved inside South Vietnam and independently of events in Laos." The Harriman-Hilsman "tacit agreement" was therefore the rock upon which all alternative strategies foundered. This was true of the Joint Chiefs of Staff's proposals, General Westmoreland's proposals, and, as Hannah relates, U.S. ambassador Ellsworth Bunker's proposals. In June 1967, Bunker "had written a personal letter to President Johnson recommending that we move into southern Laos and cut the Ho Chi Minh Trail. It hardly need be said that this proposal got short shrift in Washington."

Bunker correctly called this "a strategic mistake of the first order." As former South Vietnamese secretary of defense Tran Van Don said after the war, no strategy could have been successful unless it effectively stopped infiltration from the North, a task he thought possible. Reinforcing that belief, Lieutenant General Ngo Quang Truong, former I Corps commander, said that with hindsight, halting infiltration was the most critical requirement of the war. He believed that South Vietnam could have solved its internal problems if the infiltration had been brought under control.

But was such a strategy possible, given President Johnson's adamant refusal even to consider reserve mobilization? General Bruce Palmer believed it could

A woman and her children take to the streets as the United States Agency for International Development compound in Saigon burns down after violent clashes between government troops and Viet Cong commandos in the buildup to the fall of Saigon.

have been done without reserve mobilization. In an address to the Army War College on May 31, 1977, Palmer outlined his strategic plan. It called for a five-division force—two U.S., two ROKA, and one ARVN—along the DMZ, and three U.S. divisions deployed to extend the defensive line to the Lao-Thai border. An additional U.S. division would be required for internal security, especially in the Saigon area, and the two U.S. Marine divisions would be held in strategic reserve to reinforce the DMZ and to pose an amphibious threat to the North Vietnamese coastline.

This, Palmer pointed out, would have required four fewer U.S. divisions than the ten and two-thirds actually deployed, and the bulk of these forces would have fought on ground of their choosing in fortified defensive positions which the NVA would have to attack in order to invade the South. Given the awesome amount of artillery and air firepower available to U.S. forces, such attacks would be (as the NVA and VC discovered in any event)

tantamount to suicide. "In defending well-prepared positions, U.S. casualties would have been much fewer," Palmer said, and "the magnitude and intensity of the so-called 'Big War' involving heavy fire power [in populated areas] would have been lessened." He went on to say that a much smaller logistic effort would have been required, and much of the enormous U.S. base development would have been avoided. "Cut off from substantial out-of-country support," he concluded, "the Viet Cong was bound to wither on the vine and gradually become easier for the South Vietnamese to defeat."

Would this alternative strategy have worked? History, it has been said, does not provide its alternatives, and that question can never be completely answered. But unlike the strategy, or, more correctly, the nonstrategy that was actually followed, it not only was possible, as the Korean

As the noose around Saigon tightens, Operation Frequent Wind gets under way. Refugees from the city prepare to be evacuated by Marine CH-53 helicopters to American ships waiting offshore.

A North Vietnamese stamp bears witness to the psychological advantage which played such a crucial role in the NVA's victory. With steely determination, a Communist soldier takes aim at enemy aircraft.

experience proved, but also played to U.S. military strengths in firepower and logistics.

With the United States keeping the external enemy at bay, as in Korea, could South Vietnam have put its own house in order? As former CIA director William Colby noted in the April 27, 1995, issue of the *Washington Post*, McNamara's *In Retrospect* and other critical books such as Frances Fitzgerald's *Fire in the Lake*, David Halberstam's *The Best and the Brightest*, Neil Sheehan's *A Bright Shining Lie*, and to an extent even Stanley Karnow's *Vietnam: A History*, all ended their analysis in 1968. This, said Colby, is like ending an analysis of World War II before the battle of Stalingrad, before the Allied invasion of North

Africa, or before the battle of Guadalcanal. The war in Vietnam continued for another seven years, and the post-1968 period differed radically from the earlier years.

Unlike the largely guerrilla war that preceded it, the war after 1968 was almost entirely an NVA affair, a conventional war fought by regular forces supported by tanks and artillery. "Vietnamization" had worked, said Colby. "The pacification program freed the rural countryside of Communist guerrillas, primarily by recruiting them and arming local self-defense forces in the villages, resettling the refugees in their original communities and offering a better life of land reform and local development than Communism could provide."

Had Palmer's alternative strategy been adopted, the war would then have been at an end. The countryside was pacified and the NVA could have been kept at bay. But that was not to be. As Colby points out, "The United States withdrew its 500,000-plus combat troops between 1969 and 1972." Recognizing that they had lost the guerrilla war, the North Vietnamese then turned to a conventional cross-border invasion. When its Eastertide Offensive of 1972 was defeated by the valiant stand of the South Vietnamese Army, reinforced by massive U.S. airpower, North Vietnam agreed to end the war. In January 1973, the Paris peace accords were signed.

South Vietnam's primary strategic vulnerability had not only not been solved, however, it had been exacerbated by the terms of the agreement. The infiltration routes had not been cut, and the Ho Chi Minh Trail, now an interstate thoroughfare, remained under North Vietnamese control. Now there were no American bombers and gunships to interdict the free flow of war supplies and personnel into the South. Worse, large border areas along the infiltration routes had been ceded to North Vietnamese control, and significant numbers of regular North Vietnamese soldiers were allowed to remain within what had been the territorial boundaries of South Vietnam. In order to get the South Vietnamese to agree to such a lopsided agreement, the United States had pledged that it would react "with full force" if North Vietnam violated its terms.

When more than 20 NVA divisions rolled south in

1975, with blatant contempt for the peace accords, America looked the other way, delivering South Vietnam into the hands of its enemies. By its own inaction, it had rendered the war unwinnable. But the chain of events had been set in motion 23 years earlier, for the final invasion was exactly like the invasion that the pre-1962 U.S. Military Assistance Advisory Group Vietnam had been preparing the South Vietnamese to resist before it was ordered by McNamara's Defense Department to concentrate instead on "counterinsurgency."

The end was not inevitable, but it was invidious. Cambodian government senior adviser Sirik Matak, who was executed by the Khmer Rouge after refusing Ambassador John Gunther Dean's offer to evacuate him from Phnom Penh before its fall in April 1975, sent Dean a note that could well serve as the epitaph for the entire U.S. intervention in Indochina.

"I cannot, alas, leave in such a cowardly fashion," he wrote. "As for you and in particular for your great country, I never believed for a moment that you would have this sentiment of abandoning a people which has chosen liberty. You have refused us your protection and we can do nothing about it … But mark it well that, if I should die here on the spot and in my country that I love, it is too bad because we all are born and must die one day. I have only committed this mistake of believing in you, the Americans."

U.S. officials and Marines are evacuated from Phnom Penh shortly before the bloodbath in which most senior Cambodian government officials were slaughtered in cold blood. Pol Pot's regime of terror was to continue until December 1978, when Vietnam invaded Cambodia

Broken Promises... 1974–1975

"Perfidious Albion" is what Defense Secretary James Schlesinger said America was in danger of becoming, using the epithet coined by Napoleon Bonaparte when England reneged on the Treaty of Amiens in 1803. The United States, he told Congress on January 14, 1975, was reneging on the commitments it had made in order to secure South Vietnamese approval of the Paris peace accords.

But his argument fell on deaf ears. The United States had promised the same "swift and severe retaliatory action" against any North Vietnamese violation of the accords as it had taken to repel the NVA Eastertide Offensive in 1972. The ink was hardly dry on the accords, however, when Congress passed the Case–Church Amendment on June 19, 1973, preventing any further U.S. military involvement in Southeast Asia.

Named after its sponsors, senators Clifford Case and Frank Church, the amendment stated that "on or after August 15, 1973, no funds herein or heretofore appropriated may be obligated or expended to finance directly or indirectly combat activities by United States military forces in or over or from off the shores of North Vietnam, South Vietnam, Laos, or Cambodia." Although denounced by President Nixon, the amendment was veto-proof, having passed the House by a vote of 278–124 and the Senate by 64–26. As this was more than the two-thirds majority necessary to ensure enactment, Nixon had no choice but to sign it into law.

It was these prohibitions that later caused President Gerald Ford to renege on his predecessor's promises when the North Vietnamese Army flagrantly contravened the Paris Accords with their attack on Phuoc Long in December 1974. Instead of challenging the doubtful constitutional authority of Congress to limit presidential warmaking powers, Ford cravenly caved in, limiting his response to diplomatic notes. In a press conference on January 21, 1975, Ford said that he could foresee no circumstances in which the United States might actively re-enter the war.

Not content with blocking America's ability to counter North Vietnamese violations of the Paris accords, Congress deliberately undermined the South Vietnamese ability to counter them too. In 1972–1973, before the peace accords, U.S. military aid to South Vietnam totaled $2.1 billion. Article 7 of the Paris accords permitted South Vietnam to "make periodic replacement of armaments, munitions and war material which have been destroyed, damaged, worn out or used up after the ceasefire, on the basis of piece-for-piece, of the same characteristics or properties." At first it appeared that the United States would honor that commitment, and the U.S. contribution to the South Vietnamese military budget for Fiscal Year (FC) 1974 was set at $1.1 billion.

But in December 1973, the U.S. ambassador to Vietnam, Graham Martin, told the White House, "Before the January agreements, at the time of the January agreements, after the January agreements ... we have reiterated the commitment that we will maintain the armament level existing on a one-to-one replacement basis. Yet, almost from the beginning every action we have taken seems ... to have been calculated to convince senior [South Vietnamese] officers that we were not really serious about keeping that pledge."

Military appropriations to South Vietnam were slashed drastically. The contribution in FY 1975 was set at $1 billion in August 1974, but in September the House and the Senate appropriated only $700 million. This was to cover all shipping costs, as well as the operational costs of the U.S. Defense Attaché office in Saigon, and left only $500 million for the South Vietnamese Army. The effect on the military readiness of the latter was severe, as major cutbacks became necessary in areas such as artillery fire missions. As the NVA commander, General Van Tien Dung noted in his account of the final battles, South Vietnam had been forced to fight a "poor man's war."

Even more deadly was the effect on South Vietnamese morale, as it became increasingly apparent that the country had been abandoned by its erstwhile ally. It was not Congress' finest hour, and it seemed to confirm Senator Daniel Patrick Moynihan's earlier caustic observation that to be an enemy of the United States could be unpleasant, but to be a friend of the United States could be fatal.

The sad truth was that the American people were sick and tired of Vietnam and just wanted it to go away. These ignoble sentiments were reflected in Congress, which, even as South Vietnam fell, refused to lift a finger to help.

"The failure to support South Vietnam to the degree which we gave them to understand we would, would be a failure of a moral commitment of the United States and a failure of American foreign policy. In the past, as we withdrew our forces from Vietnam in the process of Vietnamization, we indicated to the South Vietnamese that we would give them the tools and they must do the job ... It would be a serious error on the part of the United States, and I believe, a serious moral lapse for us to contemplate the semi–abandonment of an ally by failure to provide them with the appropriate financial resources."

—James Schlesinger, 1975

James Schlesinger, defense secretary and de facto general-in-chief of the armed forces from 1973 to 1975, protests against the cutting of financial assistance to South Vietnam.

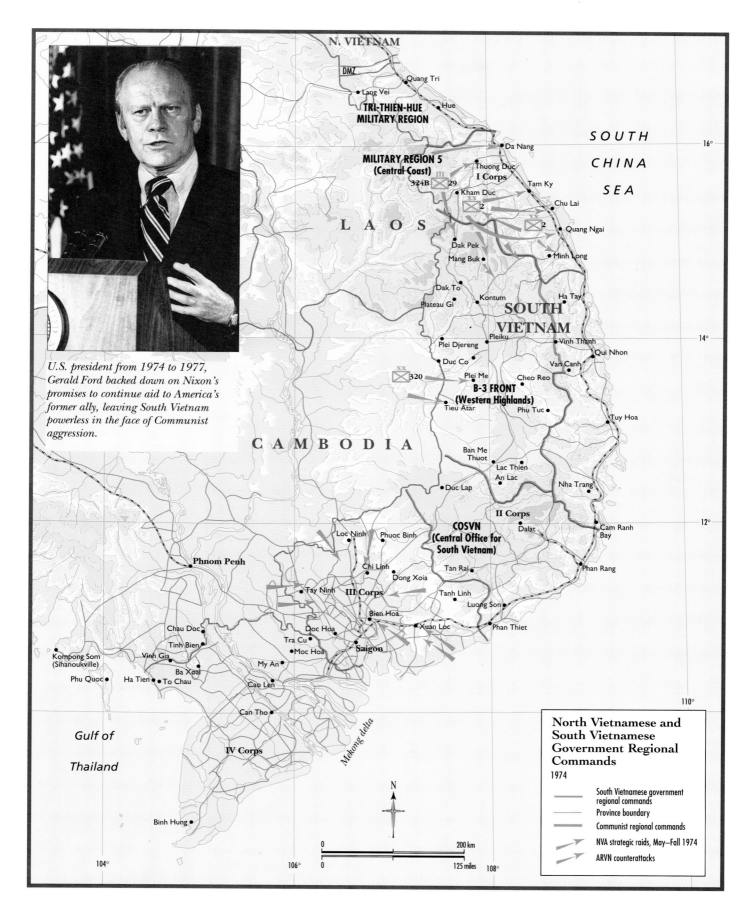

U.S. president from 1974 to 1977,
Gerald Ford backed down on Nixon's
promises to continue aid to America's
former ally, leaving South Vietnam
powerless in the face of Communist
aggression.

N. VIETNAM

DMZ

Quang Tri

Lang Vei

Hue

**TRI-THIEN-HUE
MILITARY REGION**

Da Nang

SOUTH

CHINA

SEA

16°

**MILITARY REGION 5
(Central Coast)**

324B   29   **I Corps**

Thuong Duc

Tam Ky

Kham Duc

Chu Lai

2

2

Quang Ngai

L A O S

Dak Pek

Mang Buk

Minh Long

Dak To

Kontum

Ha Tay

Plateau Gi

**SOUTH
VIETNAM**

Pleiku

14°

Plei Djereng

Vinh Thanh

Duc Co

Van Canh

Qui Nhon

320   Plei Me

Cheo Reo

**B-3 FRONT
(Western Highlands)**

Tieu Atar

Phu Tuc

Tuy Hoa

C A M B O D I A

Ban Me
Thuot

Lac Thien

An Lac

Nha Trang

Duc Lap

II Corps

Dalat

12°

Loc Ninh

Phuoc Binh

**COSVN
(Central Office for
South Vietnam)**

Cam Ranh
Bay

Phan Rang

Phnom Penh

Chi Linh

Dong Xoai

Tan Rai

Tay Ninh   **III Corps**

Tanh Linh

Luong Son

Doc Hoa   Bien Hoa

Xuan Loc

Phan Thiet

Chau Doc

Tra Cu

Tinh Bien

Moc Hoa   **Saigon**

Kompong Som
(Sihanoukville)

Vinh Gia

My An

Ba Xoai

110°

Phu Quoc   Ha Tien   To Chau

Cao Len

Can Tho

Gulf of

IV Corps

Thailand

N

Binh Hung

0   200 km

0   125 miles

104°   106°   108°

**North Vietnamese and
South Vietnamese
Government Regional
Commands**

1974

South Vietnamese government
regional commands

Province boundary

Communist regional commands

NVA strategic raids, May–Fall 1974

ARVN counterattacks

The Fall of Phuoc Long   DECEMBER 1974–JANUARY 1975

As North Vietnam prepared for the final offensive in South Vietnam, the great unanswered question was how the United States would react. The answer was critical, for the failure to predict the U.S. reaction correctly had spelled disaster for North Vietnam's Eastertide Offensive in 1972, which cost the North 100,000 casualties and one half of its tanks and heavy artillery, to no appreciable gain.

"You have my absolute assurance that if Hanoi fails to abide by the terms of this agreement, it is my intention to take swift and severe retaliatory action," said President Nixon in a note to South Vietnamese president Nguyen Van Thieu on November 14, 1972, on the eve of the signing of the Paris peace accords. But in August 1974 Nixon was out of office, brought down by the Watergate scandal. At a meeting of the North Vietnamese Politburo in October 1974, Ho Chi Minh's successor, Le Duan, took note of Nixon's removal and "drew an important conclusion that became a resolution." Having already withdrawn from the South, he said, the United States could hardly jump back in, and no matter how it might intervene, it would be unable to save the Saigon administration from collapse.

Phuoc Long Province in South Vietnam was to be the test of this conclusion. Relatively isolated, it was defended primarily by four 340-man Regional Force (local militia) battalions and a number of Popular Force (home guard) platoons. Fire support consisted of four 105mm howitzers employed in two-gun platoons throughout the sector.

Far outmatching these defenders was the attacking NVA 301st Corps, consisting of the newly formed 3rd NVA Division, the veteran 7th NVA Division, a tank battalion of Soviet-supplied T-54 tanks, an artillery regiment, an antiaircraft artillery regiment, and local sapper and infantry units. Launching its attack on December 13, 1974, the NVA defeated the South Vietnamese outposts in detail, then concentrated its attack on the airfield at Song Be.

The garrison there was reinforced by the ARVN 2nd Battalion, 7th Infantry, who were helicoptered in from their base at Lai Khe. Six additional 105mm howitzers were helilifted in as well. Later, two companies of the ARVN 85th Airborne Ranger Battalion were also flown in. But they were no match for the NVA, whose

artillery was particularly devastating. By January 3, 1975, the NVA rate of fire had increased to 3,000 rounds per day.

On January 6 the province chief and his staff withdrew from Song Be. South Vietnamese losses were staggering. Of 5,400 ARVN and RF/PF forces committed to the battle, only 850 survived and the province chief never made it to safety. About 3,000 civilians out of 30,000 or more escaped Communist control. "The few province, village, and hamlet officials who were captured," says the official report, "were summarily executed."

Tragic as these losses were, the battle had far grimmer consequences. Le Duan's "resolution" had been all too correct. In the face of this blatant violation of the Paris accords, the United States limited its response to diplomatic notes. North Vietnam had received the green light for the conquest of South Vietnam. As NVA General Van Tien Dung, who led the final attack, noted at a Politburo conference on January 8, 1975, "It was obvious that the United States ... could hardly return ... To fully exploit this great opportunity we had to conduct large-scale annihilating battles to destroy and disintegrate the enemy on a large scale." The groundwork for the final North Vietnamese blitzkrieg had been laid.

The North Vietnamese Army vastly outmatched its South Vietnamese foe in both manpower and weaponry.

"(Prime Minister) Pham Van Dong said of Gerald Ford...'He's the weakest president in U.S. history; the people didn't elect him; even if you gave him candy, he wouldn't dare to intervene in Vietnam again' We tested Ford's resolve by attacking Phuoc Long in January 1975. When Ford kept American B-52s in their hangars, our leadership decided on a big offensive against South Vietnam."

—Bui Tin, former editor of *People's Daily*

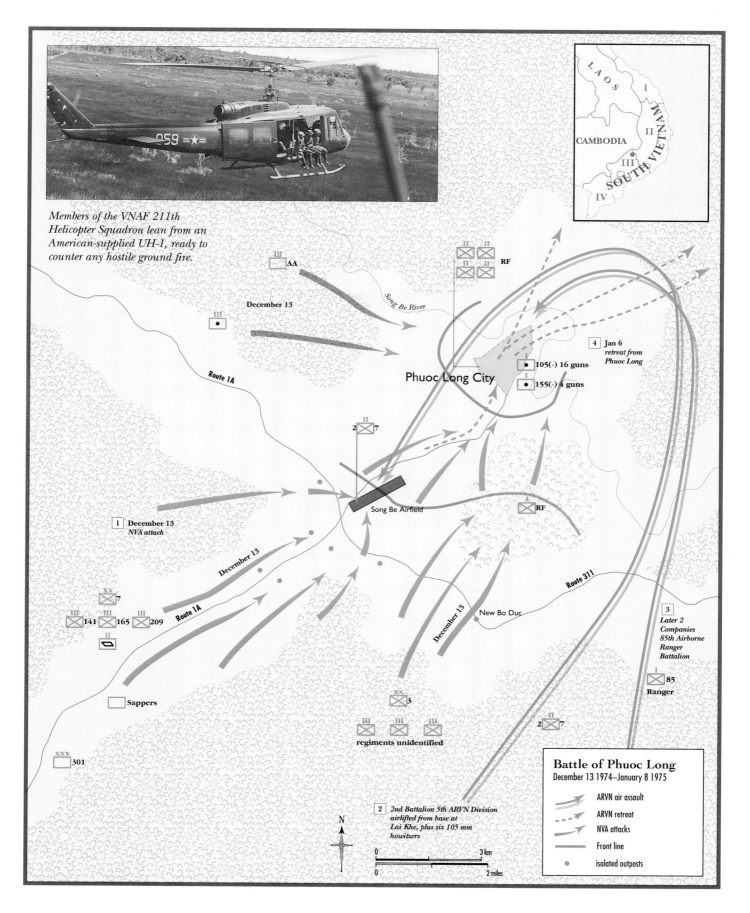

Members of the VNAF 211th
Helicopter Squadron lean from an
American-supplied UH-1, ready to
counter any hostile ground fire.

LAOS

CAMBODIA

SOUTH VIETNAM

I

II

III

IV

AA

December 13

Song Be River

RF

Route 1A

Phuoc Long City

105(-) 16 guns

155(-) 4 guns

4 Jan 6
retreat from
Phuoc Long

2 7

Song Be Airfield

RF

1 December 13
NVA attack

December 13

December 13

Route 1A

Route 311

New Bo Duc

7

141 165 209

3

Later 2
Companies
85th Airborne
Ranger
Battalion

85
Ranger

Sappers

3

2 7

regiments unidentified

301

N

2 2nd Battalion 5th ARVN Division
airlifted from base at
Lai Khe, plus six 105 mm
howitzers

0   3 km

0   2 miles

Battle of Phuoc Long
December 13 1974–January 8 1975

ARVN air assault

ARVN retreat

NVA attacks

Front line

isolated outposts

The Battle of Ban Me Thuot   MARCH 1975

The NVA battleplan for the 1975 conquest of South Vietnam began on the same note as its initial plan a decade earlier (pp. 104–105), which called for an attack eastward from its bases in Laos across the Central Highlands to the South China Sea. South Vietnam would be cut in half and the ARVN would be rendered incapable of concentrating its forces. The superior NVA forces could then overwhelm the ARVN units one by one.

The NVA tried this ploy in 1965 but was turned back by the U.S. 1st Air Cavalry Division (Airmobile), supported by massive U.S. air strikes. In 1972 (pp. 176–177), it was repulsed again at the battle of Kontum, this time by ARVN forces supported by U.S. air strikes. But now there were no American ground troops or air support to come to the rescue. Both had been forbidden by Congress in the Case–Church Amendment two years earlier.

The NVA used overwhelming combat power, committing the three divisions of its corps-level B-3 Front against the one regular ARVN regiment defending Ban Me Thuot. Guerrilla war had nothing to do with it—this was conventional war at its most fundamental level. The NVA began by isolating the battlefield. On March 4, the lifeline to the Central Highlands, Route 19 from Pleiku to Qui Nhon, was cut in two places by the NVA 3rd and 95B divisions near Mang Yang Pass, where Groupement Mobile 100 had been annihilated 20 years before. On March 5, Highway 21 between Ban Me Thuot and Nha Trang was blocked in three places by the 320th NVA Division, and on March 8 the division's 9th Regiment cut Highway 14 from Ban Me Thuot to Pleiku, establishing a roadblock north of Buon Blech. Ban Me Thuot was cut off from outside ground support.

Although the 23rd ARVN Division headquarters was at Ban Me Thuot, three of its four regiments were stationed at Pleiku, the site of the ARVN II Corps headquarters. At the beginning of March the other regiment, the 53rd, had returned to Ban Me Thuot, reinforcing the ARVN 23rd Ranger Group and the Montagnard Regional Force and Popular Force units defending the city.

At 2 A.M. on March 10, under cover of an intense artillery barrage, the NVA launched its attack. By midmorning the 320th Division had penetrated the ARVN defenses and by evening

it had a firm grip on the city center. The forward command post of the 23rd ARVN Division at Phung Duc airfield held out, however, and the NVA 316th Division joined the attack. As the encirclement tightened around the 23rd Division command post, air strikes were called in to relieve the pressure. One bomb struck the division's tactical operations center, severing communications with II Corps headquarters. By 11:30 A.M. on March 11, Ban Me Thuot was firmly in NVA hands. The 23rd Division's deputy commander, Colonel Vu The Quang, and the chief of Darlac Province, Colonel Nguyen Cong Luat, were both captured, and the 53rd Regiment was smashed.

Realizing the strategic significance of Ban Me Thuot to the survival of his country, on March 14 President Nguyen Van Thieu ordered its recapture. The 23rd Division's 44th and 45th regiments were helilifted from Pleiku to Phuoc An. Lacking armor or artillery, they were no match for the 10th NVA Division, especially when their commander, Brigadier General Le Truong Tuong, was evacuated after suffering a superficial wound, leaving his troops without a leader.

It was here that the "family syndrome" that was to destroy the ARVN's combat effectiveness first manifested itself. As General Cao Van Vien, the last chairman of the South Vietnamese Joint General Staff, noted, "Phuoc An ... was the way station for the civilian population fleeing the fighting. Here some of the [44th and 45th regiment troops] met their dependents and disappeared into the streaming flow of refugees. Others, anxious about the fate of dependents or relatives stranded in the embattled city, simply broke ranks and fled in search of their families. As a result, it was impossible to assemble a cohesive combat force for the effort. Phuoc An, the last base for a counterattack, was overrun four days later by the 10th [NVA] Division. Any hope for recapturing the city was gone."

Significantly, the ARVN 3rd Airborne Brigade, whose families were safe at their home station in Saigon, effectively blocked the advance of the 10th NVA Division at Khanh Duong. It was only on April 2, after a week of heavy fighting, that their positions were finally overrun and the NVA was able to break through to the sea.

"Because we concentrated the majority of our forces ... we achieved superiority over the enemy in this area. As for infantry, the ratio was 5.5 of our troops for each enemy soldier. As for tanks and armored vehicles, the ratio was 1.2 to 1. In heavy artillery, the ratio was 2.1 to 1 ... Thus the enemy was in a weak and isolated position."

—Senior General Van Tien Dung, NVA commander

A refugee is helped across the deck of the amphibious cargo ship USS Durham *by a U.S. Marine Corps 1st lieutenant after evacuation by a CH-46D Sea Knight helicopter.*

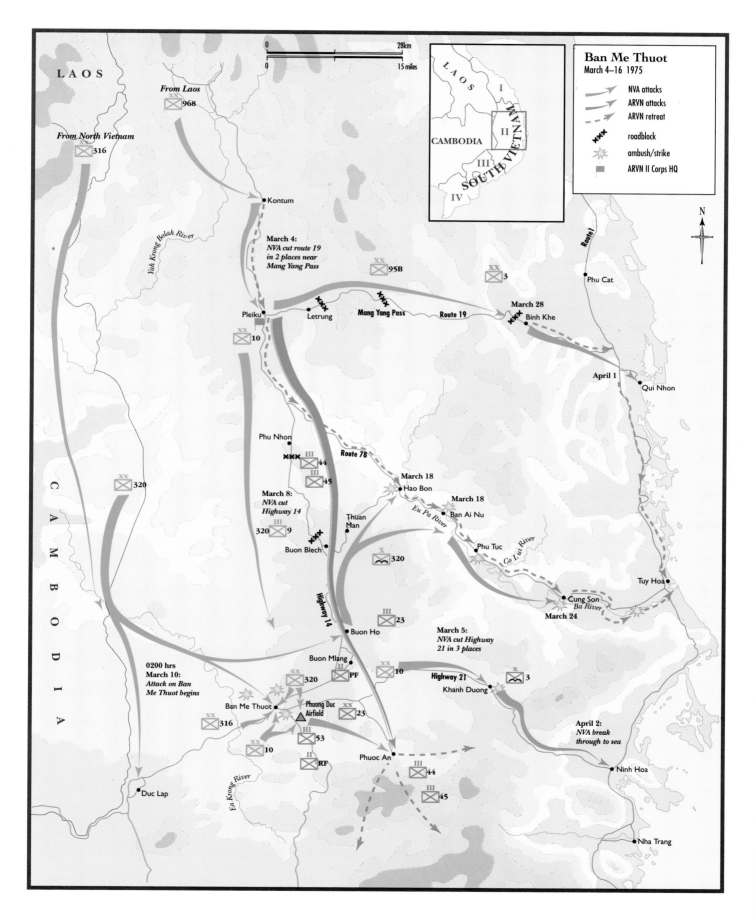

LAOS

From Laos
XX
968

From North Vietnam
XX
316

Yah Krong Bolah River

Kontum

March 4:
*NVA cut route 19
in 2 places near
Mang Yang Pass*

XX
95B

XX
3

Route 1

Phu Cat

Pleiku

Letrung

Mang Yang Pass

Route 19

March 28

Binh Khe

XX
10

April 1

Qui Nhon

Phu Nhon

XXX
III
44

Route 78

III
45

March 8:
*NVA cut
Highway 14*

III
320   9

Thuan
Man

Buon Blech

March 18
Hao Bon

Eu Pa River

March 18
Ban Ai Nu

Phu Tuc

Co Lui River

Tuy Hoa

X
3
320

Cung Son
Ba River

March 24

C A M B O D I A

XX
320

Highway 14

III
23

Buon Ho

March 5:
*NVA cut Highway
21 in 3 places*

Highway 21

X
3

Khanh Duong

0200 hrs
March 10:
*Attack on Ban
Me Thuot begins*

Buon Mlang

II
PF

XX
10

XX
320

XX
316

Ban Me Thuot

Phuong Duc
Airfield

XX
23

April 2:
*NVA break
through to sea*

III
53

XX
10

II
RF

Phuoc An

III
44

Ninh Hoa

Duc Lap

Ea Krong River

III
45

Nha Trang

Inset map

LAOS

CAMBODIA

SOUTH VIETNAM

I

II

III

IV

Legend

Ban Me Thuot
March 4–16 1975

→ NVA attacks
→ ARVN attacks
⇢ ARVN retreat
✕✕✕ roadblock
✳ ambush/strike
▪ ARVN II Corps HQ

0   28km
0   15 miles

N

The Fall of the Central Highlands   MARCH 1975

On January 8, 1975, at the conclusion of the 20-day North Vietnamese Politburo meeting, Senior General Van Tien Dung reported that "the conferees unanimously approved the General Staff draft plan, which chose the Central Highlands as the main battlefield in the large-scale widespread 1975 offensive." The loss of the Central Highlands did indeed prove to be the death blow for South Vietnam. But that loss had more to do with decisions made in Saigon than with those made in Hanoi.

On March 11, the day after Ban Me Thuot was attacked, South Vietnamese president Nguyen Van Thieu called a meeting with Prime Minister Tran Thien Khiem, security adviser Lieutenant General Dang Van Quang, and General Cao Van Vien, the chairman of the Joint General Staff. Thieu began by saying, "Given our present strength and capabilities, we certainly cannot hold and defend all the territory we want." Instead, he went on, forces should be deployed to hold and defend only populous and flourishing areas. These included all of III Corps (Saigon and the surrounding provinces) and IV Corps (the Mekong delta), as well as the continental shelf, where oil had recently been discovered.

With I Corps and II Corps, it was a matter of "hold what you can." If the territory up to Hue and Da Nang proved impossible to secure, then forces would be redeployed further south to Chu Lai or even Tuy Hoa. This plan was not without precedent—the Republic of Korea conceded far greater territory to the enemy as it retreated into the Naktong Perimeter at the beginning of the Korean War, and Seoul fell twice. But in Vietnam in 1975, one vital ingredient was missing—the support of the United States, which had been forbidden by Congress to reintervene in the war.

Thieu did not even consult the U.S. ambassador or Major General Homer Smith, the U.S. defense attaché, before ordering his plan into execution. On March 14, he ordered the II Corps commander, Major General Pham Van Phu, to redeploy his forces from the Central Highlands to Nha Trang and retake Ban Me Thuot at all costs. Phu explained that despite the efforts of his 22nd ARVN Division, Route 19, the main road from the Central Highlands to the coast, was still blocked, as was Route 14 from Pleiku to Ban Me Thuot and Route 21 from Ban Me Thuot to the coast. A secondary road, the neglected track known as Route 7B, would have to be used (p. 195).

A withdrawal while in contact with the enemy is one of the most difficult military operations, requiring the highest form of leadership. But instead of overseeing the retreat, General Phu and his staff fled, leaving the evacuation to Brigadier General Pham Van Tat. Led by the 20th Engineer Group, whose task it was to repair the road and bridges along the way, the first convoys left Pleiku on March 16, and were soon joined by thousands of civilian refugees. By the second day the column had reached Hau Bon (Cheo Reo), 60 miles away, where they were held up while engineers bridged the Ea Pa River.

Initially surprised by the withdrawal, Senior General Van Tien Dung ordered his 320th and 968th divisions in pursuit. On March 18, the 2,000-vehicle column came under artillery fire and ground attack by the 320th Division, suffering heavy casualties. On March 20, the convoy moved out again, only to become stalled again at Phu Tuc, 15 miles away. Friendly air strikes were called in but struck the column instead, killing or wounding almost an entire Ranger battalion. At Cung Son, 40 miles from Tuy Hoa, the column was stalled yet again while a pontoon bridge was erected over the Song Ba River. Crossing to Route 246 on March 22, the column fought its way through enemy roadblocks and arrived at Tuy Hoa on March 27.

The evacuation had been an unmitigated disaster. Only 20,000 of the 60,000 troops made it through, and they were combat ineffective. Only 700 of the 7,000 rangers survived, and of the 400,000 civilians, only 100,000 reached Tuy Hoa. But by March 31, the 320th NVA Division had Tuy Hoa under fire too. The feckless General Phu abandoned his new headquarters at Nha Trang, leaving the city to fall without a fight. Phu had been captured by the Viet Minh at Dien Bien Phu and later committed suicide rather than fall into enemy hands again.

Meanwhile, the ARVN 22nd Division had withdrawn along Route 19 and had been evacuated by sea from Qui Nhon to III Corps. But the remainder of II Corps, which had lost 75 percent of its fighting strength and been abandoned by its commander, ceased to exist as a fighting force.

"Moving a corps–sized column of troops, equipment and vehicles some 160 miles through the mountains and jungles of the Highlands was a hazardous task of great magnitude."

—General Cao Van Vien

Right: *Refugees struggle to board an already overloaded airplane in the frenzied evacuation from South Vietnam.*

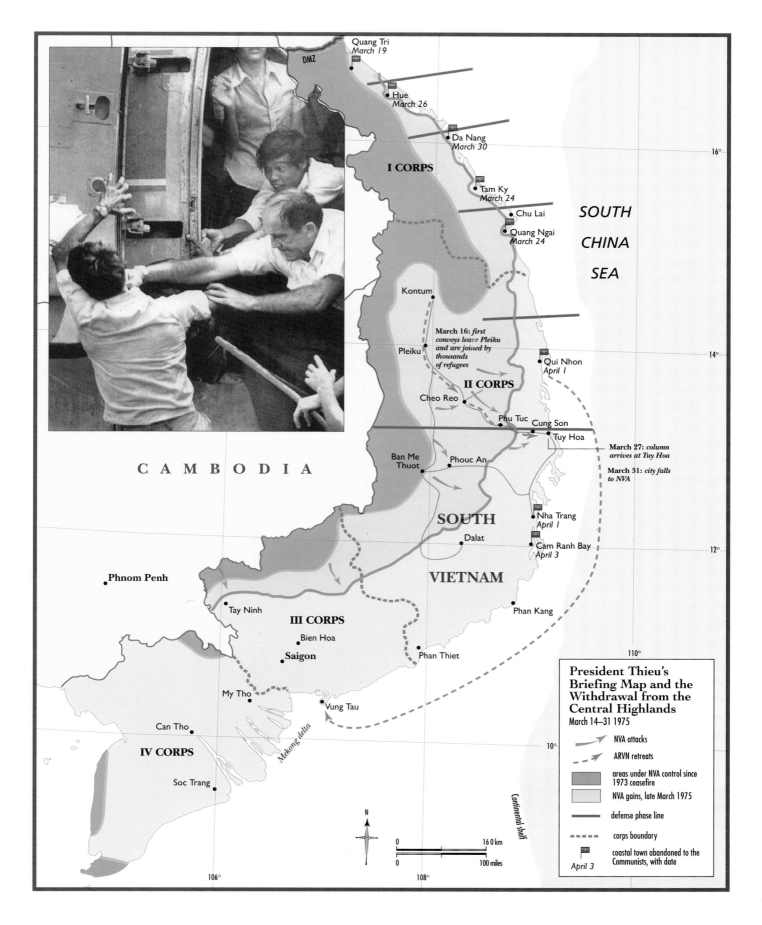

Quang Tri
March 19

DMZ

Hue
March 26

Da Nang
March 30

I CORPS

16°

Tam Ky
March 24

Chu Lai

Quang Ngai
March 24

SOUTH

CHINA

SEA

Kontum

March 16: *first*
convoys leave Pleiku
and are joined by
thousands
of refugees

Pleiku

Qui Nhon
April 1

14°

II CORPS

Cheo Reo

Phu Tuc

Cung Son

Tuy Hoa

March 27: *column*
arrives at Tuy Hoa

March 31: *city falls*
to NVA

Ban Me
Thuot

Phouc An

CAMBODIA

SOUTH

Nha Trang
April 1

Dalat

Cam Ranh Bay
April 3

12°

VIETNAM

Phnom Penh

Phan Kang

Tay Ninh

III CORPS

110°

Bien Hoa

Saigon

Phan Thiet

**President Thieu's
Briefing Map and the
Withdrawal from the
Central Highlands**
March 14–31 1975

My Tho

Vung Tau

Can Tho

Mekong delta

IV CORPS

10°

Soc Trang

⟶ NVA attacks

⤏ ARVN retreats

▨ areas under NVA control since
1973 ceasefire

▨ NVA gains, late March 1975

─ defense phase line

┈ corps boundary

🏴 coastal town abandoned to the
April 3 Communists, with date

N

0   160 km

0   100 miles

Continental shelf

106°

108°

The Fall of Da Nang MARCH 1975

The disaster in the Central Highlands was paralleled by a similar disaster in the northern provinces, which culminated in the fall of Da Nang on March 30, 1975. Like the Central Highlands debacle, it was precipitated by ill-conceived decisions by South Vietnamese president Nguyen Van Thieu. His decision, on March 12, to pull the Airborne Division, operating south and west of Da Nang, out of the line and move it south for the defense of Saigon, replacing it with the Marine Division (less one brigade) then operating in Quang Tri Province along the Demilitarized Zone, triggered a calamitous chain of events.

Although the five NVA divisions operating in I Corps had launched attacks to coincide with the offensive in the Central Highlands, these had initially been contained. But as the official U.S. Army history states, "As the Marines left, they took the courage and morale of the territorials and civilians of Quang Tri with them." A flood of refugees began moving south toward Hue, and on March 19 Quang Tri fell without a fight to the NVA forces advancing across the Demilitarized Zone.

Meanwhile, on March 13, the I Corps commander, Lieutenant General Ngo Quang Truong, widely acknowledged as one of the most capable officers in the South Vietnamese Army, met with President Thieu in Saigon. Truong was informed of the decision to abandon the Central Highlands and the northern provinces, with the exception of an enclave around Da Nang. On March 19, Truong returned to Saigon to brief his men on the contingency plans for the withdrawal. The first called for movement along Highway 1 to the Da Nang enclave. The other called for withdrawal into temporary enclaves at Hue and Chu Lai, then movement by sea to Da Nang, if road movement proved impossible. But these plans had already been overtaken by events, and General Truong was told to hold on to whatever territory he could.

Conditions continued to deteriorate rapidly. On March 17, the citizens of Hue, mindful of the atrocities committed by the Communists during their occupation of the city in 1972, began to flee south toward Da Nang. As in the Central Highlands, the 1st ARVN Division defending the city disintegrated in the "family syndrome" as the soldiers scrambled to take care of their wives and children. On March 25, Hue was abandoned.

The situation south of Da Nang was equally grim. The 3rd ARVN Division at Tam Ky and the 2nd ARVN Division at Chu Lai had also been overtaken by the "family syndrome" and now began to fall apart. Tam Ky was overrun by the advancing 711th NVA Division on March 24, sending thousands of civilian refugees and the remnants of the 3rd ARVN Division fleeing toward Da Nang. Chu Lai was evacuated on March 26, and the ARVN 2nd Division, still relatively intact, moved first to Re Island, 20 miles offshore, and then to III Corps, where they were redeployed for the defense of Phan Rang. Only the Da Nang enclave remained, a scene of total chaos as more than 2 million people clogged the streets.

On March 28, NVA artillery began to shell the city, further intensifying the panic. General Truong decided to evacuate Da Nang by sea, and on March 29 the final withdrawal began. Unable to beach because of a low tide, South Vietnamese Navy ships anchored offshore, and the troops, including General Truong, had to wade and swim to reach them. Many drowned, or were killed by NVA artillery, which zeroed in on the beaches, but over 6,000 Marines and 4,000 troops of the ARVN 3rd Division were taken on board and moved south for the defense of Saigon. Only 50,000 of the 2 million civilian refugees, however, were able to escape.

By March 30, Da Nang and all of I Corps was in the hands of the NVA. It "fell easily to the Communists," said Lieutenant General Phillip B. Davidson in his analysis of the war. "There was no heavy and prolonged fighting, no calamitous ARVN casualty lists, no great destruction—ARVN just collapsed."

"People moved about frantically in search of relief and escape. All streets were packed; vehicles were unable to move ... The chaos and disorder were indescribable. Hunger, looting and crime were widespread. On March 27 came the first U.S. commercial jet chartered for the evacuation ... Soon the airfield was besieged by a frantic crowd, deserters included, who trampled the security force, overwhelmed the guards, swamped the runways, and mobbed the aircraft. It became so unsafe for the jets themselves that the airlift had to be suspended."

—General Cao Van Vien, describing the Da Nang enclave

U.S. Marines from the consulate in Da Nang head for an airplane that will take them to Saigon. From there they were evacuated by ship, along with 40 Americans and 5,000 Vietnamese refugees.

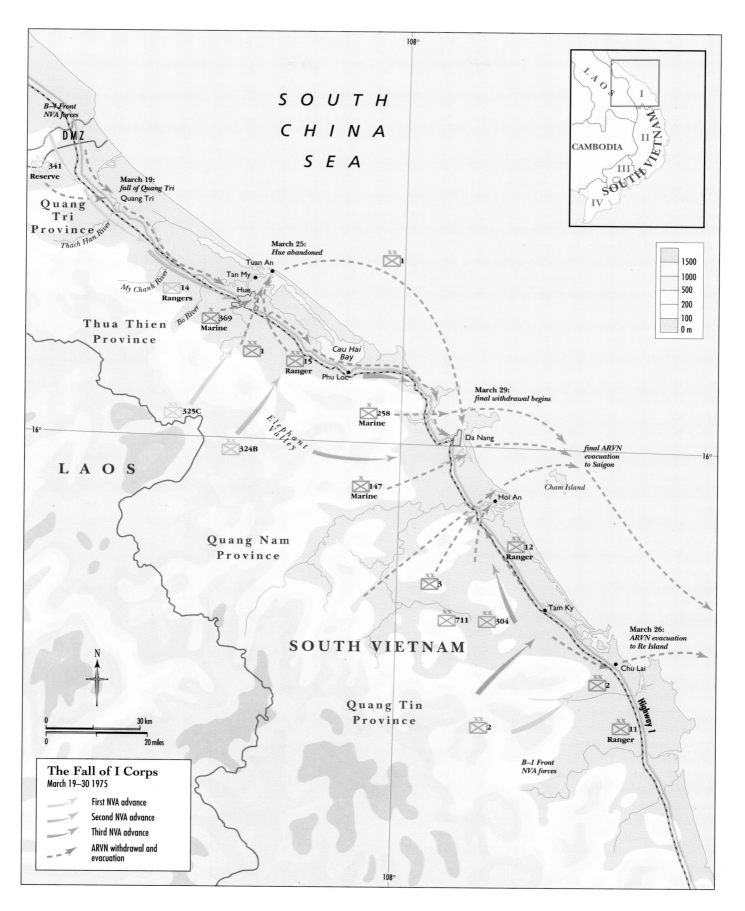

SOUTH
CHINA
SEA

*B–4 Front
NVA forces*

DMZ

341
Reserve

March 19:
fall of Quang Tri
Quang Tri

Quang
Tri
Province

Thach Han River

My Chanh River

14
Rangers

Thua Thien
Province

Bo River

March 25:
Hue abandoned

Tuan An
Tan My
Hue

369
Marine

1

1

15
Ranger

*Cau Hai
Bay*

Phu Loc

LAOS

325C

324B

*Elephant
Valley*

16°

258
Marine

March 29:
final withdrawal begins

Da Nang

*final ARVN
evacuation
to Saigon*

16°

147
Marine

Cham Island

Quang Nam
Province

Hoi An

12
Ranger

3

SOUTH VIETNAM

Tam Ky

March 26:
*ARVN evacuation
to Re Island*

711

304

N

Quang Tin
Province

2

Chu Lai

2

Highway 1

11
Ranger

*B–1 Front
NVA forces*

0   30 km
0   20 miles

LAOS
CAMBODIA
SOUTH VIETNAM
I
II
III
IV

1500
1000
500
200
100
0 m

The Fall of I Corps
March 19–30 1975

First NVA advance
Second NVA advance
Third NVA advance
ARVN withdrawal and
evacuation

The Battle of Xuan Loc   MARCH–APRIL 1975

Evoking memories of General Patton's U.S. Third Army dash across Europe in World War II, the NVA General Staff charged with planning the maneuver of Senior General Van Tien Dung's four-corps blitzkrieg worked beside a large poster that read "Lightning speed, more lightning speed; boldness, more boldness." As General Dung himself said, "Cadres of the front staff had to admit somewhat ruefully that they could not draw maps quickly enough to catch up with the advance of our forces."

That lightning speed advance was stopped short on April 9, 1975, by what General Dung called "the enemy's stubbornness." It came from an unlikely source—the 18th ARVN Division at Xuan Loc. The capital of Long Khanh Province, Xuan Loc was located 40 miles east of Saigon on Route 1, and was the home base of the 18th Division. Commanded by Brigadier General Le Minh Dao, the division consisted of its organic 43rd, 48th and 52nd regiments, plus some Ranger units and Regional and Popular Force battalions. Although it was not known for its fighting prowess, the 18th Division proved in the end to be the best division in the Republic of Vietnam Armed Forces.

Fresh from its victories in I and II Corps, General Dung's IV Corps closed in on Xuan Loc on April 9. The 341st NVA Division established a roadblock at the junction of Route 20 and Route 1, thus isolating Xuan Loc from Saigon and cutting it off from ground reinforcement. Under cover of a 4,000-round artillery barrage, the NVA now launched an infantry and armor attack on the city's northwestern perimeter. After some initial gains the NVA were repulsed with heavy losses, even though their 341st Division had been reinforced by regiments from the NVA IV Corps' 6th and 7th divisions.

By April 12 the battle seemed to be turning in the ARVN's favor. Despite their best efforts, however, and despite the commitment of three infantry and armor task forces from the 5th and 25th divisions, they were unable to clear the NVA roadblocks on Route 1, although they did succeed in weakening the NVA attack by forcing it to fight in two directions. Impressed with the ARVN resistance, Major General Homer Smith, the U.S. defense attaché in Saigon, telegrammed General George Brown, the chairman of the Joint Chiefs of Staff in Washington, to say that "The valor and aggressiveness of GVN [Government of Vietnam] troops appears to settle for the time being the question, 'Will ARVN fight?'" But Washington continued to turn a blind eye to the death throes of its former ally.

With their timetable now disrupted, the NVA intensified the attack, committing their entire IV Corps and ordering their II Corps, which on April 16 had overwhelmed the 2nd ARVN Division at Phan Rang (and captured the ARVN III Corps commander, Lieutenant General Nguyen Vinh Nghi), to push rapidly forward and join the other forces. Although it had suffered 30 percent casualties, the 18th Division, now reinforced by the 1st Airborne Brigade which had been helilifted into the city, continued to hold its ground. But with the odds now overwhelming, the end was only a matter of time. After having destroyed 37 NVA tanks, killed over 5,000 enemy soldiers, and delayed the North Vietnamese offensive for almost two weeks, the 18th Division was ordered to evacuate the city. On April 22, Xuan Loc fell to the NVA.

"The battle for Xuan Loc produced one of the epic battles of any of the Indochina wars, certainly the most heroic stand in Indochina War III ...In this final epic stand ARVN demonstrated for the last time that, when properly led, it had the 'right stuff.'"

—Lieutenant General Phillip B. Davidson

Far right: A South Vietnamese M-113 armored car lies abandoned in the center of Xuan Loc after falling foul of heavy NVA shelling.

Below: Frantic refugees cling to a CH-47 Chinook helicopter as it takes off near Xuan Loc after dropping supplies for troops fighting along Route 1.

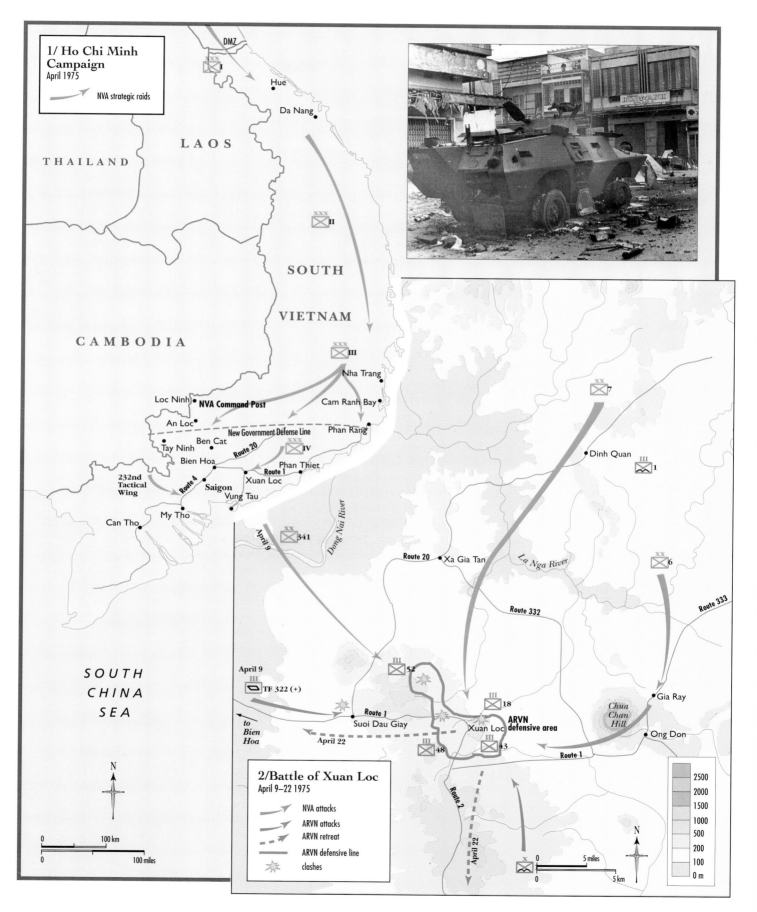

1/ Ho Chi Minh Campaign
April 1975

→ NVA strategic raids

DMZ

I

Hue

Da Nang

THAILAND

LAOS

SOUTH

VIETNAM

CAMBODIA

II

III

Nha Trang

Loc Ninh • **NVA Command Post**

An Loc • Cam Ranh Bay

New Government Defense Line

Ben Cat

Tay Ninh • Route 20 IV Phan Rang

Bien Hoa Route 1

232nd Tactical Wing Route 4 Phan Thiet

Saigon Xuan Loc

Vung Tau

April 9 341

Can Tho My Tho

SOUTH

CHINA

SEA

N

0   100 km
0   100 miles

7

Dinh Quan 1

Xa Gia Tan La Nga River 6

Route 20

Route 332 Route 333

April 9
TF 322 (+)

52

18

to
Bien
Hoa

Route 1

Suoi Dau Giay

Xuan Loc **ARVN defensive area**

April 22

Chua
Chan
Hill

Gia Ray

48 43

Ong Don

Route 1

Route 2

April 22

2/Battle of Xuan Loc
April 9–22 1975

→ NVA attacks
→ ARVN attacks
⇢ ARVN retreat
— ARVN defensive line
✳ clashes

2500
2000
1500
1000
500
200
100
0 m

N

0   5 miles
0   5 km

The Fall of Saigon   APRIL 1975

On April 23, 1975, the day after the fall of Xuan Loc, the United States in effect put its imprimatur on the NVA final offensive or "Ho Chi Minh campaign." At a speech at Tulane University, President Gerald Ford told students that "America can regain its sense of pride that existed before Vietnam. But it cannot be achieved by refighting a war that is finished as far as America is concerned."

By April 27, the NVA encirclement of Saigon was complete. To the east, having overrun Xuan Loc, the NVA IV Corps overwhelmed the ARVN 18th Division defenses at Bien Hoa while the NVA II Corps captured Long Thanh in one of the fiercest tank battles of the war. To the north, the ARVN 5th Division fell back before the NVA I Corps, while to the west the ARVN 25th Division was cut off when the NVA III Corps cut the Saigon–Tay Ninh road. Finally, Route 4 to the Mekong delta was cut by the five divisions of the NVA corps-level 232nd Tactical Force, isolating Saigon and the ARVN IV Corps at Can Tho. But instead of pressing home their attack, the NVA paused, waiting for Saigon to collapse of its own weight. They had every reason to think that this was imminent.

On April 21, President Thieu had resigned, blasting America for dishonoring itself: "The United States has not respected its promises. It is inhumane. It is not trustworthy. It is irresponsible." He likened the congressional debate on military assistance to "bargaining at the fish market," and said that he "could not afford to let other people bargain over the bodies of our soldiers." Thieu was succeeded first by Vice President Tran Van Huong, then, on April 28, by a "Third Force" candidate, General Duong Van Minh, who was convinced that the Communists would negotiate with him. It was an appropriate choice, for "Big Minh" had been instrumental in the assassination of President Diem in 1963, an act many believe to have started South Vietnam on its downhill path.

But it was too late for negotiations. On April 27, the NVA fired four 122mm rockets into downtown Saigon in the first such attack in five years, and on April 28, five captured A-37 jet bombers launched an airstrike on Tan Son Nhut air base in the suburbs. It was a clear signal that the end was on hand. At 3:58 A.M. on April 29, NVA rockets struck the U.S. defense attaché office compound at Tan Son Nhut,

effectively closing the air base and ending the fixed-wing aerial evacuation of U.S. civilian workers, third-country contract employees and their dependants, and selected South Vietnamese civilians and their families underway since April 1. At 10:40 A.M., U.S. Ambassador Graham Martin requested the final evacuation of Saigon. U.S. Marine CH-46s and CH-53s helilifted the remaining 4,395 evacuees from the compound without incident.

The situation at the U.S. Embassy in Saigon was another matter. The plan, whereby Americans at the Embassy and South Vietnamese employees at various pickup points would be moved to Tan Son Nhut for further evacuation, had gone awry. Buses were unable to get through the streets, and instead of 100 evacuees at the Embassy, there were 3,000. The task of the U.S. Delegation Four Party Joint Military Team, set up by the Paris accords to negotiate the POW/MIA issue, was to calm the evacuees and organize them for evacuation.

On the afternoon of April 29, Colonel John Madison, with the author (then a lieutenant colonel and chief of the negotiations division), his deputy, Captain Stuart Herrington, and their interpreters, Army Specialist 7 Garrett Bell, Army Master William Herron and Marine Gunnery Sergeant Ernest Pace, began to move everyone out. By 4:15 A.M. on April 30, 2,619 evacuees had been helilifted from the Embassy. But in a final betrayal, made all the more tragic by the fact that it was inadvertent, the lift was cancelled and the final 420 evacuees were abandoned: believing that there was a bottomless pit, the White House had ordered a halt. It was the Vietnam War in microcosm—good intentions but fatally flawed execution.

At 10:24 A.M., President Minh told his forces to "remain calm, stop fighting, and stay put." Just before noon an NVA T-54 tank crashed through the gates of the Independence Palace, and Minh made his second surrender speech. The war was at an end. But not all South Vietnamese forces heeded the call for unconditional surrender. Many Air Force officers flew to bases in Thailand or to U.S. aircraft carriers, and 34 Navy warships sailed to the Philippines. The IV Corps commander, Lieutenant General Nguyen Khoa Nam, and his deputy, Major General Le Van Hung, committed suicide rather than surrender.

"The people's war was over not by the work of a barefoot guerrilla but by the most conventional of military forces … The ultimate irony was that the people's war launched in 1959 had been defeated, but the soldier's war which the United States had insisted on fighting during the 1960s with massive military forces was finally won by the enemy."

—William Colby,
Head of the CIA in 1975

A U.S. helicopter crewman helps Americans and foreign nationals onto the roof of a building in downtown Saigon, from where they were flown to U.S. ships waiting offshore.

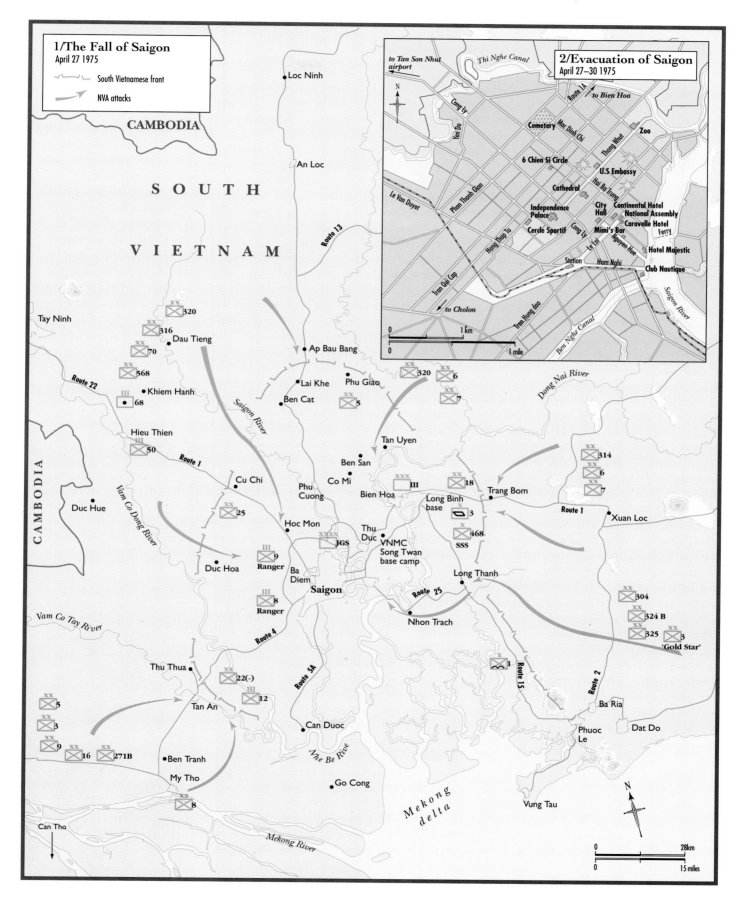

1/The Fall of Saigon
April 27 1975

⌢⌣⌢ South Vietnamese front
➜ NVA attacks

2/Evacuation of Saigon
April 27–30 1975

The Fall of Cambodia   APRIL 1975

The ultimate horrors of the Second Indochina War took place not in Vietnam but in Cambodia, a nation that had tried desperately for much of that conflict to maintain its neutrality. On April 12, 1975, five days before the surrender of Cambodia to the Khmer Rouge, U.S. Ambassador John Gunther Dean and his staff were evacuated from Phnom Penh. Most Cambodian senior government officials refused to leave and were executed in the genocidal bloodbath that followed.

Descendants of the ancient Khmer empire which occupied much of present-day southern Vietnam, the Khmers were gradually pushed into their present boundaries during the thousand-year Vietnamese "March to the South," and were only saved from extinction by French intervention in 1863. Cambodia became a French protectorate under the Indochinese Union, but gained independence in the 1954 Geneva Accords. Its ruler, Prince Norodom Sihanouk, sought to keep his country out of the Second Indochina War, but he was not strictly neutral (the Hague Convention of 1907 states that "a neutral country has the obligation not to allow its territory to be used by a belligerent") and tilted toward whichever side seemed to be winning.

In 1965, relations with the United States were severed. Three years earlier, with Sihanouk's tacit approval, NVA/VC base camps and staging areas were constructed in the northern border areas between Cambodia and South Vietnam. Later, at Chinese urging, the Sihanouk Trail was established from Sihanoukville to bases in the southern border regions. In March 1969, again with Sihanouk's tacit approval, the United States began the "secret bombing" of these areas, and in April the prince reestablished diplomatic relations with the United States. In March 1970, Khmer Rouge pressure on the Cambodian government mounted and Sihanouk was deposed by his prime minister, General Lon Nol. In April, the United States and South Vietnam invaded Cambodia to disrupt the base areas.

After the U.S. withdrawal in June 1970, Cambodia's military, the FANK (*Forces Armées Nationales Khméres*), launched a series of ineffective operations against the Khmer Rouge, the most disastrous of which was Chenla II, to lift the year-long siege of Kompong Thom north of Phnom Penh. Launching an attack up Route 6 on August 20, 1971, FANK had some initial successes. But on October 27, responding to the threat to sever the Ho Chi Minh Trail, the 9th NVA/VC Division was reinforced by the Khmer Rouge 205th and 207th regiments in an ambush on the FANK forces along the road between Kompong Thmar and Tang Kauk. Chenla II ended on December 3, with the loss of 10 FANK battalions and the equipment of a further 10 battalions. Lieutenant General Sak Sutsakhan called it "the greatest catastrophe of the war," and it was a catastrophe from which FANK never completely recovered. Although the fighting would go on for more than three years, the initiative had passed to the Khmer Rouge. FANK forces were gradually forced back into a defensive circle around Phnom Penh.

The beginning of the end came in March 1975, when the Khmer Rouge mined the Mekong River, ending the resupply convoys that had kept FANK alive. The airbase at Ponchentong near Phnom Penh also came under heavy rocket attack, which drastically reduced the flow of aerial resupply too. On April 1, the town of Neak Luong south of Phnom Penh fell, and the capital was completely surrounded. Under attack from all quarters, it fell on April 17. A tragic postlude was the Khmer Rouge seizure of a U.S. merchant ship, the *Mayaguez*, in the Gulf of Thailand, and the imprisonment of its crew on the island of Poulo Wai, 100 miles from the mainland. U.S. air strikes were flown against the airfield and port facilities at Kompong Som. A rescue mission resulted in the ship's recapture on May 15, but at the cost of 41 U.S. Marines and airmen killed in action and another 49 wounded.

But this incident paled in comparison with the horrors visited upon the Cambodian people, as the Khmer Rouge proceeded to evacuate the cities and towns and murder more than one million of the 7.2 million population. When the killings spread to the Vietnamese border areas, Vietnam launched a full-scale invasion of Cambodia on December 25, 1978, and occupied Phnom Penh on January 7, 1979. The occupation ended in September 1989, and following UN-sponsored elections in May 1993, a coalition government was formed in Phnom Penh. On September 24, 1993, Norodom Sihanouk was reinstalled as king.

"Among the characters and bona fide eccentrics who peopled the Indochina wars, Sihanouk stands out. He was a king who elected to lead Cambodia as a commoner. He was a so-so painter, a fair jazz saxophonist, and an untalented thespian who directed, acted in, and produced his own bad movies. In foreign affairs he attempted to walk the icy tightrope between China and North Vietnam on one side and the United States on the other."

—Lieutenant General Phillip B. Davidson

Far right: *Khmer Rouge soldiers patrol the empty streets of Phnom Penh on May 16, 1975, after driving the population from the city.*

One of 50 grisly photographs exhibited by Amnesty International in 1983 in order to "focus attention on the practice of murder by government." Shown here are the skulls of Cambodians murdered by the Khmer Rouge.

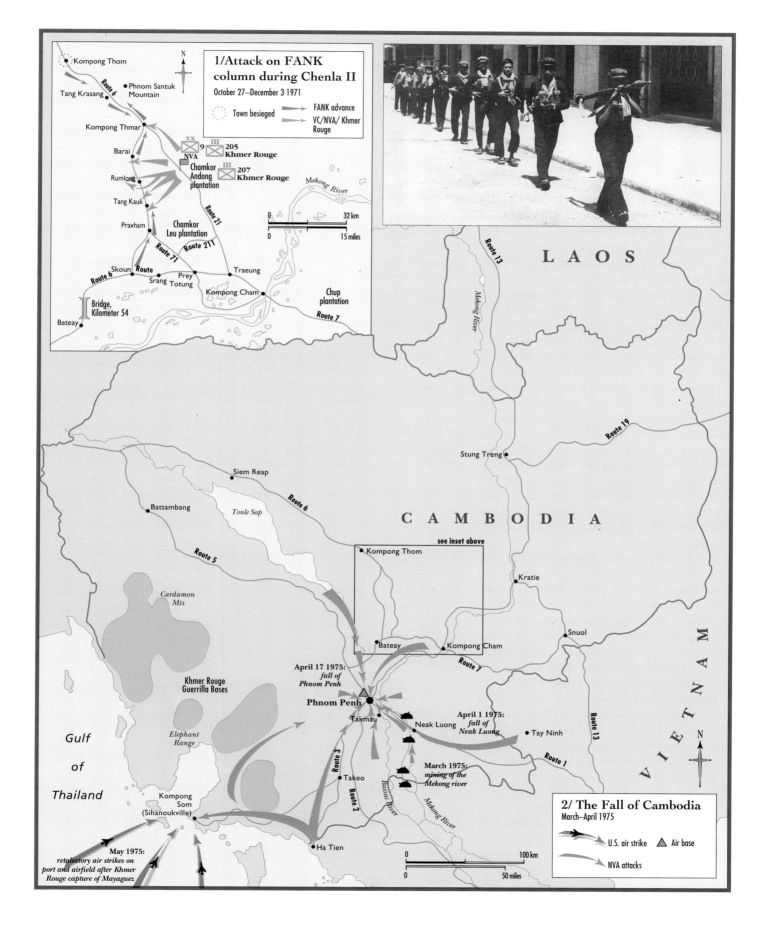

1/Attack on FANK column during Chenla II

October 27—December 3 1971

Town besieged

FANK advance

VC/NVA/ Khmer Rouge

Kompong Thom

Phnom Santuk Mountain

Tang Krasang

Route 6

Kompong Thmar

Barai

Rumlong

Tang Kauk

Praxham

Skoun

Srang Totung

Prey

Traeung

Bridge, Kilometer 54

Bateay

Route 71

Route 21

Route 211

Route 6

Route

Chamkor Leu plantation

Chamkor Andong plantation

NVA

9

205 Khmer Rouge

207 Khmer Rouge

Kompong Cham

Mekong River

Chup plantation

Route 7

0   32 km

0   15 miles

L A O S

Route 13

Mekong River

Route 19

Stung Treng

C A M B O D I A

Siem Reap

Battambang

Tonle Sap

Route 6

Route 5

Kompong Thom

see inset above

Kratie

Snuol

Route 7

Kompong Cham

Bateay

Cardamon Mts

Khmer Rouge Guerrilla Bases

Elephant Range

Gulf

of

Thailand

Kompong Som (Sihanoukville)

April 17 1975: *fall of Phnom Penh*

Phnom Penh

Takmau

Neak Luong

April 1 1975: *fall of Neak Luong*

Tay Ninh

Route 13

March 1975: *mining of the Mekong river*

Route 3

Takeo

Route 2

Bassac River

Mekong River

Route 1

V I E T N A M

N

Ha Tien

May 1975: *retaliatory air strikes on port and airfield after Khmer Rouge capture of Mayaguez*

2/ The Fall of Cambodia

March–April 1975

U.S. air strike

Air base

NVA attacks

0   100 km

0   50 miles

The Fall of Laos AUGUST 1975

While Saigon and Phnom Penh fell with a bang to enemy assaults, the Laotian capital, Vientiane, fell with a whimper on August 23, 1975, when the Pathet Lao Communists, officially known as the Neo Lao Hat Sat (Lao Liberation Front), took over the government. On December 3, the 600-year-old Lao monarchy was abolished and the People's Democratic Republic of Laos was proclaimed.

Like the Thai and the Vietnamese, the Lao peoples emigrated into the Indochina peninsula from south China. In the mid-eighth century they entered the Mekong valley and in 1353 formed the state of Lan Chang ("kingdom of a thousand elephants"), which also contained a large number of non-Lao mountain tribes. In the next few centuries, Laos came under the control first of Vietnam, then of Siam (now Thailand). On October 3, 1893, it became a protectorate of the French Indochinese Union.

The Lao kingdom, with its capital at Luang Prabang, was a backwater during the French colonial era. On May 11, 1947, it was proclaimed an independent state within the French Union, but this did not keep it out of the First Indochina War. Troops from the Viet Minh and the newly formed Pathet Lao occupied its eastern provinces, and in 1954 the climactic battle of Dien Bien Phu was fought on its northeastern border.

Laos gained full independence with the 1954 Geneva Conference, but the Pathet Lao were given virtual autonomy in the two northeastern provinces adjoining North Vietnam and, with North Vietnamese help, began to expand their forces. By the early 1960s, the country was split between the royalist forces backed by the United States and the Pathet Lao and "neutralist" forces backed by North Vietnam and the Soviet Union. With a great power confrontation in the making, another Geneva Conference was convened and a Declaration on the Neutrality of Laos, negotiated by U.S. Ambassador Averill Harriman, was signed by 14 nations, including the United States and the U.S.S.R., on July 23, 1962.

The neutrality of Laos was a farce from the beginning, with U.S. advisers and airpower supporting the Royal Lao government, and North Vietnam maintaining 80,000 soldiers in the country, mostly transport troops along the Ho Chi Minh Trail, which was their key to the conquest of South Vietnam. In December 1970, as the Second Indochina War began to wind down, the U.S. Congress forbade the commitment of U.S. combat forces or advisers in Laos, and on October 17, 1972, peace talks between the Pathet Lao and the Royal Lao government began. A peace agreement was signed on February 21, 1973, and U.S. air strikes in Laos ended the next day. A coalition government was formed in April 1974, with the Pathet Lao holding key positions. In May 1975, Pathet Lao military forces began to advance on Vientiane and government forces were ordered not to resist. On August 23, 1975, the war in Laos came to an end.

But the suffering did not end. The Pathet Lao launched a ruthless campaign against their erstwhile enemies, and 350,000 refugees, more than 10 percent of the population of Laos, fled the Communists. This exodus included a third of the Hmong tribesmen, who, under their commander, General Vang Pao, had worked closely with the CIA and U.S. Special Forces. While 150,000 people, including nearly 60,000 Hmong, were resettled in the U.S.A., about 100,000, including 55,000 Hmong, remained in refugee camps in Thailand. Twenty years later, the controversy over their forced repatriation to Laos continues.

> *"The Hmong's misfortune was to occupy the land that lay between Communist North Vietnam and the Mekong plain—a location that made them so valuable an ally, and so threatening as a possible enemy, that neither side in the war could risk leaving them to their traditional way of life … Tribal people died … in a war that served no purpose of their own."*
>
> —Arnold Isaacs,
> *Without Honor*

Neo Lao Hat Sat fighters train at a jungle base as they prepare to topple the Laotian government.

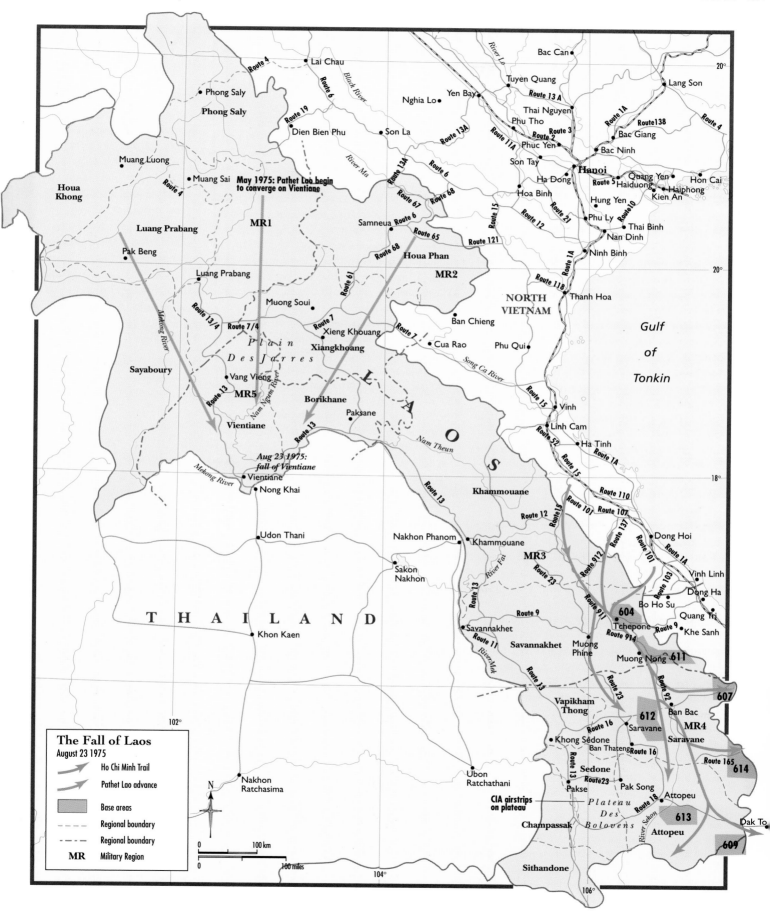

The Fall of Laos
August 23 1975

- Ho Chi Minh Trail
- Pathet Lao advance
- Base areas
- Regional boundary
- Regional boundary
- **MR** Military Region

Full Circle: The Sino-Vietnam War 1979

China had to be taken into account in every U.S. strategic decision of the Vietnam War. "Harry Truman did not take a strong personal interest in Southeast Asia until the Korean War started," noted Dean Rusk, "and even then, his interest was piqued mostly by the growth of Chinese military assistance to Ho Chi Minh's forces and by concern that China might take over its neighbors to the south ... We were concerned that the Korean War signaled the onset of a major Communist onslaught in Asia and perhaps beyond."

There were 22 official justifications for U.S. involvement in Vietnam. Fifty-seven percent of material analyzed by Professor Hugh M. Arnold of the University of Nebraska contained a reference to some form of communism, with China cited five times more frequently than Russia. Australian diplomat Coral Bell traced the roots of this to "Secretary of State John Foster Dulles' assumption ... that any extension of the area of Ho Chi Minh's control in Vietnam ... would mean a dangerous enlargement of the area of China's effective power. The U.S. saw the North Vietnamese as military proxies for China, and by that very decision made them so, without any choice on their part."

Corroborating Bell's analysis, Rusk noted that "Chinese intervention in Korea showed that Mao would use his 'volunteers' outside China ... Our China specialists stated almost unanimously that if we sent American ground forces into North Vietnam, the chance of Chinese intervention was high, and for that reason I strongly opposed U.S. ground operations against North Vietnam. ... We watched for potential mobilization of Chinese forces, avoided bombing territory adjacent to China, and tried to avoid threatening the Chinese."

The replacement of ancient emnities by a "fraternal socialist brotherhood," and public pronouncements by Moscow, Beijing, and Hanoi seemed to confirm the Marxist-Leninist tenet that communism transcended nationalism. This facade began to crumble with Nixon's 1971 visit to China. As Stanley Karnow observed, "To the North Vietnamese, Nixon's visit evoked nightmares of China's 'sellout' at the 1954 Geneva Conference—a betrayal that condemned them to the battlefield for the next decade." While these fears proved unfounded, relations continued to deteriorate. Vietnam claimed that its invasion of Cambodia in 1978 was a reaction to "China's reactionary ruling class [and its] open hostility toward Vietnam."

On February 17, 1979, China launched a "pedagogical war" to teach Vietnam a lesson, with an 85,000-man invasion of Cao Bang Province. Cao Bang fell on March 2, and Lang Son and Lao Cai on March 4. By March 16 the campaign was over. Both sides have cloaked the war in secrecy, but according to former Chinese intelligence officer Xu Meihong, China lost 58,000 soldiers in the bloody campaign. If any side learned a lesson, it was the Chinese, whose backwardness in modern warfare led to major military reforms.

The war marked the beginning of the end for the Cold War. As German war correspondent Peter Scholl-Latour observed, it "punctured the myth of 'World Communism' for ever." Another example which gives the lie to the myth of the "fraternal socialist brotherhood" is the conflicting Chinese–Vietnamese claims to the potentially oil-rich Spratley and Paracel islands. In 1974, the Chinese Navy forced the then South Vietnamese forces to evacuate the Paracels, and in 1988 China and Vietnam clashed in the Spratleys.

The question of sovereignty in the South China Sea took on a new dimension in 1995 when Vietnam joined the Association of South East Asian States (ASEAN), and was one of the main points of discussion when the Chinese foreign minister met with ASEAN in August 1995. It is a factor in U.S.–Vietnamese relations too. Ironically, the Chinese threat, once the dubious basis for U.S. intervention in Vietnam, has become the primary reason for its reintervention, this time at the behest of its former adversary. With the disintegration of the Soviet Union in December 1991, resulting in the loss of its Soviet counterbalance to Chinese domination, Vietnam turned to its erstwhile enemy, the United States, to maintain the balance of power in the area. On July 11, 1995, President Bill Clinton announced full diplomatic relations with Vietnam, and in August 1995 Secretary of State Warren Christopher made an official state visit to Hanoi to open the U.S. Embassy there. A half century after Ho Chi Minh quoted the American Declaration of Independence in a vain attempt to ally Vietnam with the United States, the circle was finally closed.

"The Sino-Vietnamese border war, in truth, was not a war so much as it was a further effort by the two to delineate their new relationship ... Gone is the centuries-old tutor-pupil relationship ... For the Vietnamese the touchstone in this process is 'independence' from China [and] abandonment of the ancient notion of the rimland barbarians' obligation of deference to the Central Kingdom."

—Historian Douglas Pike

A member of Vietnam's regional forces, armed with an aging carbine, heads for regional military headquarters after a fierce engagement with the Chinese invasion forces.

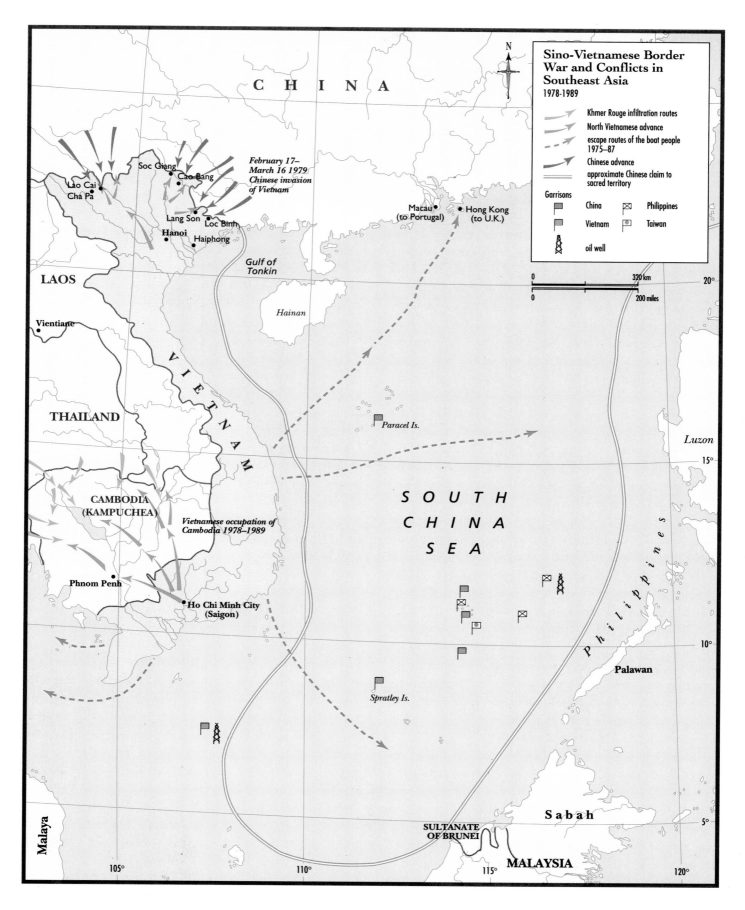

Sino-Vietnamese Border War and Conflicts in Southeast Asia
1978-1989

Khmer Rouge infiltration routes
North Vietnamese advance
escape routes of the boat people
1975–87
Chinese advance
approximate Chinese claim to sacred territory

Garrisons
China
Vietnam
oil well
Philippines
Taiwan

CHINA

Soc Giang

Cao Bang

February 17–March 16 1979 Chinese invasion of Vietnam

Lao Cai
Cha Pa

Lang Son   Loc Binh

Hanoi   Haiphong

Macau (to Portugal)   Hong Kong (to U.K.)

LAOS

Gulf of Tonkin

Vientiane

Hainan

0   320 km
0   200 miles

20°

THAILAND

Luzon

Paracel Is.

15°

CAMBODIA (KAMPUCHEA)

S O U T H
C H I N A
S E A

Vietnamese occupation of Cambodia 1978–1989

Phnom Penh

Ho Chi Minh City (Saigon)

10°

Palawan

Spratley Is.

Philippines

Malaya

S a b a h

5°

SULTANATE OF BRUNEI

MALAYSIA

105°   110°   115°   120°

VIETNAM

Epilogue by Stanley Karnow

"By God, we've kicked the Vietnam syndrome!" said President George Bush in February 1991, following America's victory in the Persian Gulf War. But two decades after the end of the tragic conflict, the memory of Vietnam continues to haunt not only the U.S. public but also the nation's civilian and military leaders. Whatever their political leanings, most Americans subscribe to the thesis "no more Vietnams."

This sentiment was dramatized in the reaction to the publication, in April 1995, of *In Retrospect*, former defense secretary Robert McNamara's memoir of the war. The only Vietnam-era official of his stature to disavow the American commitment, McNamara wrote that he and his associates in the Kennedy and Johnson administrations were "terribly wrong" to have involved the United States in Southeast Asia. He had broken his silence, he said, because he had "grown sick at heart witnessing the cynicism and even contempt with which so many people view our political institutions and leaders." But if he hoped that his admission would restore confidence in government, it seemed to have just the opposite result.

After reading McNamara's list of errors and deceptions, many Americans voiced the opinion that they are still being misled by public figures. His book confirms the extent to which Vietnam has eroded the country's faith in its politicians. Nor did his confession of guilt arouse much sympathy from the families of the young men killed in Vietnam, not to mention those who returned home crippled. As Max Cleland, who lost both legs in the war, sardonically said, "The title of his book should be *Sorry 'Bout That.*"

McNamara indirectly validated the antiwar movement, as did American figures like President Bill Clinton, who at the time dodged the draft and can now maintain that they were correct to resist a war that one of its principal architects currently repudiates. "Do you feel vindicated?" a reporter asked Clinton, to which the President replied, "Yes, yes, I do. I know that sounds self-serving but I do."

Perhaps Vietnam's major legacy has been to shatter the myth that the United States can exert its influence anywhere on earth. The roots of American intervention in Vietnam were planted in what Professor Daniel Bell of Harvard has called America's belief in its "exceptionalism." Americans have always regarded their society as unique, its democracy, natural wealth, and individual opportunities an antidote to the ideological turmoil and class tensions of Europe. The

notion of their singularity inspired in them the dream of bestowing their benefits on less privileged civilizations. The phrase "manifest destiny," which was coined in 1845 to promote the annexation of Texas, gradually came to signify the duty of Americans to assume global responsibilities.

Henry Luce, the founder of *Time* magazine, expressed the notion of the "American Century" on the eve of World War II, and the idea subsequently took various forms. In March 1947, President Harry Truman created the Truman Doctrine, his pledge to defend "free peoples" against Communism; in his inaugural address 14 years later, John F. Kennedy vowed to "pay any price, bear any burden, meet any hardship, support any friend, oppose any foe, to assure the survival and success of liberty."

But the Vietnam disaster dimmed those concepts, leaving Americans baffled and ambivalent about their international role, and other reversals further shattered their sense of supremacy. In 1973, the Middle East petroleum producers boosted oil prices, demonstrating the vulnerability of the United States and other industrial nations. Americans also saw themselves lagging behind other countries in fields such as technology, education, public health, and urban renewal. Bedeviled by an immense federal deficit, a consequence of profligate spending on Vietnam, the United States had become dependent on foreign purchases of treasury bonds. By 1989, for the first time since the end of World War I, foreign investment in America had surpassed American investment overseas. The United States, until then the world's leading creditor, was now the world's leading debtor. "The American Century," commented Daniel Bell, "foundered on the shoals of Vietnam."

Above all, Americans distressed by the Vietnam debacle lost their conviction that the United States was preeminent. No longer, Henry Kissinger warned, could they "deal with every issue simultaneously" or reconstruct the world "to American specifications." Instead, he wrote, the country "must be selective, husbanding its resources as well as its credibility." Nobody agreed more than the nation's senior military men. In 1987, I visited Fort Hood, Texas, home of the 1st Air Cavalry Division, which had fought in Vietnam. Flying in a helicopter above an exercise, I observed armored vehicles maneuvering across a terrain that resembled the plains of central Europe or a Middle East desert. The commanding general, a Vietnam veteran, said as we landed, "This is our kind of war." President Ronald Reagan's defense secretary, Caspar Weinberger, sounded a similar theme later that year. He favored a buildup of America's strategic forces, but he drew the line at backing unpopular, inept, and venal regimes in developing countries like Vietnam. Military action, he stressed, must be a "last resort," to be taken only after every diplomatic avenue had been explored. America should avoid armed conflict unless it had unwavering support of the U.S. public, and troops should not be committed without a timetable for their withdrawal.

The Weinberger Doctrine, as it was called, reflected the views of America's brass and braid, who were willing to engage in such limited operations as Panama and Grenada, yet balked at anything that even faintly smelled of Vietnam. His prestige notwithstanding, Reagan could not persuade Americans that the left-wing regime in Nicaragua posed a menace to the United States. Accordingly, his aides contrived an illegal scheme to arm the "contras." He assigned U.S. Marines to Beirut but immediately pulled them out in October 1983 when 241 of them were slain in a terrorist attack on their barracks. Lyndon Johnson, under the same circumstances, would probably have strengthened the contingent. The American forces sent to Somalia were also withdrawn after they became enmeshed in its political web.

In January 1991, when President Bush unleashed the U.S. offensive against Iraq for its invasion of Kuwait, he did so only after mobilizing United Nations support in an effort to show that America was not acting alone. Moreover, he sought to exorcise the specter of Southeast Asia by promising that "this will not be another Vietnam"—a conflict in which, he said, U.S. troops had been "asked to fight with one hand tied behind their back." But his plan was preceded by sharp splits in both Congress and public opinion that recalled the controversies that roiled America during the Vietnam War. Clearly the days were gone when Americans, convinced of their supremacy, would recoil at nothing.

Prudence similarly pervaded the United States in respect to other crises overseas. General Colin Powell, the former chairman of the Joint Chiefs of Staff, who served in Vietnam, was among the strongest opponents of American intervention in the former Yugoslavia. Polls show that Americans are overwhelmingly concerned with problems such as crime, unemployment, health care, drug abuse, and race relations. But while their priorities are primarily domestic, the majority believe the United States has a crucial stake in the security of Japan, Saudi Arabia, Russia, Kuwait, Mexico, Canada, and its traditional West European allies. Moreover, most advocate U.S. participation in United Nations peacekeeping forces. So, despite much rhetoric to the contrary, Americans

have not slid back to the isolationism of the 1920s.

If the war still haunts Americans, it has not been forgotten by the Vietnamese, who sacrificed millions of soldiers and civilians—a loss felt by every family. But they seem to have put the conflict behind them, perhaps because they have waged so many wars throughout the centuries, or would rather reconstruct their benighted land than rehash recent history. The war left Vietnam in shambles, and the Communists aggravated the devastation after their victory. Encouraged by the Soviet Union, their mentor, they wasted vast sums on unmanageable industrial projects such as steel mills rather than concentrating on agriculture and small factories. They suppressed private entrepreneurs, and by shunting peasants into big collectives sapped their initiative and stunted farm production. Out of revenge they also interned as many as 300,000 vanquished South Vietnamese officials and army officers in brutal "reeducation camps," thereby depriving themselves of valuable talent. Thousands of "boat people" fled, stark evidence that the economy was breaking down. In February 1981, when I visited Vietnam for the first time after the war, beggars filled the streets of Saigon and Hanoi, and, I was told, parts of the country were suffering from famine.

By then the Communist Party bosses recognized that they had squandered the peace and tarnished the reputation they had gained from winning the war. Desperate, they introduced an array of pragmatic economic reforms. Vietnam has since been experiencing a spectacular recovery, spurred chiefly by the determination, perseverance, and sheer hard work of its people. In the process, the Communists have scrapped their old dogmas, as I learned during a chat with General Vo Nguyen Giap in his modest Hanoi villa in January 1995. "What has happened to Marxism?" I asked, to which he responded in fluent French, "Marx was a great analyst but he never gave us a formula for running a country." I pushed him further: "And socialism? I was taught that it meant state control of the means of production and distribution." Smiling faintly, he said, "Vous savez, socialism is whatever brings happiness to the people."

Communist propagandists have also abandoned the idea of a future egalitarian paradise. To conform to the new party line, they have rediscovered one of Ho Chi Minh's hitherto unknown homilies: "The poor should get rich and the rich should get richer." Its boosters predict that Vietnam will sooner or later catch up with South Korea, Taiwan, Hong Kong, and Singapore, the dynamic "little tigers" of Asia. The cities are booming, but the rural regions, where four-fifths of the population live, lag woefully behind—and the gap is expanding. Thus Vietnam, which ranks with Bangladesh as one of the world's most destitute nations, could face a hazardous road ahead. The Communists have liberalized the economy, yet they refuse to dilute their political power. As a safety valve they tolerate a degree of criticism from such perennially disgruntled groups as students. They permit independent candidates to run in elections and allow the large Catholic minority to worship freely. But they forbid rival movements and severely censor the press.

The party has been losing its luster, however. It is blamed for the economic failures that followed the war, and has been discredited by reports of corruption and other abuses among its cadres. The collapse of the Soviet Union, once Vietnam's principal benefactor, has cast a pall over its leadership, just as it eroded Communism nearly everywhere. Nobody foresees the party's imminent demise, but its rosters have been steadily dwindling as old activists retire or die, and other temptations distract the young. As a Western diplomat told me, "Ideology is irrelevant. Only two things matter—how to make money and how to spend it."

The galloping consumer revolution has outstripped the moribund socialist revolution. Saigon, renamed Ho Chi Minh City, is bursting with free enterprise. Shops overflow with television sets, video recorders, stereo systems, cameras, wristwatches, and clothes flaunting stylish logos. Street stalls overflow with foreign cigarettes, beer, and whiskey, smuggled in by sea from Thailand or overland from China. Legally, transactions must be conducted in *dong*, the national currency, but the dollar is almighty. Taxi meters register in dollars, and one dollar buys a leisurely ride around town in a three-wheeled pedicab. At least 50,000 prostitutes ply their profession—a significant increase since 1975, when the Communists supposedly eradicated the evils remaining from the bad old days—and they demand payment in dollars as well. Deluxe hotels, restaurants, and bars are proliferating to cater to the influx of foreign businessmen and tourists. Many of the tourists are American veterans, who trek over paddy fields that were once battlegrounds; a few even meet their former enemies. Some fall prey to peddlers selling miniature U.S. airplanes made from beer cans, fake dog-tags, and Zippo lighters engraved with emblems of U.S. Army units and inscribed with slogans like "You've only lived when you look death in the face."

Hanoi creeps at a snail's pace compared to frenetic Ho Chi Minh City, but it is also embracing free enterprise. Derelict French villas have been renovated and are leased as offices and homes to foreigners at outrageous rents. The notorious "Hanoi Hilton," as the American prisoners-of-war dubbed their block-long jail, has been razed to make way for a huge office complex financed by a Singapore conglomerate. The Metropole Hotel, which fell into disrepair after the Communists took over Hanoi in 1954, has been restored to its former elegance by a French consortium. While primarily patronized by foreign businessmen, it symbolizes the city's transformation into a bastion of capitalism. Though the Communists conquered the South, the commercial spirit of the South has conquered the North.

But the urban prosperity has not filtered down to the countryside. Peasants work their fields as they have for centuries, by hand or behind plodding water buffalo. Apart from the television sets, often charged by car batteries, villages have not changed in a generation. Flimsy huts lack such basic amenities as running water and indoor toilets; extended families, from grandparents to tiny tots, sleep in the same room. Malaria and dysentery are endemic; half the children in rural areas suffer from malnutrition. Only a small fraction of Vietnam is arable, and with the population of 73 million increasing by one million a year, more and more youths are unemployed.

Commissioned by the Vietnamese government to report on Vietnam's progress, a group of Harvard economists warned that despite its remarkable rebound, the "gains achieved so far are extremely fragile." They recommended, among other proposals, that the sluggish bureaucracy be streamlined and the privileged state enterprises be dismantled so that free enterprise can flourish fully. This would entail a drastic overhaul of the Communist system—hardly a prospect for the near future. But too many senior Vietnamese officials are committed to change to allow the momentum of economic reform to halt, even if it occasionally slackens. One of the optimists is Eugene Matthews, a Harvard Law School graduate, who settled in Hanoi in 1980 and has since become a consultant to several U.S. corporations. Too young to have fought in the war or protested against it, he looks forward rather than backward. "Vietnam," he asserts, "is a country, not a war."

President Clinton endorsed that observation on July 11, 1995, when, 22 years after America's withdrawal from the divisive war that continues to scar the national psyche, he extended full diplomatic relations to Vietnam. "This moment offers us the opportunity to bind up our own wounds," he said. "We can now move onto common ground".

Right: *A duck farmer cycles to market in Ho Chi Minh City. Despite urban growth, Vietnam remains one of the deprived countries of the world.*

Bibliography

Allison, George B., *Linebacker II: A View From The Rock* (Washington, D.C., USAF Monograph Series, Office of Air Force History, 1989)

Andradé, Dale, *Ashes to Ashes: The Phoenix Program and the Vietnam War* (Lexington, MA, Lexington Books, 1990)

Andradé, Dale, *Trial By Fire* (NY, Hippocrene Books, 1995)

Arnold, James R., *Tet Offensive 1968* (London, Osprey Books, 1990)

Baldwin, Hanson W., *Strategy for Tomorrow* (NY, Harper and Row, 1970)

Barr Smith, Robert, "The Death of Groupe Mobile 100," *Vietnam*, April 1991

Barr Smith, Robert, "To Die Alone in the Silence," *Vietnam*, October 1992

Barr Smith, Robert, "A Century of French Conquest in Vietnam," *Vietnam*, December 1994

Bennett, John, "Australia's Bombing Magpies," *Vietnam*, December 1994

Berger, Carl (ed.), *The United States Air Force in Southeast Asia 1961-1973* (Washington, D.C., Office of Air Force History, 1977)

Bergerud, Eric M., *Red Thunder: Tropic Lightning* (Boulder, CO, Westview Press, 1993)

Bilton, Michael and Sim, Kevin, *Four Hours in My Lai* (London, Viking, 1992)

Blaufarb, Douglas S., *The Counterinsurgency Era: U.S. Doctrine and Performance 1950 to the Present* (NY, Free Press, 1977)

Braestup, Peter, *The Big Story* (Novato, CA, Presidio Press, 1994)

Broughton, Jack, *Going Downtown: The War Against Hanoi and Washington* (NY, Orion Books, 1988)

Brown, John, "Allies From Down Under," *Vietnam*, spring 1989

Butler, David, *The Fall of Saigon* (NY, Simon and Schuster, 1985)

Buttinger, Joseph, *The Smaller Dragon: A Political History of Vietnam* (NY, Praeger, 1958)

Buttinger, Joseph, *Vietnam: A Dragon Embittered* (NY, Praeger, 1967)

Clarke, Jeffrey J., *The United States Army in Vietnam: Advice and Support: The Final Years, 1965-1973* (Washington, D.C., Center of Military History, 1989)

Clos, Max, "The Situation in Vietnam" in the Congressional Record, April 21, 1966

Colby, William, *Honorable Men: My Life in the CIA* (NY, Simon and Schuster, 1978)

Colby, William with McCargar, James, *Lost Victory* (Chicago, Contemporary Books, 1989)

Conmy, Joseph B. Jr., "Crouched Beast Cornered," *Vietnam*, August 1990

Davidson, Phillip B., *Vietnam at War: The History 1946-1975* (Novato, CA, Presidio Press, 1988)

Davies, John Paton, *Dragon by the Tail* (NY, W.W. Norton, 1972)

Deac, Wilfred O., "Prelude to Disaster," *Vietnam*, June 1992

Deac, Wilfred O., "Losing Ground to the Khmer Rouge," *Vietnam*, December 1994

Dillard, Walter Scott, *Sixty Days to Peace* (Washington, D.C., National Defense University Press, 1982)

Don, Tran Van, *Our Endless War* (Novato, CA, Presidio Press, 1973)

Dorr, Robert F., *Air War Hanoi* (London, Blanford Press, 1988)

Dougan, Clark and Weiss, Stephen, *The Vietnam Experience: Nineteen Sixty-Eight* (Boston, MA, Boston Publishing Company, 1983)

Dougan, Clark and Lipsman, Samuel, *The Vietnam Experience: A Nation Divided* (Boston, MA, Boston Publishing Company, 1984)

Dougan, Clark and Fulghum, David, *The Vietnam Experience: the Fall* (Boston, MA, Boston Publishing Company, 1985)

Doyle, Edward and Lipsman, Samuel, *The Vietnam Experience: Setting the Stage* (Boston, MA, Boston Publishing Company, 1981)

Doyle, Edward and Lipsman, Samuel, *The Vietnam Experience: America Takes Over 1965-67* (Boston, MA, Boston Publishing Company, 1982)

Doyle, Edward, Lipsman, Samuel, and Maitland, Terence, *The Vietnam Experience: The North* (Boston, MA, Boston Publishing Company, 1986)

Ebon, Martin, *Lin Piao* (NY, Stein and Day, 1970)

Enthoven, Alain C. and Smith, Wayne K., *How Much is Enough? Shaping the Defense Program 1961-1969* (NY, Harper and Row, 1971)

Fall, Bernard, *Hell in a Very Small Place* (NY, J.B. Lippincott, 1967)

Fall, Bernard, *Street Without Joy* (Mechanicsburg, PA, Stackpole Books, 1994)

Fenn, Charles, *Ho Chi Minh* (London, Studio Vista, 1973)

FitzGerald, Frances, *Fire in the Lake: The Vietnamese and the Americans in Vietnam* (Boston, MA, Little Brown, 1972)

Ford, Ronnie E., *Tet 1968: Understanding the Surprise* (London, Frank Cass, 1995)

Fulghum, David and Maitland, Terence, *The Vietnamese Experience: South Vietnam on Trial* (Boston, MA, Boston Publishing Company, 1984)

Fulton, William B., *Vietnam Studies: Riverine Operations 1966-1969* (Washington, D.C., Center of Military History, 1973)

Futrell, Robert F., *The United States Air Force: the Advisory Years to 1965* (Washington, D.C., Department of the Air Force, 1981)

Galvin, James H., "A Communication on Vietnam," *Harpers*, February 1966

Giap, Vo Nguyen, *Dien Bien Phu* (Hanoi, Foreign Languages Publishing House, 1964)

Grant, Zalin, *Facing the Phoenix* (NY: W.W. Norton, 1991)

Greenberg, Lawrence M., "The Sea Dragon Strikes Again," *Vietnam*, December 1991

Gwin, S. Lawrence Jr., "Ambush at Albany," *Vietnam*, October 1990

Halberstam, David, *Ho* (NY, Random House, 1971)

Hall, D.G.E., *A History of South-East Asia (Third Edition)* (NY, St Martin's Press, 1968)

Hamilton-Merritt, Jane, *Tragic Mountains* (Bloomington, IN, Indiana University Press, 1992)

Hamilton-Merritt, Jane, "General Giap's Laotian Nemesis," *Vietnam*, June 1995

Hammel, Eric, *Khe Sanh; Siege in the Clouds* (NY, Crown Publishers, 1989)

Hammel, Eric, *Fire in the Streets: The Battle for Hue, Tet 1968* (Chicago, Contemporary Books, 1991)

Hannah, Norman B., *The Key to Failure: Laos and the Vietnam War* (Lanham, MD, Madison Books, 1987)

Hemingway, Albert, "A Place of Angels," *Vietnam*, February 1991

Hemingway, Albert, *Our War Was Different: Marine Combined Action Platoons in Vietnam* (Annapolis, Naval Institute Press, 1994)

Herrington, Stuart A., *Silence Was a Weapon: The Vietnam War in the Villages* (Novato, CA, Presidio Press, 1982)

Herrington, Stuart A., *Peace With Honor?* (Novato, CA, Presidio Press, 1983)

Hersch, Seymour M., *My Lai 4: A Report on the Massacre and its Aftermath* (NY, Random House, 1970)

Hinh, Nguyen Duy, *Lam Son 719* (Washington, D.C., Center of Military History, 1981)

Hooper, Edwin B. et al., *The United States Navy and the Vietnam Conflict: The Setting of the Stage to 1959* (Washington, D.C., Department of the Navy, 1976)

Isaacs, Arnold R., *Without Honor: Defeat in Vietnam and Cambodia* (Baltimore, MD, Johns Hopkins University Press, 1983)

Isaacs, Arnold R., Hardy, Gordon, and Brown, MacAlister, *Pawns of War* (Boston, MA, Boston Publishing Company, 1987)

Kalb, Marvin and Abel, Elie, *Roots of Involvement: The U.S. in Asia 1784-1971* (NY, Norton, 1971)

Kamps, Charles T. Jr., *The History of the Vietnam War* (London, Guild Publishing, 1988)

Karnow, Stanley, *Vietnam: A History* (NY, Viking Press, 1983)

Kelley, Francis J., *Vietnam Studies: U.S. Army Special Forces 1961-1971* (Washington D.C., Center of Military History, 1973)

Khuyen, Dong Van, *The RVNAF* (Washington, D.C., Center of Military History, 1980)

King, Peter (ed.), *Australia in Vietnam* (Sydney, George Allen and Unwin, 1983)

Kirkpatrick, Charles E., "Legion's War in Indochina," *Vietnam*, August 1989

Kissinger, Henry, *White House Years* (Boston, MA, Brown and Company, 1979)

Komer, Robert W., *Bureaucracy at War: U.S. Performance in the Vietnam Conflict* (Boulder, CO, Westview Press, 1986)

Kronh, Charles A., *The Lost Battalion* (Westport, CN, Praeger, 1993)

Larson, Stanley Robert and Collins, James Lawton Jr., *Vietnam Studies: Allied Participation in Vietnam* (Washington, D.C., Center of Military History, 1975)

Lavalle, A.J.C. (ed.), *The Battle of the Skies over North Vietnam* (Washington, D.C., U.S. Government Printing Office, 1976)

Legro, William E., *Vietnam from Cease-fire to Capitulation* (Washington, D.C., Center of Military History, 1981)

Lewey, Guenter, *America in Vietnam* (NY, Oxford University Press, 1978)

Lipsman, Samuel, and Doyle, Edward, *The Vietnam Experience: Fighting for Time* (Boston, MA, Boston Publishing Company, 1983)

Lockwood, Jonathan S., "The Failure of Intelligence," *Vietnam*, February 1995

Lung, Hoang Ngoc, *Indochina Monographs: Strategy and Tactics* (Washington, D.C., Center of Military History, 1980)

Maitland, Terence and McInerny, Peter, *The Vietnam Experience: A Contagion of War* (Boston, MA, Boston Publishing Company, 1983)

Mangold, Tom and Penycate, John, *The Tunnels of Cu Chi* (NY, Random House, 1985)

Marolda, Edward J., *By Sea, Air and Land: An Illustrated History of the U.S. Navy and the War in Southeast Asia* (Washington, D.C., Naval Historical Center, 1994)

McAleavy, Henry, *Black Flags in Vietnam* (London, George Allen and Unwin, 1968; NY, Macmillan, 1968)

McAlister, John T. and Mus, Paul, *The Vietnamese and their Revolution* (NY, Harper and Row, 1970)

McArthur, George, "It Became Sinful," *Vietnam*, April 1995

McAuley, Lex, "Aussies Hold The Line," *Vietnam*, December 1991

McAuley, Lex, "Long Tan Battle Royal," *Vietnam*, October 1992

McGowan, Sam, "Lifeline up in the Sky," *Vietnam*, August 1991

McGowan, Sam, "Airlifters to the Rescue," *Vietnam*, February 1993

McNamara, Robert S., *In Retrospect: The Tragedy and Lessons of Vietnam* (NY, Times Books, 1995)

Meihong, Xei, "Chinese Ordeal," *Vietnam*, October 1993

Miller, John G., *The Bridge at Dong Ha* (Annapolis, MD: Naval Institute Press, 1989)

Minor, Dale, *The Information War* (NY, Hawthorne, 1970)

Momyer, William M., *Airpower in Three Wars* (Washington, D.C., Office of Air Force History, 1978)

Moore, Harold G. and Galloway, Joseph L., *We Were Soldiers Once...and Young* (NY, Random House, 1992)

Morrocco, John, *The Vietnam Experience: Thunder From Above* (Boston, MA, Boston Publishing Company, 1984)

Morrocco, John, *The Vietnam Experience: Rain of Fire* (Boston, MA, Boston Publishing Company, 1985)

Mueller, John, "Reflections on the Anti-war movement," in Braestrup, Peter (ed.), *Vietnam as History* (Washington, D.C., University Press of America, 1984)

Murphy, Edward F., *Dak To* (NY, Pocketbooks, 1993)

Mus, Paul, *Sociologie d'une guerre* (Paris, Editions du Seuil, 1950)

Navarre, Henri, *Agonie de l'Indochine* (Paris, Plon, 1958)

Nolan, Keith W., *Battle of Hue: Tet 1968* (Novato, CA, Presidio Press, 1983)

Nolan, Keith W., *Into Cambodia* (Novato, CA, Presidio Press, 1990)

Nolan, Keith W., *The Magnificent Bastards* (Novato, CA, Presidio Press, 1994)

Noyes, Harry F. III, "Heroic Allies," *Vietnam*, 1993

Oberdorfer, Don, *Tet! The Turning Point of the Vietnam War* (NY, De Capo Press, 1983)

Palmer, Bruce Jr., *The 25-Year War: America's Military Role in Vietnam* (Lexington, KY, The University Press of Kentucky, 1984)

Palmer, Dave R., *Summons of the Trumpet: U.S.-Vietnam in Perspective* (Novato, CA, Presidio Press, 1978)

Palmer, Dave R., *The Way of the Fox: American Strategy in the War for America 1775–1783* (Westport, CN, Greenwood Press, 1978)

Pearson, Willard, *Vietnam Studies: War in the Northern Provinces* (Washington, D.C., Center of Military History, 1975)

Peers, William R., *The My Lai Enquiry* (NY, W.W. Norton, 1979)

Pike, Douglas, *PAVN: People's Army of Vietnam* (Novato, CA, Presidio Press, 1986)

Pike, Douglas, *Vietnam and the Soviet Union: Anatomy of an Alliance* (Boulder, CO, Westview Press, 1987)

Pisor, Robert, *The End of the Line: The Siege of Khe Sanh* (NY, Norton, 1982)

"Platform of the American Anti-Imperialist League, October 18, 1899," in Henry Steele Comminger (ed.), *Documents of American History* (seventh edition) (NY, Appleton-Century-Crofts, 1963)

Podhoretz, Norman, *Why We Were in Vietnam* (NY, Simon and Schuster, 1982)

Ponchaud, François (translated by Amphoux, Nancy), *Cambodia: Year Zero* (NY, Holt, Rinehard, and Winston, 1978)

Porch, Douglas, "Dien Bien Phu Reconsidered," *Vietnam*, June 1994)

Prados, John and Stubbe, Ray W., *Valley of Decision* (Boston, MA, Houghton Mifflin, 1991)

Reske, Charles, *MACV-SOG Command History Annex B: The Last Secret of the Vietnam War* (Sharon Center, OH, Alpha Publications, 1992)

Ridgway, Matthew B., *Soldier: The Memoirs of Matthew B. Ridgway* (NY, Harper and Brothers, 1956)

Rogers, Bernard William Rogers, *Vietnam Studies: Cedar-Falls–Junction City: A Turning Point* (Washington, D.C., Center of Military History, 1974)

Roy, Jules (translated by Baldick, Robert), *The Battle of Dien Bien Phu* (NY, Harper and Row, 1965)

Rusk, Dean, *As I Saw It* (NY, W.W. Norton and Company, 1990)

Safer, Morley, *Flashbacks: On Returning to Vietnam* (NY, Random House, 1990)

Sananikone, Oudone, *Indochina Monographs: The Royal Laotian Army and U.S. Army Advice and Support* (Washington, D.C., Center of Military History, 1981)

Schandler, Herbert V., *The Unmaking of a President: Lyndon Johnson and Vietnam* (Princeton, NJ, Princeton University Press, 1977)

Schell, Jonathan, *The Village of Ben Suc* (NY, Alfred A. Knopf, 1967)

Scholl-Latour, Peter (translated by Carney, Fay), *Death in the Rice Fields* (NY, St. Martin's Press, 1979)

Sheehan, Neil, *A Bright Shining Lie: John Paul Vann and America in Vietnam* (NY, Random House, 1988)

Shore, Captain Moyers S. II, *The Battle for Khe Sanh* (Washington, D.C., Historical Branch, G-3 Division, USMC, 1969)

Shulimson, Jack and Johnson, Major Charles M, *U.S. Marines in Vietnam: An Expanded War, 1966* (Washington, D.C., History and Museums Division, USMC, 1982)

Shulimson, Jack, *U.S. Marines in Vietnam: The Landing and the Buildup 1965* (Washington, D.C., History and Museums Division, USMC, 1968)

Simmons, Edwin H., "Marine Corps Operations in Vietnam, 1968," in *The U.S. Marines in Vietnam 1954-1973* (Washington, D.C., History and Museums Division, USMC, 1974)

Simpson, Charles R. III, *Inside the Green Berets: the First Thirty Years* (Novato, CA, Presidio Press, 1983)

Simpson, Howard R., *Dien Bien Phu: The Epic Battle America Forgot* (Washington, Brassey's, 1994)

Smith, Colin, *The Killing Zone: The New Zealand Infantry in Vietnam* (Auckland, Paynter Design, 1994)

Smith, Homer D., "The Final 45 Days in Vietnam," *Vietnam*, April 1995

Smith, Jack, "Death in the Ia Drang Valley," *The Saturday Evening Post*, January 28, 1967

Spector, Ronald H., *The United States Army in Vietnam: Advice and Support: The Early Years, 1941–1960* (Washington, D.C., Center of Military History, 1984)

Spector, Ronald H., *After Tet: The Bloodiest Year in Vietnam* (NY: The Free Press, 1993)

Stanton, Shelby, *The Green Berets at War* (Novato, CA, Presidio Press, 1985)

Stanton, Shelby, *The Rise and Fall of an American Army* (Novato, CA, Presidio Press, 1985)

Steinbrook, Gordon L., *Allies and Mates* (Lincoln, NE, University of Nebraska Press, 1995)

Summers, Harry G. Jr., *On Strategy: A Critical Analysis of the Vietnam War* (Novato, CA, Presidio Press, 1982)

Summers, Harry G. Jr., "The Bitter Triumph of the Ia Drang," *American Heritage*, February 1984

Summers, Harry G. Jr., "Troubled Apostle of Victory," interview with Neil Sheehan, *Vietnam*, spring 1989

Summers, Harry G. Jr., *On Strategy: A Critical Analysis of the Gulf War* (NY, Dell, 1992)

Summers, Harry G. Jr., *Vietnam War Almanac* (NY, Facts on File, 1985)

Summers, Harry G. Jr., "The Bitter End," *Vietnam*, February 1995

Summers, Harry G. Jr., "Final Days of South Vietnam," *American History*, April 1995

Summers, Harry G. Jr., *The New World Strategy: A Military Policy for America's Future* (NY, Simon and Schuster/Touchstone Books, 1995)

Sutsakhan, Sak, *Indochina Monographs: The Khmer Republic at War and the Final Collapse* (Washington, D.C., Center of Military History, 1980)

Tefler, Gary L. et al., *U.S. Marines in Vietnam: Fighting the North Vietnamese 1967* (Washington, D.C., History and Museums Division, USMC, 1984)

Thompson, Sir Robert, *Revolutionary War and World Strategy 1945-1969* (NY, Taplinger Publishing Company, 1970)

Tobin, Thomas G., Laehr, Arthur E., and Hilgenberg, John F., *USAF Southeast Asia Monograph Series: Last Flight from Saigon* (Washington, D.C., U.S. Government Printing Office, 1978)

Truong, Ngo Quang, *The Easter Offensive of 1972* (Washington, D.C., Center of Military History, 1980)

Turley, G.H., *The Easter Offensive* (Novato, CA, Presidio Press, 1985)

Vien, General Cao Van et al., *Indochina Monographs: The U.S. Advisor* (Washington, D.C., Center of Military History, 1980)

Vien, General Cao Van, *Indochina Monographs: The Final Collapse* (Washington, D.C., Center of Military History, 1983)

Vongsavanh, Soutchay, *Indochina Monographs: RLG Military Operations and Activities in the Laotian Panhandle* (Washington, D.C., Center of Military History, 1981)

Warner, Denis, *The Last Confucian* (NY, Macmillan, 1963)

Weigley, Russell F., *The American Way of War: A History of United States Military Strategy and Policy* (NY, Macmillan, 1973)

West, Francis J., *The Village* (NY, Harper and Row, 1972)

Westmoreland, William C., and Sharpe, *U.S.G. Report on the War in Vietnam* (Washington, D.C., U.S. Government Printing Office, 1968)

Westmoreland, William C., *A Soldier Reports* (Garden City, NJ, Doubleday, 1976)

Westmoreland, William C., "As I saw and now see it: a perspective on America's unique experience in Vietnam," *Vietnam*, 1990

Whitlow, Robert H., *U.S. Marines in Vietnam: The Advisory and Combat Assistance Era 1954-1964* (Washington, D.C., USMC History and Museums Division, 1977)

Wilson, William, "Massacre at My Lai," *Vietnam*, August 1991

Windchy, Eugene G., *Tonkin Gulf* (Garden City, NJ, Doubleday, 1971)

Wukovits, John F., "Debacle on the Tchepone Road," *Vietnam*, December 1990

Young, John Robert, *The French Foreign Legion* (London and NY, Thames and Hudson, 1984)

Zabecki, David T., "Battle for Saigon", *Vietnam*, summer 1989

Zaffiri, Samuel, *Hamburger Hill* (Novato, CA, Presidio Press, 1988)

Index

Figures shown below in **bold** type signify maps or pictures. Figures in *italic* refer to references in quotes.